DRIVE 5
pp68–79

FRANCE

N240
Iruña

NAVARRA
A12

A15

DRIVE 6
pp80–89
N260

DRIVE 7
pp90–97

N260

Tudela
A68

Huesca

DRIVE 8
pp98–107
AP7
A26
Figueres

Girona

ARAGÓN
A23
N240

CATALONIA
Manresa
AP7

Calatayud
A2
Zaragoza
AP2
A2
A23
N211
N232

Lleida
N240
AP2
A18
A54
Barcelona

Alcañiz
N420

DRIVE 10
pp118–127

DRIVE 9
pp108–117
Tortosa
N420
AP7

DRIVE 11
pp128–135
Teruel
AP7
Benicarló

Benicasim

Me1
Mahón

DRIVE 24
pp238–247
Ma13
Ma15
Palma

A23
AP7
Sagunto

Cuenca

Requena
A3
Valencia

**PAÍS
VALENCIANO**
A7

DRIVE 25
pp248–253
Ibiza

**THE BALEARIC
ISLANDS**

Albacete
A31

DRIVE 12
pp136–143
Xàbia
AP7

Hellín
A31
Elda
A30
Alicante

*MEDITERRANEAN
SEA*

MURCIA
Murcia
C415
A7

Lorca
AP7
A7
Cartagena

DRIVE 23
pp232–237

D1331434

Motorway
Dual carriageway
Major road
International border
Regional border

EYEWITNESS TRAVEL
BACK ROADS
SPAIN

EYEWITNESS TRAVEL

BACK ROADS
SPAIN

CONTRIBUTORS:

Mary-Ann Gallagher, Nick Inman, Phil Lee,

Chris Moss, Nick Rider, Richard Trillo,

Suzanne Wales, Greg Ward

LONDON, NEW YORK,
MELBOURNE, MUNICH AND DELHI
www.dk.com

MANAGING EDITOR Aruna Ghose
EDITORIAL MANAGER Ankita Awasthi
DESIGN MANAGER Kavita Saha
PROJECT EDITOR Trisha Bora
EDITORS Parvati M. Krishnan,
Souvik Mukherjee
PROJECT DESIGNER Shruti Singhi
DESIGNER Neha Sethi
PICTURE RESEARCH Taiyaba Khatoon
DTP DESIGNER
Rakesh Pal, Azeem Siddiqui
CARTOGRAPHY
Uma Bhattacharya,
Mohammad Hassan, Suresh Kumar,
Lovell Johns Ltd
ILLUSTRATIONS
Dev Datta, Arun Pottirayil,
Pallavi Thakur

Reproduced by Colourscan, Singapore
Printed and bound in China by
South China Printing Co. Ltd.

First published in Great Britain in 2010 by
Dorling Kindersley Limited,
80 Strand,
London WC2R 0RL
A Penguin Company

Copyright 2010 © Dorling
Kindersley Limited, London

A CIP catalogue record is available from the
British Library.

ISBN 978-1-4053-4582-8

Jacket: Sanctuary of Sant Salvador,
Mallorca, Spain

We're trying to be cleaner and greener:
- -
- we recycle waste and switch things off
- we use paper from responsibly managed forests whenever possible
- we ask our printers to actively reduce water and energy consumption
- we check out our suppliers' working conditions – they never use child labour
- -
Find out more about our values and
best practices at www.dk.com

CONTENTS

Above Valldemossa monastery complex, Mallorca

Below left Pretty balcony in Beceite **Below right** Rows of olive trees in Cazorla, Andalusia

Above left Visitors relax on Cala Deia, Mallorca **Above centre** A tunnel cuts through the Catalan Pyrenees **Above right** Windmills in Consuegra, La Mancha

Below left Intricate arches of the Palacio de Partal in the Alhambra **Below right** Hats and dresses on sale, Xàbia

Half title Cala Moraig beach near Moraira, Costa Blanca **Title** Whitewashed houses of Ronda perched at the edge of the El Tajo gorge

About this Book

Back Roads Spain aims to get visitors off the main highways, make discoveries and to get a real feel of the life and riches of Spain. The drives take visitors across Spain around all kinds of enthralling corners that lie off the well-trodden routes – fascinating old towns, placid villages in exquisite settings, and a prodigious variety of scenery, from dramatic mountain peaks and vast brown plains to idyllic green valleys and hidden beaches. On the byways of Spain you can find many of its most ancient monuments and most rumbustious local festivals, as well as the vineyards that produce its finest wines, rich traditional foods, innovative restaurants in remote places and delightful small hotels.

Getting Started

The guide begins with all the practical information you need to plan a driving holiday in Spain. This includes an overview of the best times to visit, ways to get there, the documentation that you will need, important motoring advice, and places to eat and stay. A language section at the back lists essential words and phrases, including key driving-related vocabulary.

The Drives

The 25 drives featured in this guide are spread across the whole of mainland Spain, Mallorca and Ibiza. They take visitors on leisurely tours through Spain's many and varied regions on country roads, avoiding main highways unless it is absolutely unavoidable. The drives have been selected to be accessible from different parts of the country, and to give a taste of the huge diversity of Spain – so some take you through the steep green valleys of Galicia or the Alpine mountains of Asturias or the Pyrenees, while others visit the sun-toasted villages of Don Quixote's La Mancha or the beaches and coastal villages of Andalusia. Some drives include celebrated towns and attractions like Santiago de Compostela or Granada, but then they show you how to get to the next stop along quiet, minor roads. Throughout, the emphasis is given to exploring places that have a real feel of being away from it all.

All of the featured drives in this guide can be explored with a standard-model car, and by any normally experienced driver. Country roads can be narrow, and in mountain areas they will twist and turn, but there are no great risks in getting around them, at least in good weather. In Spain, even remote valley roads are generally in fine condition.

Each of the drives presents a range of possible activities to try – market shopping, wine tasting, exploring the mountains or keeping the kids entertained on the beach – and each one also includes a route for a walk, in a special town or beautiful countryside. Drives of more than one day can also be divided into single day trips which allow visitors to return to their starting point at the end of each day. Places to stay and eat listed with each drive have been carefully selected for

Using the Sheet Map

A pull-out road map of the entire country is attached at the back. This map contains all the information you need to drive around the country and to navigate between the tours. All motorways, major roads, airports, both domestic and international, plus all the ferry ports are easily identified. This makes the pull-out map an excellent addition to the drive itinerary maps within the book. There is a map index to help you find the places. The map is further supplemented by a clear distance chart, so you can gauge the distances between the major cities.

individuality, quality and charm. And after each stop there are clear road directions to continue the drive to the next stop.

ntroducing Spain

ne essence of Spain lies in the variety it has ɔ offer. It is the most mountainous country ı Europe, and has western Europe's only real ıesert, in Almería. Behind the Atlantic coasts of ıalicia and Asturias there are still bears and wild ɔoars in the deep-green forests of oak and eech, while to the south the summer sun roasts the bare, rugged hills golden brown between the olive groves. In different parts of Spain three languages – Catalan, Basque and Galician – enjoy official status with Castilian Spanish. This linguistic variety is further reflected in the vigour of local festivals and traditions, and the delicious range of regional cuisines.

Vhen to Go

ate March to early July is an ideal me for visiting most parts of Spain, s temperatures remain pleasantly varm. In "dry Spain", from the antabrian mountains to Andalusia, ɔring sees a burst of new life before ne torrid heat of summer, with flashes f wild flowers by the roadsides. emperatures rise sharply in July and ugust, above all in the centre and ɔuth, and while there is plenty going ın – especially local festivals – vhether visitors wish to travel then ıay depend on how much they like ne heat, and the crowds. September ito October is another delightful me to visit, with clear, warm skies, ıd the grape harvest beginning in ıe-growing areas. In late autumn, ɔm mid-October on, the weather ets chillier and wetter in the north, ut many areas have seasonal attrac- ɔns at this time too, often to do with ɔecial foods. From December to larch snow and ice can make travel nore difficult in mountain areas, but nis is also the winter sports season.

imes to Avoid

he majority of Spain's population akes its holidays in late July or August, nd this is also the most popular time ɔr foreign visitors – so roads are con- ested, prices go up, and hotel rooms re harder to come by. Added to that, ı many areas the temperature lingers bove 30° C (86° F) . Country areas ot far from major cities can get very ıusy on fine weekends at any time of ear. Some monuments, museums ıd other attractions in country areas are closed from November to February or March, so check before travelling. In mountain areas such as Asturias or the Pyrenees the transitional times between the summer and winter are often rainy with poor visibility, and hence not ideal for touring.

Festivals

Easter is the most widely marked religious festival, above all in Valencia, Andalusia, central Spain and Alicante. The eve of the **Feast of St John the Baptist**, 23 June, is known for loud revelry with bonfires and fireworks. Early July sees the **bull running** of San Fermín in Pamplona, one of Spain's most famous festivals. The summer months are the most popular time for each town or village to have its *fiesta mayor*. From September cultural programmes get going in cities and towns, and many country areas have celebrations of their special products such as wine, mushrooms or ham. **Christmas** has a special touch, with traditional fairs in many places. Winter comes to an end in several towns with the raucous partying of **Carnaval**, in late February or March.

Public Holidays

New Year's Day (1 Jan)
Día de Reyes (6 Jan)
Good Friday (Mar/Apr)
May Day (1 May)
Feast of the Assumption (15 Aug)
Día de la Hispanidad (12 Oct)
All Saints' Day (1 Nov)
Día de la Constitución (6 Dec)
Immaculate Conception (8 Dec)
Christmas Day (25 Dec)

Climate

"Green Spain", extending from Galicia through Asturias and the Basque Country, and along the Pyrenees, has plenty of rain, chilly winters and warm but moderate summers. The Mediterranean coast has cold winters but the spring is generally superb, and summers are pleasant. In the south, across Andalusia to Murcia, winters are warmer, but the full summer heat is often intense. In the central plain of the two Castiles winter temperatures can be freezing, but summers can easily be as hot as further south.

eft Mountain village in Aragón **Right** People tting in a café on the main square in Altea, alencia

Getting to Spain

As one of Europe's most popular destinations, Spain is easy to reach from any part of the world. There are several major hub airports in different parts of the country, and even many small regional airports have direct international flights. Spain's excellent railways are well-connected to the European high-speed train network, and fast motorways cross over from France at either end of the Pyrenees. Direct ferry services run to the north coast from Britain. In the Mediterranean there are frequent ferries from mainland ports to the Balearic Islands and to North Africa.

Above Funicular train up to Catalor

Arriving by Air

Spain's main hub airports are Madrid, Barcelona, Málaga and Palma de Mallorca, and each has a huge range of direct flights with major and low-cost airlines, above all from the UK, Ireland and every part of Europe. In addition, the growth of low-cost airlines using smaller airports has made it very easy to fly straight to the part of Spain you wish to visit, especially from the UK, Ireland, France, Italy and Germany. Airline routes can change, but flights are now run to Santiago de Compostela, Santander, Valladolid, Zaragoza, Girona, Reus (near Tarragona), Granada and Jerez de la Frontera by **Ryanair**; to Asturias and Bilbao by **Easyjet**; to Valencia by Easyjet, **Iberia** and Ryanair; to Alicante by **British Airways**, **Bmibaby**, Easyjet, **Flybe** and Ryanair; to Murcia by Easyjet and Bmibaby; to Almería by Easyjet and Ryanair; to Seville by Iberia and Ryanair; and to Ibiza by British Airways and Easyjet.

Direct flights from North America run by **Air Canada**, **American Airlines**, and **US Airways**, and flights from other countries outside Europe, generally arrive in Barcelona or Madrid. From these cities visitors can take a connecting flight on to any of Spain's islands or regional destinations, or take a train to see more of the country. Many of the international low-cost airlines have now started operating internal flights within Spain.

Flight times to Madrid or Barcelona from different cities are: London, 2 hours; Paris, 1 hour; Amsterdam, 5.5 hours; Berlin, 2.5 hours; New York, 8 hours; Los Angeles, 15 hours; Buenos Aires, 12 hours.

Arriving by Sea

There are two direct car ferry services between Britain and Northern Spain. **Brittany Ferries** sails twice each week from Plymouth and Portsmouth to Santander (approximately 20 hours). **P&O Ferries** has three sailings a week each way between Portsmouth and Bilbao (approximately 30–33 hours). Since these are long sailings the ships are "cruiseferries": small cruise liners with comfortable berths, swimming pools and a big choice of entertainment on board.

Several Mediterranean car ferry routes connect Spain with Italy and North Africa. From Barcelona **Grimaldi Ferries** sails several times each week to Civitavecchia and Livorno (approximately 20 hours), and **Grande Navi Veloci** to Genoa (approximately 18 hours). The same company also has a weekly ferry to Tangiers in Morocco (around 26 hours), and there are several ferries serving the ports in Algeria and Morocco from Alicante, Almería, Málaga, Algeciras and Tarifa.

Balearic Islands Ferries

The ports for car and passenger ferries to the Balearic Islands are Barcelona (which has the most services), Valencia, Alicante and Denia on the Costa Blanca, which offers the shortest crossing to Ibiza. Services on most routes are frequen and are operated by several differen companies, so prices are competitiv **Acciona Trasmediterranea** is the largest company and has daily sailings to Mallorca from Barcelona (about 8 hours), Menorca and Ibiza (approximately 10 hours), from

alencia to Mallorca and Ibiza
(round 4–5 hours) and from
icante to Ibiza. **Iscomar** often has
wer fares and also runs from
arcelona and Valencia to Mallorca
nd Menorca, and from Denia to
iza and Formentera. **Baleària** also
as routes to all the islands from
arcelona, to Mallorca from Valencia
nd to Ibiza from Denia, and uses
uper fast" ferries on some routes,
hich get between Denia and Ibiza,
r example, in 2.5 hours.
Acciona Trasmediterranea also
rovides ferry services to the Canary
ands from Cádiz. Sailing time is
bout 24 hours.

rriving by Rail
omfortable "trainhotel" sleeper
ains operated by the Franco-
panish **Elipsos** company run every
ght between Paris and Madrid, and
etween Barcelona and Paris, Zurich
nd Milan. On board there is a restau-
nt car, and a bar-café. Travellers
om the UK can book tickets on the
urostar to Paris together with onward
ckets to Madrid or Barcelona through
ail Europe. Travelling time from
aris to Madrid is about 14 hours, to
arcelona 12 hours. There are several
st trains every day between Madrid
nd Lisbon, and also other, slower rail
onnections between Spain and
ther European countries. For these
ou often have to change trains at
e Spanish border.
Once in Spain, you can change
apidly at Madrid or Barcelona onto
e **RENFE**, the main Spanish railways
etwork, with which you can get to
ny part of the country. Tickets can
so be bought through international
ooking agencies. Some regional

services are slow moving, but the
ultrafast AVE high-speed train is
now the most popular way to get
between the cities of Barcelona,
Madrid, Seville and Málaga, travelling
from Madrid to Barcelona in under
3 hours. For more information on
Spanish railways and an excellent
guide to international rail travel,
check **The Man in Seat 61** website.

Arriving by Road
Spain's main highways are fully
integrated into the European road
network, but the massive mountain
barrier of the Pyrenees tends to
channel traffic entering from France
into just two large motorways at
each end of the mountains,
European route E70 (the A63 in
France, or the A8 in Spain) in the
Basque Country or route E15 (the
French A9, Spanish A7) at La
Jonquera near the Mediterranean
coast. There are no border controls
to cause delays, but these crossings
can get congested in the peak summer season, especially La Jonquera.
Drivers who have time to explore this
region, however, can find several
alternative, more attractive border
crossings between these two main
highways. Among the most spectacular are the famous Pass of
Roncesvalles above Pamplona, the
Puerto de Somport pass into the
Aragonese Pyrenees from Pau and
the road to Vielha in the Val d'Aran
from Toulouse or Tarbes.

Below far left Yatchs around a long jetty at
the lovely Port d'Andratx in Mallorca **Below
left** Escalator down to a platform at a station
in Barcelona **Below** Airport building at Eivissa,
Balearic Islands

DIRECTORY

AIRLINES
Air Canada
1-888-247-2262 (US/Canada), 914 585
568 (Spain); www.aircanada.com
American Airlines
1-800-433-7300 (US/Canada), 902 115
570 (Spain); www.aa.com
Bmibaby
0905 828 2828 (UK), 902 100 737
(Spain); www.bmibaby.com
British Airways
0844 493 0787 (UK), 902 111 333
(Spain); www.britishairways.com
Easyjet
0905 821 0905 (UK), 807 260 026
(Spain); www.easyjet.com
Flybe
0871 700 2000 (UK), 0044 1392 268
513 (from Spain); www.flybe.com
Iberia
0870 609 0500 (UK), 902 400 500
(Spain); www.iberia.com
Ryanair
0818 30 30 30 (Ireland), 807 383 811
(Spain); www.ryanair.com
US Airways
1-800-622-1015 (US/Canada), 901 117
073 (Spain); www.usairways.com

INTERNATIONAL FERRIES
Brittany Ferries
0871 244 0744 (UK), 942 360 611
(Spain); www.brittany-ferries.com
Grande Navi Veloci
00 39 010 209 4591 (Italy); www3.gnv.it
Grimaldi Ferries
00 39 081 496 444 (Italy); 902 531 333
(Spain); www.grimaldi-ferries.com
P&O Ferries
0871 6645 645 (UK), 902 020 461
(Spain); www.poferries.com

BALEARIC ISLANDS FERRIES
Acciona Trasmediterranea
902 454 645 (Spain); www.
trasmediterranea.es
Baleària
902 160 180 (Spain); www.balearia.com
Iscomar
902 119 128 (Spain); www.iscomar.com

RAIL TRAVEL
Elipsos
www.elipsos.com
Eurostar
www.eurostar.com
The Man in Seat 61
www.seat61.com
Rail Europe
www.raileurope.co.uk
RENFE
902 240 202 (Spain); www.renfe.es

Practical Information

Spain is a very easy country to travel in, with few formalities to take up your time and a comprehensive range of modern services. Even remote places often have good mobile phone and Internet coverage, and can have an ATM cash machine. There is also an extensive tourism infrastructure, with well-equipped local and regional tourist offices in most towns that can help you find accommodation, restaurants and each area's special attractions.

Above Bilingual reserved parki sign in Basque and Span

Language

Spain's main language, often referred to as *castellano* (Castilian) rather than *español* within the country, is spoken by nearly everyone. In the relevant regions, however, visitors will have more enjoyable contact with local people if they are at least aware that the locals normally speak their own, entirely separate language – *Gallego*, similar to Portuguese, in Galicia, Basque or *Euskera* in the Basque Country and Catalan in Catalonia, the Balearics and most of Valencia. In Galicia and Catalonia, especially, road and other signs in country areas are often in the local language. Since, unlike Basque, both are Latin languages, they are quite easy to understand if visitors have some knowledge of Spanish or French.

In all areas, knowledge of English has been growing fast, particularly among younger people. English-speakers are nearly always employed in tourist offices and by many other visitor services.

Passports and Visas

Nationals of all EU countries can enter Spain with only their national identity card, but UK and Irish citizens, who do not have them, must also have full passports. Citizens of the USA, Canada, Australia, New Zealand and several other countries can also enter Spain with just their full passports and do not need a visa for tourist stays of up to 90 days. Nationals of other countries must obtain a visa from a Spanish consulate in their home country or country of residence before entering Spain. Similarly, all non-EU citizens who intend to work or study in Spain, or stay longer than 90 days, should obtain the relevant visa before arriving. Visa and entry requirements can change, so check with the nearest Spanish consulate before travelling.

Travel Insurance

It is advisable for all travellers to have a comprehensive travel insurance policy, and non-EU citizens must have full medical cover. Your policy must cover you against loss or theft of money, luggage and any other belongings, personal accidents, possible legal costs in case of any dispute while travelling, and delays or cancellations of flights or ferry sailings. Most standard policies will not cover certain adventure sports such as rock climbing, rafting or, especially, skiing; so if you intend to

do any of these check carefully what your insurance covers, and whether you need a specialist sports policy.

Health

All EU citizens can make use of the Spanish national health service so long as they have a European Healt Insurance Card (EHIC). With the card you will also get a booklet that detai the level of medical treatment to which you are entitled. The EHIC is a great help in emergencies, but does not cover all kinds of treatments ane some may have to be paid for up front, leaving you to reclaim the money later. So it is a good idea to have medical cover included in you private travel insurance. Non-EU travellers should always have full mec cal cover in their travel insurance, and when necessary use public or private hospitals on a paying basis.

In any medical emergency, go to the casualty department (*Urgencias*) of the public hospital in the nearest sizeable town. Many smaller towns have clinics that can provide first-response care, but they may not operate 24 hours. If there seems to be nowhere nearby, ask at your hote or a tourist office for a (preferably English-speaking) doctor, phone

⌐ Police officers in Cangas de Onís, Asturias **Right** Spanish police car

...ur nearest consulate for a list of ...ommended doctors, or call for ...**ambulance**.

...Pharmacies, identified by large ...een or red illuminated crosses, are ...ntiful, and there is at least one in ...arly every town. Pharmacists are ...hly trained and can often advise ...treatments for minor ailments, ...nburn, bites and so on. Many phar-...acists also now speak some English. ...the windows of each pharmacy ...ere will be a list of pharmacies in ...e area that are open at night.

...sabled Travellers

...ajor efforts have been made to ...prove access and facilities for ...abled people in Spain in the last ...v years, and many hotels have ...apted rooms. There are good ...cess facilities at most city ...useums and access ramps on ...any beaches, but in small towns ...d at monuments with uneven ...ths things may still be more ...ficult. **Tourism for All** in the UK is a ...od source of information on ...ilities in some parts of Spain.

...rsonal Security

...olent crime and even petty theft is ...e in rural Spain, but as anywhere ...u should avoid leaving bags or valuables in view when you park your car. In crowded areas and at the bigger *fiestas*, be aware that there may be pickpockets and bag-snatchers around. When sitting at a pavement café, always keep your bag in view, either on the table or in your lap.

If you are robbed or become a victim of any other crime, report it immediately to the nearest police station or call the **emergency** number. In cases of theft, you must get a police statement to make an insurance claim. Spain has several police forces with varying responsibilities. In most cities the main force responsible for dealing with crime is the **Policía Nacional** (national police), but nearly every town also has its own local force (usually called **Policía Local**, Policía Municipal or Guardia Urbana), which is mainly concerned with traffic, parking and various local regulations. In most rural districts and on main highways, all areas of policing are the responsibility of the green-uniformed **Guardia Civil** (civil guard). However, in two of Spain's autonomous regions, most rural and city policing has now been taken over by separate local forces, the red-uniformed Ertzainza in the Basque Country and the blue-clad Mossos d'Esquadra in Catalonia.

DIRECTORY

PASSPORTS AND VISAS

Australia
913 536 600; www.spain.embassy.gov.au

Canada
914 233 250; www.spain.gc.ca

United Kingdom
917 146 400; www.ukinspain.com

United States
915 872 200; www.embusa.es

DISABLED TRAVELLERS

Tourism for All
www.tourismforall.org.uk

EMERGENCY

Emergencies: all services
112

Ambulance
061

Policía Nacional
091

Policía Local (most towns)
092

Guardia Civil
062

Below far left Pharmacy sign **Below left** Sign indicating beach with wheelchair access, Costa Blanca **Below middle** Tourist office sign **Below right** Street signs in Gaucín

Communications

Standard Spanish phone numbers have nine digits, and incorporate the local area code. Numbers that begin with 900 are free phone lines; those beginning 902, 906 or other combinations are premium-rate lines. Spanish mobile phone numbers all start with a 6.

Spain's former monopoly phone company Telefónica now has to compete with other phone service providers, especially for mobile phones, but it still dominates the market for landlines and provides nearly all payphones. These are easy to find, and while most still accept coins, a more convenient way to use them is with a phonecard *(tarjeta telefónica)*, which can be bought to the value of €6 or €12 from newsstands, tobacco shops *(estancos)* and other businesses. Many bars have coin-operated phones, but these tend to be expensive, as do the surcharges levied by most hotels for making a call from your room.

Mobile/cell phones *(móviles)* are enormously popular in Spain and the coverage is pretty good in every part of the country, except perhaps the most remote mountain valleys. Most mobile phones from other European countries will work in Spain via a roaming facility, but charges can be higher. It may be more economical just to buy a cheap, pay-as-you-go local mobile while in Spain. Spanish mobiles all operate on the standard European wave band, so North American phones will only work here if they have a tri- or quad-band facility.

Internet cafés are abundant in Spain, so it is easy to check your email even in small towns. In addition, broadband/ADSL provision is expanding rapidly, and many hotels even in out-of-the-way places now offer guests with laptops Wi-Fi connections, for free or for a small charge.

The Spanish postal service, *(Correos)*, has post offices all over the country, and large offices in every main town. Post boxes *(buzones)* are yellow, with a crown-and-horn insignia. Stamps can be bought at post offices, but it is generally easier to get them from tobacco shops. Larger offices provide a wide range of services and are generally open all day, Monday to Saturday; smaller offices are more limited and are often closed in the afternoons. As well as by regular post, letters and packages can be sent by express *(urgente)* or registered *(certificado)* mail.

Money and Banks

Spain is one of the many European Union countries that has adopted the euro (€) as its currency. Each euro is divided into 100 cents *(céntimos* in Spain). Euro notes are identical throughout the euro area, and are issued for €5, €10, €20, €50, €100, €200 and €500. Euro coins have a distinctive design for the issuing country on one side, and come in values of 1, 2, 5, 10, 20 and 50 cents, and €1 and €2.

Banks (virtually always with an ATM cash machine) are plentiful in all major towns and tourist areas. In the mountains and countryside, there is at least one bank branch and ATM in the largest town of each district, but they are scarce in villages, so plan accordingly. Banks generally open Monday to Friday from 8:30am to 2pm, and often on Saturdays from 8:30am to

Above Painted sign for vari[ous] facilities, Andalu[...]

1pm. Banking hours vary, however, some branches in larger towns may be open on a few afternoons each week. Larger banks and *caja* (savings bank) branches have a dedicated foreign exchange desk, where you c[an] exchange cash or traveller's cheques or withdraw cash against a credit car[d].

Outside of banking hours, in airports, main rail stations and mos[t] tourist areas there will be a range o[f] late-opening small *bureaux de chang[e]* for changing money. However, thes[e] may give poorer rates than banks.

Cash Passports, prepaid currency cards that are loaded before travelling and can be used in shops and ATMs abroad, are also gaining popularity. They are available from **Thomas Cook**, **Travelex** and various banks. Credit and debit cards are widely accepted, but note that whe[n] you use a card in shops you may b[e] asked to show your passport or oth[er] photo ID. Given the restrictive openi[ng] times of banks, the most convenien[t] way to obtain cash can also be by withdrawing it from an ATM with a card. Most Spanish ATMs accept all the major international cards (**American Express**, **Visa**, **MasterCard** and others), and display instruction[s] in English and other languages.

ove left A credit card reader in Spain **Above middle** Old town hall in a town in La Rioja **Above right** An information kiosk

ourist Information

he Spanish national tourist office as offices around the world, but urist information within Spain is enerally provided by individual ties and the various autonomous gions, which produce a huge range information and maps about tractions and activities in their area. l major towns and many small ones ave a tourist office *(oficina de turismo)*. national parks and nature reserves ere are special visitor centres which rovide a range of walking maps.

pening Hours

lost monuments and museums ose on one day each week, usually londay, although some close on uesdays. On other days smaller ghts are generally open from 10am 2pm and from 5 to 8pm, but the iggest, most famous buildings and useums are often open all day. dmission is normally charged, but hany museums are free on Sundays. ocal and smaller shops usually open om 9am to 1–2pm, and again from –5 to 8–9pm, Monday to Saturday, vith hours tending to be later in ummer. Markets open earlier, from round 7am, and often close down y 2pm. Larger city stores and hopping malls, however, are open

through the day without a break. This pattern has been copied by many shops in cities. Traditionally, only news-stands, bakeries *(panaderías)* and cake shops *(pastelerías)*, stayed open on Sundays but nowadays the big stores also stay open on some Sundays.

Tipping

It is common to leave around 5–10 per cent in restaurants. In bars, customers often leave small change. Tips are usually given to hotel porters and toilet attendants. Taxi drivers do not expect tips, but appreciate them when they are given, and a common practice is to round up the fare to the nearest euro or more, leaving a bit more for longer journeys or if the driver has helped with luggage.

Time

Spain (except for the Canary Islands) is one hour ahead of GMT during winter. It changes to and from daylight saving time on the last Sunday in March and on the last Sunday in October respectively.

Below far left Telephone booth in Andalusia **Right** Telephone shop in Xàbia **Below middle** An automatic teller machine in Andalusia **Below right** Yellow postbox of the Spanish postal service **Below far right** A terrace bar in La Pobla de Segur

DIRECTORY

COMMUNICATIONS

Directory Enquiries
11818, 11888

To call Spain from abroad
International access code (usually 00) +34 followed by the full 9-digit number

To call home from Spain
Dial 00, then the country code, and then the area code where necessary. Omit the first 0 in numbers in the UK, France and some other countries

Country Codes
Australia: 61; Ireland: 353; New Zealand: 64; UK: 44 ; USA and Canada: 1

MONEY AND BANKS

American Express
902 375 637;
www.americanexpress.com

Mastercard
900 971 231;
www.mastercard.com

Thomas Cook
www.thomascook.com

Travelex
900 948 971

Visa
900 991 124;
www.visa.com

TOURIST INFORMATION

Ireland
0818 22 02 90;
www.tourspain.co.uk

UK
79 New Cavendish Street, London W1W 6XB;
0845 940 0180;
www.tourspain.co.uk

USA
666 Fifth Avenue, 35th Floor, New York 10103;
(212) 265 8822;
www.okspain.org

Driving in Spain

At peak times on multilane highways around Madrid or Barcelona you can get caught up in horrendous congestion, but by getting off the main roads you can escape onto placid lanes between craggy hill sides and stupendous views. Carry on further, and the same road may get narrower still and wind tightly up to a tiny village. Exploring these byways is a delight, but to get the most out of your trip it is advisable to make some preparations first.

Above Sign for *autopista*, a toll motorw...

Insurance and Breakdown Cover

All car insurance policies in the EU automatically include minimum third-party insurance cover valid in any EU country. However, it is advisable to have wider cover too. For holders of fully-comprehensive car insurance most companies provide full European cover for a small extra premium; some do not charge for this, but still require you to notify them before travelling. An international "Green Card" confirming your car is insured is no longer a legal requirement, but is still useful to have, and most companies issue them when you obtain European cover.

It is also advisable to have breakdown cover with one of the Europe-wide networks with English-speaking phone lines. This can be arranged with your European insurance cover, or through a motoring organization such as the **AA** *(see p19)* or **RAC** *(see p19)*.

What to Take

You must carry your driving licence, passport, the vehicle registration document and a certificate of insurance (with a Green Card if you have one). If you are taking your own car, get it serviced before you leave your home country. If you are not the registered owner, you must have a letter of authorization from the owner. You must also carry a set of spare light bulbs and a red warning triangle. It is not yet obligatory for foreign vehicles to carry a second warning triangle or a luminous vest, but it is strongly recommended. Drivers who wear glasses should carry a spare pair. The car's country of registration should be displayed on a sticker or as part of the registration plate, and right-hand drive cars need headlamp deflectors for driving on the right, available at ferry ports and on ferries. Additional requirements apply when towing caravans or trailers *(see p20)*.

Road Systems

Main highways in Spain are either *autopistas* or *autovías*. *Autopistas* (AP2, AP7 etc) are multilane toll *(peaje)* motorways. Wherever there is a toll motorway it is flanked by a toll-free *carretera nacional* on the same route. *Autovías* (A2, A7 etc) are also multilane and generally of the same standard as *autopistas*, but they are toll-free. Several highways change between stretches of *autopista* and *autovía*, and around cities many highways are toll-free. European route numbers are also shown in green on signs alongside the Spanish numbers.

The next grade of road is the *carreteras nacionales* or national highways (N25, N230 etc). Some are just two-lane roads, but many have passing lanes. Numbering of other roads varies according to the autho... ity responsible for them (regional, provincial or local), and so changes as you cross from one area to another. Distances along all roads (and exit numbers on motorways) are marked in kilometres from the theoretical start point of the road.

Paying Tolls

On short stretches of *autopista* the toll is a flat fee, but elsewhere you take a ticket as you enter the motorway, and pay by the distance driven when you exit or leave a toll section of road. Tolls are also charged at some tunnels. At toll stations, there are three sets of lanes: *telepago/telepeaje*, for holders of pre-paid *autopista* cards; *automático*, for paying by credit card or with the exact amount in cash; and, simplest to use, *manual* lanes with staffed booths. *Autopista* tolls are quite high (€7 for Girona–Barcelona) which is why the... are often pretty empty, while nearby non-toll roads are congested.

Left Sign for a toll motorway **Right** Cars and lorries on a highway in Granada, Andalusia

Rules of the Road

Seat belts must be worn by everyone in the car, front and back. It is illegal to use a mobile phone when driving, and to sound a horn in urban areas except in an emergency. Only dipped headlights can be used in urban areas, and dipped headlights must be switched on when in tunnels. Common in small towns is a type of traffic light with electronic sensors: normally flashes yellow, but if you approach it at excessive speed it will turn to red and stop you; if you slow down, it turns back to flashing yellow. Entrances and exits on *autopistas* and *autovías* can be abrupt, so extra care is necessary, above all in a right-and-drive car. Take special care on *autovías*, because some still have junctions with quite minor roads.

If oncoming drivers flash their lights at you this usually means they are claiming right-of-way. However, this can be a friendly warning that there is a police spot-check ahead. For advice on driving or travelling abroad visit the Foreign and Commonwealth Office website *(see p19)*.

Speed Limits and Fines

Standard speed limits are 50 km/h (30 mph) in built-up areas, 80 km/h (50 mph) on urban dual carriageways,

90 km/h (55 mph) on most country roads, 100 km/h (60 mph) on dual carriageways and 120 km/h (75 mph) on *autopistas* and *autovías*. These can be modified by signs, and in many residential areas there is a limit of 30 km/h (19 mph).

Electronic speed traps and video speed checks are common in Spain. Fines are levied on the spot according to a fixed scale of charges. The legal limit for alcohol in the blood is 0.05 per cent.

Buying Fuel

Fuel stations have two or three grades of unleaded petrol (95, 97 and 98 octane) and diesel (*gas-oil or gasóleo-A*). Many have two grades of diesel, and some offer LPG fuel (*autogas*) and biodiesel. Normal diesel is a little more expensive than unleaded petrol in Spain.

Petrol stations are plentiful in cities and on main highways, but in rural areas there may only be one in the district's main town. Country stations may be closed on Sundays. Many stations have automatic pumps open 24 hours operated by credit card, but some reject non-Spanish cards. On self-service pumps you often have to tap in the amount you wish to pay before it will release fuel.

INSTRUCTIONS FOR DRIVERS

Given here in Spanish only. In the Basque Country, Galicia and Catalan-speaking regions, these signs may be written in the local languages.

Calle sin salida
Dead end, no through road

Camino/Carril cerrado
Road/lane closed

Ceda el paso
Give way, yield

Modere su velocidad
Slow down

Desviación
Detour

Precaución – Obras
Caution – road works

Salida
Exit

Sentido único
One way

Uso de cadenas obligatorio
Snow chains compulsory

Below far left Road winding past a cliff in Mallorca **Below left** Fuel station **Below middle** Sign warning drivers to use the horn **Below right** High altitude road near the Pyrenees **Below far right** A deer crossing road sign to caution motorists

Road Conditions

A great deal has been spent on upgrading Spain's roads, and even country roads are generally in very good condition. Dust can make roads slippery at speed in the full summer heat, and rain, when it comes, can be very heavy and make roads treacherous, so extra care is necessary.

Spain's main cities are all relatively small in area. Hence they and their access highways are often congested, especially on weekday mornings and evenings, and on Sunday nights. If you visit Spain's cities (above all Madrid and Barcelona), it will be more relaxing and save time to leave your car at a hotel or car park and use public transport, which is excellent. If you hire a car in a city, ask the rental company for clear directions onto highways out of town. Away from major cities, congestion is far less common, and long-distance roads often seem very empty. Exceptions are coastal roads and those leading to popular countryside areas, which get very busy in the holiday season.

Signs on country roads can be inconsistent, but are generally quite straightforward. It is not always so in towns, where local signs are often small and hard to find. Try to look for a *centro urbano* sign when entering a town, and for *todas direcciones* when you want to leave, which should lead you to a main highway.

Information on road conditions is available in Spanish only from the **Dirección General de Tráfico** (DGT) website and phone line. For Catalonia, there is more information on the regional government website. For weather information check the **Weather Channel** or **BBC Weather**.

Above Road winding under an old stone viaduct in Mallorca

Mountain Roads

Discovering many of Spain's most spectacular places involves venturing up its remarkable mountain roads, with long series of switchback hairpins. Even very remote roads now have good surfaces, with crash barriers on the sharpest bends, and have space to allow two vehicles to pass with care, but they are unavoidably steep and narrow. The main thing to take into account on mountain roads is to take time, as average speeds will often be around 40 km/h (25 mph). Drive cautiously around blind bends, and if in doubt use your horn when approaching, as many local drivers do. If you want to stop to take in the often breathtaking views, wait for a stopping place or viewpoint.

Driving in Winter

From December to March roads in mountain areas can be coated with snow and ice. Motorways are kept clear, but minor roads may be closed completely, and access to other roads may only be permitted for vehicles fitted with snow chains *(cadenas)*. This includes many highways over mountain passes. When a road is closed or chains are required it is signposted well in advance. The sta[te] of mountain roads in winter is assessed daily, so check websites before travelling.

Taking a Break

There are service areas *(areas de servicio)* with ample facilities at inter[vals] along *autopistas* and *autovías*. Along the main highways it is easy to find roadside café-restaurants. On other roads there are freque[nt] lay-bys (with a "P" sign), with more on picturesque and mountain roads, indicated as a *mirador* (viewpoint).

Warning sign for danger of snow

Breakdowns and Accidents

If you have a breakdown or accident, put hazard lights on and try to get the car off th[e] main carriageway. Place your warning triangle about 30 m (100 ft) behind the car; you should also wear a lumi[n]ous jacket, but this is not obligatory for drivers of foreign-registered cars. There are free orange emergency tele[-]phones every 5 km (3 miles) along *autopistas* and *autovías*, and operato[rs] often take calls in English. Otherwise use your mobile to call your breakdown service. In case of accidents,

ft Road signs in Andalusia **Middle** Sign for Puerto de Artesiaga in the Pyrenees **Right** Shops carved out of rocks in Mallorca

ur insurance company should have pplied copies of the European cident Statement. You and the her driver should each fill in the rm, and each should keep a copy accompany an insurance claim. t is only required to notify the lice if someone has been injured there is a dispute over what has ppened. If there is a serious dis- reement over an accident, each iver must make a statement at the cal police station.

arking

most Spanish towns parking space at a premium. Parking is prohibited here the kerb is painted yellow; -street pay-and-display spaces are arked in blue, with a ticket machine arby. Parking on the street or in unicipal car parks is usually free ring lunch hours. In many narrow eets there is free parking on differ- t sides of the street at different nes: a no-parking sign with 1–15 eneath it means parking is prohi- ed during the first half of each onth, while on the other side a milar sign will say 16–30, for the cond half. Parking space is especially arce in the old centres of cities and wns, and in cities it is best to use e of the big paid car parks. Smaller

towns have at least a few paid and free car parks.

Do not park in front of any *vado permanente* sign (*gual permanent* in Catalan), which means an entry with 24-hour right of access. If the local police tow your car away, they will leave a sticker on the kerb with a phone number and the address where you must pay a fine before retrieving the car.

Maps

The official **Instituto Geográfico Nacional (IGN)** publishes a compre- hensive road atlas, the *Mapa Oficial de Carreteras*. Also of high quality are the maps and road atlases of Michelin and Planeta. The IGN also produces regional and hiking maps, and the **Institut Cartogràfic de Catalunya** has a detailed series on Catalonia. For walk- ing and exploring the countryside, the best maps are those of Editorial Adrados (for Asturias, Cantabria, the Sierra de Gredos) and **Editorial Alpina** (Catalonia, Andalusia, the Pyrenees). Tourist offices also provide good maps.

Below far left Road signs near Nájera **Below left** Cars parked in Murillo de Reino **Below middle** Parking ticket machine **Below right** Road sign warning of falling rocks **Below far right** Visitors enjoying views of Gorg-Blau, Mallorca

DIRECTORY

INSURANCE AND BREAKDOWN COVER
AA
0800 262 050; www.theaa.com
RAC
www.rac.co.uk

RULES OF THE ROAD
Foreign and Commonwealth Office
www.fco.gov.uk/en/travelling-and-living-overseas/staying-safe/driving-abroad

ROAD CONDITIONS
BBC Weather
www.bbc.co.uk/weather

Dirección General de Tráfico (DGT)
900 123 505; www.dgt.es

The Weather Channel
www.weather.com

BREAKDOWN OR ACCIDENTS
European Accident Statement
www.insurance.fr/files/Accident_Form.pdf

MAPS
Editorial Alpina
www.editorialalpina.com

Institut Cartogràfic de Catalunya (ICC)
www.icc.es

Instituto Geográfico Nacional (IGN)
www.ign.es

Caravans and Motorhomes

Basic driving rules and speed limits are the same for caravans and motor-homes as for standard cars, with the addition that cars towing a caravan must have a yellow triangle on a blue backing near the front number plate. Also if car and caravan or trailer have a combined length of 12 m (40 ft) or more there must be yellow reflector triangles either side of the rear number plate. On roads with three or more lanes, towing vehicles can only use the two right lanes, and vehicles or combinations with a total length over 10 m (33 ft) must keep a distance of at least 50 m (165 ft) from the vehicle in front of them. Drivers towing caravans should be wary of taking on minor mountain roads, and ask at local tourist offices on their level of accessibility.

Parking a caravan or mobile home is usually only permitted in authorized sites, but there are well-equipped camp sites throughout Spain. In the peak holiday season they are very busy, so book early. Electrical voltage at sites is generally 220v, but can be less. Due to different national systems, reverse polarity can occasionally be a problem when the site's live cable connects to a caravan's neutral one, so it may be advisable to take a polarity tester, and an adaptor to use if this occurs. Calor gas is not available in Spain, but it is easy to find Campingaz, and Repsol and Cepsa petrol stations sell butane gas cylinders. You will need an adaptor to connect them to UK Calor gas equipment.

The best source of information of all kinds on travelling in Spain with a caravan or motorhome is the *Caravan*

Above Caravan parked at a camp site in Ca

Europe guide from **Caravan Club**, which includes a site guide. Volume 1 covers Spain, Portugal and France.

Motorcycles

The main traffic laws, speed limits and so on for motorcyclists are the same as for car drivers. In addition, helmets are compulsory for riders and passengers on all bikes over 125cc, and dipped headlights must be switched on at all times. *Autopista* and tunnel tolls are less for bikes, and in many towns bikes and scooters can be parked for free, so long as they do not take up a car parking space. In many towns it is legal (and free) to park bikes on the pavement if it is over 3 m (10 ft) wide, but check to see what local bike users do, as in some towns this can attract a fine.

Cycling

Cycling in Spain's cities can be terrifying, but out in the countryside conditions are ideal, and mountain biking especially is extremely popular. Officially, all riders must wear helmets, but this is loosely enforced. Tourist offices often have free guides to local mountain biking routes, and more extensive guides are published by companies such as Editorial Alpina *(see p19)*.

Many companies now offer mountain biking tours in Spain. If yo do not come with a tour or have you own bike, shops offering cycle hire *(alquiler de bicicletas)* are easy to fir especially near popular bike routes

Driving with Children

Children under age 12 and/or less than 1.35 m (4 ft 5 in) in height can only travel in the front seat of a car a child seat with a child restraint system suitable for their size. In the back, children of any age less than 1.35 m (4 ft 5 in) tall must also use child seat, not just booster cushior Seat belts must be worn at all time

Autopista service areas, and the le formal restaurant-petrol station dri ins beside national highways, often have good play areas for children.

Disabled Drivers

The European-standard blue badg for disabled drivers is also valid in Spain. However, this does not mea you can disregard parking restriction instead, you must use a designated disabled parking space, indicated b the usual wheelchair symbol. There are disabled spaces in all public an most private car parks, and usually some among on-street pay-and-display (parking ticket machines fro

Left Instructions to visitors in Parque Natural del Cap de Creus **Right** Pedestrianized street in Alcúdia, Mallorca

which customer has to buy ticket and display it on his dashboard) spaces. They are usually free, but sometimes you must pay for them at a reduced rate. The **AA** (see p19) provides a guide to using the blue badge around Europe (downloadable free from the AA website), and more information can be obtained from **Tourism for All**.

Car, Bike and Motorhome Hire

All the major car rental chains operate in Spain; there are at least a few car hire offices in every provincial capital, and many more in cities. However, if you wish to collect or drop off a car on a Sunday, you may find you can only do so at an airport or in a major city. Prices are competitive, so check around. In general, **Europcar** and **National-Atesa** have the most extensive network throughout Spain. To get the very best deals, it is best to book a car in advance through one of the online rental brokers, such as **Auto Europe** or **Argus**. Precise conditions vary, but in general to hire a car in Spain you must be over 21 and have had a driving licence for at least a year, and must present your licence, passport and a credit card against a deposit. The price quoted to you should include all taxes and unlimited mileage

(kilometraje ilimitado), which nowadays is usual practice. By law rental contracts include basic third-party insurance, but some companies now include comprehensive insurance for no extra charge. If not, it can be worth paying a bit more for comprehensive insurance and collision damage waiver (CDW) cover.

When you collect the car you will be given an emergency contact number and/or the number of a breakdown service. As well as checking the general condition of the car, check that it has the equipment required by law in Spanish-registered vehicles: a set of spare bulbs, two warning triangles and a luminous jacket. If the police discover that the car does not have them, the driver is liable for a fine, not the rental company. If you require extras such as child seats or snow chains, indicate when booking.

Motorcycle rental agencies are less common, so you have less choice of starting point. **BMW Motorental** has offices in several cities, and the more economical **Moto España** is in Barcelona, Madrid, Bilbao and Málaga. Helmet rental is usually extra.

Motorhomes can also be rented in Spain: reliable agencies include **CaravanEuropa** and **Euromotorhome**. Minimum age for drivers is usually 25.

DIRECTORY

CARAVANS AND MOTORHOMES
Caravan Club
www.caravanclub.co.uk

DISABLED DRIVERS
Tourism for All
www.tourismforall.org.uk

CAR, BIKE AND MOTORHOME HIRE

Argus
933 801 204; www.arguscarhire.com

Auto Europe
900 801 789; www.autoeurope.co.uk

BMW Motorental
www.bmwmotorental.com

CaravanEuropa
www.caravaneuropa.com

Euromotorhome
www.euromotorhome.es

Europcar
www.europcar.com

National-Atesa
902 100 101; www.atesa.es

Moto España
937 538 886 ; www.motoespana.com

Below far left Municipal camp site in Agüero
Below left Entrance to camp site, Agüero
Below right Cyclists along a trail near La Mancha **Below far right** Motorcyclist on a road in Sierra de Gredos

Where to Stay

The range of accommodation for travellers in the Spanish countryside has broadened enormously in the last few years. The long-established mix of luxurious paradors in historic buildings, beach resorts, business hotels and simple but cheap *pensiones* has been livened up with the addition of small, family-run *casas rurales* bed-and-breakfasts, allowing you to get much closer to the landscape. Even in placid old towns and remote valleys, you can find distinctive small hotels, often in stunning locations.

Above Sign for the *Casas Rurales* in Valencia

Hotels

Hotels in Spain are regulated by regional governments, so details of categorization vary. In general accommodation is divided between *hoteles* (identified by a blue plaque with an "H" on it), *hostales* ("HS") and *pensiones* ("P"). Hotels have *en suite* bathrooms in every room; *hostales* and *pensiones* do not always, but in fact many do now offer *en suite* facilities in most or even all rooms. Usually, *hostales* and *pensiones* are cheaper and have fewer facilities than hotels. *Hostal* does not mean the same as a hostel in English, with dorm-type beds, which is an *albergue*. Two other traditional names still widely used are *posada* and *fonda*. They generally indicate a traditional-inn atmosphere, but can also be used for quite grand hotels.

Hoteles are star-rated one to five. The differences between *hostales* and *pensiones* are pretty vague and they are star-rated one to two. Star ratings in all regions are based on a checklist of facilities, so are not an automatic guide to a hotel's attractiveness. A four- or five-star hotel must have extensive facilities such as swimming pools, meeting rooms and so on, but the rating will not take into account

quality of service, location or charm. Hence a good two-star can be more enjoyable than a functional three-star, and a distinctive *pensión* more attractive than a basic hotel. Many midrange hotels are owned by chains, such as **NH Hoteles** or **Sol Meliá**. They can be relied on for modern comforts, but not usually with much character.

Paradors and Other Distinctive Hotels

There are also hotels that stand out for their special appeal, many of which are conveniently grouped together in chains or associations. Oldest and best-known are the government-owned paradors, the first of which opened in 1928. Spread around the country, the most enticing paradors are in finely-renovated castles and other historic buildings. Others, especially in the mountains, are in modern buildings in spectacular locations. All paradors have very comfortable, often luxurious rooms, and provide a high level of traditional service and comfort, with restaurants that showcase regional cuisine.

In addition there are now many smaller yet unique hotels around Spain, usually for lower prices. Many

are represented by the **Rusticae** group, a quality benchmark that is a handy shortcut to finding attractive small hotels in any part of Spain. Some Rusticae hotels are boutique-style, while others have a more traditional charm, making the most of old houses and lovely settings.

Several regions have local *clubes de calidad* or small hotel associations, such as **Casonas Asturianas** in Asturias and **Cantabria Infinita** and the **Posadas Reales** in Castilla-León, while others have local quality-labelling schemes for hotels (indicated by Q de Calidad Turística).

Casas Rurales

The hotel range is supplemented by family-run *casas rurales*, country homes in villages or farms. Every Spanish region now has rural tourism schemes: classifications and local names are again confusingly varied, but usually homes are listed under *turismo rural*, *agroturismo* or something similar on regional tourism websites. This includes both bed-and-breakfast-type homes with room for overnight stays, and separate, fully equipped self-catering cottages that can usually only be rented for a few

t Outside the charming Posada el Bosque in Potes, *see p52* **Middle** Room in the Posada el Bosque, Potes, *see p52* **Right** Logo of Paradores de Turismo

ghts. Some bed-and-breakfasts are
and manor houses, while others are
ore rustic. Many offer home-cooked
ening meals with local produce.
sas rurales are listed on Spain-wide
es such as **Guíarural** and **Toprural**
well as on regional websites.

cilities and Prices

anish hotels mostly have double
oms with double beds *(cama de
atrimonio)* or twin beds *(con dos
mas)*; single rooms are scarce except
business hotels. Only a few cheap
stales and *pensiones* still have shared
athrooms. Many hotels now have
cessible rooms for disabled travel-
rs, but these are more common in
ger hotels. Breakfast is charged
parately in most hotels, but included
the room price in *casas rurales* and
any small hotels. Rates are generally
uoted per room, not per person, but
uoted prices do not normally
clude IVA tax (VAT), usually at 7
er cent. Prices vary between high
ason (Easter and July–August, and
ecember–February in winter sports
eas) and other times of year, and
me hotels have three price seasons
igh, medium or low: *alta, media,
ja)*. In country areas seasonal price
fferences are relatively modest, but
ey are far more acute on the coast.

Booking

In low season you can often get a
room in country hotels without any
prior notice, but booking is always
advisable. It is essential to book well
in advance on weekends, Easter and
in July and August. Reservations are
also necessary at nearly all *casas rurales*
and the most attractive small hotels.
For non-Spanish speakers the best
way is to book online. If you arrive without a booking, local tourist offices may
be able to assist.

Camping

Well-equipped campsites are plentiful,
especially around the coasts and popular mountain ranges. In summer, sites
must be booked well ahead. Nearly
all large sites admit caravans and
motorhomes *(see p20)*. Two annual
guides to camping sites across Spain
are the government-produced *Guía
Oficial de Campings* and the *Guía
Camping* of the Spanish camping
federation **FECC**.

Below far left El Habana around Llanes, *see p55*
Below left Interior of Casa Leonardo in Vall Fosca,
see p96 **Below middle** Stunning exterior of
Marqués de Riscal in Elciego, *see p62* **Below right**
Parador de Santo Estevo de Ribas de Sil in Galicia,
see p42 **Below far right** Sign for Bodegas Arzuaga
in Ribera del Duero, *see p148*

DIRECTORY

HOTELS

NH Hoteles
*902 115 116 (Spain), 800 0115 116 (UK);
www.nh-hotels.com*

Sol Meliá
*902 144 440 (Spain), 0800 962 720 (UK);
www.solmelia.com*

**PARADORS AND OTHER
DISTINCTIVE HOTELS**

Casonas Asturianas
www.casonasasturianas.com

Cantabria Infinita
www.calidadcantabria.com

Paradors
*902 547 979 (Spain), 0 2076 160 300
(UK); www.parador.es*

Posadas Reales
*902 203 030;
www.turismocastillyleon.com*

Rusticae
*902 103 892;
www.rusticae.es*

CASAS RURALES

Guíarural
www.guiarural.com

Toprural
www.toprural.com

CAMPING

**Federación Española de Clubes
Campistas (FECC)**
*986 472 273;
www.guiacampingfecc.com*

PRICE CATEGORIES

The following price ranges are for a
standard double room in high season:

*inexpensive: under €70;
moderate: €70–€120;
expensive: over €120*

Where to Eat

Eating out in Spain is a very social activity, and one to be enjoyed at your own pace. You can choose between lingering over a full menu for a relaxing lunch, picking and mixing tapas on a café terrace or just knocking back a beer and a *bocadillo* sandwich while sitting at a bar. The food of Spain is also enormously varied, with specialities in each region. In the last few years, refined restaurants have cropped up even in apparently out-of-the-way places, joining the satisfying traditional country restaurants.

Above Sign for Comercios a Ma

Practical Information

The first thing to adapt to in Spain is local meal times. Spaniards traditionally have only a light breakfast, a snack mid-morning and lunch around 2pm, followed by dinner around 9pm or later. Except in touristy areas, where restaurants often follow an "international" timetable, most restaurants only serve a full menu from about 1:30 to 4pm in the afternoons, and 8:30 to11pm at night. For those who find this restrictive, the natural alternatives to go for are tapas *(see pp26–7)*, available all day.

It is not usually necessary to book in mid- or lower-range restaurants, except on Friday and Saturday nights and Sunday lunchtimes, when reservations are a must. It is always a good idea to book ahead in more expensive restaurants. There is rarely any pressure to vacate a table once you have finished eating. A time-honoured part of a Spanish meal is the *sobremesa*, the time when you sit back to chat after a meal over coffee and liqueurs.

Restaurants are often closed on Sunday evenings and for one day each week, usually Monday. Many also close for a few weeks in low season. Credit and debit cards are accepted in virtually all restaurants and even many bars and cafés, but cash is preferred for paying small bills. All restaurant bills are liable to IVA (VAT) tax. This is usually included in menu prices, but some restaurants only add it to the final bill. A growing number of places include a service charge *(servicio incluído)* in bills, but elsewhere tipping is expected. Usually 7 per cent is enough in most restaurants.

Casual clothing is acceptable virtually everywhere except the smartest city restaurants. Children are also generally welcome. Not many restaurants have special menus for children, but most provide smaller portions on request. A growing number of restaurants have facilities for disabled diners, but this is still a problem in older buildings, so it is worth phoning to check.

Smoking rules are flexible. Small bars and cafés can choose to allow smoking or not, and their choice must be indicated on the door. Larger venues can be completely non-smoking, or have a separate smoking area.

Restaurants

Restaurante in Spain covers a wide range of places to eat. Most local and village restaurants also have a bar attached, as a *bar-restaurante*, and an open through the day; their full tab menu will usually only be available around Spanish meal times *(see above)*. A restaurant without a bar wi normally only be open at these times

Restaurants presenting Spain's acclaimed contemporary cuisine do not have a specific label, but are often indicated in listings as *restaurante gastronómico* or *cocina creativa* or *moderna*. A *marisquería* features fish and seafood *(mariscos)*. Old names fo local inns – *venta*, *posada*, *fonda* and especially *mesón* – are widely used and generally go with traditional oak beam decor and tasty regional dishes. Some restaurants are typical of certain regions. An *arrocería* shows cases *paella* and other rice *(arroz)* dishes of Valencia and southern Catalonia; an *asador* specializes in roast *(asado)* meats, typical of Castile

Most restaurants offer a set *menú del día* at lunchtime, with a starter *(primer plato* or *entrada)*, main course *(segundo plato)*, dessert *(postre)*, bread and a drink all included for around €8 €20. Gourmet restaurants may have a *menú de degustación* or tasting menu at the top end of the price scale.

ft Restaurant at Cal Sastre in Santa Pau, *see p104* **Middle** Sign of a bar in Teruel **Right** Vegetables on sale in the Costa Blanca

apas, Bars and Cafés

early all bars in Spain offer some nd of food – the only ones that gularly do not are nightclub-style ubs. Bar-restaurants offer a selection tapas available at all times, as well their table menus. In many bars nall complimentary tapas – olives, nunks of cheese – are served when-ver you order a drink, but more aborate tapas must be ordered nd paid for. A *ración* is a larger erving, almost as big as a restaurant ourse. Tapas, like everything, vary round the country: in many areas ney are fairly simple, but Basque ars are renowned for their arrays f intricate snacks.

Other kinds of food can be ordered bars. A *bocadillo* or *bocata* is a efty sandwich, made with a large nunk of Spanish bread filled with neats, cheese, Spanish omelette and o on. Many cafés also offer *platos ombinados*, single dishes with meat r fish, salad and other vegetables all n the same plate.

Vine and Other Drinks

pper and mid-range restaurants ake increasing care over their wine sts, but in others the choice is more mited, and it is often best to stay vith the *vino de la casa* or house

wine. Similarly, outside the main wine and sherry areas the wine range in bars that do not specialize in wine is often fairly plain.

Sidra (cider) is popular across northern Spain, and beer *(cerveza)* is available everywhere. Mineral water *(agua con gas,* sparkling, or *sin gas)* is always an option too. Excellent coffee can be ordered as an espresso *(café solo),* an espresso with a dash of milk *(cortado),* or a white coffee *(café con leche).* An *americano* is an espresso with twice the amount of water, and a *carajillo* is a *solo* with a dash of brandy or other spirits.

Shopping for a Picnic

Before heading into the countryside, buy picnic ingredients in the district's main town, especially, of course, on market days. At other times, the best one-stop shop is a *colmado* or gro-cery store (or *alimentación general,* or *queviures* in Catalan-speaking areas), which will have fresh fruit and vege-tables, cold meats *(charcutería),* cheeses *(quesos),* wine, beers and water. For bread, *panaderías* have *pan de barra,* the normal Spanish white baguette-style bread, country breads and sometimes brown bread *(pan integral).* There are also small supermarkets in many towns.

Below far left Tapas bar in Valderrobres **Below left** Inventive signs at a restaurant in Andaluía **Below middle** Restaurants, bars and other attractions advertised on a wall in Andalusia **Below right** Parador de Cambados, *see p36* **Below far right** Van selling snacks in Xàbia, Costa Blanca

The Flavours of Spain

Every part of Spain has its own distinctive dishes. Regions such as the Basque Country and Catalonia have complete cuisines of their own. Spain's adventurous modern chefs may experiment with ideas from around the world, but their creativity is nearly always rooted in traditions from their home region. Some favourites such as *tortilla* (potato omelette) and *chorizo* sausages are found in every part of Spain, but the more intriguing dishes have a strong local flavour. This creates a rich culinary landscape that is immensely enjoyable to explore.

Above Menu displaying the day's specials outside a restaurant

DIRECTORY

ON THE MENU

Ajoblanco (Andalusia)
Cold soup of garlic, almonds and often a range of other ingredients

Arròs negre (Catalan)
Black rice with squid, cooked in squid ink

Bacalao al pil-pil (Basque)
Salt cod fried in very hot oil with garlic

Botifarra amb mongetes (Catalan)
Sausage with haricot beans

Cochinillo asado (Castile)
Roast suckling pig

Empanada gallega (Galicia)
Pastry pie filled with tuna, peppers and other ingredients

Fabada (Asturias)
A rich stew of haricot beans, chorizo and pork

Fideuà (Catalonia and Valencia)
Similar to a paella, but made with noodles instead of rice

Gazpacho (Andalusia, with variations all across the south)
Cold tomato soup, usually served sprinkled with chopped cucumbers, peppers, onions and bread

Lacón con grelos (Galicia)
Pork joint with swiss chard and potatoes

Merluza a la vasca (Basque)
Hake cooked in white wine with prawns, clams, peppers and other ingredients

The North

With its rocky Atlantic coast, Galicia is famed above all for superb fish and seafood, especially hake, mussels, scallops and octopus, accompanied by the region's crisp white wines. Other Galician favourites such as *caldo gallego* (a stew made of greens, potatoes, bacon and other meats), reflect the bracing ocean climate and the often chilly, wet winter.

Neighbouring Asturias and Cantabria also draw excellent fish from the sea, and just inland is Spain's best dairy country, producing distinctive cheeses such as Asturias' pungent *cabrales*, helped down with *sidra* (cider). Hearty mountain stews are another hallmark. Asturian restaurants are also renowned for generous portions, and tapas can be as big as a restaurant course.

Refined, distinctive and subtle, Basque cuisine has traditionally been the most prestigious of all Spain's culinary traditions. It has served as an inspiration to a whole line of famous chefs. Fish and seafood such as salt cod, hake and crab, often with red peppers, are again mainstays. Basques also have a distinctive approach to tapas, known as *pintxos*. Instead of the relatively simple snacks, Basque bars serve impressive trays of carefully assembled and mixed tapas.

Navarra and La Rioja are known above all for superb wines, but also for many delicious dishes often featuring red peppers, nuts and river fish such as trout.

Along the Mediterranean

Catalonia is the Basque Country's main challenger in terms of culinary sophistication. Ferran Adrià (b. 1962) one of the world's most reputed chefs at the moment, is from Catalonia. Among the many Catalan specialities are unusual combinatio of meat and seafood. Much more use is made of vegetables here than in many parts of Spain. Along with refined creations there is also simple Catalan country cooking based around meats, especially lamb, rabb and *botifarra* sausages, grilled *a la brasa* over charcoal, and served with *all i oli* (garlic and mayonnaise).

Catalonia also produces a wide range of wines and sparkling cava. One of the most popular Catalan dishes is *pa amb tomàquet* (bread moistened by wiping it with tomatoes, olive oil, garlic and salt).

Above left Seafood on display **Above middle** Bottle of Spanish-made Ambar beer **Above right** Fish being grilled on stakes over a wood fire

e Balearic Islands also have teresting dishes, with a strongly editerranean flavour. Rich fish and ellfish stews are specialities. Valencia is known above all for the ternational symbol of Spanish food *paella*. In its Valencian homeland nd the rice lands of southern talonia) you can order *paella* in any different varieties, with a fasci- ating range of ingredients. Valencia also the home of another speciality at has conquered the whole coun- y, *turrón* (almond nougat). Made nce Moorish times, it is an essential ale to a Spanish Christmas feast.

he Centre: Castile and ragón

contrast to the complicated eations of Atlantic and editerranean Spain, the food of e two Castiles, Castilla y León, astilla La Mancha, puts the stress n simplicity. Meats such as the roast mb and suckling pig of Segovia, or perb *chuletón* steaks in Avila, are e centrepiece. Beans and other ulses appear in many sustaining otajes (stews). Otherwise, vege- bles are scarce and usually served parately as salads or first courses, nce Castilians traditionally prefer to onsume good meat on its own.

Punchy hams and sausages such as *chorizos*, *longaniza* and the *botillo* of León are also Castilian trademarks.

In Aragón, traditional cooking is simple, but with well-flavoured coun- try dishes featuring borage and other unusual vegetables.

The South

The best dishes of Andalusia reflect the region's Moorish past and the southern heat. Moorish influence is seen in the subtle use of almonds and honey. The characteristic cold soups such as *gazpacho* and the less well-known *ajoblanco* are deliciously refreshing in an Andalusian summer. Equally intertwined with the climate are the many salads, such as *pipirrana* (peppers, tomatoes, cucumber and garlic, with variations that include meat and fish). Fish and seafood such as squid and *pescadilla* (whiting) are generally cooked simply, either plain grilled or fried in batter. Inland, tradi- tional cooking makes more use of strong meats and pulses such as chick- peas *(garbanzos)*. Western Andalusia and neighbouring Extremadura are the home of the finest *serrano* hams. Murcia is known above all for the quality of its peppers and other Mediterranean vegetables, used in soups, salads and tapas.

DIRECTORY

ON THE TAPAS LIST

Albóndigas
Meatballs

Boquerones en vinagre
Fresh anchovies marinated in oil, lemon and vinegar

Calamares a la romana
Squid rings fried in batter

Ensaladilla rusa
Salad of potatoes, red peppers, onions, tuna and other ingredients in mayonnaise

Gambas al ajillo
Prawns cooked in garlic

Jamón serrano
Dry-cured ham

Patatas bravas
Deep-fried potatoes with a peppery sauce

Salpicón de mariscos
Seafood salad

Sobrassada (Mallorca)
Spicy, slightly soft red sausage

Below far left Sausages and cheese in a market **Below left** Varieties of olives on sale **Below middle left** Red peppers drying in the sun **Below middle right** Large pan of *paella* **Below right** Wine for sampling at a bodega **Below far right** Chef cooking squid over a fire

Zebre ros Villa S. Michael de d'Occa Villa vega Rocedil
Losada Franca Camino Montes Rabe Val de buentas Burgos
M. Furado Cacabelos Manzilla Seldana Melger Lara
Astorga P. de Calcadilla Villa nueva de Tramidos Cogollo
Ponferrada Reyna Carion d. los condes las caretes Venta moral Salduendo
S. Stevan P. de Domingo Monast. de la vega Villa martin Lerma Bahabon
Bollo Viana LEON Novia Torquema da Renero Lavid
Cabrera Terra Villalon Palentia Castroy od Arando de Oradara
Benavente Los Molines Valadolid Duenna Peniafuel Duero
Puebla de Sanabria Moral del reino Cabecon Villa banes Valpuesta Ventosa
Cadahoz Peradela Medina de Simacos Boezillo Avila fuente
Bragan S. Martinho Castromonte rio seco Mojadas Coca
ca Tracosas Aldea Villalat Pedroso S. Mª de nieva
Fruadoso Alcani Villalpando Tordezillas Marçotea
Caravalhes zos Çamora Tore Xambrino Antigu Villa nueva
Chasim Vimioso Miranda Duro rio Guarate Fuente sahuro Rodilana Olmedo Segovia
Mirandela Algozo Fuente Saldu Fuente saluro Medina del campo Don bierro S. Pedro Sepulveda
Frehes Moga Aldea nueva Ataquines Çorita Paja Avila Pto de
Benposto douro Termas Arcediano Fresno Helite Guadarama
Torre de Hermo selho Salamanca Aldea Ventosa Villa cast
Moncorvo Mezonero Ilva Pennaranda Herra dor Escurial Talamanc
Pejares Sagrada La moya Cardenosa Baraco Torre
Villarinho Labouela S. Martin del castag Zebreros lodo
Pena da francia nol Guguelo Paredes Redemolinos Alar
Castel V ulveste Endrinas Villa franca Aleorcoz Ma
redrigo S. Felizes de Gallegas Martin de rio Porto d. pico Cadahalso Legan
Guarda Cuidad Caparra Colmenar Las Ventas Caßarubios
Rodrigo Bonhos Quacos S. Sylvestro Cipuezelos Esquivias
Aveytaria Bodom Aldea nueva Laxarilla Xandarilla Maqueda C. d. Aquila
Galistro El villar Toril Vera de Placencia S. Olaia Cavana Borox
Coria Plazentia Oligura Bravo Anouer
S. Martinho Almaraz Talavera la reyna Burgel Toledo Yeyes
dos vinhos Alcantara Varias La calsada Caßalegas Venta de Osmo
Capara Cañaveral dar balla Pyẽte del Oropesa Velada Orgas
La barcas del coneta Las casas dd Arcobispo Villanelo Panojerbo Yuenes Huertas
Aroyo d ynercos puerto Tagus flu Rosatan Coßuegra
Malpartida Caçeres Naval villar Villar de pedrosa Malagon
Licenda Venta la vadera Venta del hospital Vent. d. los Nogalles Campo de Calatravo Vela
S. Vincente Aldealcano S. M. d. Guadahyiei Calatrava Carion
Venta Barachiva Venta de los herrerias Cihameros Herrera
Albergue Legruñaon Rio Guadiana Ciudad real Fardilla
Merida Medelin Trugilho Palazio del Rey Villa real Canalueches
Talavera Campilho Majadas Campanario el convento de calatrava
Torre de Trugilbano Cafra Vil. nu. della Serena La Puebla del coçer Almodoar del Venta la
TREMADV Mexia La parra Ruesta Curita campo reina Elvisa
res de badajoz Almendralejo Magazela Calbeça del ouey Ventas nuevas La venta Ilervela
Encina Sola Fuente de indostre NO VA La venta de los Palaci
da barca Ellarena Alcudia Vlches
rota Aroche Vlaire Belalcaçar Alhania Limares
Frexenal Cala Ynojosa Ventala Megibar Baes
Almonas ter Cumbres Realejo Alanis Sierra Morena Andujar
El cevro Xabuga maiores S. Olalla Cafre Cacalla S. Niclas Fesura S. Inhan
El villar Araçena Elpodioso Constantino Samossa Adamuz Torre de
Calamea Almaden Almera Corduba campo Alcaidate
C. de las guardias Casilblanco Villa nueva Lora Peñaflor Martos Carpio Moron Aravita
Buytron Azarcolla Cantillana Guadalcaçer Pas posadas Alcalareal
Valverde Efacena Gerenna Vacna Cabral Sequia
CONDA Mança Triana Bogodin La Rambla Montemaior Puerto lope
Niebla nilla Coria Carmona Campana Santella Isna gar S. Fee
Bollullos Sevilla Eçya Xenil Aguilar Priego

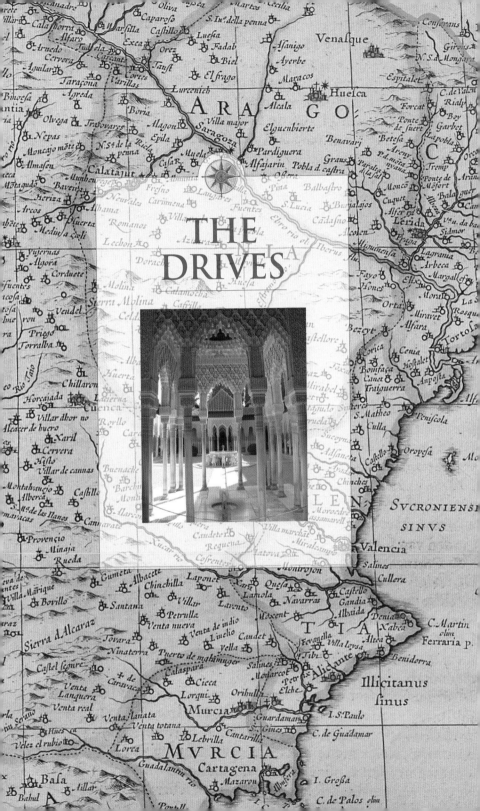

THE
DRIVES

Medieval Treasures and Golden Bays

Santiago de Compostela to Pontevedra

Highlights

- **The pilgrims' goal**
  Explore the architectural treasures of Santiago de Compostela

- **Medieval manor**
  Travel deep into the green Gallego countryside to visit the fairy-tale house and gardens of Pazo de Oca

- **Pristine beaches**
  Stroll along the lovely beaches around the Ría de Pontevedra

- **Charming street life**
  Visit one of the many excellent bars and cafés of Pontevedra's old quarter

Beaches stretch out around the
Ría de Pontevedra

Medieval Treasures and Golden Bays

The medieval city of Santiago has been a key pilgrimage destination for over a thousand years. Crammed with architectural treasures, it is less than an hour's drive from the natural beauty of Galicia's Rías Baixas. Scattered along this rugged coastline is a succession of superb beaches lining the narrow, steep-sided bays or *rías*. Pretty towns, such as Cambados and Pontevedra, offer yet more cultural gems, plus a chance to savour the area's fine cuisine and wines in their many good-value restaurants.

KEY

Drive route

0 kilometres 5

0 miles 5

Above Santiago de Compostela's grand cathedral towering over the city, *see p34*

ACTIVITIES

Forage for clams and cockles at low tide along the beach at the fishing village of Cambados

Be pampered in style at one of the luxurious spas on the tiny island of A Toxa

Soak up the sun on Galicia's longest beach, Praia de Lanzada, or rent a windsurf board and glide out into the Atlantic

Take a cruise from Sanxenxo or Portonovo out to the isolated Illa de Ons, just off the coast from Praia de Paxariñas

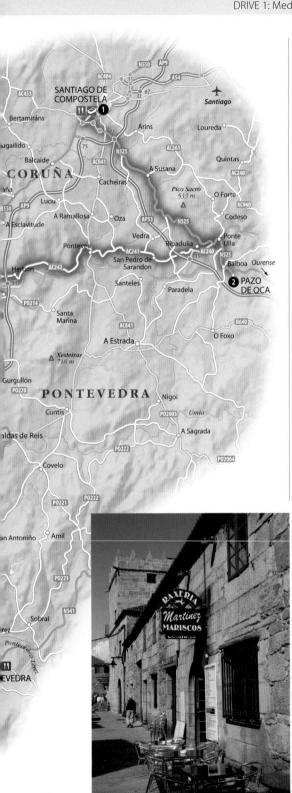

PLAN YOUR DRIVE

Start/finish: Santiago de Compostela to Pontevedra.

Number of days: 1–2, allowing half a day in Santiago.

Distances: 150 km (95 miles).

Road conditions: There are no steep climbs and roads remain passable all year round. Main roads along the coast can get crowded in summer, especially from mid-July to August.

When to go: Between May and October is the best time to visit, preferably avoiding the peak season of August.

Opening times: Most shops and museums open from 9am to 7pm daily, many closing for a couple of hours between 1 and 4pm. Churches usually stay open all day from 8am to 7pm.

Main market days: Santiago de Compostela: daily; **Cambados:** daily; **Pontevedra:** daily.

Shopping: Besides fine Albariño wines, many visitors like to take home the *tarta de Santiago* almond cakes.

Major festivals: Santiago de Compostela: Fiestas del Apóstol Santiago, 24–25 Jul; **Padrón:** Fiesta del Pimiento, first Sun Aug; **Cambados:** Festa del vino Albariño, first Sun Aug; **A Lanzada:** Romería da Lanzada, last Sun Aug; **Pontevedra:** Fiesta dos Maios, May; Fiesta de San Benito, Jul.

DAY TRIP OPTIONS

Using Santiago de Compostela as a base, spend a **leisurely day** exploring the Rías Baixas coastline, with its golden beaches, islands and pictur-esque fishing villages. **Culture** and **history lovers**, however, may prefer to head straight to Pontevedra and spend a day wandering the city's medieval alleyways. For details, see p37.

Left One of the many restaurants in Cambados, known for local wines and seafood, see p36

Above Dazzling façade of Santiago's grand cathedral looms over the Praza do Obradoiro
Below Lovely gardens of the Casa-Museo Rosalía de Castro, Padrón

VISITING SANTIAGO DE COMPOSTELA

Tourist Information
Rúa do Vilar 63, 15705; 981 555 129; www.santiagoturismo.com

Parking
The most convenient car park for the cathedral is the huge Xoán XXIII car park, a short distance north.

WHERE TO STAY

SANTIAGO DE COMPOSTELA

As Artes *moderate*
This cosy hotel is located near the cathedral. It is worth paying a little extra for one of the larger of its seven beautifully furnished rooms.
Travesa Dúas Portas 2, 15707; 981 572 590; www.asartes.com

Hostal dos Reis Católicos *expensive*
One of the oldest hotels in the world, this parador is luxurious with elegant living rooms, spectacular bedrooms and a beautiful dining room.
Plaza do Obradoiro 1, 15705; 981 582 200; www.parador.es

PADRÓN

Pension Jardin *inexpensive*
At the eastern edge of old Padrón, this fine old mansion has been tastefully converted into a very comfortable little hotel.
Avda. Franco Salgado Araujo 3, 15900; 981 810 950

① Santiago de Compostela
La Coruña; 15700

A ravishing ensemble of colonnaded stone lanes, vast squares, and mighty medieval churches, Santiago de Compostela offers a wealth of cultural treasures, along with a whirl of great places to eat, drink and sleep.

A thousand years ago, half a million pilgrims made their way each year to Santiago, walking the route known as the Camino de Santiago. The city ranked after Jerusalem and Rome as the third holiest site in Christendom, thanks to the legend that the body of the Apostle James – Sant Yago in the local Galician language – was brought here by sea after his death. Now encircled by suburbs, the city's ancient core has changed little. In its labyrinth of alleyways, each building merges organically into the next.

Towering over the Praza do Obradoiro, a large square usually packed with pilgrims, the **Catedral de Santiago de Compostela** is an amazing spectacle. Its Baroque façade dates from the 18th century. Behind, its Romanesque predecessor, six centuries older, remains largely intact. Enter via the Pórtico de Gloria, pausing to touch the carved Tree of Jesse. Relics of St James are preserved in a crypt beneath the gilded altar.

The Romanesque **Pazo de Xelmirez** *(open Mon–Sun, closed Sun afternoon)* and the Baroque church of the **Monasterio de San Martiño Pinario** *(open Mon–Sun)* in Praza da Immaculata are also worth visiting.

🚗 *From the Xoán XXIII car park, take the exit northeast on Avenue Xoán XXIII to join Santiago's ring road. Turn right at the third traffic light, following signs to Ourense on the N525. Just past the "Km 319" marker, turn right and follow signs for Pazo de Oca.*

② Pazo de Oca
Pontevedra; 36685

The best preserved *pazo* (traditional country house) in Galicia, the Pazo de Oca is enchanting. The 18th-century mansion is not open to visitors. Its gardens *(open daily)* are the attraction. Part playful, part formal, they centre on a small lake that holds a couple of boat-shaped islands. Hydrangeas and magnolias blossom on all sides, and everywhere is the trickle of running water from the irrigation channels that feed vine-clad trellises. Statues and topiary abound.

🚗 *Return to the N525 and turn left towards Santiago. Go left from Pont Ulla (direction Arzúa/Pontevea) on t AC240 which later becomes the AC24 At Pontevea, turn right and then left onto the AC242 and cross the auto-pista. Continue into Padrón. Turn rig before the railway to park outside Casa-Museo Rosalía de Castro.*

③ Padrón
La Coruña; 15900

Padrón is best known for its succulent *pimientos*, little green peppers deep-fried and served whole in tapas bars across Spain. It was home to Galicia's most famous poet, Rosalía de Castro (1837–85), who wrote in both Galician and Castilian. Her charming house, opposite the town's railway station, now serves as the Casa-Museo Rosalía de Castro *(closed Mon)*, with memorabilia downstairs and her living quarters preserved upstairs.

🚗 *Continue on the AC242 and take the N550 left in Padrón. Turn right onto the PO548. Follow signs through Vilagarcía, then after 5 km (3 miles) onto the PO549, beyond Vilaxoán, turn right onto the PO307 and cross the bridge to Illa de Arousa. Follow signs for Parque Natural de Carreiró*

Parque Natural de Carreirón

ntevedra; 36626

e Illa de Arousa, linked to the mainland by a long, low road bridge,
probably the one place in the whole of the Rías Baixas that remains
osest to its original, natural state. That is why it is worth taking the
me to stroll along the footpaths of the Parque Natural de Carreirón,
cated at the southern end of this heavily forested island. The
plated beaches, heathland and saltwater marshes of this natural
rk have been set aside as a sanctuary for migratory waterbirds.

two-hour walking tour

placard by the car park maps out
o possible loop walks around this
promontory, one of 3.6 km (2 miles)
d one of 2.5 km (1.5 miles) that
volves taking a short cut across the
ddle. Visitors are, however, unlikely
regret taking the longer route,
it allows extra time in delightful
rroundings. All the way around the
erimeter rough-hewn granite picnic
bles stand amid the pines.

Head right from the car park,
rough the woods lining the south
ore of the Enseada da Brava. A
0 m (110 yd) or so along, either
rn left to take the shorter loop, or
ontinue ahead to reach the mouth
the bay, to enjoy the ocean views
om the **Punta da Cruz** ①. To the
uthwest, the town of O Grove and
e linked island of A Toxa are clearly
sible, while yachts and fishing
bats thread their way between the
sser islets. The headland itself con-
sts of tumbled, eroded boulders

and an abundance of tidal pools. The
two loops meet again at the **Praia
das Margaritas** ②, a tiny pocket of
sand amid jumbled rocks. Continue
south, rounding the peninsula's southern tip. Immediately inland of the
Praia Lontreira ③ is a saltwater marsh
that is a good spot to watch for
wading birds, including herons and
ducks. Turning up the eastern side
of the peninsula, there are longer
strands of beach, such as the **Praia de
Salinas** ④, where swimming in summer is easy and safe. There are tremendous views along the coast from
here, with the low-lying rafts that are
used to cultivate mussels tethered in
symmetrical rows across the *rías* and
the town of Cambados sprawling
along the shore over to the east.
Continue on the trail to the car park.
🚗 *Drive back across the bridge,
to rejoin the PO549. Turn right and
5 km (3 miles) south the road enters
Cambados via the Praza de Fefiñanes.
Park on the far side of the square.*

Above Colourful boats used by local
fishermen along the Illa de Arousa's shore

VISITING PARQUE NATURAL DE CARREIRÓN

Tourist Information
There is no tourist information office,
simply a noticeboard in the park,
though the park management can be
contacted by phone.
986 805 483

Parking
Park at the end of the road at the start
of the trail.

EAT AND DRINK

SANTIAGO DE COMPOSTELA

Los Sobrinos del Padre Benito
inexpensive
This is the perfect place to try the
Gallego speciality of *pulpo a feira*
(octopus with potatoes and paprika).
*San Miguel dos Argos 7, 15704;
closed Mon*

Sant Yago *inexpensive*
In a city of great tapas bars, Sant Yago
ranks among the very best, whether it
is an order of a delicious made-to-
order tortilla, flash-fried baby squid or
a plate of ham and cheese.
Rúa da Raíña 12, 15702; 981 582 444

Don Gaiferos *expensive*
This highly atmospheric restaurant,
deep beneath vaulted stone ceilings in
old Santiago, has wonderfully attentive
service and a full menu of succulent
seafood and meat dishes.
*Rúa Nova 23, 15705; 981 583 984;
closed Sun*

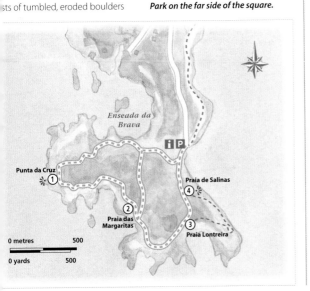

Eat and Drink: inexpensive, under €20; moderate, €20–€40; expensive, over €40

Above Capela de San Caralampio, A Toxa
Below Capela de Nosa Señora in A Lanzada

FERRIES TO ILLA DE ONS

Ferries to the island sail from
Portonovo and Sanxenxo.

Naviera Mar de Ons
986 225 272; www.mardeons.com

Cruceiros Rías Baixas
986 441 678; www.isladeons.net

WHERE TO STAY

CAMBADOS

Os Pazos *inexpensive*
Old-fashioned Os Pazos is housed
above a good-value restaurant, with
simple but spacious *en suite* bedrooms.
*Rúa Eduardo Pondal 1, 36630;
986 542 020*

Parador de Cambados *expensive*
This fine old manor house is the most
comfortable hotel in Cambados, with
pleasant gardens and a good restaurant.
*Plaza Calzada, 36630; 986 542 250;
www.parador.es*

A LANZADA

Samar Hotel *moderate–expensive*
Perched in splendid isolation at the
north end of A Lanzada beach, this
hotel has spacious ocean-view rooms
and a large terrace restaurant.
*9 Ctra. de San Vicente do Mar, 36989;
986 738 378; www.samarhotel.com*

PONTEVEDRA

Hotel Ruas *moderate*
Smart Hotel Ruas has presentable
rooms. It is ideally positioned for nightlife in one of old Pontevedra's squares.
*Rúa Padre Sarmiento 20, 36003;
986 846 416*

Parador Casa del Baron *expensive*
This inviting hotel is housed in a
majestic former palace in the lanes of
Pontevedra's ravishing old quarter.
*Rúa del Baron 19, 36002; 986 855 800;
www.parador.es*

⑤ Cambados

Pontevedra; 36630
Despite its lack of a swimming
beach, medieval Cambados is the
prettiest seaside town in the Rías
Baixas. It centres on the **Praza de
Fefiñanes**, a large flagstoned square
that is set well back from the ocean,
and is alive with bars and restaurants.
During harvest season, tractors
unload crates of the plump, white
grapes used to make Albariño wine
into the cellars of the ancient stone
mansions that line the narrow main
street. Down by the harbour, sturdy
cockle-pickers dig shellfish from the
sands exposed by each low tide.

🚗 *Head south, then right at the first
traffic light west on the PO550 from
Cambados. After 14 km (8 miles), on
reaching the peninsula that leads to A
Toxa island, turn right onto the PO316
for 4 km (2 miles) towards O Grove,
then turn right again onto the A Toxa
bridge. Head right on reaching the
island, and park alongside the hotels.*

Albariño Wine

Since Galicia's dry, elegant Albariño
was first officially standardized and
certified in 1986, it has become
firmly established internationally as
one of the most popular Spanish
wines. The Albariño grape variety
from which the wine is made was
introduced to the region by medieval German monks – the name
means "white (wine)" from the
Rhine". Thousands of farmers now
grow Albariño in small-scale vineyards concentrated mainly around
Cambados. Wineries that can be
visited include Condes de Albarei,
2 km (1 mile) south of town (*www.
condesdealbarei.com*).

⑥ A Toxa

Pontevedra; 36991
Reached by a short road bridge fro
the fishing port of O Grove, the littl
wooded island of A Toxa became
famous for its healing waters durin
the 19th century. As a result, it is no
swamped by luxury spas, hotels an
holiday villas and can become a littl
overcrowded, although it is still pos
ble to enjoy a quiet walk along the
attractive seashore. The 12th-centu
hermitage **Capela de San Caralamp**
(open daily), with its walls covered in
scallop shells, is well worth a visit.

🚗 *Recross the bridge from A Toxa,
turn left onto the PO316 to reach the
north end of Praia de Lanzada and
take a turn at the roundabout to a
large car park to the right of the roa*

⑦ A Lanzada

Pontevedra; 36989
The majestic golden crescent of the
Praia de Lanzada is the best known
of the Rías Baixas beaches. Stretchir
for around 7 km (4 miles) along the
southern shore of a slender isthmus
it is busy with swimmers, surfers an
sunbathers in high summer. For the
rest of the year, it is the perfect plac
for a long, windswept stroll, enjoyin
superb views out to the scattered o
shore islands. On the road out of A
Lanzada, between Km 27 and 26 on
the PO308, turn right (following sign
for the Capela) to get to the **Capela
de Nosa Señora** *(open daily)*.

🚗 *Go 2 km (1 mile) south along Prai
de Lanzada and come back onto the
coastal PO308. About 10 km (6 miles,
along, at a sharp bend to the left,
follow a sign to the right, down to the
car park for Praia de Paxariñas.*

Praia de Paxariñas
ntevedra; 36970

e tiny beach at Paxariñas is perhaps
e definitive example of the kind of
eltered cove that makes the Rías
xas so popular with holidaying
milies. Tucked down at the foot of
all cliffs, out of sight of a coastal
ad that is lined with little hotels, it
a wonderful spot to while away a
v hours. Take a ferry to the **Illa de**
s from either Portonovo or
nxenxo, east of Praia de Paxariñas.
e island cradles pretty beaches on
inland side, such as the Praia das
rnas, where the boats dock. The
d hillsides facing the ocean are
eal for walking.

Continue east on the PO308 and
ss through Portonovo and above
ntral Sanxenxo. After 15 km (9 miles)
m Sanxenxo, at the west end of Poio
ar Casalvito, follow a signposted
rning to the left to reach the car park.

Poio
ntevedra; 36995

hough Poio itself is only a fairly
ain modern beach town, a true gem
old Galicia survives not far up the
lside – the 500-year-old Benedictine
onasterio de Poio *(open daily)*. As
ell as an imposing church, the com-
ex includes a colonnaded cloister,
corated with a mosaic mural that
picts the history of the pilgrimage
Santiago. There is also a museum of
e world's smallest books, while a
wer annex serves as a hotel.

Return to the PO308 and turn left.
ntinue on this road to the end, follow-
g signs to Pontevedra. Turn right to
oss Ría de Pontevedra Lérez and
ach Pontevedra. Follow signs to one
the underground car parks.

⑩ Pontevedra
Pontevedra; 36000

The old city of Pontevedra is cradled
in the final bend of the Ría de
Pontevedra Lérez. A stroll through its
compact pedestrian core of cobbled
alleys introduces visitors to a succession of charming medieval squares,
ranging from the formal and spacious
Praza da Ferreria to the elegant Praza
de Teucro with its rows of orange
trees and the Praza da Verdura with its
lively cafés and bars. Prettiest of them
all is the tiny Praza da Lena, where a
fascinating museum of Gallego history
and culture, the **Museo de Pontevedra**
(open Tue–Sun), is housed in a cluster
of five neighbouring historic buildings,
one of which is in the church of Santo
Domingo a few blocks away. Among
the works on display are 15th-century
canvases by Goya and Zurbaran.

Above left View of the beach near Sanxenxo
Above right Praza de Teucro, Pontevedra

EAT AND DRINK

CAMBADOS

Yago Daporta *moderate*
Try creative Galician cuisine highlighting
local fresh seafood here.
Rúa Hospital 7, 36630; 986 526 062;
www.yayodaporta.com; closed Sun
dinner, Mon and two weeks in Nov

POIO

Casa Solla *expensive*
Enjoy Gallego favourites and views
over the bay in this elegant spot.
Avda. Sineiro 7, 36005; 986 872 884;
www.restaurantsolla.com; closed Mon,
Thu and Sun dinner

PONTEVEDRA

O Cortello *inexpensive*
Excellent tapas are available here at
exceptionally good prices.
Rúa Isabel II 36, 36002; 986 840 443

DAY TRIP OPTIONS
To break up the drive into day trips,
it is best to stay overnight in either
Santiago de Compostela at the start
of the trip or Pontevedra at the end,
both easily accessible by the AP9.

Nature's unspoilt wonders
Spend the morning on the beach of
A Lanzada ⑦. Then allow an hour to
savour the wild Illa de Arousa and its
Parque Natural de Carreirón ④. A
stop en route in the picturesque

village of Cambados ⑤, to sample
fine Albariño wines at one of the
bodegas, is a must.

From Santiago, head south towards
Padrón on the N550. Then follow the
coastal PO549 and PO550 through
Cambados to A Lanzada. Return to
Santiago the same way.

Medieval treasure trove
Walk around the labyrinth of ancient,
winding alleyways, crammed with

glorious examples of medieval architecture in Pontevedra ⑩. Beautiful
squares and fine old mansions are
punctuated by a stream of appealing
cafés and restaurants. A short round-
trip west takes in the magnificent
Monasterio de Poio ⑨.

Take the N550 or AP9 motorway south
from Santiago to Pontevedra. Poio is
4 km (2 miles) west of Pontevedra on
the PO308.

Eat and Drink: inexpensive, under €20; moderate, €20–€40; expensive, over €40

Along the Sacred Shore

Ourense to the Valle del Silencio

Highlights

- **Medieval monastery**
  Visit the cliff top Monasterio de Santo Estevo de Ribas de Síl, which now doubles as a magnificent spa hotel

- **Majestic canyon**
  Trek through the Cañón do Síl, sculpted with ancient Roman terraced vineyards

- **Gold fever**
  Take in the extraordinary stark beauty of the Roman gold mines at Las Médulas

- **Spectacular valley**
  Walk the trails of the Valle del Silencio and explore its sanctuaries and monasteries

Magnificent golden-yellow rock formations at Las Médulas

Along the Sacred Shore

In its final stretch before meeting the Miño river, not far northeast of the provincial capital of Ourense, the Síl river has carved a stupendous canyon, cloaked with ancient forests. This tour traces the sheer green walls of the gorge, which have been sculpted since Roman times with precarious terraced vineyards. The sides of the gorge are so prized for their fine, rare soils that they are known as the Ribeira Sacra (the Sacred Shore). Continuing east towards Ponferrada, the route climbs into the eerie bad lands of Las Médulas, devastated by Roman gold-mining operations. The drive finally reaches the Valle del Silencio, where early Christian churches and monasteries, linked by ravishing foot trails, lie hidden high in the woods.

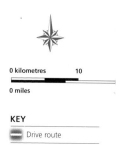

0 kilometres   10

0 miles

KEY

Drive route

Above Village of Peñalba de Santiago nestled in the mountains, *see p44*

ACTIVITIES

Walk through the woods by the Síl river or the mountains

Taste the exquisite wines of the Ribeira Sacra

Explore the ancient monasteries in the Valle del Silencio

ove Courtyard of the Monasterio de Santo Estevo de Ribas de Síl, *see p42*

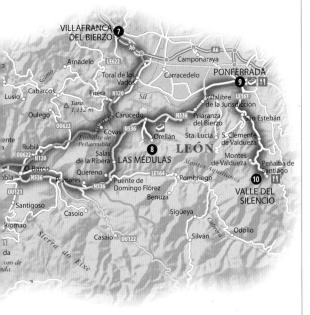

low Rugged rock formations at Las Médulas, *see p44*

PLAN YOUR DRIVE

Start/finish: Ourense to the Valle del Silencio.

Number of days: 2–3, allowing half a day to explore the Valle del Silencio.

Distance: 320 km (200 miles).

Road conditions: Roads in the Síl gorge and all mountain valleys are susceptible to ice in winter. The roads, especially on the Síl section and around the Valle del Silencio, are poorly paved and very narrow and winding at parts.

When to go: The ideal time to visit is spring for wild flowers or autumn for foliage. The Valle del Silencio is inaccessible in winter.

Opening hours: Most shops and monuments are open from 9am to 6pm with a break from 1 to 4pm.

Main market days: Ourense: 7th, 17th and 25th of every month.

Shopping: The major products on sale are earthy local foods such as figs, chestnuts, honey, strong cheeses and Ribeira Sacra wine.

Major festivals: Ourense: Festival de Cine Internacional, Oct; Ponferrada: San José Obrero de Cuatrovientos, 1 May.

DAY TRIP OPTIONS

Architecture enthusiasts will enjoy a trip to the monasteries on the Canón do Síl, while **adventure lovers** will enjoy a boat trip on the Síl river. **History buffs** will be fascinated by the rugged beauty of Las Médulas. For details, *see p45.*

Above Puente Romano, over the Miño river, in Ourense **Below** Monasterio de Santo Estevo de Ribas de Síl nestled in the mountains

WHERE TO STAY

OURENSE

Gran Hotel San Martín *moderate*
This very comfortable high-rise hotel overlooks the Parque San Lázaro.
Rúa Curros Enriquez 1, 32003; 988 371 811; www.gh-hoteles.com

MONASTERIO DE SANTO ESTEVO DE RIBAS DE SÍL

Parador de Santo Estevo de Ribas de Síl *expensive*
This magnificent monastery has rooms and a restaurant with great views over the Cañón do Síl.
Nogueira de Ramuín, 32162; 988 010 110; www.parador.es

AROUND MONASTERIO DE SANTA CRISTINA DE RIBAS DE SÍL

Reitoral de Chandrexa *inexpensive*
Near the river and 5 km (3 miles) from the monastery, this is a lovely three-room rural bed-and-breakfast.
Parada do Síl, 32747; 988 208 099; www.chandrexa.com; credit cards not accepted

CASTRO CALDELAS

Hotel Vicente Risco *inexpensive*
This charming hotel offers comfortable rooms and a good-value restaurant.
Rúa Grande 4, 32769; 988 203 360; www.pousadavicenterisco.com

A POBRA DE TRIVES

Casa Grande de Trives *inexpensive*
In a beautifully restored manor house, this bed-and-breakfast offers rooms with modern facilities.
C/ Marqués de Trives 17, 32780; 988 332 066; www.casagrandetrives.com

❶ Ourense

Ourense; 32000
The handsome city of Ourense was founded by the Romans on the south bank of the Miño river, around the city's well-known, mineral-rich thermal springs, **Fonte as Burgas**. Its hilltop historic core, a tangle of tiny stone lanes interspersed with arcaded squares, holds an appeal for visitors. The 12th- to 13th-century **Catedral de San Martiño** is the city's principal sight. Two contrasting bridges span the river – the much-rebuilt seven-arched **Puente Romano**, and the eye-catching **Puente Milenio**, unveiled in 2001, which offers great views.

🚗 *Take the N120 out of town, towards Monforte. After 18 km (11 miles), turn right onto the C546 to Luíntra. Just before Pereira, turn sharp left onto the OU0555, following signs to "Parador" and then left onto the OU0508. After 4 km (3 miles) turn left onto the OU0504 to reach Santo Estevo de Ribas de Síl.*

❷ Monasterio de Santo Estevo de Ribas de Síl

Ourense; 32164, 32747
The ancient Monasterio de Santo Estevo de Ribas de Síl *(open daily)* is perched high above an especially narrow section of the Síl river gorge. Originally built as a chapel in the 6th century, it was expanded by the Benedictine order 400 years later, which accounts for its current majestic size. While its magnificent church and three cool, quiet cloisters remain intact, other sections have been converted into a stylish parador hotel. Walking trails lead from the end of the OU504 through a superb old chestnut forest, with tremendous

views over the canyon. Hiking 11 km (7 miles) northwest goes down to the river at Os Peares, and 17 km (11 miles) east leads to the Monasterio de Santa Cristina de Ribas de Síl.

Drive back to the OU0508 and drive eastwards left past Albeguería and Cerreda; park across the road from the **Mirador de Cabezoás**. A rare break in the woods that engulf much of the OU0508, the viewpoint provides a bird's-eye view of the river's northern shore, and of the city of Monforte de Lemos on the distant plains.

🚗 *Drive east (left) onto the OU0508. At the end of the road, turn left onto the OU0605 to Parada de Síl. Turn left towards Castro, then turn right to reach Santa Cristina de Ribas de Síl.*

❸ Monasterio de Santa Cristina de Ribas de Síl

Ourense; 32747, 32765
The remote, haunting ruins of the 10th-century Monasterio de Santa Cristina de Ribas de Síl *(open daily)* stand high above the Síl valley, in the eerie silence of an ancient chestnut grove. Set just below the dead end of a precipitous road that drops from the village of Castro, the monastery is partially sheltered by a modern wooden roof. Even when its chapel and tower are locked, visitors can follow walkways to admire what is left of its former frescoes and read explanatory placards in Spanish and English.

From the monastery, go back to Castro and drive on through Parada de Síl to turn left onto the OU0605 to **A Teixeira**. The name A Teixeira, which identifies both a specific village and a municipality, comes from the Galleg

ord for the abundant yew trees on
e slopes of the Síl's south bank.

e village houses the **Casa do Viño**
*osed Sat, Sun and Mon in winter and
on in summer), a museum about local
nes, and is well worth a stop for
e remarkable view that its terraces
er of the surrounding valleys.

*Head east from A Teixeira on the
O0607. After 5 km (3 miles) turn left
to the OU903, signposted for
nforte, to reach the Ponte do Síl.*

Ponte do Síl
go; 27424

ry few roads access, let alone cross,
e gorge of the Síl river. The drive
wn to the low-slung Ponte do Síl,
ep in the inner canyon, is extremely
autiful. Cross the Ponte do Síl and
ke the OU903, which becomes
e LU903 across the river, towards
onforte. Turn left onto the LU5904
the tiny village of **Doade**. Under
e grand name of the Spatium
erpretationis Riveyra Sacrata, a mon-
nent to the wine-growing traditions
the Síl gorge marks a viewpoint on
e north bank of the river, just south
Doade. Depicting a female har-
ster weighed down by a basket of
shly-picked grapes, it overlooks a
narkable stretch of vineyards. An
ricate tracery of terraces and tracks
es all over the towering cliffs; every-
here vines cling to the rocky terrain
d a number of toiling figures can
seen tending their individual plots.
*Stay on the OU903 from Ponte do
to Castro Caldenas. Turn left follow-
g a sign "Comarcal Comercial" and
rk below the castle.*

Castro Caldelas
rense; 32760

e old quarter of the fortified hilltop
wn of Castro Caldelas is dominated
the partly restored 14th-century
stillo de Castro Caldelas *(closed
4pm)*. Visitors can stroll along its
ttlements and climb its keep to
joy panoramic views. The castle's
lls hold the **Museo Etnográfico**
en daily) displaying local crafts and
ditions. The tourist office, opposite
e main castle entrance, has displays
the region, including a relief
odel of the whole Síl canyon.
*Turn left and follow the OU536
om Castro Caldelas and after 23 km*

*(14 miles) turn left onto the OU636 to
reach A Pobra de Trives.*

6 A Pobra de Trives
Ourense; 32780

Explore the pedestrian lanes of the
older quarter of A Pobra de Trives and
visitors will find a likeable, quietly
thriving community where the bars
and cafés are geared more to locals
than passing tourists. East of A Pobra
de Trives, the OU636 drops down to
cross the Bibei river on the **Ponte
Bibei**. The remote countryside east of
A Pobra de Trives was once traversed
by a major Roman road, the **Via Nova**,
which connected Astorga with Braga.
The Ponte Bibei is a relic from that era.
Standing 25 m (75 ft) high and 75 m
(245 ft) long, it still carries traffic
across the deep valley of the Bibei.
There are two Roman columns by
the bridge – one commemorating its
construction – between AD 79 and 81
and the other honouring the Spanish-
born Emperor Trajan (AD 53–117).
*Continue on the OU636, turn left
onto the OU533 and right onto the
N120. After 50 km (31 miles) turn left
onto the A6 (direction Lugo/A Coruña)
to reach Villafranca del Bierzo.*

Above left Flower-decked columbarium in
Parada de Síl **Above right** Sleepy town of A
Pobra de Trives **Below** Colourful and cosy
restaurant in Castro Caldelas

VISITING THE PONTE DO SÍL

Catamaran Cruises
Catamaran cruises start from the
Centro Turístico Ponte do Síl and cruise
through parts of the river and gorge
that visitors would otherwise not see.
*982 254 545; www.hemisferios.es,
www.riosil.com*

EAT AND DRINK

OURENSE

San Miguel *moderate*
This Gallego restaurant specializes in
fish dishes and has a great wine cellar.
*Rúa San Miguel 12–14, 32003; 988 221
245; www.restaurantesanmiguel.com*

A POBRA DE TRIVES

La Viuda *inexpensive*
A centrally located restaurant, this place
serves a range of fish and meat dishes.
*C/ Rosalía de Castro 13, 32780;
988 330 101*

A Cepa Bar *inexpensive*
Visitors looking for tapas and a coffee
should drop by this place.
Rúa Real 6, 32780; closed Tue in winter

Eat and Drink: inexpensive, under €20; moderate, €20–€40; expensive, over €40

Top Rugged, golden cliffs at the mines in Las Médulas **Above** Thirteenth-century Templar castle at Ponferrada

VISITING THE VALLE DEL SILENCIO

Tourist Information
24415, Peñalba de Santiago; 987 424 236

Parking
There is a large car park at the edge of the village of Peñalba de Santiago.

WHERE TO STAY

AROUND LAS MÉDULAS

O Palleiro *inexpensive*
This guesthouse provides attractive rooms and hearty "Roman" dinners.
C/ San Pablo, 24444, Orellán; 987 695 395; www.opalleiro.com

PONFERRADA

Hostal La Encina *inexpensive*
Facing the Templar castle, this hotel has comfortable rooms, a bar and a café.
C/ Comendador 4, 24400; 987 409 632; www.hostallaencina.com

⑦ Villafranca del Bierzo
León; 24500

Although the town of Villafranca del Bierzo has been on the beaten track for more than a thousand years – dozens of pilgrims on the Camino de Santiago still pass through this town every day – it remains unspoiled. Stretching along the east bank of the Burbia river, and up the surrounding hillsides, its slate-roofed houses are interspersed with stately squares. Its churches range from the 10th-century Romanesque **Iglesia de Santiago**, perched where the Camino enters town, to the huge 17th-century **Convento de San Nicolás el Real** down by the main square. There is also an impressive 16th-century drum-towered **castle**, which is privately owned and not open to visitors.

🚗 *Retrace the route until O Barco. Turn onto the N536. Turn right at Carucedo, following the purple signs to Las Médulas. Then fork left and right towards Orellán, following signs to "Mirador de Orellán".*

⑧ Las Médulas
León; 24444

The steep 600-m (2,000-ft) walk from the car park up to the Mirador de Orellán offers no hint of the extraordinary devastated landscape that lies beyond the ridge at the top. The green, gorse-covered mountain looks like it has been sliced in half.

Though it resembles something from the Wild West, this landscape is far from natural. This is all that remains of a colossal Roman gold mine. During the 1st and 2nd centuries AD, the mines of Las Médulas were the most important gold mines in the Roman Empire, yielding 6,500 kgs (14,300 lbs) of gold per year.

🚗 *Drive back to Carucedo, then head 15 km (9 miles) right on the N536 to Ponferrada.*

⑨ Ponferrada
León; 24400

The town of Ponferrada, perched above the east bank of the Síl, still preserves its attractive old core. A medieval bridge reinforced with iron *(pons ferrata)*, erected for the benefit of pilgrims, gave this town its name. Its main feature is a **castle**, originally fortified by the Knights Templar during the 13th century to protect pilgrims, and repeatedly enlarged thereafter. A stroll around the battlements offers a view out to the stark ridges of the surrounding mountains. Nearby, the quiet streets hold fine mansions and an interesting museum on the region, the **Museo del Bierzo** *(closed Mon)*.

🚗 *From the castle, continue straight and turn right at the first roundabout onto the LE161. Head southwards following signs to Peñalba de Santiago.*

⑩ Valle del Silencio
León; 24415

Early in the 10th century the Bishop of Astorga, San Genadio, established a monastery at Peñalba de Santiago. The village now centres on an exquisite little church – all that is left of the long-vanished monastery. The valley that lay beyond, known as the Valle del Silencio (Valley of Silence), was already a favoured refuge of Christian hermits, and Genadio himself spent the last 20 years of his life in meditation here. This walk is a small part of the magnificent 15-km (9-mile) long trail circles the valley.

A two-hour walking tour

From the car park, enter Peñalba and take the first fork right towards the church, the **Iglesia de Santiago** ①. Turn right following the gravel road that leads down between houses. The path drops swiftly from the village, passing meadows and apple orchards. After 300 m (330 yd), turn right into the woods, along a footpath signposted "Cueva". The footpath passes beneath a heavy canopy of old chestnut, walnut, and poplar trees. It is liable to be damp and muddy all year round. It soon emerges into open country, following the contours of the hillside, with mighty bare crags looming ahead across the valley to the right. ghly 1 km (0.6 miles) out of alba the LE14 joins the path from right, and they continue ahead ether. The only sound here is likely e the wind in the trees and per- s the rush of water from the yo del Silencio (Stream of Silence) far below. Cross the **wooden kway ②** and follow the trail to a a short distance ahead, where LE14 drops to the right. Take the fork instead and climb slightly to h the stream cascading down hillside. Cross it on the rickety den walkway ③ that rests on rocks – much too rudimentary e called a bridge. Further on, the h continues to climb on the far e, although now doubling back

towards the main valley. It becomes more of a ledge than a path, roughly a third of the way up a towering cliff-face, and reaches the natural open terrace in front of the **Cueva de San Genadio ④**. The actual cave is partially walled off. On stepping through the gap, there is a small shrine to the saint with an altar carved into the stone with a simple wooden statue. The cliff is the **Peña Alba ⑤**, for which Peñalba is named. The village is clearly visible to the east from here.

To see more of the valley, visitors can take the LE14 on their walk back to Peñalba. It is a slightly longer route, with a brief stiff climb after crossing the Arroyo del Friguera, not long before reaching the southern end of the village and the car park.

Above Mountains on the way to the Valle del Silencio

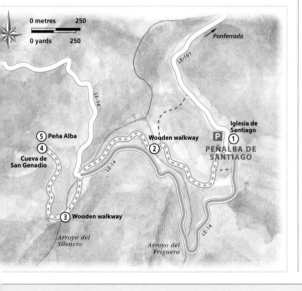

EAT AND DRINK

VILLAFRANCA DEL BIERZO

Mesón Don Nacho *inexpensive*
This is a cosy, cellar-like restaurant with a wide array of tapas.
C/ Truqueles 1, 24500; 987 540 076; www.donnacho.restaurantesok.com; closed Wed

PONFERRADA

Taberna Los Arcos *moderate*
Ponferrada's finest restaurant serves local dishes such as *botillo* (pork hotpot).
Plaza del Ayuntamiento 4, 24400; 987 409 001; www.hotelbierzoplaza.com

VALLE DEL SILENCIO

La Cantina *inexpensive*
Peñalba's only restaurant, this serves rich stew and *empanada* (a meaty pie).
C/ Bajada del Silencio, 24415, Peñalba de Santiago; 987 695 370

AY TRIP OPTIONS

he drive can be divided into several horter day trips with either Ourense n the N120) or Ponferrada (on the 6) as a base.

omanesque monasteries
rchitecture enthusiasts will enjoy he round-trip along the Síl canyon o see the medieval monasteries of anto Estevo de Ribas de Síl ❷ and anta Cristina de Ribas de Síl ❸.

eave Ourense on the N120 and follow gns for Luíntra to take the OU0508 to

Santo Estevo de Ribas de Síl. Continue on the OU0508 to Santa Cristina de Ribas de Síl. Drive eastwards, then take the LU903 to rejoin the N120 to Ourense.

Cruising along the river
For the best possible views of the Síl canyon, take a boat trip on the river. Most river cruises set off in the morning from the Ponte do Síl ❹.

Head northeast from Ourense on the N120. Then turn south at Monforte de Lemos and follow the LU903 for 19 km (12 miles) to reach the Ponte do Síl.

The Roman goldmines
The extraordinary Roman goldmines at Las Médulas ❽ are a sight worth seeing. Driving up into the hills south of the Síl river, visitors are confronted by a landscape, punctuated by rock formations and devastated by 2000-year-old mining operations.

Follow the CL536 southwest from Ponferrada. At Carucedo, 22 km (14 miles) to the west, turn left, then fork left and park 5 km (3 miles) beyond Orellán village near the viewpoint for Las Médulas.

Eat and Drink: inexpensive, under €20; moderate, €20–€40; expensive, over €40

Ocean and Mountain

Ribadesella to Llanes

Highlights

- **Awe-inspiring mountain scenery**
  Marvel at soaring peaks, precipitous gorges and lush valleys

- **Atlantic beaches**
  Jump the surf on golden ocean beaches beneath granite cliffs at Ribadesella and Llanes

- **Generous cuisine**
  Sample robust mountain dishes made with fresh produce, and washed down with fine wines or sparkling local cider

- **Remote villages**
  Discover old stone villages such as Bejes and Bulnes apparently lost in their mountain valleys, with an unbeatable tranquillity

Quiet village of Posada de Valedón, in the heart of the Picos de Europa

Ocean and Mountain

When Spanish mariners returned from their early voyages to the Americas, the first sight of land they often had from far out at sea was that of the giant summits rising up behind the Asturian and Cantabrian coasts. These summits thus gained the name "Picos de Europa". Within just 20 km (12 miles) of the Atlantic shore, rocky crags soar up over 2,000 m (6,550 ft), creating a special mix of landscapes. Each of the once-isolated valleys around the Picos has its own microclimate. This drive begins in one of the charming old ports on the Asturian coast and ends in another, passing through a breathtaking scenic display.

0 kilometres 5

0 miles 5

KEY

Drive route

Above Immense views from the winding road below Puerto de San Glorio, *see p52*

ACTIVITIES

Splash around on the beaches of Ribadesella and Llanes

Kayak down the crystal waters of the Sella river from Cangas de Onís

Take a cable car up to the massive rock plateau above Fuente Dé for an eagle's-eye view of the Picos

Explore a fabulous range of hiking trails, from the old trail through the Desfiladero del Río Cares to the peaks above Bulnes

Spot eagles circling in the sky above mountain lakes

Relax after a walk with a glass of cool cider and fresh tapas at a traditional heavy-timbered *sidrería*

Soak up the atmosphere of ancient churches and monasteries in and around Potes

Above left Charming town centre of Ribadesella, *see p50* **Above right** Basilica of Covadonga in its mountain valley, *see p50*

PLAN YOUR DRIVE

Start/finish: Ribadesella to Llanes.

Number of days: 3–4, including half a day for a walk around Soto de Sajambre.

Distances: 350 km (220 miles).

Road conditions: Well signposted and in good condition except for narrow lanes, which can be bumpy. Roads may be closed or require chains in winter.

When to go: Weather in the Picos is very changeable, but in general, skies are bright and sunny, with moderate temperatures from April to early October. Hiking trails are crowded in late July and August.

Opening hours: Most museums and monuments are closed on Mondays. On other days, they open from 10am to 2pm, and from 5 to 8pm.

Main market days: Ribadesella: Wed; Cangas de Onís: Sun; Potes: Mon; Llanes: Thu.

Shopping: The classic products of the Picos and the regions around them are cheeses, cider, honey and a wide range of hams and meats. The Liébana area around Potes is known for sweet wines and *orujo* (strong grain spirit).

Major festivals: Ribadesella: Carnaval, Feb; La Noche de San Juan, 23–24 Jun; Descenso Internacional del Sella (Kayak Race), first Sat Aug; **Cangas de Onís:** Shepherd's Festival, 25 Jul; **Santo Toribio de Liébana:** La Santuca, 2 May; **Potes:** Exaltación de la Santa Cruz, mid-Sep; **Arenas de Cabrales:** Fiesta del Queso, end Aug; **Llanes:** Vírgen de la Guía, 7–8 Sep.

DAY TRIP OPTIONS

Families will enjoy a visit to Covadonga's lakes and to Ribadesella's beachfront; **nature lovers** and **history buffs** will be drawn to driving around the valleys and mountains between Llanes and Fuente Dé, while **adventure enthusiasts** will have a great time hiking around Bulnes and then relaxing on the beaches in Llanes. For details, *see p55*.

Above Church overlooking the sea at Ribadesella **Below** Walkers heading for the Lagos de Covadonga

VISITING PARQUE NACIONAL DE LOS PICOS DE EUROPA

Information Centres
The four information centres, in Cangas de Onís, Lagos de Covadonga, Posada de Valdeón and Tama-Cillórigo (near Potes), provide maps and other information on walks and hikes in the region. *Centro de Información Casa Dago, Avda. Covadonga 43, Cangas de Onís; 985 848 614; http:// reddeparquesnacionales.mma.es*

WHERE TO STAY

RIBADESELLA

Villa Rosario *moderate–expensive*
The grandest of Ribadesella's *Indiano* mansions, an ornate 1900s fantasy house, is now a hotel.
Paseo de la Playa, 33560; 985 860 090; www.hotelvillarosario.com

AROUND RIBADESELLA

El Babú *moderate*
Subtle modern design is combined with an 18th-century farmhouse at this small hotel 19 km (12 miles) to the west from Ribadesella.
33343, Carrales, Caravia; 985 853 272; www.elbabu.com

AROUND CANGAS DE ONÍS

Aultre Naray *moderate*
A delightful, welcoming small hotel, this is in a tranquil hamlet 9 km (6 miles) north of Cangas.
33457, Peruyes; 985 840 808; www.aultrenaray.es

① Ribadesella
Asturias; 33560
Ribadesella's Old Town, behind the fishermen's quays on the east side of the Sella river, is an intimate knot of narrow streets with small shops and lively restaurants. The newer town, on the west bank, is built behind a beach lined by a promenade and old *Indiano* mansions and hotels.

Ribadesella was founded in the 13th century, but its site has been occupied since prehistory. On the west bank is the **Cueva de Tito Bustillo**, a system of caverns, discovered only in 1968, with Palaeolithic cave paintings dating back to around 20,000 BC *(open Wed–Sun from Apr to Sep; reservations recommended; 985 861 120)*. Every first Saturday in August, Ribadesella's bridge is also the finishing point for the **Descenso Internacional del Sella**, a kayak race down the Sella from Arriondas that attracts competitors from around the world.

🚗 *Follow signs to the A8 for Oviedo-Gijón-Santander on the N632. In Llovio, the road forks. Take the right fork onto the N634 to Arriondas. Turn left onto the N625 to Cangas de Onís. Follow signs to the town centre.*

② Cangas de Onís
Asturias; 33550
One of the gateways to the Picos de Europa, Cangas de Onís was the first capital of the Kingdom of Asturias. The legendary Visigothic hero of the *reconquista*, Don Pelayo, set up his court here after his victory over the Moors at Covadonga in AD 722. On its west side is an elegantly curving stone bridge across the Sella, the **Puente Romano**. Cangas is a friendly town, with excellent *sidrerías* (cider houses) and riverside restaurants to give it plenty of Asturian character.

🚗 *Follow the Avenida Covadonga out through the town to join the AS114 to Las Arenas de Cabrales. After about 4 km (2 miles), turn right on the AS262 for Covadonga.*

③ Covadonga y los Lagos
Asturias; 33589
An impressive road runs up from Cangas de Onís to the shrine of

Virgin of Covadonga, Ribadesella

Covadonga, which grew around th[e] **Santa Cueva** (Holy Cave), where D[on] Pelayo, founder of the kingdom of Asturias, is said to have prayed to t[he] Virgin. The shrine also contains his tomb. Above the shrine is a huge Neo-Romanesque basilica, built between 1877 and 1901. Beyond Covadonga there is a more drama[tic] road, which winds up past wonder[ful] viewpoints to the **Lagos de Covadonga** – Enol and La Ercina – over 1,000 m (3,300 ft) high. There a[re] many well-marked walks around th[e] lakes, from an easy circuit to hikes o[f a] few hours. Nearby are the visitor's centre and the **Minas de Buferrera**, iron mines abandoned only in 197[

🚗 *Drive back to Cangas de Onís, a[nd] take the last left turn befo[re] the Puente Romano bridge, signposted to the N625. Stay on this road as it runs through the Desfiladero de los Beyos.*

④ Desfiladero de los Beyos
Asturias–León; 33557
South of Cangas de Onís, t[he] road follows the Sella into t[he] Desfiladero de los Beyos, o[ne] of the most spectacular of the deep[,] forest-clad limestone gorges that ri[ng] the Picos de Europa. Periodically th[e] gorge widens as side lanes lead off to hillside villages, of which **Ceneya** and **Argolibio** are among the most attractive. After 30 km (19 miles), th[e] road enters the Valle de Sajambre, [a] narrow enclave within the Picos.

🚗 *Continue southwards on the N62[5] from Cangas de Onís. After Ribota, look for a steep left turn onto the CV80-8 for Soto and continue to the car park in the centre of the village.*

Soto de Sajambre
ón; 24916

ne of the most fascinating aspects of the Picos de Europa is the nstant change in landscape from one valley to another, and tween thickly wooded valley floors and windswept meadows up bove. This walk takes visitors from the sheltered village of Soto de Sajambre, tucked into a fold in the hills, up to high mountain pastures one of the emptiest parts of the Picos.

2–3 hour walking tour
e walk follows the PR–PNPE 9 otpath (with green signs and yellow d white markers) and is steep in rts. From the car park, follow the otpath signs for Vegabaño, to the ht of the school. The path begins climb out of the village with the arkling Miraño river on the right, d initially runs through hay mead-vs typical of the Picos villages. Go past an unusual red-painted ouse, **La Cubiella ①**. Rising up ahead both sides are some of the jagged anite crags of the western Picos, eña Beza to the left and Monte Neón the right. Look out for eagles and her birds of prey circling the sky. bout 1 km (0.6 miles) from Soto, the ath enters the woods. Turn right, fol-wing the yellow and white markers cross the Miraño river, and follow e path uphill through the forest. The ath twists and turns until it meets a roader dirt track. Turn left, and follow is track round until it comes out of

the trees onto the grassy meadow of **Vegabaño ②**, which is dotted with huts built as shelters by shepherds during the weeks they spent here. To the right, the track ends at a mountain refuge. Straight ahead to the east there is a glorious view of some of the most rugged peaks of the western massif of the Picos, such as Los Moledizos (2,300 m/7,550 ft) and the Picos del Verde (2,200 m/7,200 ft). The most direct way back to Soto de Sajambre and to the car park is to retrace the same route.

Return to the N625 and turn left. Beyond Soto, the main N625 road goes through Oseja de Sajambre, the valley's low-key main town, dominated by the mountain of Pica Ten. Past Oseja, the road winds up to the Puerto del Pontón. After the pass, turn left onto the LE244 for Posada de Valdeón. Drive towards the Valdeón valley through the Puerto de Panderrueda, with views from several miradors over the Valdeón and the peaks around it.

Above Footpath marker near Soto de Sajambre

ACTIVITIES IN CANGAS DE ONÍS

Kayaking and other water sports
Several agencies offer adventure trips in kayaks and other crafts, especially from Cangas de Onís and Arriondas.
www.descensodelsella.com

EAT AND DRINK

RIBADESELLA

El Cafetín *inexpensive*
An excellent choice for tapas or a good-value meal is this very popular, no-nonsense bar-*sidrería*, with a big range of satisfying dishes.
C/ Comercio 1, 33560; 985 860 283

Restaurante Arbidel
moderate–expensive
Part-hidden in one of the narrow streets of old Ribadesella is this restaurant with a delicate approach to Asturian cuisine.
C/ Oscura 1, 33560; 985 861 440; www.arbidel.com; closed Tue and Nov–Feb except Jul and Aug

CANGAS DE ONÍS

Sidrería El Polesu *inexpensive*
The oldest and most atmospheric of Cangas' *sidrerías*, this place offers classic Asturian tapas such as *boronchu* (local variant of blood sausage), seafood omelettes and *cabrales* cheese.
C/ Angel Tárano 3, 33550; 985 947 584; closed Mon in winter

El Molín de la Pedrera *moderate*
This very popular bar-restaurant presents Asturian cuisine with a fresh, modern style and plenty of rich flavour.
C/ Río Güeña 2, 33550; 985 849 109; www.elmolin.com; closed Wed, except Aug and Jan

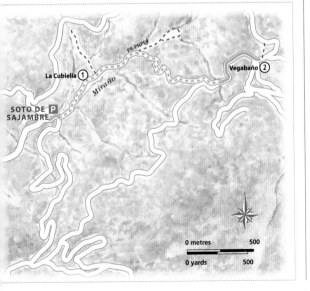
La Cubiella ① · Miraño · Vegabaño ② · SOTO DE SAJAMBRE · PR-PNPE9 · 0 metres 500 · 0 yards 500

Eat and Drink: inexpensive, under €20; moderate, €20–€40; expensive, over €40

Above Medieval monastery of Santo Toribio de Liébana **Below** Looking down to the Vega de Liébana from Puerto de San Glorio

WHERE TO STAY

POSADA DE VALDEÓN

Pensión Begoña/Hostal Campo *inexpensive*
This friendly little hotel houses Posada's best restaurant and has a country charm typical of the village.
24915, Posada de Valdeón; 987 740 502

AROUND POSADA DE VALDEÓN

Casa Cuevas *inexpensive*
A comfortable hotel with a traditional restaurant, this hotel is in the tiny, remote village of Caín, 7 km (4 miles) to the north of Posada de Valdeón and ringed by jagged grey crags.
24915, Caín de Valdeón; 987 740 500; www.casacuevas.es

VALLE DE CAMALEÑO

Posada El Bosque *inexpensive–moderate*
In a modern but traditional-style house near Santo Toribio, this is a lovely small hotel with great views over the valley.
39586, Camaleño; 942 730 127; www.posadaelbosque.com

La Casona de Cosgaya *moderate*
This massive traditional *casona* (village house) has been renovated to create distinctive bedrooms and lounge areas with a luxurious feel.
Barrio Arenós, 39582, Cosgaya; 942 733 077; www.casonadecosgaya.com

Parador de Fuente Dé *expensive*
The parador at the foot of the Fuente Dé cable car is modern and service is excellent. The restaurant has refined versions of local cuisine.
39588, Fuente Dé; 942 736 651; www.parador.es

⑥ Posada de Valdeón
León; 24915

A green hollow ringed by massive sierras, the Valdeón is one of the most enclosed of the Picos de Europa valleys, and the largest area of the Picos within the province of León. Posada de Valdeón, its main village, is a popular hiking base with hotels and restaurants and a park information centre. A narrow road continues for 7 km (4 miles) to end at **Caín de Valdeón**, a remarkable village beneath the rocky walls of the **Desfiladero del Río Cares** gorge. It is a starting point for one of the most famous long hikes in the Picos, through the Cares ravine to the north side of the mountains at Puente Poncebos. The walk is about 11 km (7 miles) long, and takes three hours in each direction, on a spectacular, but safely broad path along the often sheer rock walls of the gorge. It sometimes runs through small tunnels and crosses from side to side on narrow metal bridges.

🚗 *From Posada, follow the LE243, to the right of the Pensión Begoña out of the village. Continue on this road through Santa Marina de Valdeón and the Puerto de Pandetrave. Turn left onto the N621 at Portilla de la Reina to reach Puerto de San Glorio.*

⑦ Puerto de San Glorio
Cantabria; 39577

The differences in landscape between the northern Atlantic side of the Picos and its southern Mediterranean flanks become ever more marked as the route goes further into León. From Portilla de La Reina the N621 road runs through an

almost bare rock ravine as it climbs again up to Puerto de San Glorio, perhaps the most spectacular of all the Picos passes. A side road to the left, marked Collado de Llesba, leads to the **Mirador del Oso**, a view point with a bear statue and truly fabulous views over the Liébana valleys and ranks of sierras fading into the distance. The road then winds down to **Vega de Liébana**, a pleasant riverside village with relaxing restaurants.

🚗 *Continue on the N621. Enter Pote and turn left on the CA185, signpost for Espinama and Fuente Dé; this als leads to the centre of town. There is ample parking in the large squares just past the main historic buildings.*

⑧ Potes
Cantabria; 39577

The Cantabrian Liébana valleys in th southeastern Picos enjoy an unusua sheltered climate that has given the an especially lush, productive land-scape. Potes is the main town and tourist centre of the Liébana and th southeast corner of the Picos de Europa, with plenty of shops offerin the renowned Liébana produce – honey, sweet wines, liqueurs, sausage and cheeses. A local centre since th 9th century, Potes has a fascinating Old Town of alleys, lovely bridges and distinctive houses built precariously above the Deva river. Standing out in the middle of town, in the main square, is the **Torre del Infantado** (now the town hall), a 14th-century keep that was a stronghold of the aristocratic Mendoza clan, and the early 14th–18th-century Gothic

esia de San Vicente *(open daily)*, ich now hosts an exhibition on edieval manuscripts.

Continue on the CA185 road out of es, and then very shortly take the turn onto the CA885 signposted to nto Toribio de Liébana.

Santo Toribio de Liébana
ntabria; 39570

e protection and fertility of the bana valleys made them an impor-
nt centre of early Christianity, with veral monasteries of which **Santo** ribio *(open daily)*, above Potes, is the ost important. Founded in the 6th ntury, it became famous for the *num Crucis*, which is kept in a silver quary and is said to be the largest gment of the cross on which Christ s crucified. It was also the home of e 8th-century scholar Beatus of bana, author of the *Commentary the Apocalypse*. On an upper floor ere is a fascinating exhibition on atus and medieval manuscripts.
ll occupied by monks, the colossal pnastery has buildings from many nturies, but retains its 13th-century urch, while outside a path leads to eries of Romanesque hermitages read about the hillside.

Drive back to the CA185 and ntinue westwards on it. Follow the ad through Camaleño, Cosgaya and her valley villages to Fuente Dé.

Valle de Camaleño
ntabria; 39588

est of Potes, the Camaleño valley s some of the most exquisite sce-
ry in the Picos, with verdant woods d charming villages of red-roofed

old stone houses such as **Camaleño** itself, **Cosgaya** and **Espinama**, around which are attractive restaurants and small hotels in lovely *casa rurales*.
Mogrovejo, off the main road, is a medieval village around a 13th-century tower. There are great walks around all the villages. The road ends at **Fuente Dé**, where the popular Teleférico *(cable car; open daily)* takes visitors 900 m (2,950 ft) up to a wild rock plateau pitted with craters. As well as a fantastic panorama over the Picos, there are many hiking routes around the plateau, including one trail down the mountain to Espinama.

🚗 Drive back to Potes on the CA185, and continue on slightly out of town before turning left, back onto the N621, signed for Unquera and Santander. After about 5 km (3 miles) take a right turn signposted for Santa María de Lebeña. The church is located down a sharp turn on the left.

Above left Soaring crags above Posada de Valdeón, at the base of the Desfiladero del Río Cares **Above right** Bell tower of the early medieval church in Caín **Below** Torre del Infantado in Potes

EAT AND DRINK

AROUND POSADA DE VALDEÓN
La Posada del Montañero
inexpensive
Diners on the pretty terrace at this bar-restaurant-hotel get an imposing view of the Torre Cerredo and other peaks around Caín. Rich, meaty traditional cooking is the core of the menu.
24915, Caín de Valdeón; 987 742 711

AROUND PUERTO DE SAN GLORIO
Mesón La Vega *inexpensive*
A warm atmosphere is guaranteed at this classic timber and stone village inn by the roadside in Vega. Portions of tapas or larger dishes are generous.
39577, Vega de Liébana; 942 736 132; www.mesonlavega.com

VALLE DE CAMALEÑO
Mesón del Oso *moderate–expensive*
This giant stone inn could not be more typical of the region, and is renowned as a showcase for the traditional dishes of the Liébana, especially *cocido lebaniego*, a mountain stew with four or more meats. Booking is essential.
C/ de Potes a Fuente Dé, 39582, Cosgaya; 942 733 018

El Urogallo *moderate–expensive*
Chef Casimiro Calleja prepares some of the region's best cuisine in his restaurant in the charming Casona hotel.
La Casona de Cosgaya, Barrio Areños, 39582, Cosgaya; 942 733 077; www.casonadecosgaya.com

Above Village of Bejes, huddled at the foot of a massive rock wall **Below left** One of the narrow cobbled streets in the isolated village of Bulnes **Below right** Mozarabic Iglesia de Santa María de Lebeña

WHERE TO STAY

DESFILADERO DE LA HERMIDA

Casona d'Alevia moderate
This impressive old stone house, 4 km (2 miles) to the northwest of Panes, has been renovated with antiques and traditional fittings. The owners are very welcoming, and generous breakfasts feature fresh local produce.
33579, Alevia, Peñamellera Baja; 985 414 176; www.casonadalevia.com

BULNES

Casa del Chiflón inexpensive
To experience true mountain isolation stay over in Bulnes at this stone cottage bed-and-breakfast with snug rooms. The Casa del Chiflón is reachable only by foot or in the funicular.
33554, Bulnes; 985 845 943; www.casadelchiflon.com

AROUND LLANES

El Habana expensive
This country house 4 km (2 miles) south of Llanes has warm rooms and lounges surrounded by a garden.
33509, La Pereda; 985 400 640; www.elhabana.com; closed Nov–Easter

La Posada de Babel expensive
This hip hotel 4 km (2 miles) south of Llanes offers a change from traditional decor with stylish rooms.
33509, La Pereda; 985 402 525; www.laposadadebabel.com; closed mid-Dec–Apr

⑪ Santa María de Lebeña
Cantabria; 39583
In a magical setting above the Deva river, Santa María de Lebeña (tours Tue–Sun) is the region's gem-like oldest church, built around AD 925 in the Moorish-influenced Mozarabic style. The site had probably already been used for pre-Christian Celtic religious rituals. There are Celtic symbols on the altar beneath the beautiful Romanesque figure of the Virgin of Lebeña.

🚗 *Drive back to the N621. Turn right to go through the Hermida gorge.*

Cheeses around the Picos
Manchego may be the most famous Spanish cheese, but those of Asturias and Cantabria are far more distinctive. Asturias alone has 42 different cheeses; the best known is the wonderfully powerful cabrales, a blue-veined "three-milk" cheese (made with milk from cows, sheep and goats). Queso Picón, from Bejes and Tresviso, is similar, but a little more subtle, as is the highly-prized gamonedo from around Cangas de Onís. The quesucos of the Liébana valleys, which are mild and soft and often used as snacks, in salads and in cakes, are very different.

⑫ Desfiladero de la Hermida
Cantabria; 39580
The Liébana valleys end at another giant gorge lined by soaring grey-rock walls, the Desfiladero de la Hermida. Part-way through the gorge, a part-concealed left turn in the village of La Hermida leads up to **Bejes**, a remote village precariously placed beneath a great grey cliff. Wi Tresviso on the other side of the mountain – unconnected by road, but reachable by a footpath – this i one of only two villages with a *Denominación de Origen* to produce *Queso Picón*, the oldest of all the region's cheeses, recorded since the year 926. Return to the N621 road from Bejes and turn left to travel through the rest of the gorge to **Panes**. The Hermida gorge ends he where it meets the Cares, a densely wooded gorge that runs west to th village of **Las Arenas de Cabrales**. Drive through Panes and turn left, across a bridge, Puerto Río Cares, onto the AS114 and drive for 23 km (14 miles) to reach **Las Arenas de Cabrales**. This village is famed as the centre for the famous Asturian cheeses, *cabrales*, and there are shop selling cheeses, cider and other loc specialities all around the town.

🚗 *In Las Arenas de Cabrales turn lef on the AS264 to Puente Poncebos. Park by the funicular to take the train up to Bulnes, or turn left uphill on the CA-1 to reach Sotres and Tresviso.*

⑬ Bulnes
Asturias/Cantabria; 33554, 39580
The only way to get to Bulnes is by th funicular railway at Puente Poncebos, since it is one of the very few village in Spain still with no access by road. It is the start point for superb hikes around the awesome summit of the **Naranjo de Bulnes** (2,500 m/8,250 ft

ich has a tooth-like crest and is one the highest summits in the Picos Europa. At the bottom of the nicular, Puente Poncebos is the rthernmost point of the Desfiladero l Río Cares path from Caín.

ernatively, continuing from Puente ncebos, drive through extraordinary dscapes to two beautiful remote ages at **Sotres** and **Tresviso**, which ares a *Denominación de Origen* with es for its ancient cheese.

Return to Arenas de Cabrales and n left on the AS114. Cross Ortiguero d turn right onto the AS115 for sada. After Posada, turn right at the unction onto the AS263, passing der the A8, to reach Llanes.

Llanes
turias; 33500

join the coast at the harbour town Llanes. An important port in the

Middle Ages, it has a charming Old Town of stone-walled squares, Gothic churches and noble mansions. The harbour, still a busy fishing port, has been intriguingly decorated with multicoloured painted blocks, called *The Cubes of Memory*, by contemporary artist Agustín Ibarrola (b. 1930). Llanes also has small beaches, but the best beaches nearby are just west at **Barro** and **Celorio**, framed by the dramatic Atlantic cliffs.

Asturian Cider

Cider (*sidra*), not wine, is the traditional drink of northern Spain, and above all Asturias. Asturian cider is quite sharp, with a mix of dryness and sweetness. The best place to sample it is in a traditional *sidrería* with dark timbers and barrels around the walls, along with some *cabrales* cheese or other hearty local food.

EAT AND DRINK

AROUND DESFILADERO DE LA HERMIDA

Casa Julián *moderate*
Located beside a tree-shrouded bend in the Cares river, this place serves Asturian favourites like *fabes con almejas* (broad beans with clams).
33578, Niserias, Peñamellera Alta; 985 415 797; www.casajulian.com

Restaurante La Xana *moderate*
Specialities in this restaurant, located 14 km (9 miles) west of Panes, include salads like *pongas con jamón* (green beans, tomatoes and serrano ham).
33578, Rubena-Llonín, Peñamellera Alta; 985 415 923; reservations are essential

BULNES

Bar Bulnes *inexpensive*
With a terrace beside a babbling stream, this restaurant has some of the best tapas and sometimes larger dishes.
33554, Bulnes; 985 845 934

LLANES

Restaurante-Marisquería La Marina *moderate–expensive*
This is a lovely setting in which to enjoy local fish and seafood, prepared in many different ways.
C/ de las Gaviotas, 33500; 985 400 012; www.marisquerialamarina.es

AROUND LLANES

Llagar-Sidrería Cabañón *moderate*
A giant barn-like old farmhouse 15 km (9 miles) west of Llanes houses one of the best traditional *sidrerías*. Hefty steaks, pork loin, *chorizos* and other meats are grilled over an oak fire.
33594, Naves de Llanes; 985 407 550

Left Lofty peaks encircle Bulnes and its lonely farms

DAY TRIP OPTIONS

The coastal towns of Ribadesella and Llanes (both near the A8) make great oases for the short trips that this drive can be divided into.

Beaches to high mountain lakes
Spend a day on Ribadesella's ❶ beachfront, then visit Cangas de Onís ❷ for a leisurely lunch, before driving to Covadonga y los Lagos ❸ to see the beautiful lakes.

From Ribadesella, follow the N634, then the N625 to Cangas de Onís, then the AS114 and the AS262 to Covadonga.

History and culture
With Llanes ⑭ as base, a visit to the Liébana valleys of the Cantabrian Picos, the shops and charming old streets of Potes ❽, the ancient churches and monasteries of Santo Toribio de Liébana ❾ and Santa María de Lebeña ⑪ and the walks and fine restaurants along the Valle de Camaleño ⑩ to Fuente Dé make for a great trip.

From Llanes, follow the N634 eastward and then the N621 southwest to Potes, driving through the Hermida and Liébana valleys and visiting the

monastery of Santa María de Lebeña on the way. From Potes follow the CA885 and the CA185 to Santo Toribo de Liébana and the Camaleño valley and Fuente Dé.

High peaks to the harbourside
For hiking in the Picos head for the vistas around Bulnes ⑬ or start with a hike around Bulnes, and then relax on the beautiful beaches around Llanes ⑭.

From Llanes follow the AS115 to Las Arenas de Cabrales, then take the AS264 to Bulnes and Tresviso.

Eat and Drink: inexpensive, under €20; moderate, €20–€40; expensive, over €40

The Land of Rioja

Laguardia to Quintanar de la Sierra

Highlights

- **Enchanting town**
  Dive into La Rioja's wine culture in the medieval town of Laguardia

- **Cutting edge architecture**
  Marvel at the new breed of bodegas from the world's top architects

- **Medieval monasteries**
  Discover ancient monasteries tucked in the folds of forests and mountains

- **Majestic mountains**
  Explore the little-known Sierra de la Demanda, a nature lover's paradise

Vineyards near Laguardia, capital of La Rioja Alavesa, sheltered by the hills to the north

The Land of Rioja

Famous the world over for its wine, the tiny region of La Rioja has everything visitors could want from a holiday in northern Spain. Encircled by the swooping hills of the Sierra de la Demanda, the region is rich with crystalline rivers full of fish, medieval villages and monasteries nestled in pretty valleys. The gastronomy is on a par with the neighbouring Basque region and the countryside presents no great difficulties for once-a-year walkers and cyclists. At the end of the day's sightseeing, a bottle of La Rioja's delicious eponymous product is always at hand.

Above Rows of vines around Haro, see p63

ACTIVITIES

Sample famous wines at the hundreds of bodegas scattered throughout La Rioja Alavesa

Learn about how wine is made at the Museo de Cultura de Vino in Briones

Watch storks nest in the rooftops of Haro

Trek through the forests between the Yuso and Suso monasteries

Stroll across a mountain top to a glacial lagoon in Neila

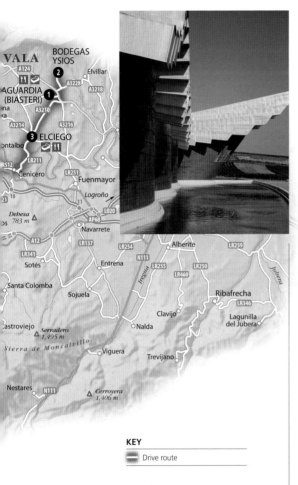

VALA

BODEGAS
YSIOS ②

AGUARDIA
(BIASTERI) ①

③ ELCIEGO

Elvillar

Cenicero
Fuenmayor

Logroño

Debesa
783 m

Navarrete

Sotés
Entrena
Alberite

Santa Colomba
Sojuela
Ribafrecha

Clavijo
Lagunilla
del Jubera

astroviejo
Serradero
1,495 m
Nalda

Sierra de Moncalvillo
Viguera
Trevijano

Nestares
Cerroyera
1,406 m

KEY

━━ Drive route

Above Contemporary structure of the bodega in Ysios, *see p61* **Below** Rooftop view of the village of Villavelayo, *see p67*

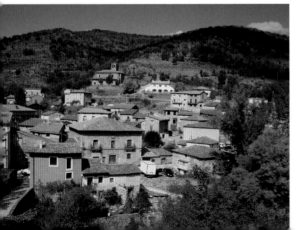

PLAN YOUR DRIVE

Start/finish: Laguardia to Quintanar de la Sierra.

Number of days: 4–5, allowing half a day to explore the monasteries of Yuso and Suso.

Distances: 225 km (140 miles).

Road conditions: The roads are generally good around this region. There are mountain roads in the Sierra de la Demanda, with narrow stretches and lots of curves.

When to go: Spring and summer are the best times to go. The *vendimia* (harvest) takes place in October and is the best time to see the vineyards of La Rioja. Expect snow in the Sierra de la Demanda in winter.

Opening hours: Most museums and monuments are closed on Mondays. Shops are open from 9:30 am to 1:30pm, and from 4 to 8pm. Restaurants are open from 2 to 4pm, and from 8 to 11pm.

Main market days: Laguardia: Tue; Haro: Tue, Sat; Santo Domingo de la Calzada: Sat; Nájera: Thu.

Shopping: Ezcaray is famous for its wine, woollen blankets and scarves. Wine-related objects (bottle openers, glasses, etc.) are available in many village shops and bodegas.

Major festivals: Haro: La Batalla de Vino, 29 Jun; **San Millán de la Cogolla:** Traslación de las Reliquias, 26 Sep; **Anguiano:** Danza de los Zancos, 22 Jul and last week Sep; **Quintanar de la Sierra:** San Cristobal, 10–12 Jul.

DAY TRIP OPTIONS

Wine lovers should visit the towns and villages of Laguardia, Elciego and Briones and taste some of their world-renowned wines at old-fashioned bodegas. **History enthusiasts** should make their way to see the ancient church at Santo Domingo de la Calzada, the twin monasteries of San Millán de la Cogolla and the Monasterio de Valvanera. For more details, *see p67*.

Above Walls around the town of Laguardia

VISITING LAGUARDIA

Tourist Information
*Palacio Samaniego, Plaza San Juan,
s/n, 01300; 945 600 845; www.
laguardia-alava.com; open daily*

Parking
Parking is available in front of Puerta
de Páganos.

SHOPPING IN LAGUARDIA

Casa & Vino
Pick up tablecloths and all sorts of
wine paraphernalia such as bottle-
openers and decanters from this shop.
It also has a range of woollen rugs and
scarves from nearby Ezcaray and
various grape-based beauty products.
C/ Mayor 1, 01300; 945 600 667

Enoteca Arbulu Uriate
This shop has a wide selection of
wines from the Alavesa region as well
as La Rioja's famous *conservas* – jars of
preserved red peppers, artichokes
and asparagus.
Plaza Mayor 1, 01300; 945 600 791

WHERE TO STAY

LAGUARDIA

Hotel Villa de Laguardia *moderate*
A four-star hotel which has plush
and comfortable rooms, a pool, a spa
and a superb in-house restaurant
with wonderful views of the area.
*Paseo de San Raimundo 15, 01300;
945 600 560; www.
hotelvilladelaguardia.com*

Castillo El Collado *expensive*
This eight-roomed hostelry in an
18th-century palace is located just
outside Laguardia's walls, and affords
great views of the Cantabrian mountains. Rooms are decorated with fine
period furniture, maintaining the
original regal ambience of the building.
*Paseo el Collado 1, 01300; 945 621 200;
www.hotelcollado.com*

❶ Laguardia (Biasteri)
Álava; 01300

The main town of La Rioja Alavesa, the part of the Rioja wine regio
within the province of Álava, Laguardia (Biasteri in Basque) makes
splendid start to the journey into Spain's most famous wine count
Viniculture is alive and well everywhere, from the wine shops and
bars, to the fields of vineyards surrounding Laguardia's walls and fina
the underground bodegas. This little medieval town's encircling ra
parts, towers and fortified gateways are visible from afar. The Gothi
portal of Iglesia de Santa María de los Reyes is a treat for all art enth
siasts. The following walk can be done at any time of the day.

A one-hour walking tour

Start at the car park in front of Puerta
de Páganos and walk to the Plaza San
Juan, also the location of the tourist
office. At the centre of the plaza is the
13th-century **Capilla de la Virgen del
Pilar e Iglesia de San Juan Bautista** ①.
From the front of the church turn left
into Calle Mayor to the small Plaza de
la Cárcel. Bear left via Calle de la Cárcel
and through Paseo San Juan. Turn
right to **Puerta de San Juan** ② – one
of Laguardia's five gates – to the other
side of the walls for a fine view of the
craggy Cantabrian mountain range.
Turn left following the wall to the
frontón (Basque handball or *jai alai*)
court and go back into the village via
the 15th-century **Puerta Nueva** ③ on
the left. After 50 m (55 yd), cross Calle
de Santa Engracia to come to the
Plaza Mayor ④ where the 16th-

century *ayuntamiento* (town hall)
is located. A few steps further on is
the current town hall with its charm
ing carillon clock whose dancing
figurines appear at the stroke of mi
day and at 2, 5 and 8pm. Continue u
Calle de Santa Engracia and take the
first left onto Calle Traversia de Sant
Engracia. Then turn right onto Calle
Mayor and walk to the end of the
street. This is the site of the **Iglesia c
Santa María de los Reyes** ⑤ *(closed
Mon)*. Built between the 12th and
15th centuries, it incorporates differe
styles, from Gothic to Renaissance. It
celebrated portal, with intricate figur
of the apostles, was not painted un
the 17th century, which partly explai
its near-perfect state. To the left of
the church is the **Torre Abacial** ⑥, a
13th-century defence tower that ha
an underground passage to the

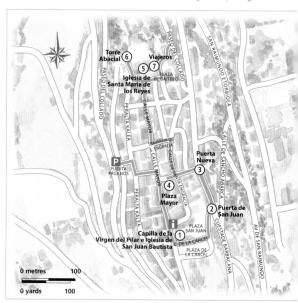

urch. To the right of the church
 pretty garden on Plaza El Gaitero
ntaining **Viajeros** ⑦, a sculpture
:allation of various types of shoes
d bags, the work of a local culture
up. Next to the garden is another
all plaza with an antique water
l and water basin. Cross the plaza
d go down the steps. Turn left to
:h the lovely garden at Paseo
 Collado where there is a bust
Félix María Samaniego (1745–
)1), a Laguardian writer famous
 his fables (his old palatial home
ow the tourist office). After stop-
g here for a while, go back to
 car park.

*From Laguardia take the A124
rthwest in the direction of Vitoria-
steiz. This will lead to a crossroad
h a sign which says "Elvillar/Kripan".
n right and immediately left and
ow signs for Bodegas Ysios till the
park.*

Bodegas La Fabulista

he underground Bodegas La
abulista *(Plaza San Juan s/n; 945
21 192)* is located next to the tourist
ffice – the ancestral home of the
ble writer Félix María Samaniego,
aguardia's most illustrious son. It
 a part working winery and part
ourist attraction. A tour takes
sitors through the extensive
nnels where the wines are created.
raditional methods are still used
ere: the grapes are crushed by
ot and the machine used to
eparate their stalks dates from
)03. At the end of the visit, guests
e invited to taste some of La
abulista's wines. Visitors can also
uy some wine to take home.

② Bodegas Ysios
Álava; 01300

The first of a handful of spectacular
contemporary bodegas now dotting
La Rioja, Ysios is the work of Santiago
Calatrava, the Spanish architect who
designed the stadium in Athens for
the 2004 Olympic Games. With the
craggy Cantabrian mountains as a
backdrop, it is a wonderful sight. The
low-rise wooden structure is crowned
with an undulating metal roof and
protruding peaked "wings", lending it
an articulated, church-like quality. A
simple water-filled moat frames its
sculptural form. The bodega can be
toured, but visitors need to book in
advance *(open daily; 945 600 640)*.

🚗 *Return to Laguardia on the A124
and follow this road around the town.
At the junction with the A3216, take
the A3210 signed for Elciego.*

Above left Dancing clock in the Plaza Mayor,
Laguardia **Above right** Typical La Rioja
landscape lined with vineyards and mountains
in the background **Below** Bodega Ysios amid
rows of vines near Laguardia

EAT AND DRINK

LAGUARDIA

Biazteri *moderate*
Tasty regional dishes and local wines
are served in rustic surroundings here.
Try the stews: either white beans with
clams or potatoes with chorizo, and
leave room for their delicious wine-
infused desserts.
*C/ Berberana 1, 01300; 945 600 026;
www.biazteri.com*

Posada Mayor de Migueloa
expensive
This restored 17th-century palace of
Viana now houses a small hotel and
one of northern Spain's best restaurants.
The cuisine is a Basque-La Rioja fusion,
strong on fish and seafood. Try the
baked hake.
*C/ Mayor de Migueloa 20, 01300; 945
621 175; www.mayordemigueloa.com;
closed mid-Dec–7 Jan*

Eat and Drink: inexpensive, under €20; moderate, €20–€40; expensive, over €40

Above left Façade of the Hotel Marqués de Riscal, Elciego **Above right** Arcades in Plaza de la Paz, Haro **Below** Museo de Cultura de Vino in Briones

WHERE TO STAY

ELCIEGO

Hotel Marqués de Riscal *expensive*
As would be expected from a work by Frank Gehry, the rooms and common areas in this destination hotel are as stunning as its exterior and well worth the cost. The in-house spa specializes in vinotherapy – wellness treatments using varieties of grape-based products.
C/ Torrea 1, 01340; 945 180 880; www.marquesderiscal.com

AROUND HARO

Señorío de Casalarreina *expensive*
Located in Casalarreina, a village 7 km (4 miles) outside Haro on the road to Ezcaray, this stylish *casa rural* is situated in the old college of the Monasterio de Nuestra Señora de la Piedad. The rooms retain many of their original stone walls and wooden beams, with bathrooms featuring jacuzzis.
Plaza Santo Domingo De Guzmán 6, 26230, Casalarreina; 941 324 730; www.alojamientos conencantodelarioja.com

❸ Elciego
Ávala; 01340
This pretty little village boasts one of the most acclaimed buildings in Spain, the **Hotel Marqués de Riscal** by Canadian-American architect Frank Gehry. Located on top of a natural terrace, the interesting main structure is wrapped in the architect's trademark titanium "ribbons" in glittering pink and gold colours (a metaphor for those of a wine bottle) that stand out for miles around. The interior is off limits for those who are not guests (or have at least booked for the in-house restaurant or spa), but visitors can tour the **Marqués de Riscal bodega**, which is adjacent. The original winery dates from 1858 (though modern additions

have been made) and produces some of the most renowned wine the region. The highlight is the "Cathedral" where bottles of every vintage produced since the bodega's foundation are reverently displayed *(tour by prior reservation only)*.

🚗 *Continue on the A3210 (which becomes the LR211 after it crosses into La Rioja) until it meets the LR5 outside Cenicero. Turn right and drive through Cenicero to meet the N232. Then turn right onto this road and follow it to Briones.*

❹ Briones
La Rioja; 26330
The first thing that visitors will notice as they drive into Briones is the Baroque bell tower of the **Iglesia de Nuestra Señora de la Asunción**. As well as a handful of other buildings of note, such as the **Palacio de los Marqués de San Nicolás** (now the town hall), Briones hosts the best museum in the area. Located in a striking modern building on the main road to the village, the **Museo de la Cultura de Vino** *(closed Mon; reservation recommended; 902 320 001)* is a fascinating trip into the world of wine – from the harvest to bottle – and shows how methods have changed over the centuries. At the end of the visit guests will be offered a glass of wine from the Vivanco bodega.

🚗 *Leave Briones, right, on the N232 and follow signs for Vitoria. After 8 km (5 miles), take the N124. Turn right and follow this road. Park on the street.*

The Wines of La Rioja

La Rioja is the most internationally known Spanish wine region, with over 300 bodegas dotting the Rioja area. The region is best known for its red wines which are matured to a distinctive vanilla mellowness. Today La Rioja produces over 250 million litres (55 million gallons) of wine a year, the large majority of it red. All of it falls into three categories: *crianza* (young wine), *reserva* and *gran reserva* (matured). A DO (*Denominación de Origen* or qualified designation of origin) was decreed for La Rioja's wine in 1902 and today three exist (La Rioja Alavesa, Rioja Alta and Rioja Baja) that identify exactly where the wines are produced and their style.

Haro

La Rioja; 26200

With its romantic hanging balconies and central square featuring an elegant rotunda, Haro is a graceful town on the Ebro river. Haro became the nucleus of La Rioja's wine-making industry over 130 years ago when a railway was built to Bilbao, facilitating exportation to the rest of Europe. The legacy is the charming **Barrio de la Estación**, a clutter of period bodegas set around the old railway station, many of which are open to the public. In the historic quarter, storks flock to the nests they have made in the Baroque crowns and cornices of Haro's abundant Baroque architecture. At the top of the hill is the Gothic **Iglesia de Santo Tomás**, which has a portal featuring the Way of the Cross.

Every June, Haro hosts its La Batalla del Vino festival, when boisterous crowds throw wine at each other.

🚗 *Leave Haro on the LR111/N126 on the west side of town. Continue on this road around Casalarreina to Santo Domingo de la Calzada. Park on the outskirts of the village.*

6 Santo Domingo de la Calzada

La Rioja; 26250

The little town of Santo Domingo de la Calzada owes its existence to the pilgrimage to Santiago de Compostella. In the Middle Ages a hermit named Domingo set up a hospice here to aid pilgrims, and out of that a town was born. His remains are buried in the 12th-century cathedral *(closed Sun)*, which also has a cage containing a pair of hens against the wall. Legend has it that Domingo resuscitated a pilgrim who had been unjustly sent to the gallows. When the townsfolk went to the judge to relate the miracle, the judge believed it to be nonsense, and explained that the condemned pilgrim could be no more alive than the roast chicken he was eating, at which point the chicken stood up and crowed. Opposite the cathedral is the 18th-century clock tower **Torre Exenta**, the tallest in La Rioja, and a hermitage with a Renaissance retable.

🚗 *Continue south on the LR111 (Avenida Alfonso Peña within Santo Domingo) and follow this road through Ojacastro for 3 km (2 miles) to Ezcaray.*

Above Tapas bars line the street to the Iglesia de Santo Tomás, Haro **Below left** The modern Marqués de Riscal wine spa at Elciego **Below right** Elaborately carved portal of the Monasterio de Nuestra Señora de la Piedad in Casalarreina near Haro

EAT AND DRINK

ELCIEGO

Hotel Marqués de Riscal *expensive*
Booking a table at this restaurant is certainly the best way to experience Frank Gehry's amazing architecture if visitors are not staying at the hotel. The cutting-edge menu has been created by the Michelin-starred Francis Paniego, of Echaurren *(see p65)* fame.
C/ Torrea 1, 01340; 945 180 880; www. marquesderiscal.com; reservations recommended; closed Mon and Sun

HARO

Las Cañas *inexpensive*
This recently renovated bar near Haro's cathedral is lined with old photos of the town's *peñas* (social clubs). The excellent tapas fly out of the kitchen at lightning speed and the *tigres* (individual mussels coated in béchamel) are to die for.
Plaza San Martín 5, 26200; 941 311 001

Right Courtyard and fountain of the Iglesia Santa María la Mayor, Ezcaray

VISITING THE MONASTERIES OF SAN MILLÁN DE LA COGOLLA

Visitors need to book in advance for both monasteries; for Suso at 941 373 082 and Yuso at 941 373 049. Tickets are sold at the Yuso office. Entry to the smaller Suso monastery is limited, so it is best to book online or by telephone. The monasteries are located 1 km (0.6 miles) apart. Visitors can drive, take a shuttle bus or walk, following the "Ruta de Gonzalo de Berceo."
Agustinos Recoletos, 26326; 941 373 049; www.monasteriodeyuso.org; open daily

SHOPPING

EZCARAY

Hijos de Cecilio Valgañón
Ezcaray has a long tradition of textile weaving and this factory shop sells luxurious blankets, shawls and scarves in vibrant colours and different wools, such as mohair or cashmere, at a fraction of what you would pay in high-end boutiques.
C/ Gonzàlez Gallarza 12, 26280; 941 354 034; open daily

WHERE TO STAY

EZCARAY

Hotel Echaurren *moderate*
Considered one of the best hotels in La Rioja, there are 21 comfortable and tasteful rooms located inside this medieval mansion. The atmospheric lounge has an open fireplace and there are two famed restaurants on the ground floor.
C/ Pedro José García 19, 26280; 941 354 047; www.echaurren.com

AROUND NÁJERA

Real Casona de las Amas *expensive*
Located 8 km (5 miles) west of Nájera in the village of Azofra, this luxury hotel in a beautiful 17th-century mansion boasts genuine antique furniture. Many rooms have either a jacuzzi or a private terrace.
C/ Mayor 5, 26323, Azofra; 941 416 103; www.realcasonadelasamas.com; closed mid-Dec to mid-Jan

SAN MILLÁN DE LA COGOLLA

La Posada de San Millán *inexpensive*
This up market *casa rural* is located on the grounds of the Monasterio de San Millán de Yuso and has a large garden with views over the valley.
26326, San Millán de la Cogolla; 941 373 161; www.ascarioja.es/laposada

⑦ Ezcaray
La Rioja; 26280
The gateway to **Valdezcaray** in the upper Oja valley, Ezcaray is La Rioja's only ski resort. The town is surrounded by striking verdant forests and skirted by the Oja river and it is well worth visiting in the off-season. In the centre of the town is the atmospheric Plaza de la Verdura with a pretty 1900s fountain surrounded by medieval houses with porticoes and wooden relief carvings. Ezcaray had an important woollen textile industry up until the beginning of the 1800s. Only one factory remains, the **Real Fábrica**. Built in 1752, it has been well preserved and can be seen from the outside. Also worth a visit in Ezcaray is the 15th-century **Iglesia Santa María la Mayor**, which houses a museum of religious artefacts.

Weaving from Ezcaray

🚗 *Return to Santo Domingo de la Calzada on the LR111, and then turn right on the N120 (direction Logroño) for Nájera.*

⑧ Nájera
La Rioja; 26300
The old town of Nájera, west of Logroño, was once the capital of the Kingdom of Navarra, which at its height ruled over a huge part of northern Spain. With many shops and facilities, Nájera is a good place to stock up on anything that might be required before heading into the

Sierra de la Demanda. With the Najerilla river cutting straight throug it, flanked by *paseos* and grassed are Nájera is a lovely place to spend an hour or so. The town's most important monument is the **Monasterio Santa Maria la Real** *(closed Mon)*; members of the royal families of Navarra, Léon and Castille are burie here. According to legend, a statue of the Virgin was found on this site the 11th century. The present buil ing dates from the early 15th century and contains Gothic and Renaissance elements.

🚗 *Take the LR113 from Nájer heading south towards Bobadilla. In Bobadilla, turn right on the LR331, following signs to San Millán de la Cogo*

⑨ San Millán de la Cogolla
La Rioja; 26326
The little village of San Millán de la Cogolla is known for its two mona teries. The monasteries, among the oldest in Spain, grew up around th former hermitage of San Millán, a 6th-century hermit, who, over his 101-year life, attracted many schola disciples. Their scribes created an important collection of manuscrip most notably the 10th-century *Glos Emilianenses*, the first written exam ples of the Castilian language. Som of the manuscripts are on display i the treasury.
Located in the Cárdenas valley is the **Monasterio de San Millán de**

o. The monastery was home
ionzalo de Berceo, who in the
n century wrote the first Castilian
try. This has led San Millán to be
·bed "the cradle of Castilian", and
 o is now home to Aula de la
 gua Castellana, which promotes
 nish-language studies. The mon-
·ry itself was rebuilt from the
 n to the 18th centuries in a mix
 enaissance and Baroque styles,
 lent in the immense plaza and
 numental doors leading to the
 rch, and a Rococo sacristy, where
 n-century paintings are hung.
·r visiting the monastery, follow
 s on the LR421 to the Monasterio
 ان Millán de Suso.
 ocated in the depth of a pine
 st on a hillside above San Millán
 ne **Monasterio de San Millán de**
 o. Dating from the 10th century,
 the original site of San Millán's
 nastic community. Etched out of
 k sandstone in the Romanesque
 e, the saint's tomb is located
 de, along with those of the
 ·ven Infants of Lara" who, accord-
 to legend, were beheaded by
 Moors. The richly painted doors
 ne altarpiece depict scenes from
 life of San Millán and the
 dhood of Jesus.

Retrace the route to Bobadilla on
LR331, and turn right onto the
13, following signs for Anguiano.
·r the village of Anguiano, drive
m (9 miles) and turn right onto

the LR435, following signs to the
Monasterio de Valvanera. Park outside
the monastery.

Anguiano Dancers

The archetypal mountain village of
Anguiano is one of the prettiest in
the Sierra de la Demanda. Anguiano
hosts a famed tradition, celebrating
its patron saint's (Mary Magdalene)
day with a bizarre fiesta. Every year
on 22 July nine local youths dress up
in colourful, harlequin-like costumes
and perform the *Danza de los*
Zancos. Perched on pointed stilts,
they twirl down a precarious crest,
in time to music, performing an
ancient rite of passage. The ritual is
repeated on the last Saturday of
September, when the image of
Mary of Magdalene is returned to
her shrine for the winter.

Above Monasterio de San Millán de Suso
Below left Textile loom in a factory in
Ezcaray **Below right** Spire of the Monasterio
de San Millán de Yuso

EAT AND DRINK

EZCARAY

El Rincon del Vino *moderate*
This restaurant serves delicious
traditional Riojan cuisine with an
emphasis on seasonal produce
including mushrooms and truffles.
C/ Jesus Nazareno 2, 26280; 941
354 375

El Portal del Echaurren *expensive*
Local chef Francis Paniego has earned
a Michelin star for his creative take on
local cuisine. Special dishes include
solomillos de rape negro sobre
purrusalda (monkfish with leeks).
C/ Pedro José García 19, 26280; 941
354 047; www.echaurren.com; closed
Sun dinner and Mon and Tue in
Jan–Jun

AROUND SAN MILLÁN DE LA
COGOLLA

El Mirador *moderate*
Located 1 km (0.6 miles) outside the
village of Berceo, north of San Millán
de la Cogolla, this restaurant serves
local dishes such as *pisto de piquillo*
with cod and *patatas la riojana*.
Ctra. de San Millán s/n, 26327, Berceo;
941 373 008

La Cañada *inexpensive*
On the main road just north of
Anguiano, 19 km (12 miles) from San
Millán de la Cogolla, this is a favourite
stop for hunters and walkers, so meals
come hot, hearty and in large portions.
Ctra. Anguiano, Km 49; 941 745 003

Eat and Drink: inexpensive, under €20; moderate, €20–€40; expensive, over €40

WHERE TO STAY

QUINTANAR DE LA SIERRA

Posada Las Mayas *inexpensive*
A charming hotel with 10 cosy, well-equipped rooms in a fine old stone house in the middle of Quintanar, with a surprisingly sophisticated restaurant using fresh local produce.
C/ El Cerro 5, 09670; 947 395 609; www.lasmayas.es

⑩ Monasterio de Valvanera
La Rioja; 26322

This impressive Gothic monastery *(open daily)* located 1,000 m (3,300 ft) above sea level on a mountain top, is home to the patron saint of La Rioja, the Virgin of Valvanera. The faithful queue up to light a candle at the feet of the Virgin, allegedly sculpted by Saint Lucas in AD 71 although most historians believe the statue dates from the 11th century. Unusually, the feet of baby Jesus, who is seated on the Virgin's lap, are twisted the opposite way to the direction He is facing. Surrounded by lush forests and backed by the jagged peaks of the Sierra de San Lorenzo, the monastery has magnificent views and hiking tracks, one of which winds all the way through the mountains to the town of Ezcaray *(see p64)*.

🚗 Return to the LR113 and turn right towards Mansilla de la Sierra. Park at the lookout point for the Embalse de Mansilla.

⑪ Embalse de Mansilla
La Rioja; 26329

This extensive dam was constructe in the 1950s by the regime of Gene Franco. Mansilla was located at the crossroads of two important rivers Najerilla and Cambrones. A dam w required to irrigate the area, and it was decided that the village aroun it would need to be submerged. T inhabitants were relocated to high ground. At low tide the remains of the church, town hall and other bu ings of the original village from the old Ermita de Santa Caterina are visible. The "new" Mansilla is locatec further uphill, a less atmospheric doppelgänger of its former self bu has spectacular views.

🚗 Continue along the LR113 in the same direction. In Villavelayo, turn I onto the LR334, following signs for Neila. Pass Neila and turn left onto BU822 (direction Quintanar). Drive 4 km (2 miles) and turn right, follow signs for the Lagunas Altas de Neila

Above left Interior of the Monasterio de Valvanera **Above right** Archways in the Monasterio de Valvanera **Below left** Monasterio de Valvanera located dramatically high up in the hills **Below right** Typical scenery of the Sierra de la Demanda

Lagunas Altas de Neila
Rioja, Burgos; 09679

The four natural lagoons that make the Lagunas Altas de Neila are enclosed in a post-glacial cirque and for many years were seen solely by shepherds and wood collectors. Now an asphalt road (a popular stretch for cycling events) leads to their threshold on the peak of La Campina, over 2,000 m (6,550 ft) above sea level and surrounded by spine-tingling views of the sierra. On ascending, a sign will direct visitors to the Larga and Negra lagoons, which are the most impressive. Visitors will need to then walk to the Larga lagoon, which goes a short way over the mountain top. On the way, there are breathtaking views of the black water of the Negra lagoon, located on a natural terrace below. To explore the other lagoons, return to the car park and take the opposite track. The lagoons freeze over in winter; for many this is the most spectacular time to see them. There are plenty of pretty picnic spots on the road leading from Neila through a green countryside with constant views of the majestic Sierra de la Demanda.

Return to the BU822 and turn right into the province of Burgos. Follow signs to Quintanar de la Sierra.

Quintanar de la Sierra
Burgos; 09670

Surrounded by mountains and rivers, this sizeable town located in the province of Burgos is a popular hub for outdoor sports. Quintanar de la Sierra's old quarter has retained some of its original architecture, such as old stone homesteads with distinctive conical chimney stacks, the 16th-century **Iglesia de San Crístobal** and an attractive Plaza Mayor with a central bandstand.

Just south of Quintanar de la Sierra, turn left onto the CL117, following signs to the **Necrópolis de Cuyacabras**. This is one of the most rewarding archaeological treasures in Spain: the remains of over 160 anthropomorphic tombs and niches carved out of rock in the midst of a pine forest. There is evidence that the site was in use in the 10th century, but historians believe the first tombs were created here 200 years earlier by Christians fleeing into the mountains from Muslim invaders.

> ### Villages of the Sierra de la Demanda
> The Sierra de la Demanda is dotted with historic villages (collectively known as Las 7 Vilas or "Seven villages") whose sheer isolation has kept their ancient homesteads and monuments incredibly well-preserved. One of the prettiest is Canales de la Sierra (reached via an exit on the LR113, 11 km/7 miles past Embalse de Mansilla), which is crisscrossed with bubbling streams and stone bridges. In Villavelayo (also on the LR113, 6 km/4 miles past Embalse de Mansilla) the Baroque Ermita de Santa Aúrea boasts a façade peppered with sculptures of saints. Visitors come to these villages to enjoy activities such as fishing and walking.

Above Façade of Ermita de Santa Aúrea in the village of Villavelayo

VISITING QUINTANAR DE LA SIERRA

Tourist Information
Plaza Mayor 1, 09670; 947 395 045; www.turismoburgos.org; open daily 10am–2pm only from Jul to Sep

EAT AND DRINK

There are very few restaurants in this region. Most of the hotels listed have their own restaurants. Visitors can also take picnic supplies with them from the nearest town as there are many pretty picnic spots en route.

DAY TRIP OPTIONS

There are two options for day trips in this region: an expedition to the wine-growing towns or a visit to the monasteries. Visitors can be based either in Laguardia or Haro to do these day trips. The N232 in the north and the LR113 in the south access most of the stops in this drive.

Wines of La Rioja Alavesa
Start the day with a walk around Laguardia ❶, soaking up the atmosphere of this splendid medieval hilltop town. Visit the bodegas around Laguardia including Bodegas La Fabulista and Bodegas Ysios ❷.

Then head to Elciego ❸ for lunch at Frank Gehry's exclusive Hotel Marqués de Riscal. Drive to Briones ❹ to visit the excellent wine museum.

From Laguardia take the A124 northwest for Bodega Ysios. Return to Laguardia on the A124. At the junction, take the A3210, signed for Elciego. Continue on the A3210/LR211 until it meets the LR512 outside Cenicero, and turn right and drive through the village to meet the N232. Turn right for Briones.

Ancient monasteries
Visit the 12th-century cathedral in Santo Domingo de la Calzada ❻ and head to San Millán de la Cogolla ❾ to visit the monasteries of Yuso and Suso, which are among the oldest in Spain. After this, drive to the Monasterio de Valvanera ❿, a Gothic monastery located in the mountains.

Leave Haro on the LR111/N126 to Santo Domingo de la Calzada. From Santo Domingo take the N102 to join the N120 for Nájera. In Nájera, get onto the LR113 (south). In Bobadilla turn right onto the LR331 for San Millán de la Cogolla. Return to Bobadilla on the LR331 and turn right, following signs for Anguiano. After Anguiano, turn right onto the LR435 to the Monasterio de Valvanera.

Eat and Drink: inexpensive, under €20; moderate, €20–€40; expensive, over €40

A Circuit around Navarra

Zangoza to Lizarra

Highlights

- **The pilgrim's path**
  Discover Zangoza, Roncesvalles and Lizarra, all important stopovers on the Camino de Santiago

- **Mountain scenery**
  Explore the mountains of Navarra and the breathtaking valleys that are full of wildlife

- **Caves with history**
  Visit the Zugarramurdi caves, shrouded in tales of witchcraft

- **Powerful Iruña**
  Enjoy Navarra's capital, famous for its bull-running fiesta

Way down from the witches' cave in Zugarramurdi

A Circuit around Navarra

Once a powerful, independent kingdom, Navarra is blessed with rich history and great natural beauty. Its most northerly region, bordering France, is mountainous and scantily populated, with tiny hamlets that are bastions of Basque language and culture, including the Basques' celebrated cuisine. This tour takes visitors from the *cuenca* (basin) around Iruña to high country and back again. Expect enthralling scenery, ancient forests ideal for walking and inspiring medieval monasteries, hospices and churches that were built to accommodate Navarra's first tourists: the pilgrims on the Camino de Santiago.

Above High mountain road in the Navarrese Pyrenees, *see p72* **Below** Shop for pilgrims' accessories in Puente la Reina, *see p78*

ACTIVITIES

Listen to monks performing moving Gregorian chants in the Monasterio de Leyre

Take a walk through the remarkable Lumbier gorge

Enjoy Roncal cheese in the village of the same name

Go bird-watching in the magical Bosque de Irati

Trek through the serene Parque Natural de Bertiz

Taste local wines and *pintxos* in Iruña

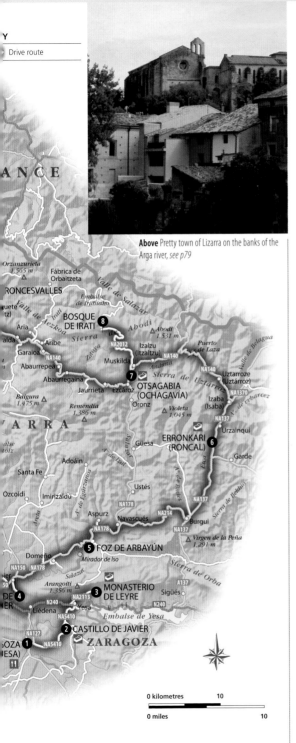

Above Pretty town of Lizarra on the banks of the Arga river, see p79

PLAN YOUR DRIVE

Start/finish: Zangoza to Lizarra.

Number of days: 4–5, allowing half a day to explore Iruña.

Distances: 425 km (265 miles).

Road conditions: There are lots of curves on the mountain roads between Erronkari and Bera. In the high mountain areas around Roncesvalles and Belagua the roads are very narrow. Some mountain roads may be closed, or require snow chains in the winter.

When to go: July and August have the most festivals and the weather will be temperate to warm. Winter is not a good time to visit as the mountain roads may be closed.

Opening hours: Most monuments and museums are open from 10:30am to 5:30pm, while shops are open from 9:30am to 1:30pm and 4 to 8pm.

Main market days: Zangoza: Fri; Elizondo: every second Sat; **Iruña:** daily; Puente La Reina: Sat; Lizarra: Thu.

Shopping: The region is known for its cheeses (especially from Roncal) and charcuterie.

Major festivals: Zangoza: San Sebastián, 11–17 Sep; **Otsagabia:** Natividad de Nuestra Señora, 8 Sep; **Iruña:** San Fermín, 6–14 Jul; **Lizarra:** San Andrés, last week Nov.

DAY TRIP OPTIONS

Using Iruña as a base, there are many day trip options in the Navarra valley. The Valle del Baztán and the Bertiz estate are beautiful stopovers and **those interested in walking** can explore the Jardín de Señorío de Bertiz and the adjacent Parque Natural de Señorio de Bertiz. The adjoining valleys of Roncal and Salazar and the magnificent Bosque de Irati are ideal for the **lovers of countryside**. For details, see p79.

WHERE TO STAY

CASTILLO DE JAVIER

Hotel Xabier *moderate*
This three-star hotel, which in many ways feels like a four- or five-star, is located in the gardens of the castle complex and has a lovely outdoor restaurant with a terrace on the ground floor. The sizeable rooms are decorated with antiques, fine textiles and rugs over hardwood flooring.
31411, Castillo de Javier; 948 884 006; www.hotelxabier.com

MONASTERIO DE LEYRE

Hotel Hospedería de Leyre *moderate*
The rooms in this monastery hotel are comfortable and seem good value considering its historic setting. Guests will be well placed to listen to the monks' daily chants.
31410, Yesa; 948 884 100; www. hotelhospederiadeleyre.com

Above Imposing battlements of the Castillo de Javier **Below** Romanesque exterior of the Monasterio de Leyre

❶ Zangoza (Sangüesa)
Navarra; 31400
When the Camino de Santiago gained momentum in the 12th century, so did Zangoza, which owes much of its development to the popularity of the Christian pilgrimage. Even today, *bastón*-carrying pilgrims are seen all over the town, guided by the bronze scallop shell medallions set into the ancient streets (the *vieira* or scallop is a symbol of the route). There are two important churches here. **Santa María la Real** features a decorated portal depicting the Last Judgement. The tourist office is located opposite it.
Santiago el Mayor was built between the 7th and 13th centuries. It has a fortified tower and a stone statue of the saint, discovered in the church foundations in 1965. For a change of style, seek out the ornately Baroque **Palacio de Ongay-Vallesantoro** and the **Casa Consistorial**, the 16th-century city hall.
🚗 *Take the NA5410 east to Castillo de Javier.*

❷ Castillo de Javier
Navarra; 31411
The impressive structure of the Castillo de Javier *(open daily)* is surrounded by rolling green hills and forests. It dates back to the 11th century, but was added to and altered up to the 16th century and has been well preserved.

Statue of Saint James in Zangoza

It was the birthplace of Saint Franc Xavier, who, as well as being co-founder of the Jesuit order, has a special place in Basque religious culture as the patron saint of sports men. Once over the footbridge and inside, explore the castle, its paint ings, medieval furniture and macabre skeleton murals in the chapel *(Mass daily at 1pm)*. The castle also houses a magnifi cent 13th-century crucifix. During the first two weeken of March, a pilgrimage, the Javierada, is made to here from Zangoza.
🚗 *Continue on the NA5410 to Yesa. Turn left onto the N240 towards Iruña (Pamplona), ar immediately there will be sign to turn right (on the NA2113 to reach the Monasterio de Leyre. Follow signs and park*

❸ Monasterio de Leyre
Navarra; 31410
Surrounded by limestone cliffs and manicured lawns and with views of the Yesa reservoir, the Monasterio d Leyre is an impressive sight. Leyre wa founded as a Benedictine monaster but later came to be in the hands o Cistercian monks. Monks still reside here, and part of the original comple built between the 11th and 12th centuries, has been heavily restored and now contains a hotel. Visitors ar allowed access to the 11th-century church and mausoleum. The church dedicated to Santa María, features

e of the most renowned portals in
varra, an elaborate composition of
ange beast, bird and human forms,
ough inside it is remarkably austere.
e mausoleum, where the early kings
Navarra are buried, is an eerie place
th a series of symmetrically placed
ches. Leyre's monks are famous for
eir Gregorian chant, which they
rform here *(open Mon–Fri, from
15am to 2pm, and 3.30 to 7pm, Sat–
n, from 10:15am to 2pm, and 4 to 7pm;
ants performed Mon–Fri at 7.30am, 9
d 7pm, Sat–Sun at 8am, noon and 7pm).*

Return to the N240, turn right in
dena and cross the bridge. After
dena, turn right towards Iruña
mplona). At the second roundabout,
n right onto the NA150. At Lumbier,
low signs for the Foz de Lumbier.
ave the car in the parking area.

Foz de Lumbier
varra; 31440

e Foz de Lumbier, a majestic gorge
rrounded by rock walls over 150 m
0 ft) high, is one of the most cele-
ated beauty spots in Navarra. A
in used to run through it, but this
e is no longer in use and the tracks
ve been removed, leaving a 1,300-m
400-yd) path for walkers, joggers
d cyclists. The gorge's craggy walls
rout thyme and lavender plants
d at its arched entrance there are
undant poplars. Visitors can spot
e odd fox or *jabalí* (wild boar).

Return to Lumbier, cross the river
d at the roundabout turn right onto
e NA178 towards Navascués. After
e village of Domeño, follow signs off
is road to the Foz de Arbayún.

⑤ Foz de Arbayún
Navarra; 31454

Unlike the Foz de Lumbier, the
Arbayún gorge cannot be traversed,
but a lookout point, the Mirador de
Iso, has been installed directly above
it. This 6-km (4-mile) long gorge was
formed by the Salazar river eroding
the rock of the Sierra de Leyre. Blessed
with a microclimate, the gorge is blanketed with a diverse variety of trees,
which come alive with vivid colours
during autumn. It is also home to a
large community of vultures.

Return to the NA178 and continue
along it as far as Navascués where
there is a right turn onto the NA214 in
the direction of Burgui. At Burgui, turn
left on the NA137 for Erronkari (Roncal),
and park at the base of the village.

Above Stone carvings at the Castillo de Javier
Below left Breathtaking view of the Foz de
Arbayún **Below right** Intricately carved portal
of the Monasterio de Leyre

Above View of the picturesque hamlet of Otsagabia amid the mountains **Below** Old stone church in Erronkari village

WHERE TO STAY

ERRONKARI

Txarpa Etxea *inexpensive*
This *casa rural* in an old town house in the heart of Erronkari has four attic-style rooms with exposed beams, pretty throws and comfortable beds.
C/ Irionda 17, 31415; 948 475 068

OTSAGABIA

Hostal Orhy Alde *inexpensive*
A lovely hostel, which overlooks the river, decorated with antiques and assorted bric-a-brac. The attic, which sleeps up to six, is a good option for families or friends travelling together.
Urrutia 6, 31680; 948 890 027

Camping Osate *inexpensive*
This extensive campsite has good bathroom and laundry facilities and a bar-restaurant on site, which is popular with locals.
NA130 s/n (follow the signs from the village), 31680; 948 890 184; www.campingosate.net

RONCESVALLES

Casa de los Beneficiados *moderate*
The original 18th-century pilgrims' hospice, adjacent to the Colegiata Real, has been renovated and stripped back to show natural wood beams and floors and brick walls.
Orreaga-Roncesvalles, 31650; 948 760 105; www.casadebeneficiados.com

AROUND LAS CUEVAS DE ZUGARRAMURDI

Sueldegia *inexpensive*
Sueldegia, a *casa rural* in Zugarramurdi's main square, offers spacious *en suite* rooms, a comfortable common area and outdoor garden.
Lapizteguia s/n, 31710, Zugarramurdi; 948 599 088

---

⑥ Erronkari (Roncal)
Navarra; 31415

The valley of Roncal is famous throughout Spain for the cheese it produces with the milk of the Lacha breed of sheep that inhabit the rolling green pastures of this mountainous part of Navarra. At the heart of the valley is the sleepy village of Roncal. It is a wildly pretty place, with stone streets and houses on a curious Y-shaped layout ending at the Esca river and surrounded by forests. The shepherd-turned-opera singer Julián Gayarre (1844–90) was from here and a museum on his life and work, the **Casa-Museo Gayarre** *(open Tue–Sun)*, has been set up in Roncal.

🚗 *Leaving Erronkari, continue along the NA137 for Izaba (Isaba), and turn left on the NA140. Go through Uztarroze (Uztárroz) and through many bends until the T-junction. Turn left, on the NA140. Go through Itzaltzu (Izalzu) to reach Otsagabia (Ochagavía). Park in the village.*

The Cheese of Roncal

The celebrated cheese from the Roncal valley was the first in Spain to receive its own DO or *Denominación de Origen*: an official standard that means no other region can use its name or produce a cheese with its particular qualities. Just north of Roncal, in the village of Uztarroze, a local cheesemaking family has set up a museum on cheesemaking, Ekia *(open daily)*, where visitors can also buy their products.

⑦ Otsagabia (Ochagavía)
Navarra; 31680

The picture-perfect hamlet of Otsagabia is located in the Salazar valley, which is named after the rive that runs through it. The village is renowned for its six medieval stone bridges and its white houses cappe with pointed slate roofs. The lovely 12th-century **Ermita de Nuestra Señora de Muskilda** on the outskirts the village is topped by an unusual cone-shaped tower, lending it a fair tale appearance. Every September, th village's famous *danzantes* (traditiona dancers) perform in the honour of th Virgin of Muskilda in traditional attire.

🚗 *From Otsagabia, take the NA201. mountain road, which ascends to the Bosque de Irati. Park at the entrance t the forest where there is a small infor mation office.*

⑧ Bosque de Irati
Navarra; 31670

The Irati forest occupies a special plac in Basque folklore. It spreads over 170 sq km (65 sq miles) of the Aezkoa and Salazar valleys and stretches all the way into France, making it one o the largest forests in Europe. Over 2 species of birds inhabit the Irati, which is made up of surprisingly large beech and fir trees. Wildlife includes red dee wild boar and foxes. The informatio centre can advise visitors on hikes through the forest and bird-watchin trails. Visit the **Ermita de la Virgin de las Nieves**, a pretty hermitage, a short walk from the car park.

🚗 *Return to Otsagabia and get onto the NA140. Cross the river twice and turn right following signs for Jaurriet and Burguete (Auritz), still on the same road. Go through Garaioa and Garralda until it meets the main N135. Turn right here for Roncesvalles.*

Roncesvalles
varra; 31650

s ancient mountain border village
s mythologized in the medieval
ic *Chanson de Roland* as the place
ere the heroic knight Roland died
hting against the Moors with
arlemagne's army in 778. However,
tory has shown that it was the
sques, not the Moors, who attacked
arlemagne's men in Roncesvalles.
:er the discovery of Saint James's
mb in Galicia a century later,
ncesvalles became the main point
entry for pilgrims from France into
ain on the Camino de Santiago.
e most important building is the
legiata Real *(open daily 10am–2pm,
0–7pm)*, where Sancho VII, the King
Navarra (r. 1194–1229), is buried.

   *Return from Roncesvalles along
e N135 and beyond Burguete (Auritz)
ntinue straight on this road towards
ña (Pamplona). At Zubiri, turn right
to the N138 towards Eugi to reach
tasun. Turn left here onto the NA2520
Olague. Turn right onto the N121A
Olague. Go through two tunnels
d turn right onto the NA2540,
rough Berroeta. Follow this road to
eet the N121B for Elizondo.*

Elizondo
varra; 31700

is village of 18th- and 19th-century
wn houses and red-shuttered
omesteads (known as *caserios*) is
e gateway to the Valle de Baztán,
oreathtaking valley lined by moun-
ns and ancient oak trees. The Baztán
er runs through the valley, making
oopular with walkers and water
orts enthusiasts. Straddling the
er, Elizondo is a pleasant place

to walk around. Visit the 20th-century
Iglesia de Santiago, built in the Neo-
Baroque style, and the 18th-century
Palacio de Arizcunera. The town is
famous for its *urrakin egina* (hazelnut
chocolate) and holds a food fair
in October.

   *Continue on the N121B past
Elizondo until the left turn for Urdazubi
(Urdax), off the main road. Follow signs
for Zugarramurdi on the NA4402 and
then the NA4401. Park at the public
car park on the outskirts of the village.*

⑪ Las Cuevas de Zugarramurdi
Navarra; 31710

The caves of Zugarramurdi, more
commonly known as La Cueva de las
Brujas (the Witches' Cave) *(open daily
9am to dusk)*, are one of the most
unusual sights in Navarra. At 120 m
(130 yd) long and surrounded by
thick green forest, the caves are an
impressive natural wonder. In the
late 1600s they were an alleged
meeting place for witches. During the
Inquisition, 300 women from the area
were arrested and accused of witchcraft. Many were tortured and
eventually executed in an act that
was intended to rid Navarra of black
magic. Near the caves, the **Museo de
las Brujas** *(closed Mon)* puts these
events in context.

   *Leave on the NA4401, which then
joins the N121B, to Dantxarinea on
the French border. Turn left and enter
France briefly and follow the local D4
wide road left to Sare. Continue on the
same road to re-enter Spain and
arrive at Bera (Vera de Bidasoa). Park
in the Plaza Juan de Alzate at the
entrance to the village.*

Above Wooden doorway of the 12th-century
Ermita de Nuestra Señora de Muskilda,
Otsagabia **Below** Forest around the Witches'
Cave in Zugarramurdi

EAT AND DRINK

RONCESVALLES

La Posada de Roncesvalles
inexpensive
Located in a 17th-century farmhouse,
La Posada serves up hot and hearty
local dishes to pilgrims. Recommended dishes are the roasted red
peppers, wild mushrooms and game
including pigeon and boar.
*Roncesvalles-Orreaga, 31650;
948 760 225; www.
laposadaderoncesvalles.com*

**AROUND LAS CUEVAS DE
ZUGARRAMURDI**

Altzatenea *moderate*
The speciality here is large succulent
steaks, which come cooked to perfec-
tion from an outdoor grill. There is a
flower-filled outdoor terrace for dining
on warmer evenings.
*C/ Basaburua 3, 31710, Zugarramurdi;
948 599 187*

Above Homestead with a colourful, flower-filled balcony, Bera **Below** One of the old *carboneras* in the Parque Natural de Señorio de Bertiz

⑫ Bera (Vera de Bidasoa)
Navarra; 31780

Bera is the largest of the famous *cinco villas* (five towns) that dot the Valle de Bidasoa. Its close proximity to France has played an important part in Bera's prosperity, allowing it to flourish through trade. Stately *caseríos* (homesteads), many bearing colourful coats of arms, flank its main street, which also has a good selection of shops. The illustrious Baroja family have their roots in Bera.

Their most famous members were the novelist Pío Baroja (1872–1956), his painter brother Ricardo and the nephew the anthropologist Julio Caro Baroja (1914–95).

🚗 *From Bera head towards Iruña (Pamplona) on the N121A for 25 km (16 miles), and then turn left for Oronoz. Drive to the centre of the village. Turn right at the petrol station, crossing the bridge and following signs for Parque Natural de Señorio Bertiz. Park in the car park.*

⑬ Parque Natural de Señorío de Bertiz
Navarra; 31720

With giant oaks, beech and chestnuts, pretty streams and waterfall and a large community of woodpeckers, the nature reserve is a magical place to take a walk. The Jardín de Señorío de Bertiz lies on the edge of the Parque Natural de Señorío de Bertiz. The following easy to moderate 6-km (4-mile) walk consists of forest paths and tracks, all well signposted. This walk can be done any time of the day, but be sure to carry water.

VISITING PARQUE NATURAL DE SEÑORÍO DE BERTIZ

Tourist Information
The Oficina de Turismo de Señorío de Bertiz is located in the car park of the Jardín de Señorío de Bertiz. Guided visits are also available.
31720, Bertiz; 948 592 421; www.parquedebertiz.es; open 10am to 8pm in summer and 10am to 6pm in winter

WHERE TO STAY

BERA

Hotel Churrut *moderate*
An 18th-century building that the Churrut family has converted into a comfortable hotel. The gallery is an eye-catching feature with comfortable wicker armchairs and floor-to-ceiling windows that offer great views of the garden.
Plaza de los Fueros 2, 31780; 948 625 540; www.hotelchurrut.com

PARQUE NATURAL DE SEÑORÍO DE BERTIZ

Hostal Bertiz *moderate*
Located on the edge of the park, this 16th-century stone guesthouse is surrounded by a flower-filled garden and has tastefully decorated rooms.
C/ San Juan Bautista 16, Oieregi, 31720; 948 592 081; www.hostalbertiz.com

A two-hour walking tour

From the car park take the tarmac road past the old guard house to the remains of the **carbonera** ①. The inhabitants of the villages surrounding the park used to collect wood in the forest to burn to charcoal in mounds such as these. Concerned about anything that might halt the regeneration of the forest, Pedro Ciga, the last lord of the manor, employed wardens to stop this practice, as he did the collection of acorns. Two paths branch out from this point. Take the Irretarazu path to the

Parque Natural de Señorío de Bertiz sign

left and walk uphill. Almost immediately there will be many oak trees. Oaks were felled here from the 16th to the 18th centuries for use in shipbuilding, and since then as firewood. Since the time of Pedro Ciga, this practice too has stopped. Continue walking uphill, onto a natural elevated terrace with some great views of the Valle de Bertiz. The track leads to an area of the forest dominated by chestnut trees, some a century old. Keep walking and the oak trees will become scarcer and beech will begin to dominate. Continue to where the

tarazu path crosses with the
rburua path and take the latter.
s goes through the valley floor
ere alder and ash trees can be
en, and which is crisscrossed by
scades and streams. Almost at
e end of the path is the **Suspiro
terfall** ②, formed by a spring of
e same name. Continue to the junc-
n with the Suspiro path. This point
s halfway through the walk. Turn
ht and follow the signs to the car
rk. The path leads to an ancient
ne **drinking fountain** ③ and
nch, turning into a cobblestoned
d lined with plane trees that goes
ck to the starting point.
Before leaving, stop at the magical
dín de Señorío de Bertiz ④ at
e entrance of Parque Natural de
ñorío de Bertiz. This 19th-century
tanical garden, one of the most
autiful in Spain, stands on land
at had been gifted to the noble Ciga
mily by King Charles II in the 17th
ntury. Pedro Ciga was an ardent
ture lover and pioneer ecologist
o, with his wife Dorotea, planted
e garden and rebuilt the ancestral
me, the **Palacio de Bertiz** ⑤, in Art
ouveau style before gifting it to the
ate in 1949. The garden's diversity is
tounding, with exotic trees and

plants such as cedar, gingko biloba,
liquidambar, cypress, lemon and an
abundance of bamboo. Flowers
bloom from every nook. The manor
is occasionally used for exhibitions
and the old chapel has been converted into an information centre
(open daily). After visiting the garden,
go back to the car park.

🚗 *Return to the N121A and follow
signs to Iruña (Pamplona). Follow
"Centro Urbano" and "Todas
Directions" signs to park. Use a private
car park as street parking is prohibited.*

Above Giant tree in the Parque Natural de Señorío de Bertiz

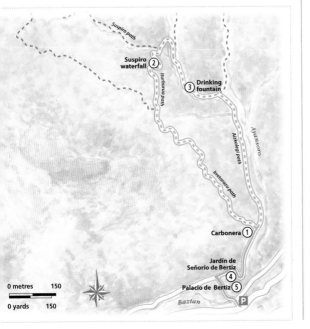

EAT AND DRINK

BERA

Restaurant Miguel *moderate*
Located on the second floor of a
modern building on the outskirts of
the village, the dining room is enclosed
by large windows which offer some
wonderful views of the rolling countryside. Although the cuisine uses local
produce, it is often presented in surprising, innovative ways. Try the
bacalao al ajoarriero, chopped salt cod
cooked with potatoes, garlic, peppers,
oil and herbs.
C/ Ibardin, 31780; 948 631 394

Eat and Drink: inexpensive, under €20; moderate, €20–€40; expensive, over €40

Above Five-arched medieval pilgrim's bridge at Puente la Reina **Below** Romanesque structure of Palacio de los Reyes de Navarra, Lizarra

VISITING IRUÑA

Tourist Information
C/ Hilario'n Eslava (corner of Plaza San Francisco); 848 420 420; www.turismo. navarra.es; open daily from 10am to 2pm and, from 4 to 7pm, and in summer from 9am to 8pm Mon–Sat, and from 10am to 2pm Sun.

Parking
Directions to commercial car parks are posted on all main arteries into Iruña. Central ones include the Plaza de Castillo, the Auditorio Baluarte and the bus station at the Ciudadela.

WHERE TO STAY

IRUÑA

Hotel Castillo de Javier *inexpensive*
A step up from the plethora of budget hostels in Iruña's Old Town, this hotel offers small but bright rooms.
C/ San Nicolás 50-52, 31100; 948 203 040; www.hotelcastillodejavier.com

PUENTE LA REINA

Bidean *moderate*
Located on Puente La Reina's main street, this *casa rural* offers cosy accommodation in stylish rustic surroundings. There is a good restaurant on site, which is popular with pilgrims.
C/ Mayor 20, 31100; 948 340 457; www.bidean.com

⑭ Iruña (Pamplona)
Navarra; 31110

Iruña, or Pamplona as it is more commonly known, the capital of Navarra, is said to have been founded by the Roman general, Pompey. It is probably best known for its yearly San Fermín festival, or the running of the bulls. It is a handsome town, and well worth stopping in for an afternoon or even overnight, even when the festival is not on, in order to try its famous tapas bars.

A good starting point for a quick tour is the central **Plaza de Castillo**. From here, it is easy to explore the main sights, which are signposted throughout the old city. The most important are the Gothic **Catedral de Santa María la Real** *(open daily)*, the massive 16th-century *ciudadela* (citadel) built in ochre-coloured stone, and the Neo-Classical **Palacio del Gobierno de Navarra** *(by appointment only)*, which is now the seat of Navarra's regional government. This is where Iruña's mayor heralds the beginning of San Fermín.

Once back at the Plaza de Castillo, take a break at the famous Cafe Iruña, a *Belle-Époque* café Ernest Hemingway frequented while writing *The Sun Also Rises*. A bronze life-size statue of the author sits at the entrance.

🚗 *Leave Iruña (Pamplona) via the PA30 ring road, following the*

directions to Tarragona. Take the ex to the A12, following the directions Logroño/Madrid. Leave the A12 at e 18 and follow the signs to Puente La Reina. Park in the street.

San Fermín

The most famous festival in Navarra, and possibly the whole of Spain, is San Fermín, otherwise known as the running of the bulls. The whole city practically closes down for the week-long event in early July, and what may seem like madness to an outsider is actually taken quite seriously by Spaniards, with daily bull runs (called *encierros*) shown live on television. In honour of Navarra's patron saint, people spill out onto the streets for spontaneous partying, a parade of *gigantes* (towering figures dressed in traditional costumes) and, on 7 July, the carrying of the effigy of San Fermín in procession to the cathedral amid great ceremony.

⑮ Puente la Reina
Navarra; 31100

A major stop on the Camino de Santiago, this village gets its name from the elegant humpbacked ston pedestrian bridge spanning the Arg river that was built for pilgrims in th 11th century by royal command. Visitors can reach it by walking to th end of Calle Mayor. About halfway along this street, the Plaza Julian

Where to Stay: inexpensive, under €70; moderate, €70–€120; expensive, over €120

Left Running before the bulls in Iruña's famous San Fermín festival

SHOPPING

IRUÑA

Visit the shops around the cathedral for pottery and ceramics, textiles and other paraphernalia related to the San Fermín festival.

LIZARRA

Carmelo Boneta Lopetegui
Visit Carmelo Boneta's *taller* (workshop) near the cathedral. He sells intricately-carved pieces of wooden furniture and objects inspired by Basque symbolism as well as religious artifacts.
C/ La Rúa 19, 31200; 948 551 481

EAT AND DRINK

IRUÑA

Rodero *expensive*
This contemporary-cuisine restaurant is considered one of the best in the city. The menu includes dishes such as wild pigeon with figs.
C/ Emilio Arrieta 3, 31002; 948 228 035; www.restauranterodero.com; closed Sun and Easter

Tapas bars
There are dozens of tapas bars lining the old streets. Most specialize in *pintxos*, a Basque style of tapas that generally consists of small morsels served on a round of bread.

LIZARRA

Bar-Restaurante Casanova
inexpensive
This family-run place is as popular with locals as tourists for its dishes such as roast suckling pig and red bean stew.
C/ Fray Wenceslao de Oñate 7, 31200; 948 552 809; closed Mon

---

ena contains a handful of bars underneath its porticoes. The 12th-century **Iglesia del Crucifijo** (open ...ly), supposedly built by the ...ights Templar, is named after the ...haped wooden crucifix of Christ ...th arms upraised, which resides ...side, and is said to have been a gift ...m a German pilgrim in the 14th ...ntury. The **Iglesia de Santiago** ...en daily), located on the main ...rrow street of Puente la Reina, has ...gilded statue showing the saint ...a pilgrim.

Return to the A12 and at exit 36, ...e the right onto the NA1110 to ...arra (Estella). Pass the modern ...riphery and park in the street.

Lizarra (Estella)
...varra; 31200

...perhaps one of the earliest exercises ...mass tourism, Sancho V Ramírez

(r. 1063–1094), King of Navarra, founded Lizarra in the 11th century to attract pilgrims on their way to Santiago. Lizarra has most of its major attractions across the Arga in a compact *conjunto monumental* (historic centre). Climb the dozens of steps to get to the portal of the **Iglesia de San Pedro de la Rúa** (closed for renovation at the time of going to press). The church boasts rich 13th-century carvings of plant and figurative motifs. It has a Cistercian Mudéjar-influenced sculpted doorway. Opposite is the **Palacio de los Reyes de Navarra**, the only secular Romanesque work in Navarra and now the location of the tourist office and a **museum** (closed Mon) dedicated to the painter Gustavo de Maeztú (1887–1947). Next to it is the San Martín square with its famous Fuente de Chorros, a good place to relax in the shade.

DAY TRIP OPTIONS

The Navarra valley offers two day trip options. The Valle de Baztán and the Bertiz estate are both easily reached via a well-paved motorway from Iruña. Another option is to visit the valleys of Roncal and Salazar and the Bosque de Irati.

Valle de Baztán and the Bertiz estate

Drive at a leisurely pace through the enchanting Valle de Baztán in the Basque Pyrenees. Stop off and stroll around the village of Elizondo ⑩. Then head to Parque Natural de

Señorío de Bertiz ⑬ to explore this wonderful nature reserve and the Jardín de Señorío de Bertiz.

From Iruña's PA30 ring road, take exit 3 to the N121A, then the N121B to Elizondo. To reach the Bertiz estate, return along the N121B to Oronoz and drive to the centre of the village. Turn right at the petrol station, crossing the bridge and following signs for Parque Natural Señorío de Bertiz.

Erronkari, Otsagabia and the Bosque de Irati

Visit Erronkari ⑥ and Otsagabia ⑦,

which are popular Sunday destinations for Pamploneses, who come to walk and cycle around the villages that dot the valleys. Leave a few hours for walking through the dense Bosque de Irati ⑧, following signed footpaths from the car park.

From Iruña take the N21 then the N240 eastwards. At the junction of the NA178, turn left and follow signs to Erronkari. To reach Otsagabia from Erronkari, continue on the NA137 to Isaba following signs to Otsagabia. To reach the entrance to the Bosque de Irati, ascend the NA2012 road from Otsagabia.

Eat and Drink: inexpensive, under €20; moderate, €20–€40; expensive, over €40

To the Roof of Aragón

Castillo de Loarre to Hecho

Highlights

- **Castles in the air**
  Discover Loarre and Jaca, the rocky strongholds of the kings of Aragón

- **Breathtaking scenery and wildlife**
  Watch eagles, vultures and other large birds of prey glide over Los Mallos de Riglos

- **Romanesque architecture**
  Visit old churches and monasteries in San Juan de la Peña and Santa Cruz de la Serós

- **Local wines**
  Taste the little-known but surprisingly good wines of Aragón

Spectacular rock formations of Los Mallos de Riglos dominate Riglos village

To the Roof of Aragón

Forming a giant wall along the French border, the Aragonese Pyrenees dramatically cap Huesca, Aragón's northernmost province. This drive starts with the magnificent Castillo de Loarre, impressively situated overlooking the wide, flat Ebro plain and goes through tiny villages, awe-inspiring rock formations and majestic gorges. En route, visitors will see the Monasterio de San Juan de la Peña, hidden in an overhanging cliff and reputed to have been an early guardian of the Holy Grail. The tour also goes through the medieval city of Jaca, gateway to the High Pyrenees and comes to an end in the valleys of Ansó and Hecho.

Above Majestic 11th-century Castillo de Loarre offering spectacular views, *see p84*

ACTIVITIES

Take a walk in the Pyrenees, from easy 1- to 2-hour strolls to more arduous hikes

Go rock climbing at the stunning rock formation of Los Mallos de Riglos

Try white water rafting and canoeing around Biniés and Berdún

Above Thick forest around San Juan de la Peña, *see p86*
Below left Sweet shop in Jaca, *see p88* **Below right**
Iglesia de San Pedro in Ayerbe, *see p84*

Borau

Castiello
de Jaca   Villanovilla

N330
Albarín
1,551 m
Banaguás   Baraguás
Guasa
JACA

Barós
Navasa
Oroel
1,770 m
Puerto de
Oroel

A1205

Bernués

HUESCA

Moro

Javierrelatre

Gállego
Caldearenas
Rasal

KEY

 Drive route

0 kilometres   5

0 miles   5

de Loarre
Pusilibro
1,597 m

**CASTILLO
DE LOARRE**
Aniés

HU313

alse de
avás

A1206

ales

PLAN YOUR DRIVE

Start/finish: Castillo de Loarre
to Hecho.

Number of days: 3–4, allowing half
a day to explore San Juan de la Peña
and half a day for visiting Jaca.

Distances: 180 km (110 miles).

Road conditions: Most roads are in
good condition, but with lots of hairpin
curves and bends, which make it slow.
In winter some mountain roads may
be closed, or require snow chains.

When to go: The best time to visit this
region is between spring and autumn.
Spring will see the rivers at their fullest
for water sports enthusiasts.

Opening hours: Most museums
and monuments are closed on
Mondays. Shops are open from 9:30
to 11:30am, and from 4 to 8pm.
Restaurants are open from 2 to
4pm, and from 8 to 11pm.

Main market days: Jaca: Fri;
Hecho: Wed.

Major festivals: Murillo de Gállego:
Santo Domingo, third weekend Aug;
Jaca: Fiestas Patronales, last week Jun;
Ansó: Fiesta del Traje, last Sun Aug;
Hecho: Natividad de la Virgen, Sep.

DAY TRIP OPTIONS

Culture and **history buffs** will
love the old San Juan de la Peña
Romanesque sanctuary. **Nature
lovers** will be enthralled by the
magnificent forest of Oza and the
villages of Ansó and Hecho. For
details, *see p89*.

VISITING LOARRE

Take the A132 northwest from Huesca to Ayerbe, and turn right onto the A1206, following signs to Loarre.

WHERE TO STAY

AROUND CASTILLO DE LOARRE

Hospedería de Loarre *moderate*
This small, 12-room hostelry is located in a medieval mansion in the centre of Loarre, with a fine restaurant on the ground floor specializing in regional dishes. The thyme-flavoured ice cream is a must.
Plaza Miguel Moya 7, 22809, Loarre; 974 382 706; www.hospederiasdeloarre.com

AGÜERO

Camping Municipal Peña Sola *inexpensive*
Campers wake up to the magnificent sight of the Peña Sola at this camp located at the base of Agüero village.
Ctra. 534 s/n, 22808; 974 380 533

MURILLO DE GÁLLEGO

Hotel Los Mallos *inexpensive*
Popular with outdoor sports enthusiasts, this well-kept and homey hostel offers a great value *media-pensión*, which includes breakfast and lunch or dinner.
Ctra. de Jaca s/n, 22808; 974 383 026

Above Hill town of Agüero sheltered by a crag, the Peña Sola **Below** Gigantic red-hued cliffs of Los Mallos watching over the village of Riglos

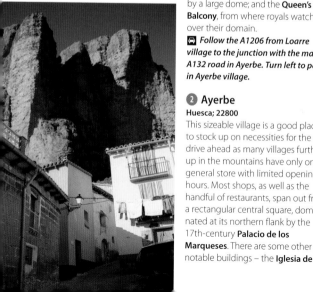

① Castillo de Loarre
Huesca; 22809

The majestic 11th-century Castillo de Loarre *(open daily)* sits high above the village of the same name. It started out as a fort but was converted to a monastery during the reign of Sancho Ramírez (c.1042–94), one of the first kings of Aragón. Perched over 1,000 m (3,300 ft) above sea level, with spectacular vistas of surrounding orchards and reservoirs, much of the complex is surprisingly well preserved. Visitors are free to wander all the rooms, passageways and turrets. Highlights of the castle include the **Iglesia de San Esteban** with its magnificent external apses; the **Royal Chapel**, a perfectly symmetrical space crowned by a large dome; and the **Queen's Balcony**, from where royals watched over their domain.

🚗 *Follow the A1206 from Loarre village to the junction with the main A132 road in Ayerbe. Turn left to park in Ayerbe village.*

② Ayerbe
Huesca; 22800

This sizeable village is a good place to stock up on necessities for the drive ahead as many villages further up in the mountains have only one general store with limited opening hours. Most shops, as well as the handful of restaurants, span out from a rectangular central square, dominated at its northern flank by the 17th-century **Palacio de los Marqueses**. There are some other notable buildings – the **Iglesia de San Pedro**, a 16th-century church, and the Baroque **Torre de Reloj** (clock tower). The Nobel Prize-winning physician Santiago Ramón y Cajal (1852–1934) spent his youth in Ayerbe, and there is a small museum dedicated to him in the house where he lived *(C/ Rafael Gasset 19, 22800, closed Mon, and Tue in winter)*.

🚗 *Continue along the A132, signposted for Jaca, for about 6 km (4 miles), and then turn right onto HU310/Z310 (unsigned), following signs for Riglos and Los Mallos de Riglos. Park at the entrance of Riglos.*

③ Los Mallos de Riglos
Huesca; 22808

The tiny village of Riglos is dominated by one of the most extraordinary sights in Aragón – Los Mallos de Riglos. These eight red-hued, 300-m (985-ft) high vertical rock formations rule over the area, which was baptized El Reino de los Mallos or "Kingdom of Mallos". They rank among the best rock-climbing territories in Europe and the views from the top are astounding. On any given day, dozens of climbers can be seen ascending over their massive surface. Watching the climbers is a fascinating way to spend an hour or two. The sheer number of birds of prey darting in and out of Los Mallos' jagged crevices will enthrall nature lovers.

🚗 *Return to the A132 and turn right and then very shortly fork left again on the Z534/HU534 (unsigned) for Agüero. Park at the base of the village.*

Romanesque Architecture

specially common throughout the
yrenees, Romanesque is an artistic
yle that flourished across Europe
om the 11th to the 13th centuries.
ater, it morphed into the early
othic style. Across northern Spain,
omanesque architects were most
ctive in the building of churches,
nonasteries and hermitages, many
n or near the route of the Christian
ilgrimage route to Santiago de
ompostela. Romanesque build-
ngs stand out for their simplicity
nd sturdiness: thick stone walls,
ounded arches, barrel vaults.
omanesque artists excelled at
reating richly carved portals and
ighly graphic, colourful murals,
esigned to communicate the scrip-
ures to a largely illiterate population.

Agüero
esca; 22808

e attractive little hill town of Agüero,
ich also forms a part of the El Reino
los Mallos, is sheltered by another
vering crag of stone known as the
ña Sola. The extraordinary 13th-
ntury **Iglesia de Santiago** is located
a forest outside the village (follow
ns) and is considered a stellar
ample of Aragonese Romanesque
hitecture for its exquisitely carved
rtal depicting scenes of Salome
ncing. Most experts have attri-
ted this work to the same sculptor
o worked on the Monasterio de
n Juan de la Peña *(see p86)*.
   *Return to the A132 and turn left
gnposted for Iruña). Park at the
se of Murillo de Gállego.*

⑤ Murillo de Gállego
Zaragoza; 22808

A picturesque village of stone
houses, Murillo de Gállego gets its
name from the Gállego river, which
runs directly through it. Walk up to
the main plaza, where there is a handy
children's playground and the majestic
11th-century **Iglesia de El Salvador**
(open for Mass only). The church was
later expanded in the 16th century.
Some original polychrome paintings
still remain on the capitals on either
side of the crypt, one of which depicts
a scene of two women arguing.
🚗 *Stay on the A132 till Santa María
(also indicated as Las Peñas de Riglos)
and turn right onto the A1205 (Ctra.
de Jaca a Santa María). After 25 km
(16 miles), is Bernués, near which
there is a left turn on the A1603
(unsigned) for San Juan de la Peña.*

Above left Stone portal of the 13th-century
Iglesia de Santiago in Agüero **Above right**
Majestic Iglesia de El Salvador in Murillo
de Gállego **Below** Approach to the town
of Loarre

EAT AND DRINK

AROUND CASTILLO DE LOARRE

Casa O' Caminero *inexpensive*
A popular local eatery located in a
whitewashed homestead in Loarre,
this restaurant serves up hot and hearty
menu del día (fixed price, three-course
meals). Particularly good are the
chuletas (grilled lamb chops), game
dishes and rabbit *paella*.
*Plaza San Pedro 14, 22809, Loarre;
974 382 696*

MURILLO DE GÁLLEGO

Reino de los Mallos *moderate*
This local *bodega* offers tastings of
their excellent product and creative
cuisine in stylish surroundings
overlooking their vineyards.
*Ctra. A 132, 22808; 974 383 015;
www.reinodelosmallos.es*

Eat and Drink: inexpensive, under €20; moderate, €20–€40; expensive, over €40

Above Tenth-century Real Monasterio de San Juan de la Peña

VISITING SAN JUAN DE LA PEÑA

Tourist Information
974 355 119; www.turismodearagon. com; www.monasteriosanjuan.com

Parking
Park in front of the Monasterio Nuevo, on an open field that also has picnic facilities. Parking is not permitted outside the old monastery. There is a shuttle service that runs every 20 minutes between the new and old monasteries of San Juan de la Peña (cost is included in the entry fee).

WHERE TO STAY

MONASTERIO DE SAN JUAN DE LA PEÑA

Hospedería San Juan de la Peña *expensive*
Located inside the 17th-century monastery, this hotel boasts contemporary decor with modern facilities.
22711, Monasterio de San Juan de la Peña; 974 374 422; www. hospederiasdearagon.com

SANTA CRUZ DE LA SERÓS

El Mirador de Santa Cruz *expensive*
All rooms in this luxury guest house have pretty, antique furniture and private terraces with views over the valley. There is also an in-house spa and an outdoor pool.
Ordana 8, 22792; 974 355 593; www.elmiradordesantacruz.com

⑥ Monasterio de San Juan de la Peña
Huesca; 22711

This imposing monastery complex actually consists of two sites: the incredible old Real Monasterio de San Juan de la Peña (Royal Monastery of Saint John of the Rock), a Romanesque sanctuary literally carved into the side of the cliff face, and the Monasterio Nuevo, dating from the 17th century. The monasteries are located in the middle of a nature reserve of the same name. With constant views of the Pyrenees in the distance and massive rock formations bursting out of forests, the location is as exciting to explore as the medieval chamber

A one-hour walking tour

Start the walk from the car park in front of the **Monasterio Nuevo** ① *(open daily)*. After a fire destroyed the Royal Monastery in the 17th century, a new one was built further up the hillside, on a wide field known as Llano de San Indalecio. Although the new monastery contains none of the dramatic stony carvings of the original San Juan de la Peña, it is noted for being a fine piece of monastic architecture and has maintained its elegant Baroque façade. The interior has been heavily altered and restored, with much of it given over to a four-star hotel and temporary exhibitions on art and history. To the right of the new monastery is a well-marked

Stone capital in the old monastery cloister

path stretching northwards. This goes through a thick forest of pine, holly, beech and maple to the **Balcón de Pirineo** ②, a panoramic lookout point across the valleys of Ansó and Ordesa with the mountains framing the horizon. An indicator will help visitors identify each one, including France's Midi d'Ossau. Return to the new monastery and go past the Centro de Interpretación located next to it. The visitor centre, housed in the **Ermita de San Homónimo** ③, provides information on the mountains and countryside that surround the complex. Take the south-leading track directly in front of the visitor centre. This zigzagging track will lead to a hermitage and *mirador* (lookout point), the **Ermita**

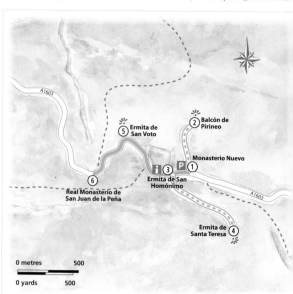

A1603

Ermita de San Voto ⑤

Balcón de Pirineo ②

Monasterio Nuevo ①

ℹ ③ P ①

Ermita de San Homónimo

⑥

Real Monasterio de San Juan de la Peña

A1603

Ermita de Santa Teresa ④

0 metres 500
0 yards 500

Santa Teresa ④. The hermitage
•lf lies in ruins, but it has fine views
'he valleys and mountains of the
-Pyrenees, including the village of
arre *(see p82)*.
Return to the Ermita de San
Mónimo. Follow the main tarmac
d to the west that leads to the
monastery. About 50 m (165 ft)
er the turn-off to the Tozal de San
vador take the route, marked by a
ine indicator, to the **Ermita de San
to** ⑤, a simple stone structure
th another *mirador* with further
ws of the Pyrenees. From here,
n up again with the main road
at goes to the **Real Monasterio
San Juan de la Peña** ⑥.

The Real Monasterio de San Juan
la Peña, or royal monastery, was
inded in the 10th century by a
bup of hermit monks fleeing the
borish invasion. Seeking sanctuary
the folds of an overhanging rock,
ey chiselled out a church in
bzarabic style on the ground floor.
e church later expanded to an
portant holy site under the order
the Benedictines. Legend has it
at the Holy Grail – the chalice that
as used in the Last Supper – was
dden here from the Moors; a
olica is on display in the central
ise in the upper church. The
onastery was a customary stop for
grims on the Camino de Santiago.
the 18th century, a Neo-Classical
antheon featuring some exquisite
ief carvings was built on the site of
medieval necropolis. The highlight
the structure is the Romanesque
bister. Conceived to represent New

Jerusalem, this space features 20
Romanesque capitals with carved
scenes from the scriptures by an
anonymous artist known simply
as El Maestro.
After visiting the old monastery,
either walk or take the shuttle service
back to the car park in front of the
Monasterio Nuevo.

🚗 *Continue on the A1603 to Santa
Cruz de la Serós. Park in the street at
the entrance to the village.*

⑦ Santa Cruz de la Serós
Huesca; 22792
A wonderfully intact little village,
Santa Cruz de la Serós is made up
of typical mountain houses. Built
entirely of stone, they feature cylindrical chimney stacks nicknamed
espantabrujas (something that is
believed to scare off witches). There
are two important Romanesque
monuments here. The first, on the
main road to the entrance of the
village, is the tiny 11th-century **Iglesia
de San Caprasio**, whose simple
interior can be viewed from behind
a grid at the entrance. The second,
in the middle of the village, is the
11th-century **Iglesia de Santa María**.
Carved in the centre of its portal is a
crismón, a compass-type symbol
common in Romanesque imagery
that depicts the beginning and end
of the universe. The town also has
some good bed-and-breakfasts and
high quality restaurants.

🚗 *Leave Santa Cruz de la Serós on
the A1603 and follow it until it meets
the N240. Turn right and follow signs
to the citadel in Jaca.*

Top Intricately-carved exterior of the Real
Monasterio de San Juan de la Peña **Above**
Sturdy exterior of the 11th-century Iglesia de
Santa María, Santa Cruz de la Serós **Below**
View of the elegant and simple Monasterio
Nuevo in San Juan de la Peña

SHOPPING IN SANTA CRUZ DE LA SERÓS

Embarrarte
A wide range of ceramicware and
pottery is on display from local artists
with modern designs in vibrant blue
and gold. There is also a range of
traditional designs.
Plaza 1, 22792; 974 363 106

EAT AND DRINK

SANTA CRUZ DE LA SERÓS

O' Fogaril *inexpensive*
This restaurant serves delicious food.
Try local dishes such as *pochas* (white
beans in a thick soup).
*C/ Baja 6, 22792; 974 361 737; closed
Mon–Fri in winter*

Above Ornate altar in the 16th-century Iglesia de San Pedro in Ansó **Below left** Eleventh-century castle in Biniés **Below right** Sign for the *casa rural* Hotel Barosse in Jaca **Bottom right** Exterior of the excellent Restaurante Gaby, Hecho

VISITING JACA

Tourist Information
Avda. Regimiento Galicia, 22700; 974 360 098; www.jaca.es

Parking
Private car parks are located in the Paseo Manuel Gímenez Abad behind the Ciudadela and on Calle Tierra de Biescas on the western flank.

Water sports
UR Pirineos offer rafting, canoeing, kayaking and canyoning on the Veral and Gállego rivers. They also have an office in Murillo de Gállego.
Avda. Primer Viernes de Mayo 14, 22700; 974 383 048; www.urpirineos.es

WHERE TO STAY

AROUND JACA

Hotel Barosse *moderate*
Hosts Jose and Gonzalo make guests feel thoroughly at home at their bed-and-breakfast, 4 km (2 miles) south of Jaca, where every detail has been meticulously conceived for comfort.
C/ Estiras 4, 22700, Barós; 974 360 582; www.barosse.com

ANSÓ

Posada Magoria *inexpensive*
This is the best place to stay in the village, with a rear garden overlooking the river.
A1602 s/n, 22700; 974 370 049; www.posadamagoria.com

8 Jaca
Huesca; 22700

Founded in the 2nd century, Jaca was the first capital of the kingdom of Aragón and is the gateway to the High Pyrenees. The town is home to the **Ciudadela de Jaca** *(open Tue–Sun)*, a massive pentagonal citadel built in the 16th century, and one of only two of its kind remaining in Europe. It has remained perfectly intact and can be visited despite it still having a military role.

Cross the Avenida Primer Viernes de Mayo into the old town, the site of the town's 11th-century **Catedral de San Pedro** *(open daily)*, one of Spain's oldest and the first in the country to be built in the Romanesque style. Its cloisters contain the **Museo Diocesano**, which holds many fine examples of Gothic and Romanesque frescoes and sculpture. The museum is currently closed for renovation. The picturesque pedestrianized streets surrounding the cathedral contain an eclectic range of cafés and bars, as well as shops specializing in cakes, sweet delicacies and unique local wines.

🚗 *Return to the N240 and retrace the route back to the junction with the A1603. Continue through Puente la Reina as far as Berdún (34 km/*

The Hecho coat of arms

21 miles). At Berdún, turn right on the A1602 (Carretera de Berdún) ar follow signs for Biniés. Park at the entrance to the village.

9 Biniés
Huesca; 22773

The picturesque Valle de Ansó is considered the most beautiful vall in the region. Its bucolic villages a typically made up of red-roo stone houses, and Biniés is no exception. Located 68C (2,250 ft) above sea level, Biniés is home to the Baroc **Iglesia de San Salvador** *(op for Mass only)*, which sits on the village's main square. A the rear of the village is an 11th-century castle, now privately owned. There is a walking track around its perimeter, which affords some magnificent views and a couple of picnic spots.

Continue along the same road tc the dramatic **Foz de Biniés**, which i signposted, but also easily recogni: able by two natural stone overhan ing arches. This majestic gorge is over 50 m (165 ft) long and enclose by rocky crags over 200 m (655 ft) high. Running through it is the Ver. river, a popular spot for fishing, wh water rafting and canoeing.

🚗 *Continue along the A1602 and fo left on the A176 to Ansó. Park in the car park in the outskirts of the villag*

EAT AND DRINK

JACA

Casa Fau *inexpensive*
Underneath ancient stone arches, this popular place serves mounds of mouth-watering tapas and *pinchos* such as prawns in béchamel sauce, stuffed red peppers and wild mushrooms with *foie gras*.
Plaza Catedral 3, 22700; 974 361 594

HECHO

Restaurante Gaby *moderate*
Gaby is a renowned cook who has turned her mountain home into a tiny restaurant and small hotel. Her clients come from far and wide to taste her dishes prepared from local produce.
Plaza Palacio 1, 22720; 974 375 007; www.casablasquico.com; bookings are essential

Above Isolated and picturesque mountain village of Ansó **Below** Breathtaking view over the mountains with the town of Jaca in the distance

Ansó

esca; 22728

archetypal mountain village ated in the Pyrenean foothills, só is made up of stone chalets ch hanging balconies, intricately ved shutters and doors, cobble- ned streets and steep tiled roofs. só remained very isolated for nturies due to poor road links, ich lead to a strong sense of dition and even its own dialect, led *cheso*, passed down the gen- tions. On the first floor of the th-century Gothic **Iglesia de n Pedro** is the **Museo del Traje sotano**, which displays medieval ditional costumes. On the last nday of August, the villagers dress traditional costume and parade ough the streets, a spectacle that aws a sizeable crowd. For those ho feel like a dip, there is a lovely unicipal pool in the village.

Return to the junction with the 602 and turn left, still on the A176 Hecho. Park on the outskirts of e village.

⑪ Hecho

Huesca; 22720

The village of Hecho rivals Ansó for sheer atmosphere, with a cluster of yet more charming old houses with hanging balconies brimming with pots of red geraniums. One of them contains the Restaurante Gaby, con- sidered the best place in the Valle de Hecho for traditional local dishes. The impressive 18th-century **Iglesia de San Martín** was probably built on the site of an original Romanesque structure. On the outskirts of the city there is an open-air sculpture garden, the work of noted French artist Pedro Tramullas (b. 1937). The garden also includes the works of several other artists of the region.

Just north of Hecho in the village of **Siresa** is the Romanesque **Iglesia de San Pedro**. Further north, the **Selva de Oza** is a great place to take a walk, with giant oak and pine trees and a thick vegetation of ferns. Just before the entrance to the forest, there are signs to the **Boca de Infierno** (Hell's Mouth), an impressive gorge.

DAY TRIP OPTIONS

With a base in Jaca visitors have the option of two day trips: a day in San Juan de la Peña, and another day exploring the Aragonese villages, Ansó and Hecho. Jaca is best approached by the N240.

Culture and history buffs
Visit the Monasterio Nuevo in San Juan de la Peña ⑥ in the morning, then have a picnic lunch in its

gardens. Go down to the nearby Real Monasterio de San Juan de la Peña, and then return in the shuttle bus that runs between the two.

Return to Jaca on the same route, via the A1603, then the N240.

Villages and forests
Visit Ansó ⑩ first, taking the incredible drive along the A1602. After visiting the neighbouring

village of Hecho ⑪, head to the Selva de Oza to take a walk in this forest of ferns, giant oak and pine trees.

From Jaca take the N240 to Berdún. Turn right onto the A1602 to Ansó. From Ansó take the A176 to Hecho. To visit the Selva de Oza take the HUV2131 from Hecho northwards in the direc- tion of Siresa. Return to Hecho, then take the A176 back to Puente la Reina, then the N240 back to Jaca.

Eat and Drink: inexpensive, under €20; moderate, €20–€40; expensive, over €40

Mountains and Valleys

La Seu d'Urgell to La Pobla de Segur

Highlights

- **Stunning scenery**
  Lose yourself in the idyllic blend of peaks, lush forests and glittering lakes in the Parc Nacional d'Aigüestortes i Estany de Sant Maurici

- **Romanesque marvels**
  Discover gems of early medieval art in the remote villages of Barruera, Durro, Erill la Vall and Boí

- **Valley villages**
  Experience the calm, clear air of the tiny, picturesque villages around the high mountains

Church spire stands tall above the mountain village of Llessui

Mountains and Valleys

Each part of the Pyrenees has its own distinctive character. The eastern Pyrenees in Catalonia have a special beauty, with a centrepiece in Parc Nacional d'Aigüestortes i Estany de Sant Maurici, where soaring rock pinnacles over 2,000 m (6,550 ft) high are offset against gem-like lakes left by the last Ice Age. This magnificent hiking country is easily accessible from the main roads. The once-isolated valleys between the mountains have a long human history too, and their importance 1,000 years ago is reflected in the Romanesque churches found even in remote villages. Just a brief circuit around the mountains goes through a fascinating variety of landscapes and ancient grey-stone towns.

Above Medieval church in the mountain town of Sort, *see p94*

ACTIVITIES

Hike through Parc Nacional d'Aigüestortes i Estany de Sant Maurici to look down over glittering mountain lakes

Go white water rafting through the rapids of the Noguera Palleresa

Ride a mountain bike through the woods and villages of Val d'Aran

KEY

 Drive route

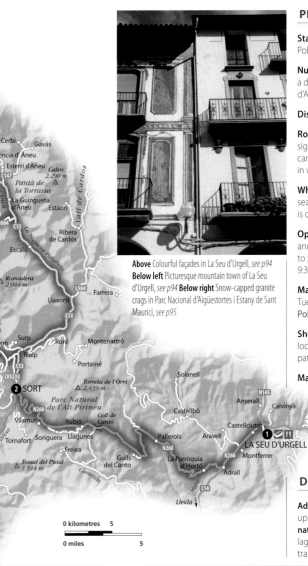

Above Colourful façades in La Seu d'Urgell, *see p94*
Below left Picturesque mountain town of La Seu d'Urgell, *see p94* Below right Snow-capped granite crags in Parc Nacional d'Aigüestortes i Estany de Sant Maurici, *see p95*

PLAN YOUR DRIVE

Start/finish: La Seu d'Urgell to La Pobla de Segur.

Number of days: 3–4, allowing half a day for the walk in Parc Nacional d'Aigüestortes i Estany de Sant Maurici.

Distance: 370 km (230 miles).

Road conditions: Roads are well signposted and in good condition, but can be slow. Snow chains are required in winter.

When to go: April to October is hiking season in Aigüestortes. Normal hiking is dangerous during winter.

Opening hours: Most monuments and museums are open from 10:30am to 5:30pm, while shops are open from 9:30am to 1:30pm, and from 4 to 8pm.

Main market days: La Seu d'Urgell: Tue, Sat; **Sort:** Tue; **Vielha:** Thu; **La Pobla de Segur:** Wed.

Shopping: Val d'Aran produces various local specialities: liqueurs, mushroom patés, cheeses and honey.

Major festivals: La Seu d'Urgell: Carnaval, Jan–Feb; **Sort:** Sant Feliu, 1 Aug; **Llavorsí:** Festa Major, late Jul; **Vielha:** Carnaval, Jan–Feb; **Vall de Boí:** Las Fallas, mid-Jun in Durro; **La Pobla de Segur:** Diada dels Raiers, first weekend in Jul.

DAY TRIP OPTIONS

Adventure buffs will enjoy hiking up to the peaks of Aigüestortes, while **nature lovers** should explore the villages in the Val d'Aran and the contrasting Vall de Boí. For details, *see p97*.

Top Romanesque cathedral in La Seu d'Urgell
Above Peak of Pui Pla, above the Estany de la Ratera **Below** Hikers by the pristine Estany de Sant Maurici

WHERE TO STAY

LA SEU D'URGELL

Hotel Andria *moderate*
This charming hotel has been a landmark on La Seu's main promenade since the 19th century. With a lovely terrace and garden, the hotel is exceptional value.
Passeig Joan Brudieu 24, 25700; 973 350 300; www.hotelandria.com

Parador de La Seu d'Urgell *expensive*
A luxurious parador around the remains of a Dominican friary in La Seu, with the former cloister as an impressive centrepiece.
C/ Sant Domènec 6, 25700; 973 352 000; www.parador.es

ESPOT

Hotel Els Encantats *moderate*
This hotel in the middle of Espot has been renovated with different imaginative decor in each of its 14 well-equipped bedrooms. Guests can take advantage of a range of guided hikes.
Ctra. de Espot s/n, 25597; 973 624 138; www.hotelencantats.com

❶ La Seu d'Urgell
Lleida; 25700

An important Pyrenean crossroads since Roman times, La Seu d'Urgell has a charming old town of narrow streets and stone arcades around the Romanesque **Catedral de Santa Maria d'Urgell** (*seu* is an old Catalan word for cathedral). Beside the Segre river there is a "water park", the **Parc Olímpic del Segre**, built for the kayaking events of the 1992 Olympics. A typically Catalan *rambla* (promenade), **Passeig Joan Brudieu**, bonds the old and new towns.

Southwest of La Seu d'Urgell the road soon climbs into dramatic mountain scenery as it leaves the Segre valley to cross over to the Noguera Pallaresa valley through the pass of **Coll de Cantó**. There are many twists and turns on the way.

🚗 *From the town centre follow signs south for Lleida onto the N260. In Adrall turn right to continue on the N260 (a steep climb) for Sort (47 km/29 miles).*

❷ Sort
Lleida; 25560

Sort was the stronghold of the medieval Counts of Pallars, and the remains of their castle, at the top of the old town, are currently being restored. Modern Sort is a centre for hiking, rafting and other mountain sports. Its tiny former prison is now a museum, **El Camí de la Llibertat** (*open daily Aug, Tue, Sat and Sun rest of the year*) commemorating the role of the Pyrenean valleys as an escape route

from Nazi-occupied Europe during World War II. Exit Sort on the C13 just north of town, look out for a le turn onto the LV5233. This road go into the Vall d'Assua and to the gorgeous mountain village of **Lless** (park at the entrance to the village), with a winter sports centre nearby. From Llessui, rejoin the C13 and tu left, signed for Vielha, continuing through the rugged Noguera gorg to **Llavorsí**, a riverside town that is popular adventure sports centre.

🚗 *Go through Llavorsí on the C13 a after 12 km (7 miles) turn left on the LV5004 for Parc Nacional d'Aigüestor i Estany de Sant Maurici and Espot. In Espot, park by the visitor centre.*

❸ Espot
Lleida; 25597

The main gateway to the Parc Nacional d'Aigüestortes i Estany de Sant Maurici, Espot is a charming grey-stone mountain village in a de valley with a watchtower and a brid from the early Middle Ages. It make an excellent base for exploring the park. Staff at the visitor centre (Casa del Parc) provide maps and ideas fo longer or shorter walks. A 4WD taxi service runs from the village to the park entrance (4 km/2 miles) and then up to the Sant Maurici lake (another 1 km/0.6 miles). Driving to the park entrance and then walk up to the lakes, will add over an hour to the walk.

🚗 *Take one of the 4WD taxis to Estany de Sant Maurici for the walk.*

Parc Nacional d'Aigüestortes i Estany de ▮nt Maurici
da; 25597

▮ending over 140 sq km (55 sq miles), the Parc Nacional
▮igüestortes i Estany de Sant Maurici contains some of the most
▮quisite scenery in the entire Pyrenees, dotted with towering, snow-
▮pped granite peaks and over 200 sparkling-blue glacial lakes, fed
▮ countless mountain streams. This circuit around the most cele-
▮ted of the lakes, Estany de Sant Maurici, goes into the heart of a
▮eathtaking alpine landscape. The walk is best done in the morning.

▮wo–three hour walking tour
▮ 4WD stops at the **taxi stop ①** by
▮ park warden's hut. The panorama
▮m here is dazzling, with the lake or
▮any of Sant Maurici backed by a
▮g of mountains. Take the footpath
▮nposted "Cascada de la Ratera" to
▮ left of the park warden's hut (for
▮easier walk, follow the broader
▮ck right of the hut). The footpath
▮s through a fir forest right beside
▮ lake until it meets the **Cascada de
▮atera ②** stream and turns right to
▮nb up beside it. The path then veers
▮nt, slightly away from the stream,
▮t climbs to meet the main track,
▮ere a sign points left to the **Estany
▮ la Ratera ③**, a little pool in an
▮ine meadow and a fine place to
▮t birds. To get here takes a little
▮er an hour. This is the best place to
▮n back on a shorter walk, and return
▮the Estany de Sant Maurici by the
▮in track. To continue, follow the
▮-and-white GR11 footpath signs
▮und the tributary lake, **Estanyola
▮ la Ratera ④**, and turn left, under
▮massive tree trunk, back across the

ridge toward Sant Maurici. At a
crossing of paths, where the GR11
goes off to the right, take the path
left, signed **Mirador de l'Estany ⑤**,
a viewpoint far above Sant Maurici.
Beyond the mirador, take the path
signed "Volta de l'Estany–Portarró de
l'Espot". It narrows to run across a giant
bank of rocky scree, before climbing
again to another crossing, where a
path right leads to the Portarró pass.
Turn left instead (following "Volta de
l'Estany") for the descent back to Sant
Maurici. The path becomes smoother,
crossing the flower-filled meadow of
Subenuix ⑥. It then crosses the
Barranc de Subenuix ⑦ stream. For
the quickest way back, find the path
left across the dam; otherwise, follow
the main track past the **Refugi
Mallafré ⑧** mountain refuge, then
turn left on the Espot track and follow
this back to the taxi stop.

🔲 *From Espot, return to the C13 and
turn left. Near Esterri d'Àneu, follow
the C13 (which becomes the C28) left.
The road climbs up over Port de la
Bonaigua into the Val d'Aran.*

Above Tiled stone streets in medieval Llessui

VISITING PARC NACIONAL D'AIGÜESTORTES I ESTANY DE SANT MAURICI

Private vehicles are not allowed beyond
the National Park entrances at Espot
and Boí. The best way to get to the
heart of the park is to leave the car in
Espot or Boí and use one of the 4WD
taxi services that run from each village.
*Casa del Parc d'Espot, Prat del Guarda,
25597, Espot; 973 624 036; http://
reddeparquesnacionales.mma.es*

ACTIVITIES IN VALL D'ASSUA

Adventure Sports
Rafting and kayaking are the most
popular adventure sports in the valley.
Look up Assua Activa in Sort *(www.
assua.com)* and Rocroi in Llavorsí
(www.rocroi.com).

EAT AND DRINK

LA SEU D'URGELL

El Menjador *moderate–expensive*
Contemporary art decorates the walls
to complement the inventive dishes.
*C/ Major 4, 25700; 606 922 133;
www.elmenjador.com*

ESPOT

Casa Palmira *inexpensive*
This little restaurant provides local
dishes such as grilled meats with *all
i oli* (garlic mayonnaise).
C/ Marineta 2, 25597; 973 624 072

Restaurant Juquim
inexpensive–moderate
Espot's best restaurant, Juquim's
specialities are wild boar fillet grilled
with herbs and dry-cured duck.
Plaça Sant Martí, 25597; 973 624 009

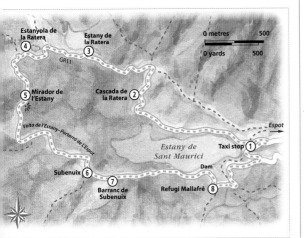

Above Thirteenth-century church and a typical house in the Aranese village of Salardú
Below Congost dels Collegats gorge between La Pobla de Segur and Gerri de la Sal

WHERE TO STAY

VAL D'ARAN

Hotel deth Pais
inexpensive–moderate
This traditional 18-room hotel is located by the main square in the old village of Salardú. The rooms are attractively decorated.
Plaça dera Pica, 25598, Salardú; 973 644 500

Hotel Albares *inexpensive–moderate*
In a typical Aranese town house in the old part of Vielha, this friendly hotel has 15 comfortable rooms.
Passeig dera Llibertat 11, 25530, Vielha; 973 640 081; www.hotelalbares.com

VALL DE BOÍ

Ca de Corral *inexpensive*
Bright colours and quirky fittings are common features of this relaxed *casa de pagès*, with a pretty garden.
C/ Pradet, 25528, Taüll; 973 696 176; www.cadecorral.com

AROUND LA POBLA DE SEGUR

Casa Leonardo
inexpensive–moderate
Located in the village of Senterada, 10 km (6 miles) from La Pobla de Segur, this charming café and bed-and-breakfast is full of an extraordinary range of antiques. It also makes a great base for exploring the mountains.
C/ la Begoda, 25514, Senterada; 973 661 787; www.casaleonardo.net

5 Val d'Aran
Lleida; 25598, 25530

The C28 climbs into **Port de la Bonaigua**, which at 2,050 m (6,800 ft) is one of the highest and most dramatic passes in the Pyrenees and the gateway to the Val d'Aran. The C28 continues up to a broad, windswept plateau, before descending into the lush valley to the west. The Val d'Aran is a major winter sports area. There is a ski station at Bonaigua, and a little further on is **Baqueira-Beret**, one of Spain's most fashionable ski resorts. Baqueira boasts more than 100 km (60 miles) of skiing slopes. The C28 then goes on to **Salardú**, a lovely Aranese village with a fine 13th-century church, which has murals dating from the 16th century. Follow the same road, the C28, into Vielha. There is a car park to the right before the main river bridge.

Capital of the Val d'Aran, **Vielha** boasts distinctive architecture in its tiny old town, with chalet-style houses flanking the Nere river. The **Església de Sant Miquèu** has a fine Gothic altarpiece and, its greatest treasure, the *Crist de Mijaran*, a 12th-century painted figure of Christ. Another tower tops a 17th-century house that is now the **Museu dera Val d'Aran** *(closed Mon except Jul–Aug)*, a museum of Aranese history and customs.

🚗 *At the roundabout on the west side of Vielha turn left (south) on the N230, signed for Lleida and Vilaller. Follow this road through the tunnel into the Vall del Noguera Ribagorçana, and after 24 km (15 miles) take the left*

turn onto the L500 Vall de Boí road. The L501 turn-off leads to Boí.

6 Vall de Boí
Lleida; 25526, 25527, 25528

The Vall de Boí is an idyllic closed valley that became a centre for art in the early Middle Ages. The 11th–12th-century churches in its villages of **Barruera**, **Durro**, **Erill la Vall** and are gems of Romanesque architecture, and since 2000 have collectively been a UNESCO World Heritage Site. Several had magnificent fresco paintings, the originals of which are now in the Museu Nacional d'Art de Catalunya in Barcelona. There are, however, copies of the original paintings in most of the churches. The valley is also the western entrance to the Aigüestortes and Sant Maurici national park, with a park information centre in Boí. There is also a multilingual information centre on the valley's history in Erill la Vall, the **Centre Romànic de la Vall de Boí** *(open daily)*. From Erill la Vall, carry on up to Boí, and then stay on the L500 road to Taüll.

Taüll deserves special attention as the most beautiful of all the Vall de Boí villages. It has two spectacular churches, the **Església de Santa Maria** within the maze-like village and the **Església de Sant Climent** just outside it, with a six-storey tower that visitors can climb. Sant Climent's mural of Christ, the *Crist de Taüll* (now in Barcelona, although there is a copy in the church) is one of the finest early medieval European paintings.

Retrace the route to the N230 and left for Pont de Suert.

Rafters of the Pyrenees

For centuries one of the traditional occupations in the Noguera Pallaresa valley was cutting timber in the mountains and transporting it downriver in log rafts (or *rais*). This dangerous trade died out in the early 20th century. However, since the 1970s, the craft of the loggers has been revived, and this ancient way of life evoked with an annual festival, the Baixada dels Raiers, in the first weekend of each July. The festival invites log-rafters from around the world.

Pont de Suert
Lleida; 25520

Pont de Suert has a fascinating old quarter of secluded squares and tunnel-like alleys leading down to the Noguera Ribagorçana river.

Leave Pont de Suert and turn left onto the N260 (signed) for La Pobla de Segur via the pass at **Coll de la Creu de Perves** (1,350 m/4,450 ft). The road winds up into dramatic scenery soon as it leaves the valley to climb a mountain ridge up to the pass. There are stunning views all along this road, especially at the pass itself and the remarkable villages of **Viu de Llevata** and **Sarroca de Bellera**. The road descends down to laid-back **Senterada** at the entrance to the **Vall Fosca**, another lovely valley leading towards Aigüestortes from the south. *Keep following the N260 through Senterada. Take a left turn signed for to enter La Pobla de Segur.*

Above Bell tower in the idyllic village of Boí

❽ La Pobla de Segur
Lleida; 25500

A historic Pyrenean crossroads, La Pobla de Segur has a Romanesque hermitage and the impressive **Casa Maurí**, a complex combining a mansion and olive oil mill built in the Catalan Modernist (Art Nouveau) style in 1907. Its mosaics have been finely restored. The building now serves as the town hall and tourist office. Also in La Pobla is the **Museu dels Raiers** *(open Tue–Sat)*, commemorating the skilled timber raftsmen of the Noguera Pallaresa valley. The heart of the old town, Carrer Major, has several stately medieval houses.

Northeast of La Pobla the road passes through a red-walled gorge, the **Congost dels Collegats**, very different from the high-mountain scenery further north, to a valley village, **Gerri de la Sal**. The village has a medieval bridge and *salines*, stone pans once used for drying salt.

EAT AND DRINK

VAL D'ARAN

El Molí *inexpensive–moderate*
Specialities at El Molí are charcoal-grilled meats and Catalan-style *pa amb tomàquet* – toasted tomato bread with ham, mushroom and other toppings.
C/ Sarriulera 24, 25530, Vielha; 973 641 718; closed Mon

VALL DE BOÍ

Mallador *inexpensive*
This restaurant offers platters of lamb chops, *botifarra* sausages and other traditional Catalan meat favourites cooked over an open grill.
Plaça Sant Climent, 25528, Taüll; 973 696 028

LA POBLA DE SEGUR

La Cuineta *inexpensive–moderate*
A very individual little restaurant where chef Montse Blesa prepares imaginative and light Catalan cuisine.
Passeig de la Riba, 25500; 973 680 256; www.restaurantlacuineta.com; open Mon–Sat lunch, Sun by prior reservation

DAY TRIP OPTIONS

Driving along mountain roads takes time, and there are no fast short cuts between the main valleys, so to retrace the same routes to the initial start will take a lot out of a day. Visitors can be based either in La Seu d'Urgell or Vielha, in the north, to do the following day trips.

Mountain towns

Experience the varied Pyrenean landscape by beginning at La Seu d'Urgell ❶ and following the main route to Sort ❷ and Espot ❸, although there may not be time

for a long walk in Parc Nacional d'Aigüestortes i Estany de Sant Maurici ❹ if visitors are returning to La Seu d'Urgell the same day. Alternatively, from Sort head down to La Pobla de Segur ❽ on the road south to Lleida.

Return from Espot to Sort and then take the N260 east back to La Seu d'Urgell, or the same road to La Pobla de Segur.

Explore the Val d'Aran
The Val d'Aran ❺ is a natural area to explore in a day – especially if entering on the quicker road, the N230,

from the northern, French end. Take a look around Vielha, capital of the Val d'Aran, before going up to the ski towns of Salardú and Baqueira. If time permits, visitors can leave the valley by the tunnel from Vielha and turn into the beautiful Vall de Boí ❻. Stop by picturesque valley villages such as Barruera, Durro, Erill la Vall and Boí to visit their magnificent 11th–12th-century churches.

From Vielha, take the C28 road, signed for La Seu d'Urgell, as far as Salardú and Baqueira. Return to Vielha and then take the N230 south to reach Vall de Boí.

The Catalan Heartland

Girona to Cadaqués

Highlights

- **Girona's old quarter**
  Get lost in the stone warren of El Call, Girona's alluring Jewish quarter

- **Volcanic scenery**
  Traverse a landscape of long-extinct volcanoes, now covered in forest and dotted with pretty villages

- **Romanesque gems**
  Admire the spectacular Romanesque monasteries of Ripoll and Sant Joan de les Abadesses

- **Surrealism at its best**
  Be dazzled by the originality and playfulness of Salvador Dalí at his museum in Figueres

- **Whitewashed Cadaqués**
  Relax in the charming fishing village of Cadaqués

Harbour at Cadaqués, a favourite with artists

The Catalan Heartland

According to tradition, Guifré el Pilós (Wilfred the Hairy) founded Catalonia from his strongholds in the eastern Pyrenees in the 9th century. This drive explores the magnificent monasteries he founded at Ripoll and Sant Joan de les Abadesses, as well as the glorious mountain scenery that surrounds them. The ancient city of Girona retains its enchanting medieval core, and the nearby lake of Banyoles has become a serene summer retreat, with parks and natural swimming pools. One of the most famous Catalans of all time, Salvador Dalí, created a spectacular museum at Figueres, and his exquisite home can be found near the utterly delightful fishing village of Cadaqués.

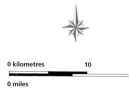

0 kilometres 10

0 miles

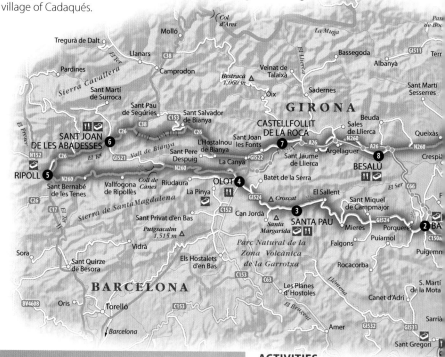

ACTIVITIES

Take a dip in the giant natural swimming pool at Banyoles lake

Go up, up and away in a hot-air balloon over the volcanic hills around Olot

Hike up volcanoes, through Pyrenean valleys, or around the dramatic Cap de Creus

Rent a boat at Cadaqués to explore the tiny cove around the cape

Tuck into hearty mountain dishes in local restaurants all over this region

Left Tiny medieval village of Mieres near Santa Pau, *see p103*

Above Narrow lane in the historic centre of Banyoles, *see p103* **Below** Pont Vell in Sant Joan de les Abadesses, *see p105*

PLAN YOUR DRIVE

Start/finish: Girona to Cadaqués.

Number of days: 3–4, allowing half a day to explore Girona.

Distance: 265 km (165 miles).

Road conditions: Most of the roads are well paved and signposted. There are a few stretches of steep terrain with hairpin bends. In the winter, there can be snow in the Ripoll/Sant Joan de les Abadesses region.

When to go: May and June are ideal, not too hot or crowded. Girona is wonderful year-round, but Cadaqués is best avoided in July and August as it is too crowded then.

Opening hours: Museums are open from 10am to 1pm, and from 4 to 6pm. Shops are open from 9:30am to 1:30pm and from 4 to 8pm. However, most museums in this region are closed on Mondays.

Main market days: Girona: Tue, Sat; Olot: Mon; Ripoll: Sat; Figueres: Thu; Cadaqués: Mon.

Shopping: The Catalan heartland is famous for its cured sausages (including *fuet*) and wines.

Major festivals: Girona: Sant Narcís, late Oct; Olot: Corpus Christi, Jun; Festa del Tura, 8 Sep; Ripoll: Festa Major, 11–12 May; Sant Joan de les Abadesses: Festa Major, second Sun of Sep; Besalú: Sant Vicenç, 22 Jan; Festa Major, last weekend Sep; Figueres: Santa Creu, 3 May; Cadaqués: Festa Major d'Estiu, first week Sep.

DAY TRIP OPTIONS

Visitors interested in walks and **hiking trails** can explore Olot and the volcanoes as a day trip. **Art enthusiasts** should head to Figueres to visit the Dalí Museum and then onto Cadaqués to see his charming home. **Families** will enjoy the resort of Banyoles, where kids can play in the lake. For details, *see p107*.

Above Steps leading up to Girona's impressive Gothic cathedral

VISITING GIRONA

Tourist Information
Rambla de la Llibertat 1, 17004; 972 226 575; www.ajuntament.gi/turisme

Parking
Parking is available in Plaça de Catalunya, in the pay-and-display car park near the train station (follow signs for RENFE) and near Pont de Sant Feliu.

WHERE TO STAY

GIRONA

Pensión Bellmirall inexpensive
The charming little Bellmirall occupies a historic town house right in the heart of Girona's atmospheric old quarter.
C/ Bellmirall 3, 17004; 972 204 009

AROUND GIRONA

Hotel Masferran expensive
Located in a 17th-century farmhouse, this is a lovely Rusticae hotel just 7 km (4 miles) west of Girona.
C/ Cami de la Bruguera, 17150, Sant Gregori; 972 428 890; www. masferran.com

BANYOLES

Hotel Mirallac moderate
A pleasant hotel, built in the 1960s and traditionally furnished, Mirallac is located on the lakeside in Banyoles.
Passeig Darder 50, 17820; 972 571 045; www.hotelmirallac.com

❶ Girona
Girona; 17004

The prosperous and elegant little city of Girona is handsomely set on the banks of the Onyar river. At its heart is El Call, the former Jewish quarter, a warren of narrow streets and tiny passages crowned by a magnificent Gothic cathedral. The city is well known for its fine traditional cuisine, which can be sampled in numerous restaurants, cafés and bars. The best time to do this walk is late afternoon, as the city is particularly pretty at dusk.

A two-hour walking tour

Park in Plaça de Catalunya and cross the bridge to see the tourist office on the left, on the Rambla de la Llibertat, an elegant, bustling boulevard with plenty of delightful terrace cafés. Stroll up to the Plaça del Vi, which is overlooked by the **ajuntament** ① and the **Teatre Municipal** ②. Continue along Carrer Ciutadans to reach another charming little square, the Plaça de l'Oli, with a diminutive fountain.

From here, plunge into the Jewish quarter, taking Carrer B. Carreras Peralta, which leads into Carrer de la Força. This street, one of the most atmospheric in the city, was the very heart of the Jewish ghetto. The history of the Jews of Girona, once famous throughout Europe for their great learning, is documented in the **Museu dels Jueus** ③ (open

Tapestry of the Creation, Catedral de Girona

daily) in the Centre Bonastruc Ça Porta at No. 8 Carrer de la Força. As the narrow street climbs, visitors will see the interesting **Museu d'Història de la Ciutat** ④ (open Tue–Sun) on the left at No. 27. Carrer de la Força opens out into a beautiful square, the Plaça de la Catedral, dominated by flank of steps leading to the **Catedral de Girona** Although the façade is Baroque, the rest of the cathedral is Catalan Gothic at its purest. The cathedral museum contains several fine treasures, including a celebrated 11th-century tapestry depicting the Creation. There is more wonderful medieval art, as well as later works, in the excellent **Museu d'Art** ⑥ (open Tue–Sun), housed in the nearby Palau Episcopal. Return to the Plaça de la Catedral and take the gateway near the curiously truncated **Església de**

nt Feliu ⑦. On the left are the
th-century Arabic-style baths
nys Àrabs ⑧ *(open daily)*. Beyond
little bridge is the Romanesque
glésia de San Pere de Galligants ⑨,
w converted into a beautiful
heological museum *(closed Mon)*.
urn to the Banys Àrabs and bear
the left to get to the **Jardins de la
ncesa ⑩**, small gardens that are
e of several access points to the
sseig Arqueològic, a panoramic walk-
y atop the old city walls. Bear right
find the walls and then walk south-
rds along them all the way to Plaça
neral Mendoza. From here walk
ck along the river to the car park.
   *Leaving Girona, follow signs for
nyoles onto the NIIa (Avinguda de
nça), and then turn left onto the
6. At Banyoles, follow signs for
tany" (lake). Park next to the lake.*

Banyoles
ona; 17820

nyoles has a charming medieval
re and a lake. The lake has been a
ourite summer vacationing spot
ce the 19th century, and its shores
still dotted with small *pesqueres* –
hing huts built right onto the water.
ere are a couple of natural bathing
ots, a footpath and cycle track right
und the lake. Visitors can rent bikes
re. A short stroll around the Old
wn throws up a handful of pretty
manesque and Gothic churches,
caded streets and several delightful
uares to relax in.
   *Leave Banyoles by the southern
d of the lake, following signs for the
524 towards Mieres and Santa Pau.
rk outside the village.*

Parc Natural de la Zona Volcànica de la Garrotxa

The GI524 is a stunning stretch of
road twisting through the Parc
Natural de la Zona Volcànica de la
Garrotxa towards the distant, violet
shadows of the pre-Pyrenean mountain ranges. The boundary of the
nature reserve starts at Mieres, a
tiny stone village wrapped around
a church. The Parc Natural de la
Zona Volcànica de la Garrotxa
encompasses a beautiful landscape
of long-extinct volcanoes, now
thickly covered with forest and
scattered with tiny villages including Santa Pau. Some of the best
walking trails start at the park information office in the midst of a
beech forest.

EAT AND DRINK

GIRONA

Boira *inexpensive–moderate*
Enjoy tasty Mediterranean cuisine here
with views over the colourful houses
that line the river bank.
*Plaça de la Independència 17, 17004;
972 490 487*

Divinum *inexpensive–moderate*
This is a hip little bar and restaurant,
serving delicious Catalan cuisine. There
are designer tapas to go with the excellent selection of wines in the downstairs bar, with more substantial fare
available in the restaurant.
*C/ General Fournàs 2, 17004; 872
080 218*

El Celler de Can Roca *expensive*
One of the finest restaurants in Spain,
with two Michelin stars, this place combines sleek decor with modern cuisine
accompanied by a stellar wine list.
*C/ Can Sunyer 48, 17004; 972 222 157;
www.cellercanroca.com*

BANYOLES

Taverna Can Pons *inexpensive*
This welcoming little tavern serves an
excellent fixed-price lunch menu.
Plaça Major 7, 17820; 972 581 063

Above People relaxing around the lake at
Banyoles **Below** Arcades framing the Plaça
Major in Banyoles

Eat and Drink: inexpensive, under €20; moderate, €20–€40; expensive, over €40

Above Seven-arched bridge at Besalú **Below left** Ornate window in a Modernista mansion in Olot **Below right** Twelfth-century church in Sant Joan de les Abadesses

WHERE TO STAY

SANTA PAU

Cal Sastre *moderate*
This is a sweet little inn in a restored stone house.
C/ Cases Noves 1, 17811; 902 998 479; www.calsastre.com

AROUND OLOT

Mas Garganta *moderate*
Located 5 km (3 miles) from Olot, this is a lovely bed-and-breakfast.
Ctra. A Riudaura, 17179, La Pinya; 972 271 289; www.masgarganta.com

RIPOLL

Mas Isoles *inexpensive*
This *casa rural* in a stone farmhouse offers bed-and-breakfast rooms.
Camí Sant Antoni s/n, 17500; 608 744 016; www.masisoles.com

SANT JOAN DE LES ABADESSES

El Reixac *moderate*
Housed in a beautiful farmhouse, this hotel has rooms with kitchenettes.
El Reixac, 17860; 972 720 373; www.elreixac.com

BESALÚ

Els Jardins de la Martana *moderate*
This glorious 19th-century mock castle is set next to Besalú's famous bridge.
C/ Pont 2, 17850; 972 590 009; www.lamartana.com

③ Santa Pau
Girona; 17811
A perfectly preserved medieval village perched on a low hilltop, Santa Pau is the jewel of the Garrotxa region. The village grew up around a 12th-century castle, with thick stone walls and crenellated towers, which still dominates the centre. Densely wooded hills spread out in every direction, sheltering some of the loveliest walking paths in all of Catalonia. Many of them go up to the craters of extinct volcanoes: the best are Santa Margarida and the Croscat.

🚗 **Continue on the GI524 towards Olot. After about 10 km (6 miles) the road will lead directly to Olot's town centre where there is a pay-and-display parking next to the Mercat Municipal.**

④ Olot
Girona; 17800
The prosperous market town of O is beautifully set in the gentle wood hills of the extinct volcanic zone o' Garrotxa. The soft light inspired a generation of 19th-century artists, known as the Olot School, whose works are on view at the **Museu Comarcal** *(closed Mon)*. The museu is housed in an 18th-century hospic The narrow streets, with their winsome, early-20th-century Moderni mansions, old-fashioned shops an bakeries, are a delight to explore.

🚗 **Take the ring road out of Olot, following signs "Totes Direccions" across two roundabouts until there are signs for the N260 for Vallfogon de Ripollès. Continue past Vallfogo into Ripoll and follow signs for "Centre". Park in the main square.**

⑤ Ripoll
Girona; 17500
Ripoll contains one of the great jewels of Catalan Romanesque architecture: at the very centre of town is the 10th-century **Monestir de Santa Maria** *(open daily)*, established by Guifré el Pilós, legendary founder of Catalonia. The magnifi cent portal miraculously survived t destruction of the church followin the dissolution of the monastery ir 1835. It is carved with biblical scen and a menagerie of beasts.

🚗 **From Ripoll head north along th C26, following signs for Sant Joan d les Abadesses. Approaching the tow**

tre, follow signs for the
tacionament Gratuit", to find the
park on the left, next to the bridge.

Burial ground of the Count-Kings of Catalonia

Numerous early Catalan rulers,
including Guifré el Pilós, were
buried in the crypt of the Monestir
de Santa Maria in Ripoll, but their
tombs were desecrated after the
monastery was closed in the 1830s.
After the church was rebuilt in the
late 19th century, plaques were
erected in their memory on either
side of the main altar. The small
sarcophagi of Catalan counts still
line the nave.

Sant Joan de les Abadesses

rona; 17860

ow a sleepy country town, Sant Joan
e les Abadesses grew up around an
portant abbey, founded by Guifré el
ós in the 9th century for his daugh-
r, Emma. Dim and austere, it is easy
visitors to imagine themselves back
the Middle Ages while visiting this
urch. Behind the main altar is a
th-century sculpture depicting the
escent from the Cross, composed of
riously modern articulated figures.
e town is another excellent base for
alkers, with a host of good walking
ails. To the east is Vall de Bianya, a
alley with a sprinkling of farms and a
utch of Romanesque churches.

*Follow the C26 out of Sant Joan
e les Abadesses through the Vall de
anya. Turn left at the big round-
bout at La Canya, following signs for
e GI-522 for Sant Joan les Fonts and
astellfollit de la Roca. At Castellfollit,
ark in the municipal car park on the
ft at the entrance to the village.*

⑦ Castellfollit de la Roca

Girona; 17856

Castellfollit de la Roca is perched
alarmingly on a sheer lava cliff which
plunges dramatically to the river
below. From the riverside, visitors can
gaze up at the medieval village, its
stone houses strung vertiginously
along the cliff edge. Castellfollit's
sleepy streets are perfect for an
aimless stroll, and offer more splendid
views of the rolling landscape.

*Continue through the village,
following signs for the N260/A26,
towards Figueres and Girona. Fork
right at exit 67 onto the Carretera
d'Olot straight to Besalú. Park at the
entrance of the village; the centre is
closed to tourist traffic.*

⑧ Besalú

Girona; 17850

A picture-postcard medieval walled
town, Besalú is firmly on the tourist
trail. However, even the crowds of
day-trippers from the nearby Costa
Brava cannot dim its ancient charm.
A splendid medieval seven-arched
bridge, punctuated with towers,
spans the river and leads into the
cobbled streets of the Old Town. The
Plaça de la Llibertat is handsomely
fringed with 16th-century arcades,
and the village boasts the only surviving *mikveh*, a Jewish ritual bath-
house, in Spain.

*From Besalú, return to the N260/
A26 (no longer an autovía highway
from this point), and follow signs for
Figueres. In the city centre, roadside
parking is fairly easy to find, but there
is a large pay-and-display car park near
the RENFE train station. From here, it is
a 10-minute walk to the Dalí Museum.*

Above Graceful Església de Sant Esteve in
Olot **Below** Cloister of the Monestir de Santa
Maria in Ripoll

ACTIVITIES IN THE GARROTXA

Walking in the Fageda d'en Jordà
Walking trails in this beech forest start
at the Can Jordà park information office,
down a forest road 4 km (2 miles) west
of Santa Pau. Maps and leaflets are
available in local tourist offices.

Hot-air balloon rides in Olot
Several companies offer hot-air
balloon rides in the Garrotxa region.
www.voldecoloms.cat

EAT AND DRINK

SANTA PAU

Portal del Mar *moderate*
The restaurant serves Mediterranean
cuisine prepared with local produce.
C/ Vila Vella 16, 17811; 972 680 442;
www.portaldelmar.es

OLOT

Les Cols *expensive*
This award-winning restaurant serves
superb cuisine using local ingredients –
from wild trout to wild mushrooms.
C/ de la Canya s/n, 17800; 972 269 209;
www.lescols.com; closed Mon evening,
Sun, 2 weeks in Aug

SANT JOAN DE LES ABADESSES

Casa Rudes *inexpensive*
A good place to try out Catalan
mountain dishes, such as *trinxat*
(vegetables with bacon).
Ctra. Major 10, 17860; 972 720 115;
www.santjoandelesabadesses.com

BESALÚ

Cúria Reial *moderate*
A traditional restaurant serving
local cuisine and specializing in *carns a
la brasa* (meat cooked over hot coals).
Plaça de la Llibertat 14, 17850; 972 590
263; www.curiareial.com

Eat and Drink: inexpensive, under €20; moderate, €20–€40; expensive, over €40

Top Beach in the resort town of Roses
Above Surrealistic towers of the Dalí Museum in Figueres **Below** Sixteenth-century fortress in Roses

WHERE TO STAY

AROUND FIGUERES

Mas Falgarona *expensive*
A beautiful country house hotel, Mas Falgarona is located in a village just 5 km (3 miles) west of Figueres.
Avinyonet de Puigventós, 17600; 972 546 628; www.masfalgarona.com

CADAQUÉS

Hotel Blaumar *moderate*
The family-run Blaumar is just a few minutes' walk from the town centre.
C/ Massa d'Or 21, 17488; 972 519 020; www.hotelblaumar.com; closed Nov–Feb

L'Hostalet de Cadaqués
inexpensive–moderate
A trendy new hotel located in the town centre, which has eight double rooms.
C/ Miquel Rosset 13 , 17488; 972 258 206; www.hostaletcadaques.com

Rural accommodation
This region boasts a range of rural accommodation – from farmhouses to renovated *finques* (country houses).
www.ruralcatalunya.com,
www.rusticae.es

⑨ Figueres
Girona; 17600

The Old Town in Figueres and its busy *rambla* (promenade) have an understated charm, but there is only one big reason to visit the city: the fabulous **Teatre-Museu Dalí** *(closed Mon Oct–May; www.salvador-dali.org)*. This occupies an old theatre, converted by the celebrated artist himself, surreally topped with diving figures and enormous eggs. Within, the museum is equally eccentric, with galleries leading off a central patio in which a car with a warbling diva is the main exhibit. In the Mae West room, visitors are invited to climb a ladder and view the furnishings morph into the features of the celebrated actress.

🚗 *To leave the city, follow signs "totes direccions", which will lead to the NII ring road. Take the exit for the C260, following signs for Roses. Near Castelló d'Empúries, take the bridge on the left to cross the La Muga river to reach the centre of the town where parking can be found.*

⑩ Castelló d'Empúries
Girona; 17486

This pretty stone town still retains the vestiges of its medieval walls, along with a cluster of fine churches and medieval mansions gathered around delightful squares. The beautiful **Basílica de Santa Maria** is one of the jewels of Catalan Gothic architecture, its sublime arches succeeding elegantly in the airy nave. An amble around the historic centre, now largely pedestrianized, reveals handsome

convents and arcaded squares. The town is also the starting point for the Parc Natural dels Aiguamolls de l'Emporda, protected wetlands which shelter numerous bird speci

🚗 *Return to the C260, and turn righ for Roses. There is free parking next the market on Carrer Doctor Ferran.*

Parc Natural dels Aiguamolls de l'Emporda

The wetlands of the Parc Natural dels Aiguamolls de l'Emporda extend for much of the Bay of Roses. Wooden trails wind between lakes and marshes to scattered observation points, where there are flamingos, herons and the extraordinary jewel-coloured purple swamphen. The park also has rarer species such as the endangered bittern and the Garganay duck. From Castelló d'Empúries, follow signs for the Parc Natural dels Aiguamolls de l'Emporda and park near the information office *(El Cortalet, 17486; 972 454 222)*.

⑪ Roses
Girona; 17480

The largest resort town on this stretch of coast, Roses is big and blowsy, with just a few scattered remnants to remind visitors of its ancient history. The oldest of these the **Conjunt Megalític**, a collection magnificent dolmens which date back 5,000 years. The massive, squa **Ciutadella** is a Renaissance fortress, erected in 1543 over the ruins of an 8th-century Arabic citadel. Within a scattered remains attesting to the numerous ancient civilizations, fror

Greeks to the Romans, who have
tled here. Most people come to
ses for the glorious golden beaches.
tors can rent a small boat to
plore the surrounding *cales* – tiny,
obly bays which, if they are lucky,
ey might even have to themselves.

*From Roses, return in the direction
Figueres, following signs for the
514. Just before Cadaques, follow
ns to Cap de Creus on the left, on
iny road which twists up over the
d and beautiful natural park.*

Parc Natural del Cap
e Creus

rona; 17489

e Cap de Creus is a magnificent
adland formed by the last gasp of
e Pyrenees as it plunges into the
editerranean. Wind-whipped and
aggy, it is one of the most beautiful
rners of Catalonia, and now pro-
cted as a nature park. The wild
rrain still bears vestiges of the ter-
ces laid out by the monks of the
stere **Monestir de Sant Pere de
des**, near the town of Port de la
lva. The monastery houses the
urist information office *(open daily;
2 193 191)* of the nature park.

*Continue on the Gl614 to Cadaqués.
is best to park on the outskirts and
alk to the centre, as parking can be
fficult in the high season.*

Cadaqués

irona; 17488

adaqués is an exquisite fishing village
urved around a perfect bay and
rowned with a simple church. Its
xtraordinary light has drawn artists
ncluding Picasso and Dalí since the

early 20th century. Dalí's intimate
home *(visits must be booked in advance;
972 251 015)*, which he converted from
a cluster of whitewashed cottages,
overlooks the adjoining bay at Port
Lligat. The views from the little square
in front of the church at the top of
Cadaqués are sublime, stretching out
across the huddled rooftops to the
shimmering sea beyond.

The Dalí Triangle

The Dalí Museum in Figueres, the
artist's private home near Cadaqués,
and a converted medieval castle in
Púbol make up the Dalí Triangle.
The tiny village of Púbol is a short
excursion from Girona. This is where
Dalí's wife and muse, Gala, lived in
queenly splendour in the Castell
Gala Dalí, *Púbol-la-
Pera; 972 488 655)*. Her husband was
required to make appointments in
advance, and Gala would receive
him while seated on her throne.

Above Lighthouse at the tip of the wild Cap
de Creus

ACTIVITIES ON CAP DE CREUS

Hiking
Two long-distance footpaths meet
at Cadaqués, the GR11 across the
Pyrenees, and the GR92 along the
Mediterranean coast.

EAT AND DRINK

FIGUERES

Hotel Empordà *moderate–expensive*
This restaurant serves some of the
finest cuisine in the region. Try the
paella with lentils and crayfish.
*Avda. Salvador Dalí, 17600; 972 500
562; www.hotelemporda.com*

CADAQUÉS

Casa Nun *moderate*
Overlooking the bay of Cadaqués, this
restaurant occupies a thin house on
the seafront. Locally caught fish is the
highlight of the menu here.
C/ Port-dixos 6, 17488; 972 258 856

DAY TRIP OPTIONS

With a base in Girona, there are
many places in this drive that are
easily accessible as a day trip. The
AP7 motorway (toll) is a useful
north–south route, which links
Girona with Figueres, but most
destinations are reached on the
smaller roads.

Olot and the volcanoes
The relaxed country town of Olot ❹
is surrounded by the surreal, flattened
peaks of long-extinct volcanoes. The
nearby Garrotxa Volcanic Zone is a

nature park with hiking trails and
pretty little villages.

*Follow the C66 from Girona to Banyoles,
then take the Gl-524 to Olot through
the stunning volcanic zone. Return via
the fast A26 and then down the C66.*

On the Dalí trail
Head to Figueres ❾ to visit the Teatre-
Museu Dalí, before heading to the wild
coast of the Cap de Creus ⓬ and the
white fishing village of Cadaqués ⓭.

*Take the AP7-E15 to Figueres, then head
east along the C68. Just before reaching*

*Roses, turn inland on the Gl614 to reach
Cadaqués.*

Lakes and bridges
Families will enjoy the pretty, verdant
resort of Banyoles ❷, where kids
can splash around in the clear
natural lake, or take hikes around its
lovely shores. Beyond Banyoles, the
village of Besalú ❽ with its perfectly
preserved old bridge is a delight to
explore on foot.

*Take the C66 directly from Girona to
Banyoles, and then on to Besalú.*

Eat and Drink: inexpensive, under €20; moderate, €20–€40; expensive, over €40

Vineyards and Gothic Treasures

Sant Sadurní d'Anoia to Delta de l'Ebre

Highlights

- **Home of cava**
  Visit the renowned vineyards and cava cellars of the Penedès

- **Monasteries and walled town**
  Experience a medieval world in three great Gothic monasteries and the walled town of Montblanc

- **Compact paradise**
  Explore the twisting valleys and soaring crags of the Priorat, and sample fine wines from its vineyards

- **Delta perspectives**
  Spot flamingos and experience a dramatic change of landscape in the vast wetlands of Delta de l'Ebre

Twelfth-century monastery at Santes Creus

Vineyards and Gothic Treasures

Between Barcelona and the mouth of the Ebre river lies an astonishing variety of landscapes: the broad vine-clad hills of the Penedès, the steep narrow valleys and massive yellow-stone *mesas* of the Priorat and Montsant, the broad Ebre valley and finally the vast flatness of the Delta de l'Ebre. A thousand years ago this region was the frontier between Christian and Muslim lands. Its rich history can be traced in magnificent Gothic monasteries and walled towns, and in the Moorish fortress of Tortosa. This is also a land of superb food and fine wines – from the famous labels of the Penedès to the characterful vintages of the Priorat – that make its discovery a catalogue of pleasures.

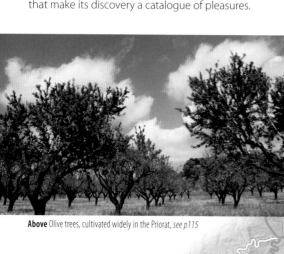

Above Olive trees, cultivated widely in the Priorat, *see p115*

ACTIVITIES

Discover how cava gets its sparkle at a winery in Sant Sadurní d'Anoia

Pick out the symbols in the stunning Gothic carvings in the monasteries of Santes Creus and Poblet

Look down at the world from the heights of Siurana

Hike up into the hills of Montsant, richly scented with Mediterranean herbs

Taste and compare wines on a slow tour around the Priorat's hillside vineyards

Ride a bike through the Delta de l'Ebre, scanning the horizon for flamingos and other wild birds

Y

Drive route

BARCELONA

Cervera

merà

Conesa · Les Piles de Gaià

La Llacuna

Masquefa

vella · Sarral · Querol

SANT SADURNÍ D'ANOIA ❶

NTBLANC · El Pont d'Armentera · Valldossera · Torrelles de Foix

Sant Pau d'Ordal

El Pla de Manlleu · Pacs del Penedès

Les Pobles

❸ SANTES CREUS

La Múnia

VILAFRANCA DEL PENEDÈS ❷

Fontscaldes · Vila-Rodona · Sant Jaume dels Domenys

Canyelles

Valls · Alió

Montferri

L'Arboç

Sitges

lmoll

El Vendrell

Vilanova i la Geltrú

Calafell

Torredembarra

Tarragona

rada

Above Gothic cloister of the monastery at Santes Creus, *see p112*
Below Rugged landscape of the Priorat, *see p115*

PLAN YOUR DRIVE

Start/finish: Sant Sadurní d'Anoia to Delta de l'Ebre.

Number of days: 3–4, including half a day in Montblanc and Tortosa.

Distances: 340 km (210 miles).

Road conditions: Mostly well-signed roads, although signs can be unclear in rural areas. The Priorat's winding roads make travel slower.

When to go: April to October is the best time, but July and August can be very hot and crowded with tourists. The smaller vineyards may be too busy for visitors during the grape harvest in September and October.

Opening times: The opening hours of the major attractions vary between seasons, but in general the major monasteries and museums are closed on Mondays. Wine cellars are often closed on Mondays and Tuesdays.

Main market days: Sant Sadurní d'Anoia: Thu; Vilafranca del Penedès: Sat; Montblanc: Fri; Prades: Tue; Falset: Tue; Móra d'Ebre: Fri; Tortosa: Mon.

Shopping: Wine is the region's top buy and is sold at most vineyards. Sant Sadurní, Vilafranca, Escaladei, Gratallops and Falset have shops with good stocks of local vintages.

Major festivals: Sant Sadurní d'Anoia: Festa de la Fil·loxera, early Sep; Semana del Cava, second week, Oct; Vilafranca del Penedès: Carnaval, Jan–Feb; Fira de Santa Llúcia, Dec. Montblanc: Sant Antoni Abat i Tres Tombs, Jan; Carnaval, Jan–Feb; Festes de Sant Maties, May; Prades: Festa del Cava, Jul; Falset: L'Encamisada, Jan; Fira del Vi, May; Tortosa: La Festa del Renaixement de Tortosa, end Jul.

DAY TRIP OPTIONS

For **wine** and **culture lovers**, a day of cava and culture in Sant Sadurní and Vilafranca make an easy trip from Barcelona. **History enthusiasts** can combine Santes Creus, Vallbona and Poblet. The Priorat is a mecca for **wine buffs**, while **fans of birdlife** might explore Tortosa and the Delta. For details, *see p117*.

Left Thirteenth-century Església de Sant Miquel, Montblanc **Right** Caves Cordoniu, Sant Sadurní d'Anoia

VISITING CAVES CODORNIU

Avda. Jaume Codorniu s/n, 08770, Sant Sadurní d'Anoia; 938 913 342; www.codorniu.com

VISITING BODEGUES TORRES

The winery offers exclusive tours with professional guides.
M. Torres 6, 08720, Vilafranca del Penedès; 938 177 400; www.torres.es

WHERE TO STAY

SANT SADURNÍ D'ANOIA

Fonda Neus moderate
In Sant Sadurní itself, the renovated Fonda Neus is a reliable traditional hotel, with an ambitious restaurant.
C/ Marc Mir 14–16, 08770; 938 910 365; www.casafonda.com

AROUND SANT SADURNÍ D'ANOIA

Can Bonastre Wine Resort expensive
A 16th-century estate, 19 km (12 miles) north of Sant Sadurní, it has its own vineyard and gourmet restaurant.
Ctra. B-224, Km 13, 21, 08783, Masquefa; 937 728 767; www.canbonastre.es

AROUND VILAFRANCA DEL PENEDÈS

Arianel.la de Can Coral moderate
Housed in an old farmhouse, 13 km (8 miles) north of Vilafranca, this hotel has a pretty garden and pool.
Avda. Can Coral, 08787, Torrelles de Foix; 938 971 579; www.arianelladecancoral.com

AROUND SANTES CREUS

Hostatgeria de Celma expensive
Located in a hamlet 5 km (3 miles) above Santes Creus, the hotel has rooms that are lavishly decorated.
C/ Angel Guimerà 2–4, 43815, Les Pobles; 977 639 458; www.hostatgeriadecelmahotel.com

MONTBLANC

Fonda Cal Blasi moderate
A comfortable, friendly hotel in the Old Town, it serves generous breakfasts.
C/ Alenyà 11, 43400; 977 861 336; www.fondacalblasi.com

Mas Carlons moderate
An imposing country house in its own vineyard, just outside Montblanc, Mas Carlons has spacious rooms and a swimming pool.
43400, Montblanc; 977 860 045; www.mascarlons.com.

① Sant Sadurní d'Anoia
Barcelona; 08770

Sant Sadurní is the capital of cava, Catalan sparkling wine, with over 80 producers in and around the town. Many cellars are in the town centre, but the largest ones are on the outskirts. Most spectacular is the huge **Caves Codorniu** (visits by reservation only), with graceful buildings built in 1902–15, designed by the great Catalan architect Josep Puig i Cadafalch (1867–1956). There are several other engaging Modernista buildings in Sadurní, including the town hall built in 1900.

🚗 **From the centre of Sant Sadurní d'Anoia follow signs for Vilafranca onto the C243a. Turn left when this road joins the C15 to enter the town of Vilafranca del Penedès.**

Historic advertising at Caves Cordoniu, Sant Sadurní d'Anoia

② Vilafranca del Penedès
Barcelona; 08720

Historic capital of the Alt Penedès comarca (district), Vilafranca is known more for its still wines and brandy than for cava. There are cellars and vineyards all around the town, including the famous **Bodegues Torres** (daily tours), 4 km (2 miles) north on the road to Pacs del Penedès. Vilafranca was an important town in the Middle Ages, still evident from the distinguished Gothic **Basílica de Santa María**, beside which is a 14th-century mansion, the Palau Baltà. The 13th-century Palau Reial or royal palace now hosts a wine museum, the **Vinseum** (open Tue–Sun).

🚗 **Follow the Avinguda Tarragona through Vilafranca and at the first large roundabout turn right onto th Carretera de Sant Jaume dels Domer (B212). This becomes the TP2125. Before Sant Jaume dels Domenys, tu right onto the TP2442 for El Pla de Manlleu. Follow the road, which becomes the T244, and at the next junction turn left onto the TV2441 f Santes Creus.**

③ Santes Creu
Tarragona; 43815

The majestic **Monestir de Santes Creus** (open Tue–Su, that dominates thi village was founde in 1158. It no longe houses a religious community, but is almost complet intact. The delicately decorated 17 century Bishops' Palace now serves as a town hall. Visitors enter the mo astery through its magnificent Got cloister, with an intricate variety of beasts, figures and symbols carved on its columns. The 13th-century church houses the tombs of seve kings of Aragón. Other parts worth visiting include the monks' dormito with its wonderfully elegant arche

🚗 **From the village, stay on the same road to meet the TP2002. Turn left to Vila-Rodona, pass through th town and go under the motorway to meet the C51. Turn right for Valls. Follow signs onto the N240 towards Montblanc. Go left around the city walls and park behind the tourist offic**

Montblanc

agona; 43400

ntblanc is a medieval jewel. It stands within a ring of fortified
ls and 31 towers that were begun in 1366 on the orders of King
e III "the Ceremonious", at a time when this town was already an
portant military stronghold and merchant centre.

wo-hour walking tour

d left from the car park towards
13th-century **Antiga Església de
t Francesc** ①. Start the tour by
king around the walls. Go past
small gate of Portal de Sant Jordi
he 14th-century **Església de Sant
çal** ②, which is partly set into the
l. Keep right, passing below battle-
nts at Baluard de Santa Anna,
se to the Pont Vell (Old Bridge)
r the Francolí river. On the east
e of the Old Town, the walls past
striking **Torre dels Cinc Cantons** ③
partly obscured by newer build-
s, but re-emerge near the **Portal
Bové** ④. From here, walk back
ards Sant Francesc.
urn right into the Carrer Major to
s inside the walls. On the right is
15th-century **Palau-Fortalesa del
tlà** ⑤, built for Montblanc's military
ernors, and the 13th-century
lésia de Sant Miquel ⑥. Go up
turn left into Pere Berenguer de
ranca to **Plaça Major** ⑦, site of a

Friday market and the 13th-century
Casa de la Vila (town hall). Head up
Carrer Hortolans to reach **Església de
Santa Maria la Major** ⑧, a striking
example of a 14th-century Catalan
Gothic church with a 17th-century
Baroque façade. Exit the square to the
left of the church and continue uphill
to **Pla de Santa Bàrbara** ⑨, from
where there are great views. Descend
via Travessera de la Pedrera back to
Carrer Major, and turn right. Opposite
Pere Berenguer, turn left into **Plaça
dels Àngels** ⑩, then left down Carrer
dels Jueus, the remains of a Jewish
ghetto. Pass the 14th-century Gothic
mansion **Palau Alenyà** ⑪ and turn
right into Carrer Font de la Vila, then
left into Carrer River to come to Portal
de Bové. Go right along Muralla de
Jaume II to Carrer Major and turn left
to return to the car park.

🚗 *Go back to the N240. At the first
roundabout take the C14 for Tàrrega.
After Solivella turn left onto the
TP2335/LP2335 for Vallbona.*

Above City walls of the medieval town
of Montblanc

VISITING MONTBLANC

Tourist Information
*Antiga Església de Sant
Francesc, 43400; 977 861 733;
www.montblancmedieval.org*

Parking
Approaching from Valls on the N240,
follow the road left around the town
walls to find the tourist office in the
Antiga Església de Sant Francesc.
Behind it there is a free car park.

EAT AND DRINK

SANT SADURNÍ D'ANOIA

Cal Blay Vinticinc *expensive*
An elegant modern restaurant in an
old wine cellar, combining adventurous
cuisine with Penedès wine traditions.
*C/ Josep Rovira 27, 08770; 938 910 032;
www.calblay.com; open Wed–Mon for
lunch, Fri and Sat dinner*

AROUND SANT SADURNÍ D'ANOIA

Cal Xim *expensive*
Located in a village, 5 km (3 miles)
from Sant Sadurní d'Anoia, this
restaurant serves Catalan fare.
*Plaça Subirats 5, 08739, Sant Pau
d'Ordal; 938 993 092; www.calxim.
com; open Mon–Sat for lunch, Fri and
Sat dinner*

SANTES CREUS

Cal Mosso *inexpensive*
This convivial restaurant has *calçotades*
in season, salads and Catalan snacks.
*Plaça Santa Llúcia 1, 43815; 977 638
484; closed Mon in summer*

MONTBLANC

El Call de Montblanc *expensive*
Located in a 14th-century house near
the old Jewish quarter of Montblanc,
the restaurant serves Catalan, Basque
and international dishes.
*C/ Sant Josep 15, 43400; 977 860 120;
www.elcalldemontblanc.com; open
Tue–Sun lunch, Fri and Sat dinner*

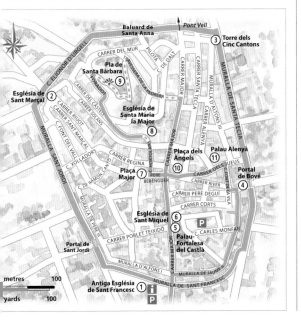

Eat and Drink: inexpensive, under €20; moderate, €20–€40; expensive, over €40

Right Cistercian monastery in Vallbona de les Monges **Below** Romanesque church of Siurana with the hills in the north

WHERE TO STAY

AROUND MONESTIR DE POBLET

Hostal Fonoll *moderate*
Opposite the monastery and run by the same family for over a century, the rooms here are simple but good value. The bar-café runs out onto a pretty terrace and there is a big restaurant that is open for lunch only.
Plaça Ramon Berenguer IV 2, 43448; 977 870 333; www.hostalfonoll.com

PRADES

Cal Crispí *moderate*
Owners Sergi and Eva have used great taste and imagination in transforming this old house into a charming and comfortable bed-and-breakfast. They can advise on all kinds of walks and activities in the area. Guests also have the use of a kitchen.
C/ Nou del Pont 5, 43364; 977 868 097; www.calcrispi.com

SIURANA

La Siuranella *moderate–expensive*
The view from the balconies in this smart hotel in Siurana is hypnotic, and can justify a stay just by itself. Rooms are also very comfortable, and there is an attractive restaurant for enjoying the local wines.
43362, Siurana; 977 821 144; www.siuranella.com; closed Jan

AROUND ESCALADEI

Cal Compte *moderate*
Anna Figueras and her family have lovingly restored this magnificent 18th-century mansion in the town of Torroja, 8 km (5 miles) south of Escaladei. Once the home of a local aristocrat, it is now a distinctive *casa rural* that caters to a wide range of needs. There are stylish double rooms as well as larger suites with kitchens for longer stays. Guests are also welcome to use the main kitchen.
C/ Major 4, 43737, Torroja del Priorat; 619 023 779; www.calcompte.com

AROUND VILELLA BAIXA

Cal Llop *moderate–expensive*
This distinctly chic, modern boutique hotel has been created in a town house in the cramped stone alleys at the top of Gratallops, 5 km (3 miles) south of Vilella Baixa. The stylish restaurant serves creative Catalan cuisine. Wine tourism is a speciality here and there is an excellent selection of vintages available.
C/ de Dalt, 43737, Gratallops; 977 839 502; www.cal-llop.com; closed 10 Jan–10 Feb

⑤ Vallbona de les Monges
Lérida; 25268

The road north leads through very different, more arid and empty countryside to the region's smallest royal monastery, **Monestir de Santa María de Vallbona** *(closed Mon, except Aug)*, with an impressively remote feel. While Poblet and Santes Creus were men's monasteries, from 1175 Vallbona was a women's convent *(de les Monges* means "of the nuns"). It received endowments from Catalan queens, especially the wife of Jaume I Violant of Hungary (1216–51), who is buried here. It is still home to a community of nuns, but visitors can see the main parts of the building, including the intimate **cloister** and its rare Gothic domes.

📷 *Continue along the LP2335 from Vallbona to Maldà, turn left, and then almost immediately left again onto the L220 through Els Omells de na Gaia. Just past this village, drive onto the L232/T232 for Senan and L'Espluga de Francolí. Approaching L'Espluga, follow signs for Poblet.*

⑥ Monestir de Poblet
Tarragona; 43448

Grandest of the region's three great monasteries, the **Monestir de Poblet** *(open daily)* looks more like a castle than a monastery. It was also the most treasured by the medieval Catalan monarchs, many of whom were buried here. Founded in 1150, it was closed in 1835, but since 1940 Cistercian monks have again been its resident, giving it a special atmosphere. Many parts of the complex can be visited, beginning with the cloister and early

Gothic chapterhouse. The royal tombs in the massive church are unique, with effigies of the monar in rows on shared sarcophagi raise on columns beside the altar. Abov the cloister are the spectacular arch scriptorium, where the monks on copied manuscripts, and the snug 14th-century palace built for King Martí I (1356–1410).

📷 *Turning to the left from the Monestir de Poblet entrance, take t T700, which is well signposted for Riudabella and Prades.*

⑦ Prades
Tarragona; 43364

Past Poblet, the landscape change radically as the road winds up throu thick plantations of Mediterranea pines on the slopes of the Muntany de Prades range, with superb view on either side. Prades itself is a unique town, known as the *Vila Vermella* or "red town" thanks to th strange colour of the local stone used in its tightly packed building which include a Gothic-Baroque church and a Renaissance fountai The lovely arcaded Plaça Major ha enjoyable bars and restaurants. Th drive to the west from Prades towa Albarca, the great flat slab of the Se de Montsant looms ever larger ahe a spectacularly rugged backdrop t the winding road.

📷 *Follow the main road out of Prad now the T701, signed for Cornudel de Montsant and Reus. At Albarca, turn left onto the C242. Just before Cornudella, turn left onto the TV32 for Siurana.*

Siurana

Tarragona; 43362

The scenery becomes ever more rugged beyond Albarca on entering the **Priorat**, an area of steep, vineyard hills, ravine-like valleys and dramatic crags, where it is impossible to travel fast. A side road twists and turns up to the extraordinary village of Siurana. A natural fortress, on a crag 735 m (2,400 ft) above the valley floor, with sheer drops on three sides, this was the last Muslim stronghold in Catalonia, taken in 1154. Remains of a Muslim cemetery can still be seen near the Romanesque church in the village. There are spectacular walks around Siurana, and the views on all sides are unforgettable. Return to Cornudella and head 17 km (11 miles) west on the TV7021. Just off the road, to the right, is La Morera de Montsant, the starting point for hikes up into the Serra de Montsant Nature Park (open Mon–Fri).

From La Morera de Montsant, turn right back onto the TV7021, which then becomes the TV7022, for Escaladei.

Escaladei

Tarragona; 43379

The delightful little village of Escaladei is surrounded by vineyards and has great little wine shops. A road from the village leads to the Carthusian monastery, **Cartoixa d'Escaladei** (open Tue–Sun), which once had

Wines of the Priorat

Until the late 1980s, the red wines of the Priorat were a Catalan secret. Conditions in its vineyards are almost unique – a combination of staircase-steep terraces and special soils that produces distinctive wines that are robust but very subtle. Winemaking had gone on here for centuries, but a big change came in 1989, when winemakers such as Alvaro Palacios (with labels such as *Les Terrisses*) and Carles Pastrana (*Clos de l'Obac*) began to combine new techniques with the Priorat's long traditions. Since then, Priorat wines have won worldwide acclaim, and many more small wineries have opened up, although production on the terrace-vineyards is necessarily small. The Montsant wine region, which surrounds the core of the Priorat, is less known but also enjoys a growing reputation.

authority over the area. Founded in 1194, it was rebuilt in Baroque style in the 17th and 18th centuries, but is now an atmospheric ruin.

Return to Escaladei village and turn right to join the T702. Turn right again at the fork for Vilella Baixa.

⑩ Vilella Baixa

Tarragona; 43379

A gorgeous drive leads on to Vilella Baixa, one of the most extraordinary Priorat villages. Set along a steep rocky ridge, it has created its own vertical style of architecture, with such tall houses that it has been labelled "the New York of the Priorat". Continuing on the road through Vilella Baixa then turning right onto the T710 leads to **Gratallops**, another striking hilltop village, again surrounded by fine vineyards.

Continue south on the T710 from Gratallops to reach Falset.

Above Village of Siurana, high up on a crag
Below Entrance to the monastery in Escaladei

EAT AND DRINK

PRADES

L'Estanc *moderate*
A charming restaurant on Prades' lovely main square, L'Estanc has rustic decor which goes well with the good-value Catalan country cooking, including a rich *escudella* (meat and vegetable stew) and delicious home-made desserts.
Plaça Major 9, 43364; 977 868 167

AROUND SIURANA

El Balcó del Priorat *inexpensive*
This large, modern restaurant, 17 km (11 miles) from Siurana, serves Catalan country dishes and excellent, all-local wines, but the greatest attraction is its fabulous location, with stunning views of the Montsant and the valleys below.
C/ Bonrepòs, 43361, La Morera de Montsant; 977 827 211; www.balcodelpriorat.com; open lunch Wed–Mon, dinner Sat only

VILELLA BAIXA

El Racó del Priorat
inexpensive–moderate
A friendly, relaxed village restaurant with attractive traditional menus, featuring fresh seasonal ingredients, including strictly local game such as wild boar and an impressive selection of fine local wines.
C/ Priorat 9, 43374; 977 839 065; open lunch Wed–Mon, dinner Sat only

Eat and Drink: inexpensive, under €20; moderate, €20–€40; expensive, over €40

Above Roadside bar in Gandesa's town centre

VISITING TORTOSA

Tourist Information
*Plaça Carrilet 1, 43500; 977 449 648;
www.turismetortosa.com; open
Tue–Sun*

Parking
Parking is very limited in the old city. It
is usually easier to cross the Mil·lenari
bridge and park in the newer part of
the city, and then walk up.

WHERE TO STAY

AROUND FALSET

Mas Ardèvol *moderate*
This bed-and-breakfast, located 1 km
(0.6 miles) outside Falset, has lovely
rooms and serves meals prepared
from garden produce.
*Ctra. de Falset a Porrera, 43730; 630
324 578; www.masardevol.net*

Mas Figueres *moderate*
Comfortable rooms and great views
are offered at this eccentric house
just 3 km (2 miles) south of Falset.
*Ctra. de Falset 2, 43775, Marçà; 977
178 011; www.masfigueres.com*

TORTOSA

**Parador de Tortosa – Castell de la
Zuda** *moderate–expensive*
Housed in the castle high above the
city, this parador's modern rooms blend
well into the medieval architecture.
*43500, Castell de la Zuda; 977 444 450;
www.parador.es*

AROUND TORTOSA

Villa Retiro *expensive*
An extravagant fantasy-palace of a
country house 15 km (9 miles) north
of Tortosa, this is now a luxury hotel.
*C/ dels Molins 2, 43592, Xerta; 977 473
003; www.rusticae.es*

DELTA DE L'EBRE

Delta Hotel *inexpensive*
This is a modern hotel on an "island"
beside the town of Deltebre.
*Avda. del Canal, 43580; 977 480 046;
www.deltahotel.es*

⑪ Falset
Tarragona; 43730

Although it is the capital of the
Priorat *comarca*, Falset lies within
another wine *Denominación de
Origen*, Montsant. At the top of its
hill are the remains of a 12th-century
castle, below which is a placid old
town with distinguished Renaissance
and Neo-Classical buildings, such as
the 17th-century palace that is now
the town hall. Falset's most impressive structure, though, is the
Modernista **Cooperativa Agrícola**
built by architect Cèsar Martinell in
1919. The building can be visited.
Enquire at the tourist office for details
about visiting times. Falset also has
excellent wine shops.

🚗 *Leave Falset on the N420 towards
Móra la Nova and Alcañiz. West of
Falset the road emerges from moun-
tains into more open, rolling country,
moving much faster down to the great
Ebre river and cross it at Mòra d'Ebre.
The N420 climbs up again to reach the
next stop at Gandesa.*

⑫ Gandesa
Tarragona; 43780

The centre of the Terra Alta wine
region, Gandesa is home to another
great wine cellar, the **Cooperativa
Agrícola** *(for tours contact tourist office
977 420 910)*. The town was also the
hub of the 1938 Battle of the Ebro
in the Civil War, commemorated in
a museum, the **Centre d'Estudis de
la Batalla de l'Ebre** *(open Tue–Sun)*.

South from Gandesa, the C43 lead
to one of the finest Cèsar Martinell
wine cellars at Pinell de Brai *(open
Mon–Fri to visitors)*, fronted by a
marvellous mosaic frieze by Xavier
Nogués. Continuing south there are
more fine views and another sudden
change of landscape as the road
drops back to the Ebre, to run beside
the river through orange groves.

🚗 *Keep on the C43 to meet the C12
and turn right for Tortosa. Stay on
the road past the town, then turn left
and cross the Ebre by the Pont del
Mil·lenari (C42). Turn left following
"Centre Ciutat" signs to the old city.*

⑬ Tortosa
Baix Ebre; 43500

The main city of southern Catalonia, Tortosa was already a key
crossing point over the Ebre in Roman times. It was also a stronghold of Andalusia's Muslim rulers until it was taken by the armies of
Ramon Berenguer IV of Catalonia in 1148. With summer temperatures often over 30° C (86° F), it is a city with a very southern feel.

The Moorish **Castell de la Zuda**, built
on a steep crag with a commanding
position above the Ebre, was captured
and incorporated into a later Christian
castle, part of which is now a parador
hotel. Views from the castle
are superb, and allow
visitors to see many more
fragments of the city's old
walls and fortifications.

On the east of the castle
away from the river, narrow
streets and stone steps
lead down into the old
city. The **Reials Col·legis**
(Royal Colleges) on Carrer
Sant Domènec, now a
historical archive, have a
16th-century patio carved
with a remarkable collection of
often strange faces and figures.
Below the castle is the rather bizarre

**Portico of the Catedral
de Tortosa**

Catedral de Tortosa, which was begun
in the 14th century and has a massive
17th-century Baroque façade. The
building was never quite finished,
and has been left with only a simple
flat roof. Many more
smaller details can also be
seen around the old city,
including Muslim inscrip-
tions and relics of the
medieval Jewish quarter.
Outside the narrow streets
there is a pleasant riverside walk.

🚗 *Recross the Ebre on the
Mil·lenari bridge and turn
left onto the C12 for
Roquetes, then left again
for Amposta. Cross the
river again on the southernmost bridge
(on the N340) and immediately turn
right onto the TV3454 for Deltebre.*

The Wine Cathedrals

around 1910, Mancomunitat, one of Catalonia's regional authorities, set about an ambitious programme to support small local vineyards by setting up cooperatives to make and sell their wine. To give these institutions the dignity they deserved, they were housed in extraordinary Modernista-style cellars, many designed by the architect Cèsar Martinell, a student of Gaudí. They were dubbed *catedrals del vi*, wine cathedrals, because of their grandeur, but many also resemble the great cathedrals of the Middle Ages in both their structure and style.

Delta de l'Ebre

Aragon; 43870, 43580

Beyond Amposta, with the last bridge over the river, there is yet another utterly different world in the Ebre delta, of flat fields of rice stretching off as far as the eye can see towards broad misty horizons. At the centre of this vast stretch of land is the sleepy municipality of **Deltebre**, where there is a river ferry to **Parc Natural del Delta L'Ebre**. It also has the information centre of the park *(C/ Martí Buera 48, 43870; 977 489 679; open daily)*.

The delta wetlands make an ideal habitat for all kinds of wild birds, including flamingos, which are a common sight around the lagoons. The flat delta is also a perfect spot for cycling, and bicycles are available for hire in Deltebre. Boat trips from Deltebre are also popular.

Beyond Deltebre, the road winds down to **Riumar**, where there are beaches with good seafood restaurants beside the river.

EAT AND DRINK

FALSET

Hostal Sport *moderate*
The dining room at Falset's foremost traditional hotel is plain, but comfortable. It has a reputation as a showcase for local food and wines.
C/ Miquel Barceló 4–6, 43730; 977 830 078; www.hostalsport.com

AROUND GANDESA

Cal Pelegrí *moderate*
Local gourmets make a detour to this restaurant in Corbera d'Ebre, 5 km (3 miles) north of Gandesa. Specialities include roast goat and seafood.
Avda. Llibertat 8, Corbera d'Ebre, 43787; 670 246 460; www.cal-pelegri.com

TORTOSA

Sidrería Amets
inexpensive–moderate
This Basque-style *sidrería* (cider house) offers excellent wines and the food runs from tapas to meat and seafood dishes.
Passeig Joan Moreira 13, 43500; 977 446 699; www.sidreriaamets.com; closed Sun dinner, Sun all day Jun–Aug

El Paiolet *moderate*
Variations on the Ebre delta's rice dishes and delicious salads are served here.
Rambla Felip Pedrell 56, 43500; 977 446 653; www.paiolet.com

DELTA DE L'EBRE

Bar-Restaurant Galatxo
inexpensive–moderate
One of the area's best places to enjoy local rice dishes and seafood.
Desembocadura de L'Ebre, 43580, La Cava; 977 267 503; www.galatxo.net

Left Rooftops of Tortosa, with a view of the unique flat roof of the cathedral

---

DAY TRIP OPTIONS

The AP7 and the AP2 offer quick and easy access to every part of this route. The AP7 runs from Barcelona through the Penedès and down to Amposta; the AP2 turns off west of Vilafranca.

Cava and Gothic treasures

Visit some cava houses in Sant Sadurní d'Anoia ❶ and Vilafranca del Penedès' ❷ wine museum. Then wander into the countryside to the Monestir de Santes Creus ❸.

Take the AP7 from Barcelona to Sant Sadurní and Vilafranca. Go south on the B212; turn right onto the TP2442, which becomes the TP244 and then left onto the TV2441 for Santes Creus.

The Cistercian trail

Get immersed in splendid medieval monasticism amid the Gothic glories of Santes Creus ❸, Vallbona de les Monges ❺ and Poblet ❻, and wander around the impressive walls of Montblanc ❹.

Drive to Santes Creus from Barcelona on the AP7 and AP2. Follow the itinerary from here. Join the AP2 at junction 9, near Montblanc, to return.

Wines and lost valleys

Lovers of wines and rural calm can spend a perfect day on a slow drive around Siurana ❽, Escaladei ❾, Vilella Baixa ❿ and Falset ⓫, dropping in on vineyards and marvelling at the extraordinary cliff top locations of its villages.

From Barcelona, take the AP7 to junction 34, then take the N420 Gandesa road and turn right on the C242 to Siurana. Return from Falset on the N420.

Moorish castles and birding spots

For a varied trip, explore old Tortosa ⓭ and its Moorish Castell de la Zuda in the morning, then head to the Delta de l'Ebre's ⓮ beaches and bird-filled lagoons.

Take the AP7 south to Amposta, turning right on the C12 for Tortosa and left on the TV3454 for the Delta.

Eat and Drink: inexpensive, under €20; moderate, €20–€40; expensive, over €40

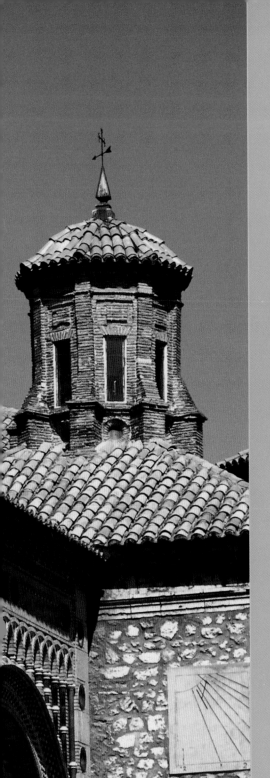

From the Mountains to the Plains

Alcañiz to Albarracín

Highlights

- **Breathtaking scenery**
  Visit ancient villages tucked away
  in the Matarraña National Park

- **Majestic birds of prey**
  Witness the rare sight of hundreds of
  vultures swooping down from the
  mountains at feeding time in Mas de
  Bunyol, near Valderrobres

- **Amazing architecture**
  Marvel at the engaging mix of Moorish
  and Modernista architecture in Teruel

- **Fortified village**
  Get lost amongst the ancient stone
  monuments and edifices of Albarracín

View of the towers and rooftops of the
Mudéjar Iglesia de San Pedro in Teruel

From the Mountains to the Plains

The largely undiscovered area of Matarraña is one of abundant wildlife, medieval villages, waterfalls, rivers and constant views of Els Ports (the gates), an ancient mountain range. From the mountains, this drive takes visitors across the plains of lower Aragón to Teruel, another little-known gem with an intriguing Moorish past. The drive finishes in Albarracín, one of the most beautiful of Spain's fortified towns.

0 kilometres 10

0 miles 10

Above View of the village of La Fresneda in the distance, *see p122* **Below** Turret of the cathedral in Albarracín, *see p127*

KEY

⬛ Drive route

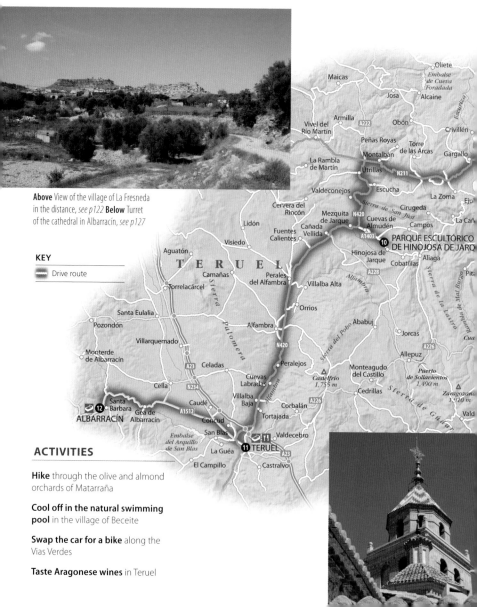

ACTIVITIES

Hike through the olive and almond orchards of Matarraña

Cool off in the natural swimming pool in the village of Beceite

Swap the car for a bike along the Vías Verdes

Taste Aragonese wines in Teruel

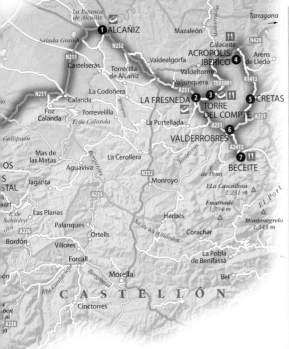

PLAN YOUR DRIVE

Start/Finish: Alcañiz to Albarracín.

Number of days: 3–4, allowing half a day to explore Teruel.

Distances: 290 km (180 miles).

Road conditions: Roads are generally well paved and signposted; there is some steep terrain and hairpin bends in Matarraña.

When to go: Matarraña can get cold in winter and in summer the water-falls and streams can be dry. Autumn and spring are the best times to visit the region.

Opening hours: Shops are open from 9:30am to 1:30pm, and from 4 to 8pm. Restaurants are open from 2 to 4pm, and from 8 to 11pm. Most museums and monuments are closed on Mondays.

Main market days: Alcañiz: Tue; La Fresneda: Wed, Sat; Cretas: Mon; Beceite: Fri; Teruel: Thu; Albarracín: Wed.

Shopping: *Jamón* (ham) and beautiful Mudéjar-style green and bronze tiles are available in Teruel. Pick up cheese, *embutidos* (charcuterie), olive oil and almonds from Matarraña.

Major festivals: Alcañiz: Fiestas Patronales, 8–13 Sep; Teruel: Fiestas del Ángel, second Sun Jul; Albarracín: Fiestas Patronales, 8–17 Sep.

Above Houses in Albarracín perching on a lofty cleft, *see p127* **Below** Arches framing an alley in Beceite, *see p124*

DAY TRIP OPTIONS

Nature lovers will enjoy driving through the northern part of this drive and visiting the charming villages of Alcañiz, La Fresneda, Vallderrobres and Beceite. **Architecture enthusiasts** and **history buffs** will be enthralled by the towns of Teruel and Albarracín. For details, *see p127*.

Above left Plaza Mayor in La Fresneda
Above right Ornate altarpiece of the Ermita de San Antonio Abad Below Courtyard of El Castillo in Alcañiz

WHERE TO STAY

ALCAÑIZ

Hotel Guadalupe *inexpensive*
Located right opposite the cathedral in Alcañiz, this 3-star hotel has rooms that are functionally comfortable. There is a great bar downstairs specializing in *pinchos* or local tapas.
Plaza España 8, 44600; 978 830 750

LA FRESNEDA

Camping La Fresneda *inexpensive*
This is a small camp site surrounded by almond trees and overlooking the Les Ports mountain range. A small bar-restaurant serves simple fare.
Partida Vall de Pi, 44596; 978 854 085; www.campinglafresneda.com; closed end Oct–mid-Mar

El Convent *moderate*
As the name suggests, this high-end hostelry is located in an old convent dating from 1613.
C/ Convento 1, 44596; 978 854 850; www.hotelelconvent.com

TORRE DEL COMPTE

La Parada del Compte
moderate–expensive
A wonderful *casa rural* which accommodates its guests in cozy wood-lined bungalows in lovely verdant surroundings.
Finca la Antigua Estación del Ferrocarril, 44597; 978 769 072; www.hotelparadadelcompte.com

AROUND ACROPOLIS IBERÍCO

La Raconet de la Plaça *inexpensive*
This simple and comfortable rustic-style villa in the heart of Calaceite is of exceptional value.
Plaza Espanya 9–19, 44610, Calaceite; 978 851 519; www.ruralceit.com

① Alcañiz
Teruel; 44600
An archetypal Aragonese castle-town located by the Gaudalope river, Alcañiz has a splendid array of monuments for its size, all neatly tucked around the central Plaza de España. The largest is the **Iglesia de Santa Maria Mayor** *(open daily)* with its soaring Gothic tower and ornate Baroque portal, a work of Basque sculptor Juan Bengoechea. Next to it is **La Lonja** *(closed to the public)*, another Gothic treasure that once served as a commodities exchange. Follow signs to the 13th–14th century castle, **El Castillo**, once a stronghold of the Knights of the Order of Calatrava. Though it is now a hotel, visitors can wander around the grounds. Across the river, the **Atrivm** *(closed Mon)*, a new visitor centre, tells the history of the region through multimedia and expositions.

🚗 *Take the N232 in the direction of Tarragona. Bear left on the A231, signposted for Valjunquera and Valderrobres, to reach La Fresneda.*

② La Fresneda
Teruel; 44596
With its pretty 16th-century portico along the Calle Mayor and cobblestoned squares, La Fresneda is one of Matarraña's most colourful villag Highlights include the gargoyle-dotted *ayuntamiento* (town hall), t **Iglesia de Santa Maria Major** and remains of the castle at the very to of the village's steep streets. Also worth a visit are a couple of ancier dungeon-like jails on the Plaza Mayo Ask at the tourist office (on the Plaz Mayor) for opening times, which ter to vary for all sights in the village.

🚗 *Continue along the A231. After 1 km (0.6 miles) take the turn-off on the left onto the narrow TEV3001 (unmarked) for Torre del Compte. Cc tinue on this road for 4 km (2 miles).*

③ Torre del Compte
Teruel; 44597
A small village, Torre del Compte h a fine 14th-century church, a town hall, a museum and a stylish rural hotel, the **Parada del Compte**. The **Centro Etnográfico** *(open daily 11am 1pm, ring the doorbell)* contains a collection of everyday items and ephemera from the region's fiestas, industries, workshops and farms. A around Torre del Compte there are magnificent views of the olive and almond orchards that blanket Matarraña, with the majestic Els Ports mountain range providing a beautiful backdrop.

🚗 *Continue on the TEV3001 till the N420 again. Turn right and follow signs to Calaceite. On approaching th town turn right onto the A1413 for th Acropolis Iberíco, signposted Poblad Iberico de San Antonio.*

Acropolis Iberíco

el; 44610

fascinating Acropolis Iberíco is
remains of an Iberian village
ch had reached its height in the
d century BC; the ancient streets
homes' foundations can be
arly imagined from what one can
today. Joan Cabre discovered
m in 1903, and a museum
dicated to his work is located in
ghbouring Calaceite *(open Thu–*
). At the high point of the Iberian
is the tiny **Ermita de San Antonio**
ad dating from 1798. The larger
lding on the opposite hill is the
h-century **Ermita de San**
stóbal. Its interior was ransacked
ring the Civil War. All that remains
he saint's original statue is a sev-
d hand, which has been laid at
base of a replacement statue.
Continue on the A1413, following
signs to Cretas.

The Iberians

he Iberians were the original
paniards. They populated the
eninsula between the 6th and 1st
enturies BC and flourished in agri-
ulture and the arts before the
Roman conquest. Archaeologists, on
xcavating in the Bajo Aragon, have
discovered vestiges of this ancient
ulture. There have been initiatives
o present them to the public with
multilingual signages and exhibition
paces for artifacts. In Cretas an information centre has been set up with
a small museum on the Iberian language. Visitors can pick up a map of
Bajo Aragon's *Ruta de los Iberos*, an
tinerary that contains over 20 sites.

⑤ Cretas

Teruel; 44623

This once-walled village has
preserved three of its original gates:
Valderrobres, San Roque and San
Antonio. The late Gothic **Iglesia de**
la Asunción *(open for Mass only)* was
ransacked during the Civil War; when
the war ended, the village's inhabitants donated a percentage of their
olive crops until enough funds were
gathered to commission a new
retable. Just in front of the church is
the majestic arch of the **Casa Sapera**,
the threshold to the **Plaza de España**.
Noble stone mansions dating from
the 15th and 16th centuries flank the
village's main square. In the square's
centre is a curious column, brought
here in 1962. Its origins are unclear,
bar the decorative cross – a sign of
the Order of Calatrava, *patrones* of
the village until the 12th century.

🚗 *Leave Cretas on the A1413 and*
continue along it until the A231. Turn
right here and follow signs to the
village of Valderrobres.

Above left Bell tower of the Iglesia de Santa
Maria Major in La Fresneda **Above right**
Richly decorated doorway of the cathedral in
Alcañiz **Below** El Castillo looks over the town
of Alcañiz

EAT AND DRINK

ALCAÑIZ

La Oficina *inexpensive*
This excellent value *mesón* (inn)
specializes in traditional, homemade
food using local produce, including
the area's famed olive oil. Highlights
include meat dishes with options such
as steak with Roquefort sauce.
Avda. de Aragón 12, 44600; 978
870 801

TORRE DEL COMPTE

La Parada del Compte *expensive*
Creative cuisine using locally sourced
ingredients is complemented by wine
from the restaurant's own bodega.
The menu is small, but generally
includes a variety of salads for starters
and meat, pork or fish dishes for mains.
Leave room for the delicious panna
cotta and fig dessert.
Finca la Antigua Estación del
Ferrocarril, 44597; 978 769 072;
www.hotelparadadelcompte.com;
closed Jan

Eat and Drink: inexpensive, under €20; moderate, €20–€40; expensive, over €40

Above View of the village of Valderrobres with its castle Below Façade of the old church in Beceite

⑥ Valderrobres
Teruel; 44580

Located on the banks of the Pena river, Valderrobres is the grandest of Matarraña's villages. Ancient stone town houses flank the banks of the river. Cross over the medieval bridge and through the grand **Torre San Roque** into the Old Town to come directly into the main square and the **Casa Consistorial**, a 16th-century building conceived in the Aragonese Mannerist style. At the top of the Old Town is the Catalan Gothic **Iglesia de Santa Maria del Mar Mayor** (open for guided visits only when visiting the castle), which has a huge rose window. Next door is the 13th-century **castle** (open winter: Tue–Sat, summer: Tue–Sun), which was commissioned by the archbishops of Zaragoza. It still has a large swath of its original ramparts.

🚗 *Take the A 2412 (unsigned) to reach Beceite.*

Feeding the Vultures

One of the most remarkable experiences in Matarraña is to be had just outside of Valderrobres in the tiny locality of Mas de Bunyol. Since the 1990s, a local couple has been coaxing a population of magnificent leopard vultures to swoop down and feed off butchers' cast-offs. Today, over 300 of these astounding creatures have been known to descend from the mountains and feed. A special observatory has been built for visitors to watch the spectacle, one of only two of its kind in Spain.

⑦ Beceite
Teruel; 44588

Dramatically perched in a valley surrounded by mountains and striking ridges, this sleepy little village is blessed with views that take the breath away. In its narrow streets exposed brick *casas* with hanging wooden balconies jostle for space with more modern structures. Highlights include the 18th-century **Ermita de Santa Ana** with arched entrance and a belfry, and Baroque **Iglesia de San Bartolomé** (open for Mass only). Cross the old sto bridge down Arrabel del Puente to **Antigua Fabrica Noguera**, an old paper mill now turned into an arts and craft gallery. Visitors who feel l a dip, or even a lovely walk, should follow signs from here to **El Parriza** a natural park that traces the cours of the Matarraña river and crosses dozens of waterfalls and natural poc About 1 km (0.6 miles) along this unmarked road is the **Piscina Natu de L'Assut**, a man-made pool of wate diverted from the river. The walk is simple and suitable for all age group

🚗 *Drive back along the A2412 to Valderrobres, then the A231, passing La Fresneda till the N232. Head for Alcañiz. At Alcañiz take the N211 at the roundabout on the western side of town, following signs for Teruel. Continue for 47 km (29 miles) on this road and then take the TEV8215 towards the "Grutas del Cristal" and Molinos. Park on the outskirts of Molinos.*

WHERE TO STAY

MOLINOS

Hostal de la Villa *inexpensive*
A comfortable old-world hostel located inside an 18th-century building offering basic rooms and hearty, home cooked meals in its first-floor dining room.
Plaza Mayor 5, 44556; 978 849 234

Where to Stay: inexpensive, under €70; moderate, €70–€120; expensive, over €120

Molinos
uel; 44556

s wildly picturesque little hamlet,
tled in a valley, is bereft of the
nd housing developments that
ght many villages in the area, and
ome to a surprising museum.
terio Blasco Ferrer (1907–93) was
oted Spanish Expressionist whose
rk hangs in major museums
und the world. Although
n in Teruel, his mother lived
Molinos and for this reason
village's town hall houses a
all, light-filled gallery of his
rks. Like the rest of the
able buildings in Molinos, it
be viewed by guided tours
y. Tours of the village start
ront of the church on Plaza
yor, where the Tourist
ice is located *(978 849 085;*
ly tours at 12:30, 4, 5:30 and
n during high season; ring
ad for other times).
Follow the TEV8215 and signs
the "Grutas de Cristal".

Grutas de Cristal
uel; 44556

covered in 1961, these crystal caves
end over 620 m (680 yd) and are
ted for their large variety of forma-
ns, especially vertical stalactites, and
sils. They are also home to a large
mmunity of bats *(978 849 085; open*
mer: 11am to 1pm and 4 to 6–7pm;
ter: two guided visits daily Mon–Fri).
Go back to Molinos on the TEV8215
d turn left onto the TE41 to reach the
11. Continue towards Montalbán.
er Montalbán, turn left onto the
20 towards Teruel. After about 20 km
miles) take the A1403 in the direc-
n of Aliaga to Hinojosa de Jarque.

⑩ Parque Escultórico de Hinojosa de Jarque
Teruel; 44157

The sweeping plains and sculptured
cornfields of this agricultural swath
of Aragón are home to one of its most
special sites: the Parque Escultórico, a
sculpture park in and around the tiny
village of Hinojosa de Jarque. Dozens
of Spanish artists took part in the
project which is dedicated to
the "memory, myth and legend"
of Aragonese villages, over four
years in the mid-1990s, creating the 36 abstract pieces that
now dot the landscape. Locals
fed and accommodated the
artists while they worked,
making it a community
achievement. A tour includes a
visit to the shrine of El Pilar
in the village.

Figure in the church of Molinos

🚗 *Return to the N420 via*
the A1403 and turn left.
Continue for about 50 km (31 miles)
to reach Teruel.

Above Portal of the church in Molinos
Below left Carved balcony door in Beceite
Below right Main town square in the village
of Valderrobres

Left Remains of an abandoned castle in Albarracín **Right** Interior of the Mausoleum de Los Amantes, Teruel **Below** Arabic exterior of the Iglesia de San Pedro in Teruel

VISITING TERUEL

Tourist Information
C/ San Francisco 1, 44001; 978 641 461
www.turismodearagon.com

Parking
Park in the private car park at the Estación de Autobuses (bus station). The largest car park is located at the Estación de Ferrocarril (train station) from where it is a five-minute walk into the Old Town. Others are located inside the Old Town in front of the Torre de San Martin on the Plaza Pérez Pedro, the Plaza San Juan. Parking on the street is not recommended.

WHERE TO STAY

TERUEL

Hospedería El Seminario *inexpensive*
The modest rooms in this 18th-century religious building in the centre of Teruel offer exceptional value.
Plaza Pérez Prado nº 2, 44001; 978 619 970; www.hospederiaelseminario.com

Spa Hotel *moderate*
Located on the outskirts of town, rooms here are stylishly modern.
Ctra. Zaragoza (Poligono de la Paz), 44001; 902 100 300; www.spahotel-teruel.com

ALBARRACÍN

Hotel Albarracín *moderate*
This three-star hotel belongs to the small Gargallo chain, and is located in a brick palace in the historical centre.
C/ Azagra S/N, 44100; 978 710 011; www.hotelalbarracinteruel.com

⑪ Teruel
Teruel; 44001

The city of Teruel is one of the last of Spain's undiscovered secrets. Free of mass tourism, Teruel is an enchanting place located on a naturally elevated terrace. On approach, its most distinctive featu. is its four ornate Mudéjar towers. These reign over even more UNESCO-classified Baroque, Gothic and Modernista architectural gems in Teruel's compact and easy-to-navigate old town. A large university ensures a vibrant nightlife in the city.

A one-hour walking tour

From the car park walk down the busy Ronda de Ambeles to the cylindrical **Torreón de San Esteban** ①, the entrance to the old Jewish quarter. Turn right up Calle Abadia to get to the Plaza Breton; the **Casa Bayo** ②, an elegant blue apartment block in a restrained Art Nouveau style, is on the right. Turn right into Matias Abad, a tiny lane that leads to the tourist office and two of Teruel's most extraordinary sights – the **Mausoleum de Los Amantes** ③ *(open daily)* and the stunning **Iglesia de San Pedro** ④. The mausoleum encloses the mummified cadavers of Diego and Isabel who, legend has it, literally died of broken hearts but are preserved here

for eternity clutching each other's hands in an exquisitely carved pie of marble by sculptor Juan de Áva (1911–2006). Adjacent to the mau leum is the dazzling Iglesia de San Pedro built in the 14th century. Th building was constructed by the city's Mudéjar population, who offe their skills to the city's authorities in exchange for special privileges afte Teruel was taken by the Christians. Every surface of the church has be embellished with the most vivid Arab-inspired motifs, in deep gold and jewel colours to stunning effe. The adjacent San Pedro tower *(op daily)*, the oldest in the city, is equ. rich, featuring intricate tiles and gla bricks on its columns and borders.

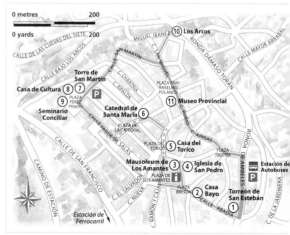

k back to the tourist office, turn
nt and then right again into the
za del Torico with its central foun-
u sporting bronze bulls' heads. The
tty **Casa del Torico** ⑤,
the right, is the city's
st emblematic Art
uveau building. Go
che top of the plaza and
n left into the Plaza de
Catedral. The **Catedral de**
ta Maria ⑥ is a complex
ucture, spanning eight
uturies of different styles. The
most striking feature is an
ricately carved wooden ceiling,
vering the entire central nave, a
gnificent piece of work with
mic and Gothic influences. The
able, by French artist Gabriel Joly,
tes from the 16th century and
picts the life of Christ in Renaissance
lle. On the opposite side of the
za turn right into Calle Yagüe de
as and walk to the end. Here are
ee important monuments. On the
nt is the **Torre de San Martín** ⑦,
ich is richly embellished in deco-
ve brickwork and Islamic motif. In
nt is the **Casa de Cultura** ⑧, now
e city's public library, and to the
: is the **Seminario Conciliar** ⑨, an
ch-century Jesuit College con-
ed into a hotel. Turn right past
e Torre de San Martín into Calle
n Martín and follow it as it veers to
e right. Turn left and then fork right
Calle San Miguel. On the right is
s **Arcos** ⑩, a 16th-century aque-
ct. Retrace the route on Calle San

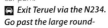

**Detail of Iglesia
de San Pedro**

Miguel and continue down to the
Plaza Fray Anselmo Polanco. This is
the site of the **Museo Provincial** ⑪
(open Tue–Sun), which is worth perus-
ing for its eclectic collection
of artifacts and antique toys.
Continue straight ahead on
Calle Rubio and Calle Ainsas
to Plaza Judería. From here
take a left to reach the Ronda
de Ambeles and the Estación
de Autobuses, back to the
car park.

🚗 *Exit Teruel via the N234.
Go past the large round-
about. Take the A1512 in the direction
of Albarracín. Park at the bottom of
the village.*

⑫ Albarracín
Teruel; 44100
The gateway to the Montes
Universales mountain range, this pink-
hued medieval city literally spills out
over a lofty crest, with its awesome
ramparts snaking even further up
into the sierra. Park at the base of the
village and walk up to its small yet
atmospheric **Plaza Mayor** where
there are a handful of bars and restaurants. The peak of the village is the
location of the 16th-century **cathedral**
(open daily), which contains a small
museum of tapestries, and the **Palacio**
Episcopal *(closed for renovation at the
time of going to print)* with its Baroque
portal. For breathtaking views, ascend
further to the remains of the **castle**,
carved into the rock in the 11th
century by a powerful Berber family.

EAT AND DRINK

TERUEL
Cafeteria Sarto *inexpensive*
Start the day at this buzzing cafeteria
with hot egg and ham rolls, fluffy
tortilla de patatas, fresh orange juice
and great coffee.
C/ Joaquin Costa 12, 44001; 978 602 039

Aqui Teruel *inexpensive*
This tapas bar specializes in local
produce such as Jamón de Teruel and
cheeses and wine from Aragón.
*C/ Yagüe de Salas 4, 44001; 978 612
365; www.aquiteruel.com*

Yain *moderate*
Creative, expertly crafted dishes are
served here in a modern setting. A
three-course menu with wine is
offered for both lunch and dinner.
*Plaza de la Judería 9, 44001; 978 624
076; www.yain.es*

Below Vibrant Plaza del Torico in Teruel

DAY TRIP OPTIONS
This drive can clearly be divided
nto two shorter day trips. The A221
ccesses all the stops in the north
nd the A23, in the south. Visitors
an base themselves in either
Alcañiz or Teruel to do the following
day trips.

Charming villages
Start the day from the castle-town of
Alcañiz ① and visit its church and
castle. Then drive to the colourful
village of La Fresneda ②. Head
o Vallderrobres ⑥, located on the
banks of the Pena river, to watch a
ocal couple feed leopard vultures as
hey swoop down in hundreds. Then

drive to Beceite ⑦ for lunch,
after which take a relaxing walk to
El Parrizal, a natural park by the
Matarraña river. The walk is approximately four hours long and can be
done by anyone.

*Leave Alcañiz on the N232 following
signs to Tortosa. At the junction of the
N420, take the A231 to La Fresneda.
From La Fresneda, drive south on the
same road straight to the town of
Vallderrobres. At Vallderrobres, take the
A2412 to Beceite. Return to Alcañiz the
same way.*

History and architecture
Spend the morning taking in the

fabulous architecture and visiting
the many sights in Teruel ⑪. After
a lazy lunch at one of its many
restaurants, drive to the mountain
town of Albarracín ⑫, where the
setting sun washes the ancient stone
buildings with incredible pinkish
hues. There are some gorgeous
views from the remains of the castle.
Visit the cathedral and Palacio
Episcopal and spend the evening in
the Plaza Mayor, which has a handful
of restaurants and bars.

*Exit Teruel via the N234 on the western
side of the town. Go past the large
roundabout, then take the A1512 in
the direction of Albarracín.*

Eat and Drink: inexpensive, under €20; moderate, €20–€40; expensive, over €40

The Land of the Templars

Morella to Ares del Maestre

Highlights

- **Enchanting walled town**
  Explore Morella – bordered by medieval walls and crowned by a magnificent castle

- **Medieval Mirambel**
  Take a stroll back into the Middle Ages in this perfectly restored village

- **Limestone landscapes and dry-stone architecture**
  Take in the endless views of crags, valleys and plateaux

- **Stunning panoramas**
  Climb up to the Maestrazgo's most spectacular viewpoint, Ares del Maestre

Small hilltop village of Ares del Maestre

The Land of the Templars

During the centuries of war against the Muslim rulers of southern Spain, the Grand Masters (*maestres*) of the Knights Templar and other military orders were put in control of the austerely beautiful upland region straddling the borders of Aragón and Valencia. This thus became known as the Maestrazgo (or the *Maestrat* in Valencian). This route sets out from the "capital", Morella, and traverses the mountains north to south to visit two handsome, historic seigneurial towns, taking visitors across landscapes characterized by their dry-stone wall architecture. There are few main roads and no cities in the Maestrazgo, making this back roads country *par excellence*.

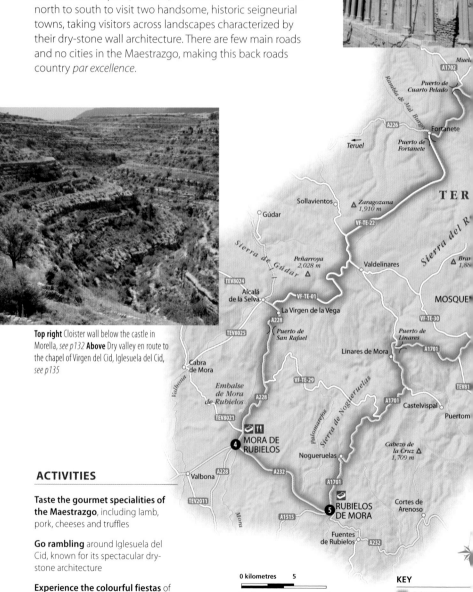

Top right Cloister wall below the castle in Morella, *see p132* **Above** Dry valley en route to the chapel of Virgen del Cid, Iglesuela del Cid, *see p135*

ACTIVITIES

Taste the gourmet specialities of the Maestrazgo, including lamb, pork, cheeses and truffles

Go rambling around Iglesuela del Cid, known for its spectacular dry-stone architecture

Experience the colourful fiestas of the region

KEY

Drive route

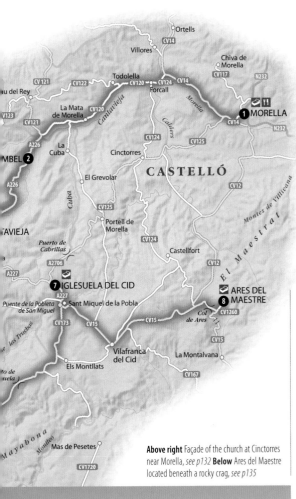

Above right Façade of the church at Cinctorres near Morella, *see p132* **Below** Ares del Maestre located beneath a rocky crag, *see p135*

PLAN YOUR DRIVE

Start/finish: Morella to Ares del Maestre.

Number of days: 2–3, allowing for half a day in Morella.

Distance: 250 km (155 miles).

Road conditions: Generally reasonable but parts of the road between Mosquerela and Iglesuela del Cid are in poor condition.

When to go: Spring to autumn are ideal. In winter, the Valdelinares section may be blocked by snow.

Opening hours: Most churches are open for Mass only but if visitors are interested, they can find the person who has the keys to open them. Monuments and museums are closed on Mondays.

Main market days: Morella: Thu, Sun.

Shopping: This region is famous for its traditional textiles, ham, charcuterie, cheese and pastries.

Major festivals: Morella: Sexenni, Aug, every six years, next in 2012; **Mirambel:** Fiestas Patronales en Honor a San Lamberto y San Roque, Aug; **Mora de Rubielos:** Fiestas de San Miguel, Sep.

DAY TRIP OPTIONS

Nature lovers will find Morella an ideal base for exploring the northern mountains, while **families** and **history buffs** will enjoy a visit to the churches of Rubielos de Mora and Mora de Rubielos. For details, *see p133*.

Right Typical timber-framed house in Morella
Far right Gothic monastery of Convent de
Sant Francesc, Morella

VISITING MORELLA

Tourist Information
*Plaçeta de Sant Miquel s/n, 12300; 964
173 032; www.morella.net*

Parking
Park as close to the gateway as
possible, above Portal de Sant Miquel.
There is limited access for cars into
Morella because streets are narrow.

WHERE TO STAY

MORELLA

Cardenal Ram *moderate*
This remodelled 16th-century building
is now a hotel and restaurant, which
dominates the main street of Morella.
*C/ Cuesta Suñer 1, 12300; 964 173 085;
www.cardenalram.com*

CANTAVIEJA

Balfagon *inexpensive–moderate*
This Balfagon has 46 rooms on three
floors. The attic rooms have more
character and are quieter than the rest.
*Avda. Maestrazgo 20, 44140; 964 185
076; www.hotelbalfagon.com*

MORA DE RUBIELOS

Jaime I *moderate*
All the rooms of this hotel are
individually styled and some have
terraces or balconies.
*Plaza de la Villa, 44400; 978 800 184;
www.hoteljaime.com*

La Trufa Negra *moderate*
La Trufa Negra is a slick, contemporary
hotel with spa facilities.
*Avda. Ibañez Martín 8–10, 44400; 978
807 144; www.latrufanegra.com*

① Morella
Castelló; 12300

A first view of Morella, the main town of the Maestrazgo, never fail
to impress. Raised up dramatically from the surrounding landscap
it consists of a fan-shaped labyrinth draped around a rock outcrop
on which stands a ruined castle.

A 90-minute walking tour

This walk can be done any time
but it is wise to avoid midday in
summer. From the car
park walk to the
tourist information
office and turn right
onto the Plaçeta de
Sant Miquel. Across this
square is the **Portal de Sant
Miquel** ①, one of the old
gates through the medieval
walls. Turn left at the corner, go
uphill a few steps and turn left by
the souvenir shop into Carrer de Don
Juan Giner. Bear right on the upper
fork into Carrer Mare de Déu del Pilar.
After passing the **ajuntament** ②, a
14th–15th-century mansion, the
street becomes Carrer Segura

*A medieval sundial
in Forcall*

Barreda, then Carrer Marquesa Fuer
del Sol before feeding into the po
coed Carrer Blasco d'Alagó. The
town's main restaurant
are all on or just off th
street. When the porti
coes end, take the flig
of steps on the right.
Turn right at the top of t
first flight up a second,
broad flight of steps into
square, Plaça Sant France
Across the square is the 13th-centu
Gothic monastery, the **Convent de
Sant Francesc** ③, which has a
beautiful cloister. Climb up the slop
to the **Castillo de Morella** ④, a 13th-
century Moorish fortification which
includes a courtyard, governor's
quarters, dungeons and a tower.

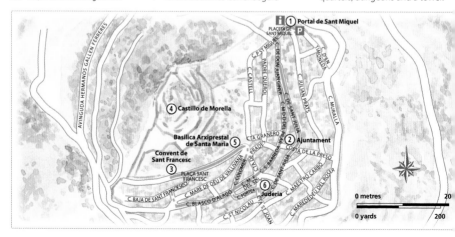

ce back from the castle, turn left
m the monastery and walk down-
to the **Basílica Arxiprestal de Santa
aría** ⑤. This church has a magni-
ently decorated carved spiral stair-
se leading to the choir loft.

ake the steps opposite the church
d continue down Carrer Colomer
meet the porticoed main street,
rrer Blasco d'Alagó. Almost directly
oss the street, between a souvenir
op and a bar, is a narrow, dark flight
roofed steps. Go down these and
rn left into the **Judería** ⑥, Morella's
edieval Jewish quarter. Go through
e arch and follow the street down-
l. Turn right down the stepped
eet at the end and take the first
t, Carrer de Noguer/Sant Julià (it
s two names). This leads to a fork
a shrine to St Julià, patron saint of
orella. Take the upper road, which
ns behind the town hall. This road
erges with Carrer Juan Giner. Carry
aight on to the souvenir shop on
e corner. Turn right onto the Plaçeta
Sant Miquel and to the car park.

*Take the CV14 northwest from the
wn. After 10 km (6 miles), turn left
to the CV124 to Forcall. Turn right
to the CV120 at Forcall and follow it
st La Mata de Morella. Turn left onto
e A226 (TE810) to reach Mirambel.*

Mirambel
ruel; 44141
rtly preserved, partly restored,
rambel seems frozen in the Middle
es. Upon entering through the
rtal de las Monjas Agustinas, look
to see the intricate carving above.
not miss looking into the shop
ehind the ruined castle), which is a
th-century baker's, now stocked
th regional Maestrazgo produce
cluding cheeses and hams.

*Continue southwest on the A226 to
ach Cantavieja. Park in the Plaza de
paña, just outside the Old Town.*

Cantavieja
ruel; 44140
e Old Town of Cantavieja is
etched along a ridge high above a
ver valley. Its main point of interest
the Plaza Mayor, the square which
ontains the town hall and is enclosed
three sides by beautiful buildings
golden stone. Off the main street,
alle Mayor, are several large houses

built by the rural nobility in the
17th and 18th centuries.

🚗 *Leave Cantavieja for Mora de
Rubielos on the A226, a dramatic
road, signed for Fortanete and Teruel,
to reach the Puerto de Cuarto Pelado
(1,650 m/5,450 ft). Turn left onto the
VF-TE-22 before Fortanete for
Valdelinares. Drive over the Puerto
Fortanete (1,800 m/5,950 ft) and at
the T-junction, turn left towards
Valedelinares. Turn right onto the
VF-TE-01 at the next junction, signposted "Estación de Esqui", which
goes through the ski resort (rather
than the town) of Valdelinares. At the
roundabout at the bottom of the hill,
turn left for Mora de Rubielos onto the
A228, which passes through La Virgen
de la Vega and Puerto de San Rafael
(1,550 m/5,100 ft) and leads to Mora
de Rubielos.*

④ Mora de Rubielos
Teruel; 44400
The main road into Mora de Rubielos
from the north is deflected around the
great square 14th-century Castillo de
Mora de Rubielos. Behind this, across
a pretty square, is the former collegiate
Església de Santa Maria la Mayor,
built in Gothic style. The rest of the
town, which includes some atmospheric streets and squares, and four
old gateways, shelters beneath these
two monumental buildings.

🚗 *Take the A232 southeast from the
town to Rubielos de Mora.*

Top Església de Santa Maria la Mayor, Mora de
Rubielos **Above** Intricate lattice work in Mirambel
Below Main gate to the 14th-century castle in
Mora de Rubielos

EAT AND DRINK

MORELLA

Fonda Moreno *moderate*
A simple, stylish place, this serves the
staples of Morella's cuisine: lamb, pork,
sausages, ham and truffles.
*Sant Nicolau 12, 12300; 964 160 105;
www.lafondamoreno.com*

Meson El Pastor *moderate*
This is a centrally located restaurant
serving the specialities of Morella,
including meat cooked with truffles.
*Cuesta Jovani 5 y 7, 12300; 964 160
249; www.mesondelpastor.com; open
for lunch only, except Sat; closed Wed*

MORA DE RUBIELOS

El Rinconcico *moderate*
Traditional Mediterranean cuisine with
Aragonese influences is served here.
*Santa Lucía 4, 44400; 978 806 063;
www.elrinconcico.com; closed Tue and
first fortnight of July*

Eat and Drink: inexpensive, under €20; moderate, €20–€40; expensive, over €40

the town hall. Be sure to make a stop at the church, **Ex-Colegiata de Santa Maria la Mayor** *(closed for restoration until 2012)*, which has the second widest Gothic nave in Spain. On a walk around the village, visitors will find many more well-preserved historic stone and timber buildings. Enjoy the spectacular view over the rooftops of Rubielos de Mora from the road towards Castelló.

Leave Rubielos de Mora and head northwards on the A1701. Along this road are two venerable villages, **Nogueruelas** and **Linares de Mora**. The latter has an ancient castle, vestiges of its walls and gateways, and an 18th-century clock tower.

🚗 *Continue on the same road, the A1701, as it goes through the Puerto de Linares (1,700 m/5,650 ft) to reach the next stop, Mosqueruela.*

Above left Puerto de Linares on the road to Mosquerela **Above right** Intricately-carved wooden window in Rubielos de Mora **Below** Looking over the rooftops of Rubielos de Mora

WHERE TO STAY

RUBIELOS DE MORA

La Villa *moderate*
Housed in a castle-like 16th-century house, La Villa has a fine restaurant.
Plaza del Carmen 2, 44415; 978 804 640; www.hotel-de-la-villa.com

IGLESUELA DEL CID
Hospederia de La Iglesuela del Cid *moderate*
More plush than the Maestrazgo's other hotels, this is a 17th-century mansion with a great restaurant.
Ondevilla 4, 44142 ; 964 443 476; www.arturocantoblanco.com

ARES DEL MAESTRE

Hotel d'Ares *inexpensive*
Located on the town square, this is a 12-room hotel with a restaurant.
Plaza Mayor 4, 12165; 964 443 007

Dry-stone Architecture
The natural abundance of limestone blocks littering the landscape, coupled with the need to control flocks of sheep, has left the Maestrazgo a legacy of dry-stone architecture, which UNESCO is considering adding to its World Heritage list. Around Iglesuela del Cid and Vilafranca del Cid, lengthy strings of walls, all without mortar, divide up the pastureland and enclosed droving lanes. Most ingenious of all are the circular shepherds' cabins with their domed rooms formed out of delicately balanced stones.

⑤ Rubielos de Mora
Teruel; 44415
That Rubielos was a well-to-do place between the 15th and 17th centuries can be seen in the opulence of its grand seigneurial mansions. One of the best of them, a beautiful Renaissance building, serves as

⑥ Mosqueruela
Teruel; 44410
The charm of this town lies in the fact that it has not yet been gentrified or restored and so gives a glimpse of the Maestrazgo before modernity arrived. There are some porticoes off the square beside the beautiful 13th- and 14th-century church and stretches of the town wall, together with five gateways, which are still intact.

Leave Mosqueruela on the A1701. There are many dry-stone walls and cabins on the stretch of road over the Puerto de Mosqueruela pass (1,500 m/4,850 ft).

🚗 *Continue on the A1701 which becomes the CV173 across the provincial border. The road is now narrower and rougher. Follow signs for the "Camino del Cid" (a tourist route that links places associated with the medieval hero, El Cid) near the chapel on the outskirts of the town; do not take the road which turns off to the left for Cantavieja. At the T-junction for Iglesuela del Cid, turn left onto the A227 for the town, or stop to see the Puente de la Pobleta de San Miguel, a 14th–16th-century humpbacked bridge, on the right.*

⑦ Iglesuela del Cid
Teruel; 44142
This small town has a nucleus of fine civic buildings around the church and town hall dating from its heyday

ween the 16th and 18th centuries. m the "back" of town (through the tal San Pablo), there is a good walk drive (3 km/2 miles each way) oss a bridge over a dry valley to the lated **Capilla de la Virgen del Cid**. m Iglesuela del Cid retrace the ute on the A227 to the junction the bridge and turn left onto the 15 for **Vilafranca del Cid**. The town s a museum explaining the dry- ne architecture of the region. er Vilafranca del Cid continue on e CV15 towards the Col de Ares ss (1,500 m/4,950 ft).

Continue on the CV15 and turn at the Col de Ares pass onto the 1260 for Ares del Maestre.

Ares del Maestre

stelló; 12165

e approach on the CV1260 to Ares l Maestre offers a breathtaking view the village. It is spectacularly situ- d beneath a 1,300-m (4,300-ft) high ck of the Mola d'Ares mountain. ghts of interest include the Gothic untamiento (town hall), the Neo-

Classical parish church, and the remains of a castle. Once at the village, an option is to climb up to the castle from where there is a great view of a massive sweep of uplands. To get there, take the narrow street to the left of the church, near the town hall. The path setting out from the right of the church is longer.

Above left Church spire in the town of Iglesuela del Cid **Above middle** Statue of a knight in Ares del Maestre **Above right** Classic medieval chapel just outside Mosqueruela **Below** Shepherds' cabins built into dry-stone walls beside the road near Iglesuela del Cid

EAT AND DRINK

There are very few restaurants in this region. Most of the hotels listed have their own restaurants.

DAY TRIP OPTIONS

For those who can only spend a night in the region, the itinerary can be divided into two parts with either Morella (on the N232) and Rubielos de Mora (on the A1701) as base.

Explore the northern mountains
Use Morella ➊ as a base and take a couple of hours to explore this old town before setting off. Drive to Mirambel ➋ and Cantavieja ➌, Iglesuela del Cid ➐ and finally to

Ares del Maestre ➑, the village sited beneath a spectacular high rock.

Follow the route to Mirambel and Cantavieja then take the A227 to La Iglesuela del Cid. Either return to Morella via Cinctorres on the CV125 or take the CV15 (as per the route) to Ares del Maestre and return on the CV12.

Two southern towns
Explore the beautiful Renaissance town of Rubielos de Mora ➎ to see

the church, and then head north on the A1701 road to Linares de Mora. From here, pick up the route to the town of Valdelinares and head through La Virgen de la Vega on the VF-TE-01 and then the A228 to arrive in Mora de Rubielos ➍. Visit the church, then the castle or just wander around its atmospheric streets and stop for a lazy lunch break.

Return along the A232 to Rubielos de Mora.

Eat and Drink: inexpensive, under €20; moderate, €20–€40; expensive, over €40

Behind the Costa Blanca

Xàtiva to Xàbia

Highlights

- **The Borgia dynasty**
  Discover the history of the infamous popes of Xàtiva

- **Mysterious caves**
  Explore a man-made labyrinth of caves chiselled into the side of a mountain in Bocairent

- **Secluded coves**
  Unwind on the secluded beaches of the Costa Blanca

- **Valencian cuisine**
  Enjoy delicious *paella* in its birthplace – the Valencian region

View of Bocairent from the Covetes dels Moros

Behind the Costa Blanca

The Costa Blanca is one of Spain's most popular tourist destinations, but the lush mountain terrain that lies in its interior is virtually unexplored. Those who do venture into its interior will discover sweeping plains dotted with mountaintop villages, castles and forts from centuries of Moorish rule. They will also stumble upon Baroque churches and townhouses characteristic of Valencia and Alicante. This drive starts in the rugged rural interior and sees the rocky, pine-covered mountains and gorges of the Sierra de Aitana open out onto the breathtaking blue of the Mediterranean Sea.

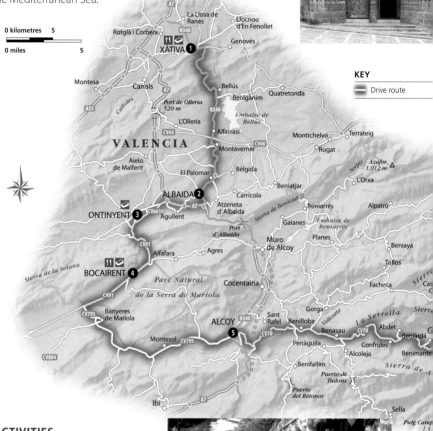

ACTIVITIES

Walk up to Xàtiva's famous castle

Explore the ancient caves in Bocairent

Hike or cycle through the Parc Natural de la Serra de Mariola

Go shopping in Gata de Gorgos, the "bazaar of the Costa Blanca"

Bask in a secluded cove in Xàbia

Entrance to the Gothic Església de Sant Bartomeu in Xàbia, *see p143* **Above** Steeple of the
ésia de l'Assumpció de Nostra Senyora overlooking Albaida, *see p141* **Below right** Steps
ing to the prison in the castle in Xàtiva, *see p140* **Below left** Colourful flamenco dresses and
ddresses at a stand in Xàbia, *see p143*

PLAN YOUR DRIVE

Start/finish: Xàtiva to Xàbia.

Number of days: 2–3, allowing half
a day to explore Xàtiva.

Distance: 175 km (110 miles).

Road conditions: Mostly well paved
and signposted with some steep
terrain and hairpin bends. There are
many roundabouts and one-way
streets in villages.

When to go: July and August can
be very hot. April to June and
September to late November are
good times to visit this region.

Opening hours: Shops are open
from 9:30am to 1:30pm, and from 4
to 8pm; restaurants open from 2 to
4pm, and from 8 to 11pm.

Main market days: Xàtiva: Tue;
Xàbia: Thu.

Shopping: Look out for handmade
jewellery and other local crafts in
Xàbia, and locally crafted hats, bamboo furniture, basketware and local
moscatel wine in Gata de Gorgos.

Major festivals: Xàtiva: Las Fallas,
16–19 Mar; Fira de agosto, 14–20
Aug; Xàbia: San Juan, 24 Jun; Moros Y
Cristianos, third weekend Jul.

DAY TRIP OPTIONS

Nature lovers and **adventure
enthusiasts** will enjoy exploring the
labyrinth of caves in Bocairent and a
visit to the Parc Natural de la Serra de
Mariola, while **families** will have a
great time on the beaches on the outskirts of Xàbia. For details, *see p143.*

Above Façade of the 15th-century Església de Sant Francesc, Xàtiva

VISITING XÀTIVA

Tourist Information
Alameda Jaume I, 50, 46800; 962 273 346; www.xativa.es; open Tue–Sun

Parking
Parking is available on Avinguda de la República Argentina, below the Old Town.

WHERE TO STAY

XÀTIVA

La Maga *inexpensive*
This hotel has stylish rooms decorated in neutral tones, and a Mediterranean cuisine restaurant.
C/ de les Animes 56, 46800; 962 288 292; www.grupolamaga.com

Hotel Mont Sant *moderate–expensive*
Xàtiva's best hotel is located at the base of the castle.
Subida al Castillo s/n, 46800; 962 275 081; www.mont-sant.com

ONTINYENT

Kazar *moderate*
This grandiose hotel, inspired by a Moorish palace and visited by the King of Spain, has lush and regal interiors.
C/ Dos de Mayo 117, 46670; 962 382 443; www.hotelkazar.com

BOCAIRENT

L'Estació *moderate–expensive*
Once a train station, this charming 13-room hotel with a restaurant has smartly decorated rooms and enchanting gardens.
Parc de L' Estació s/n, 46880; 962 350 000; www.hotelestacio.com

Les Casas de L'Agora *moderate*
This hotel is housed in a pretty Art Nouveau building and has period furniture to match.
Sor Piedad de la Cruz 3, 46880; 962 355 039; www.lagorahotel.com

❶ Xàtiva
Valencia; 46800

Dominated by the ruins of a Moorish-Gothic castle, Xàtiva is a plac steeped in history. The town is famed for its association with the region's most notorious family, the Borjas, better known by their Italian name as the Borgias. The two Borgia popes Calixtus III (1378 1458) and the famously corrupt Alexander VI (1431–1503), father o Lucrezia and Cesare Borgia, were both born here.

A one-hour walking tour

Mid-morning is the best time to start this walk. From the car park walk south on Carrer Baixada del Carme and then on Portal de Lleó to **La Seu** ①, Xàtiva's massive Mannerist-style cathedral with bronze sculptures of the two Borgia popes at its main entrance. Across the square is the 15th-century **Hospital Real** ②. Turn left into Carrer Noguera to arrive at the **Plaça del Mercat** ③, Xàtiva's main square. Exit via Carrer de les Botigues, and turn left into Calle del Peso to reach the **Museo de l'Almodí** ④, the municipal museum *(closed Mon)*, located in a mid-16th-century Renaissance-style building. Return to Carrer de les Botigues and walk downhill on Carrer Font d'Alós to a small square with a Baroque-style fountain. Across the square is the **Església de Sant Francesc** ⑤, a 15th-century church *(open for Mass only)*, and opposite this is **Café Sirope** ⑥, which serves great *horchata*, a drink made from crushed tiger nuts, and is a good place to take a break. Turn right into Carrer Montcada to see the **Palau del Marqués de Montortal** ⑦,

a medieval palace. Continue along the street to reach the **Plaça de la Trinitat** ⑧, a small square with a Gothic fountain bearing the Kingdo of Valencia's coat of arms. Continu in the same direction to reach thre pleasant squares. The first is Plaça Alexandre VI, named after the Borg pope Alexander VI, whose *casa na* (childhood home) is the austere 14th-century mansion on the righ Adjacent is the Plaça Benlloch with the **Font d'Almodar** ⑨, a fountain dating from the 18th century. Last there is the Plaça Sant Pere, which contains two important sites – the **Església de Sant Pere** ⑩ *(open daily for Mass)*, an impressive 15th-centu church, and the **Ex-Convento de S Onofre el Nou** ⑪, an attractive 18t century building topped by a fetch ing Baroque bell tower. The walk c be extended by a visit to Xàtiva's famous castle *(closed Mon)*. Turn rig on Carrer Fuente and right again in Carrer de San Cristòbal. Turn left ar then right onto Carrer de San José Bear to the left to emerge onto Carrer Rinconada Collar de la Palor then take the first left and walk up

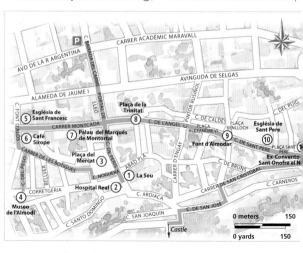

castle. It is a fairly steep climb on
. This lofty location, first fortified
he Iberians and Romans, bears
ence of Moorish occupation and
Gothic period. Divided into the
er and lower wings and spread
r a precarious U-shaped peak, this
contains chapels and prisons,
ets and ramparts, grottoes and
dens; it also has superb views of
surrounding countryside. Don't
s the **Capilla de Santa Maria**
ere the 11th Count of Urgell is
ed. After exploring the castle, go
k to Carrer de Sant Pere, and to
car park.

Follow the signs from the Plaza
anya (the busy roundabout next
he bullring) to the N340 towards
dia/Alicante. At Montaverner turn
onto the CV640 and then right
o the N340 to follow it southwards
Ibaida.

Albaida

ncia; 46860
village of Albaida has an
resting *casco antiguo* (Old Town)
ts size. Walk up the stairs to Carrer
t Miguel to the workshop of local
st **Rafael Amorós**. Further up is the
a Major and the Gothic **Església**
'Assumpció de Nostra Senyora
n daily). Behind it, the Plaça Pintor
rrelles features a couple of eclectic
seums. The first is the **Museu José**
rrelles *(closed Mon and Sun after-*
n), the ceramic-embellished *casa*
al of a local painter famous for his
ercolours. The second is the **Museu**
rnacional de Titelles *(open daily)*, a
ppet museum.
From the roundabout at the town's
e, follow signs onto the A7, then
u left onto the CV6610 to Ontinyent.

Ontinyent

ncia; 46870
tinyent is famous for its festival of
os y Cristianos, during which the
n hall dons a faux fortress-like
ade in commemoration of the
nquista. This sizeable town has an
iguing *casco antiguo* with ancient
ne portals, maze-like streets and
ding stairways laid out over differ-
levels, which give way to small pla-
shaded by clusters of palm trees.
oldest part of the town, La Vila,
es back to the 14th century and is

dominated by the majestic **Església**
de Santa Maria *(open for Mass only)* .
From the Plaza Major follow signs
onto the C40 that changes to CV81 and
then onto C3316 to reach Bocairent.

❹ Bocairent
Valencia; 46880
This atmospheric hilltop town is home
to two of the region's most fascinating sites. The first is the **Covetes dels**
Moros (Moors' Caves) *(closed Mon;*
guided tours only), a labyrinthine network of man-made caves chiselled
into a cliff face, connected to each
other on various levels and with
windows looking out over the valley.
The intention with which this awe-
inspiring structure was constructed is
still being debated, although the
general consensus is that the town's
original Arabian inhabitants used the
caves for storing harvested grain. The
second is the **Cava de Sant Blai** *(winter:*
closed Mon-Fri, summer: closed Mon), an
underground ice cave where snow
was sold for food preservation.
Continue along the same road, the
CV81. After 9 km (6 miles), turn left onto
the CV795 and drive through Banyeres
de Mariola, the entry point for the Parc
Natural de la Serra de Mariola, a nature
reserve, en route to Alcoy.

Above Ontinyent skyline punctuated with
church spires **Below** Ceiling of the Cava de
Sant Blai in Bocairent

EAT AND DRINK

XÀTIVA

Pebrenegre *moderate*
This restaurant specializes in rice
dishes – from the ubiquitous *paella* to
arroz negre (rice cooked in squid ink)
and *arroz a banda* (rice in fish stock).
Alameda Jaume I, 56, 46800; 962 280
723; www.pebrenegre.com

Carpanel *expensive*
A reputable restaurant, this place has
an exposed-brick interior courtyard
and an extensive range of local wines.
C/ Sant Francesc 38, 46800;
932 281 585; closed Mon

BOCAIRENT

Ca L'Alegre *moderate*
This stylish restaurant in Bocairent's
Old Town serves creative cuisine with
local wines. Set menus are available for
both lunch and dinner
C/ Bisbe Miró,10, 46880; 962 905 346;
www.calalegre.com; closed Mon

Restaurant L'Estació *moderate*
Fresh salads, pastas and soups
complement heartier meat and fish
dishes in this lovely restaurant, housed
in the L'Estació hotel.
Parc de L' Estació s/n, 46880; 962 350
000; www.hotelestacio.com

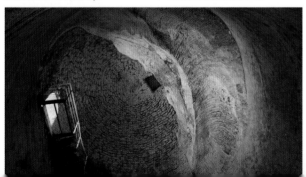

Above Pristine beach in Xàbia **Below left**
Belfry of the Església de Nuestra Senyora de
Asunción, Guadalest **Below right** Sunflower
field near the picturesque village of Mariola,
en route to Alcoy

Verdant Wilderness

The village of Banyeres de Mariola,
through which the route passes, is
the gateway to the Parc Natural de
la Serra de Mariola. The park has
majestic mountains and valleys with
fields of wild flowers, archaeological
finds, ancient hermitages and bub-
bling streams. Information on walks
and cycling in the park can be
obtained in Banyeres at the Centre
d'Interpretació Ull de Canals *(965 566
531; www.llardemariola.com)*. Located
in a historic farmhouse, the centre
also has a restaurant, bicycles for
hire and accommodation.

⑤ Alcoy
Alicante; 03801
Straddling two rivers and known as
the "city of bridges", Alcoy (Alcoi in
Valencian) is the largest town in the
region and a good spot for picking
up supplies, with a good selection of
shops and corporate-type hotels.
Alcoy has a handful of sights worth
seeking out. The gigantic **Església de
Santa Maria** *(open daily)* dominates the
cityscape with its glittering blue
dome, while the **Plaça de Dins** features
elegant porticoes and outdoor cafés.

🚗 *Leave via the CV70 to the east of
the city, following signs straight to
Benasau and Guadalest. It changes to
CV755 near Benimantell. Park in the
main plaza on the outskirts.*

⑥ Guadalest
Alicante; 03517
The approach to the dramatic clifftop
village of Guadalest is spectacular. The
old part of this village is accessible
only on foot through a single entry:
a sloping tunnel cut into the rock on
which the ruins of a Wagnerian castle

and the belfry of the church, the
Nuestra Señora de la Asunción are
precariously perched. The **Castell d
Guadalest** *(open daily)*, originally a
Moorish fort, was partially destroy
by an earthquake in the 17th centu
After exploring the castle, access t
which is through the Casa Orduña
wander around the plaza on the
village's upper plateau and take in
the views of the gorges and rocky
mountains, some of which are the
highest in the sierra. The **Museo de
Micro-Miniaturas** *(open daily)* displ
copies of Goya's *Le Maja Desnuda*
(The Nude Maja) painted on the
wing of a fly and *Los Fusilamiento c
3 de Mayo* (The Shootings of May
Third) painted on a grain of rice.

🚗 *Follow the CV755 out of Guadale
through the Sierra de Aitana mount
range to turn left onto the AP7 mot
way. Follow signs for Xàbia and lea
the highway at exit 63 (right) to tur
left onto the N332 to Gata de Gorgo*

⑦ Gata de Gorgos
Alicante; 03740
The little whitewashed village of Ga
de Gorgos is known as the "bazaar
the Costa Blanca" for its strong arti
heritage. Shops line its streets selli
hats, bamboo furniture, colourful
basketware and local *moscatel* win
At the end of September, during th
festival of **San Miguel**, the town ho
an artisan fair.

🚗 *Leave on the N332 and turn righ
onto the CV734, following signs to
Xàbia. Parking is available at the Pla
de la Constitución Española.*

Xàbia

cante; 03730

hough, like many of Spain's coastal destinations, Xàbia (Jàvea in stilian) has been urbanized, its Old Town, long, sandy beaches and Iden coves make for a wonderful stop along the Costa Blanca.

rrently undergoing a major facelift, ia's Old Town, originally a walled age, is being steam-cleaned and eled back to its former glory. The vn centre is perched on a hill, a rt way inland, on the site of a h-century Iberian walled settle- nt. Steep streets, with whitewashed Idings and handsome brick town uses, lead to the **Església de Sant tomeu** (closed Thu, Sun), which dates ck to the 16th century and was tified to serve its congregation as efuge in times of invasion. It has enings in the doors through which ssiles could be aimed at attackers. xt to this is the ajuntament (town l), with a range of architectural ments from the medieval he Neo-Classical. Close by, the **iseo Soler Blasco** (closed Mon) is elegant edifice containing nological artifacts pertaining the region.

Xàbia's port curves around the rious **Platja de la Grava**, a picture- stcard sandy beach skirted by a menade and lined with dozens of tdoor cafés. At its northern end is narina and the **Duanes del Mar**, ere local fishermen sell their daily tch. Dazzling views of the bay of bia, whose beaches are free of gh-rise buildings, can be seen from highest point, the **Cap de Sant toni**. Walking tracks sprawl out all

over this small cape through a nature park known as the **Parc Natural de El Montgó**, after the mountain peak at its centre. A popular route is the one- hour, mid-level **Ruta de Sant Antoni- Molins**, which takes visitors to one of the town's many landmarks, a cluster of abandoned windmills, most of which date back to the 14th century. The remains of 12 windmills, 11 of which are within the Parc Natural de El Montgó, overlook the cape. With a decline in wheat production by the end of the 18th century, these wind- mills went out of use and their iron mechanisms and fans were disman- tled, leaving only the massive brick bases guarding the bay of Xàbia. Given their proximity to each other, they are a striking sight.

Above Boats moored at the northern end of the port in Xàbia **Below** Locally crafted basketware on display in Gata de Gorgos

VISITING XÀBIA

Tourist Information
Plaça de la Iglesia 4, 03730; 965 794 356; www.xabia.org

EAT AND DRINK

XÀBIA

Posit Restaurant moderate
This seafood restaurant serves up succulent paella and other rice dishes local to this part of the coast.
Plaza Alimirante Bastarreche 11, 03730; 965 793 063

Restaurant El Rodat expensive
Try the menu desgustación, at this restaurant housed in the Hotel El Rodat, for a full taste of the highly creative cuisine.
Ctra. Cabo de Nao, 03730; 966 470 710; www.elrodat.com

DAY TRIP OPTIONS

This route can be easily divided into two distinct day excursions, the first covering the inland countryside behind the Costa Blanca and the second the coast itself, combined with a visit to the famous castle of Guadalest. The main access road for Xàtiva is the A7 while Xàbia is served by two main roads: the paying AP7 and the toll-free N332.

Caves and parkland
Using Xàtiva ❶ as a base, head to Bocairent ❹ to see the astounding labyrinthine Covetes del Moros.

Continue to Banyeres de Mariola, the gateway to the Parc Natural de la Serra de Mariola, which offers several walking and cycling routes.

From Xàtiva follow signs to the A7/ CV645 from the roundabout at the Avinguda de les Corts Catalans. Continue along the A7/CV645, turn right onto the CV6610 and then the CV81 to pass Ontinyent and follow the signs to Bocairent. After visiting Bocairent, continue on the same road, then turn off into the CV795 and follow signs to Banyeres de Mariola, the gateway to the Parc Natural de la Serra de Mariola.

Castle and beaches
With Xàbia ❽ as a base, visit the many beaches and coves that are located on its outskirts. Guadalest ❻ is a popu- lar excursion from Xàbia. It is best to go in the afternoon when it is quieter and there are fewer bus tours.

From Xàbia, follow the Carretera de la Granadella to its southernmost point to reach the Cala de la Granadella. To reach Guadalest, take the CV734 then the N332 to the AP7 in the direction of Benidorm. Take exit 64, then follow the CV755 mountain road to the Castell de Guadalest.

Eat and Drink: inexpensive, under €20; moderate, €20–€40; expensive, over €40

Along the Duero

Peñafiel to Clunia

Highlights

- **Charming town**
  Wander around the streets of Peñafiel and visit the impressive castle perched high above the town

- **The wine route**
  Stop by the bodegas of La Ribera del Duero for a taste of their world-renowned wines

- **Gastronomic delights**
  Excite your tastebuds in Aranda del Duero with great *asadores* or restaurants specializing in local delicacies

- **Ancient ruins**
  Explore the ruins of the city of Clunia, which date back to the pre-Roman occupation of the Iberian Peninsula

Medieval Castillo de Peñafiel in the lush Duero valley

Along the Duero

Located in the southerly swath of the regions of Burgos and Valladolid, La Ribera del Duero gets its name from the Duero river that snakes through it. The river runs all the way to Oporto in neighbouring Portugal, and throughout history has been the lifeblood of the agriculture and the crafts around it. High-quality wine is produced in this region and its production started here over 2,000 years ago. With its blankets of vineyards and hundreds of bodegas hugging the river's edge, La Ribera del Duero is a popular destination for day-tripping Madrileños who come here for a Sunday lunch of *lechazo* (slow-roasted lamb) in one of the many famed *asadores* (restaurants that specialize in Castillian-style roast meats) that dot the region. Afterwards, there are forests and valleys to stroll through, castles to explore and ancient villages to discover.

Above Timber-framed Plaza de los Duques in Peñaranda de Duero, *see p150* **Below** Renaissa façade of Iglesia de Santa María in Gumiel de Izán, *see p150*

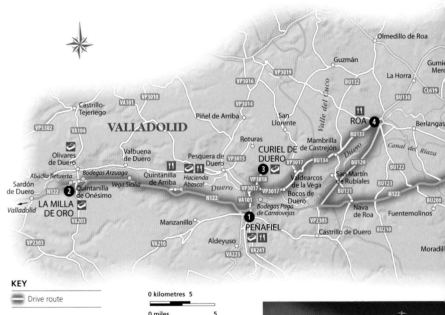

KEY

━━ Drive route

0 kilometres 5

0 miles 5

ACTIVITIES

Drive up to the hilltop castle in Peñafiel

Go wine tasting in La Ribera del Duero's many bodegas

Take a walk around Curiel, located in the verdant Valle del Cuco

Enjoy a lazy picnic beside the Duero river

Wander the grounds at the ancient Monasterio de Santa María de la Vid

ve left Site of Roman ruins in Clunia, *see p151* **Above right** Old-fashioned bodega in Aranda de ro, *see p150* **Below** Traditional stone bodegas in Peñafiel, *see p148*

PLAN YOUR DRIVE

Start/finish: Peñafiel to Clunia.

Number of days: 2–3, allowing half a day to explore Peñafiel.

Distances: 175 km (110 miles).

Road conditions: The roads here are very good. There is some heavy traffic along the N122.

When to go: September is when the grapes ripen. The warmest months are from May to Jul.

Market days: Peñafiel: Thu; Roa: Tue; Aranda de Duero: Sat; Peñaranda de Duero: Fri.

Shopping: Wine is available from the bodegas to speciality shops in the villages. The tourist offices in Peñafiel and Aranda de Duero have inform-ation on which bodegas are open to the public for tours and tastings.

Opening hours: Shops are open from 9:30am to 1:30pm, and from 4 to 8pm. Restaurants are open from 2 to 4pm, and from 8 to 11pm.

Major festivals: Peñafiel: Fiestas de Nuestra Señora y San Roque, 14–18 Aug; **Roa:** Romería de la Virgen de la Vega, 8 Sep; **Aranda de Duero:** Fiestas Patronales, 8–16 Sep.

DAY TRIP OPTIONS

Wine lovers can drive along La Milla de Oro, the golden route for wine, and visit the many bodegas that dot the area. **History buffs** should head to Aranda de Duero, Peñandra de Duero, the Monasterio de Santa María de la Vid and Clunia to see their castles, churches and Roman ruins. For details, *see p151.*

Above Peñafiel castle in the Duero valley

VISITING PEÑAFIEL

Tourist Information
*Plaza San Miguel de Reoyo 2, 47300;
983 881 526; open daily*

Parking
Visitors can park in the public car park at the base of castle.

WHERE TO STAY

PEÑAFIEL

Hotel Convento Las Claras *expensive*
Set in the historic heart of Peñafiel, this hotel is housed in a converted convent.
*Plaza Adolfo Muñoz Alonso s/n,
47300; 983 878 168;
www.hotelconventolasclaras.com*

LA MILLA DE ORO

Casa Rural El Agapio *inexpensive*
This is a cheerful *casa rural* offering rustic charm and comfort.
*C/ Santa Maria 11, 47359, Olivares de
Duero; 983 680 495; www.agapio.com*

Hacienda Abascal *expensive*
An avant-garde structure that rises up from among the vines, this wine hotel is located by the Duero.
*Ctra. N122, Km 321, 5, 47360,
Quintanilla de Arriba; 902 109 902;
www.agapio.com*

Hotel Arzuaga *expensive*
Surrounded by vineyards, this five-star hotel has a wine-therapy spa and lets guests participate in the grape harvest and hunting deer on the hotel grounds. It also has a great restaurant.
*Ctra. N122, 47350, Quintanilla de
Onésimo; 983 681 146; www.
arzuaganavarro.com*

CURIEL DE DUERO

Residencia Real Castillo de Curiel
expensive
The old castle overlooking Curiel has been converted into a luxury hotel.
*Camino de Curiel s/n, 47316; 983 880
401; www.castillodecuriel.com*

❶ Peñafiel
Valladolid; 47300

Built along the verdant banks of the Duero river, dominated by an ancient castle and with a surprisingly eclectic clutch of specialist museums, Peñafiel is the best introduction to the region of La Ribera del Duero.

A two-hour walking tour

Start at the car park and ascend on the marked track to the **Castillo de Peñafiel** ①. Dating from the 15th century, it offers impressive views over the entire region. The structure of the castle has often been compared with that of a huge boat. The castle also houses the Museo Provincial del Vino *(closed Mon)* in its patio.

Go back down to the car park and follow the perimeter of the Parque de San Vicente to the left. Walk down Calle Varquilla and then take a left to enter **Plaza del Coso** ②. This wide, sand-covered plaza is often used for bullfighting and festive events and is flanked by traditional housing, with decorative hanging balconies and wooden adornment. Backtrack along Calle Derecha al Coso, passing the medieval **Casas Hidalgas** ③ on the left and the quaint chimney-like ventilation shafts of ancient underground **bodegas** ④ on the right. Continue on this road, which soon turns left, till the **Iglesia de Santa María** ⑤, a 17th-century church with a Baroque bell tower. The church houses a Museo Comarcal de Arte Sacro *(open daily)*, with a collection 12th–15th-century religious objec[t] made from precious metals. Turn le[ft] up Calle Episcopal and walk down Calle Reoyo to the Plaza de San Miguel Reoyo. This is where the tourist office and the **Museo de la Radio** ⑥ *(open daily)*, with exhibits covering the history of the mediu[m] are located. On the right is the 16th century **Iglesia de San Miguel** ⑦ *(open for Mass only)*, whose austere Romanesque walls hide a rich interio[r] with Baroque retables. Cross the Duero via the Puente de la Judería. Under the bridge is a parkland whe[re] visitors can have a picnic. Cross the bridge to reach the 17th-century **Convento de Santa Clara** ⑧, which has now been converted into a ho[tel.] Retrace the route to the car park.

🚗 *Head northwest on Calle de Subi[da]
al Castillo and turn right on the N12[2.]
At 1 km (0.6 miles) towards Aranda [de]
Duero, turn right to reach Bodegas
Pago de Carraovejas.*

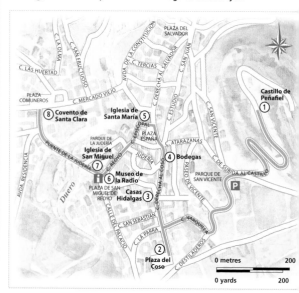

La Milla de Oro
lladolid; 47340

s stretch of road, locally known as Milla de Oro (Golden Mile), offers ood insight into the region's wine ture. The first vineyard that comes just outside Peñafiel is **Bodegas ço de Carraovejas**. After a stop here urn to the N122 and turn right vards Valladolid. At 4 km (2 miles) er Quintanilla de Arriba is **Hacienda ascal**, an adobe-style bodega, ich also houses a good hotel d restaurant. Return to the N122 d soon the **Vega Sicilia** will come on the right. The estate has a plant- on of 2.5 sq km (1 sq mile) of eyards. After a stop here, return to e N122 and turn right towards intanilla de Onésimo. Get onto rretera de Soria on the right for the owned **Bodegas Arzuaga**, which various tours offers, from wine tings to visiting the vineyards and e production facilities. Just before rdón de Duero is **Abadía Retuerta**, ineyard located in a beautiful th-century abbey.

Return to the N122 and head back *Peñafiel. On approach, follow signs* *the VA101. Then turn right onto the* *3017/VP3018 to the village of Curiel* *Duero. Park near the Iglesia de Santa* *ría at the entrance of the village.*

Curiel de Duero
lladolid; 47316

e tiny village of Curiel de Duero is e of the prettiest in the Valle del co, a picturesque valley of forests,

wheat and sunflower fields, and home to foxes, rabbits and partridges. The valley is popular with locals for walking and hunting. Curiel's most striking building is the Gothic-Mudéjar **Iglesia de Santa María** *(open for Mass only or ask at the tourist office during the summer months)*. On the highest point of Curiel and perched on a rocky platform is the 12th-century fortress-like castle, now converted into a hotel.

🚗 *Leave Curiel on the VP3018 and turn left onto VP3017. At Valdearcos de la Vega, take the BU134. Get onto the BU133 after Mambrilla de Castrejón and follow signs to Roa. Park on the outskirts of the village.*

④ Roa
Burgos; 09300

The bustling, largely industrial little village of Roa has a secret gem: the **Colegiata de Nuestra Señora de la Asunción** *(open Jul–Aug, rest of the year open for Mass only)*. Situated on Roa's Plaza Mayor, this imposing 16th-century building exudes typical Castilian sobriety from the exterior, with its massive stone walls and rectangular bell tower. In contrast, the church's interior of bare ivory-coloured walls, soaring columns and elegant, carved vaults is simple and uplifting. Some noted decorative pieces here are attributed to a celebrated sculptor of the period, Gil de Siloé.

🚗 *Exit Roa on the BU120. When it joins the N122, turn left, following signs to Aranda de Duero. Park on the outskirts of the old city by the river.*

VISITING THE BODEGAS

Bodegas Pago de Carraovejas
Camino Carraovejas s/n, 47300, Peñafiel; 983 878 020; www. pagodecarraovejas.com

Hacienda Abascal
Ctra. N122, 47360, Quintanilla de Arriba; 902 109 902

Vega Sicilia
Ctra. N122, 47359, Valbuena de Duero; 983 680 147; www.vega-sicilia.com

Bodegas Arzuaga
Ctra. N122, 47350, Quintanilla de Onésimo; 983 681 146; www.arzuaganavarro.com

Abadía Retuerta
Ctra. N122, 47340, Sardón de Duero; 983 680 314; www.abadia-retuerta.es; tours need to be booked in advance

EAT AND DRINK

PEÑAFIEL

Molino de Palacios *expensive*
This is the best place in Peñafiel to try *lechazo*, baby lamb that has been slow-roasted in a clay oven.
Avda. de la Constitución 16, 47300; 983 880 505; www.molinodepalacios.com

LA MILLA DE ORO

Durius River Cafe *moderate*
Housed inside the Hacienda Abascal winery, this restaurant offers imaginative cuisine using local ingredients.
Ctra. N122, 47360, Quintanilla de Arriba; 902 109 902; www.haciendas-espana.com

ROA

Restaurante Nazareno *expensive*
The Restaurante Nazareno serves the most succulent *lechazo* in Ribera del Duero.
Puerta Palacio 1, 09300; 947 540 214

Above View of the Duero river over the Puente de la Judería, Peñafiel **Below** Iglesia de Santa María in Curiel de Duero

Above left Magnificent Monasterio de Santa Maria de la Vid **Above right** Bodega in Peñaranda de Duero **Below** Roman amphitheatre in Clunia

WHERE TO STAY

ARANDA DE DUERO

Hotel Tres Condes *moderate*
This landmark hotel is located in the new part of town. Rooms are functional and have been recently spruced up.
Avda. de Castilla 66, 09400; 947 502 400; www.hoteltrescondes.com

AROUND ARANDA DE DUERO

Hotel Tudanca Aranda *moderate*
One of the best near the city, the Tudanca Aranda is located 6 km (4 miles) south of Aranda de Duero. The rooms in this hotel are spacious and comfortable, and the in-house restaurant is highly recommended.
NI (Autovía del Norte) Km 152, 09470, Fuentespina–Aranda de Duero; 947 506 011; www.tudanca-aranda.com

AROUND GUMIEL DE IZÁN

El Rincón de la Tía Elena *inexpensive*
This cheerful *casa rural*, located in Oquillas, 7 km (4 miles) north of Gumiel de Izán, offers homespun comfort and wholesome home-cooked meals.
C/ Real 31, 09350, Oquillas; 685 920 955; www.elrincondelatiaelena.com

PEÑARANDA DE DUERO

Posada Ducal *moderate*
A 12th-century building, this hotel is decorated in regal style, with antiques and period features. It also has an excellent in-house restaurant.
Plaza Mayor 1, 09410; 947 552 347; www.laposadaducal.com

MONASTERIO DE SANTA MARÍA DE LA VID

Hospedería El Vid *moderate*
The residence inside the Monasterio de Santa María de la Vid is a good place for a simple and quiet stay.
Ctra. Soria La Vid de Aranda, 09471; 947 530 510; www.monasteriodelavid. org; minimum stay of two nights

⑤ Aranda de Duero
Burgos; 09400
Although small in size, the capital of La Ribera del Duero has much to offer with its good selection of shops, restaurants and a maze of ancient underground bodegas. The town's main sight is the imposing 15th-century **Iglesia de Santa María** *(open for Mass only)*, with a richly rendered threshold. Behind the church is another important religious edifice, the **Iglesia de San Juan Bautista** *(closed Mon in Jan and Feb)*, which houses a **Museo de Arte Sacro** *(closed Mon)*. Opposite this, is the **Casa de las Bolas** *(closed Mon)*, which has a collection of paintings from the 15th to the 20th centuries. Walking in the opposite direction will lead to Aranda's main square, which is a good place to relax.
🚗 *Leave town on the N1A and turn right onto the A1 heading northwards towards Burgos. Take exit 171 and follow signs to Gumiel de Izán.*

⑥ Gumiel de Izán
Burgos; 09370
Santo Domingo de Guzman (1175–1221), the monk who founded the order of Dominicans is Gumiel de

Izán's most famous resident. He spe[nt] his infancy in a medieval home th[at] still stands in the village's main squa[re.] It is one of a handful of well-preserv[ed] whitewashed structures with column-like supports which form arcades. Opposite is the **Iglesia de Santa María** *(open daily Jul–Sep, and open for Mass only for the rest of the ye[ar] or by request; 947 544 018)*, an impos[ing] structure, considering the size of t[he] tiny village, built between the 14th and 17th centuries with an elabor[ate] Renaissance portal.
🚗 *Leave Gumiel de Izán on the BU922 and turn left on the BU912. G[o] through Villanueva de Gumiel on th[e] BU912 following signs to Peñarand[a] de Duero. Go through Quemada an[d] turn left onto the BU925 towards Peñaranda de Duero.*

⑦ Peñaranda de Duero
Burgos; 09410
Behind the remains of the ancient stone walls of this little village lies [a] real surprise: the elegant **Plaza de l[os] Duques** (Plaza Mayor) which is line[d] with porticoed timber-framed buil[d]ings. Set among the traditional me[di]eval homes is the **Iglesia de Santa**

Where to Stay: inexpensive, under €70; moderate, €70–€120; expensive, over €120

a *(closed Mon)*, which features
man busts, transferred here from
digs at nearby Clunia, and heavy
oque detailing on the portal.
posite is the superb Renaissance
acio de los Zuñiga y Avellanda
sed Mon), once home of the noble
nily of Zuñiga y Avellanda. Stroll
to the castle (car access is
icult) overlooking Peñaranda de
ero which affords great views of
area.

Take the BU924 when coming
of the Plaza Mayor towards the
nasterio de Santa María de la Vid.
ce there, park outside the monastery.

Monasterio de Santa
aría de la Vid
gos; 09471

e impressive monastery, located
the banks of the Duero, is home
one of the oldest monastic orders
pain. The monastery was inspired
a group of French monks devoted
San Norberto, though today it is
by the Order of Augustines. The
fice spans from the 12th to the
h centuries, and has a variety of
es from Romanesque to Gothic,
aissance and Neo-Classical. Visitors
wander around the lovely gar-
ns that surround the monastery.
see the library (one of the largest
religious manuscripts in Spain),
ister and museum *(closed Mon)*,
tors will need to take a tour, which
s about an hour.

Leave on the BU923 north from the
nastery. At Peñaranda de Duero
n right onto the BU925 and keep on
s road. After Coruña del Conde look
for a sign indicating Clunia.

⑨ Clunia
Burgos; 09454

The site of Clunia, on a ridge 1,000 m
(3,300 ft) above sea level, had first
been occupied by the Iberians. Many
centuries later, when the Romans
took over, it became one of the most
important strongholds in Hispania
Tarraconensis. Forty thousand people
lived there between the 1st and 3rd
centuries AD. The Romans' logical
urban planning of Clunia is evident
from what remains today, especially
the surprisingly intact **amphitheatre**,
which was cleverly placed in order to
incorporate a view of the Sierra de la
Demanda as a backdrop, and **Los
Arcos** *(closed Mon)*, the expansive thermal baths. Three impressive mosaic
works, which once graced the floors
of private homes, still stand.

Above View of the valley below from the
castle in Peñaranda de Duero **Below** Façade
of the Iglesia Colegio in Peñaranda de Duero

EAT AND DRINK

ARANDA DE DUERO
Tapas in Aranda de Duero
inexpensive
The old city in Aranda de Duero is
swarming with good tapas bars. Try
morcilla (a local sausage similar to
English black pudding) or *pimientos del
piquillo* (roasted red peppers).

El Lagar de Isilla *moderate*
An eatery that offers great tapas in the
front bar, a formal rear dining room
and an ancient underground bodega.
C/ Isilla 18, 09400; 947 510 683;
www.lagarisilla.es; closed Sun dinner

GUMIEL DE IZÁN
El Zaguan de Gumiel *moderate*
Home-cooked fare of grilled meat and
gigantic salads are the highlights here.
Try the local *torta de anis* for dessert.
C/ Real 54–56, 09370; 947 544 141

PEÑARANDA DE DUERO
Señorio de Velez *moderate*
The Señorio de Velez serves comfort
food favourites such as grilled lamb
chops, fish soup and rice pudding.
Plaza Duques de Alba 1, 09410;
947 552 201

DAY TRIP OPTIONS

his drive can be divided into two
ay trips with visitors being based
ither in Peñafiel or in Aranda de
Duero. The autovía (A1) and the
J122 easily access all the sights
this area.

Wine tasting

tart the day at the ancient town
f Peñafiel ① and explore its many
nuseums and the castle. Then spend
he rest of the day visiting, tasting
nd buying wine at the many
odegas along La Milla de Oro ②.

Leave Peñafiel on the N122 west
towards Valladolid to visit the bodegas
and return the same way.

Churches, monastery and
Roman ruins
Visit the churches in the capital of La
Ribera del Duero, Aranda de Duero ⑤,
and stop by its many restaurants and
bodegas. Head to the Monasterio de
Santa Maria de la Vid ⑧, located on
the banks of the Duero river. Take a
stroll around its lovely grounds. Visit
Peñaranda de Duero ⑦, a tiny village
crowned by a castle with great views

of one of the most charming villages
in Burgos. Then head north to Clunia
⑨ to see the ancient Roman ruins,
and the amphitheatre which is still in
spectacular condition.

Take the N122 from Aranda de Duero
to the Monasterio de Santa María de la
Vid. Then head north on the BU923 for
Peñaranda de Duero. From Peñaranda
take the BU925. After Coruña del
Conde look out for a left for Clunia. To
return to Aranda de Duero, keep on the
BU925, which goes back to the town.

Eat and Drink: inexpensive, under €20; moderate, €20–€40; expensive, over €40

The Spine of Castile

Toros de Guisando to Ciudad Rodrigo

Highlights

- **Mountain landscapes**
  Explore some of the least visited parts of Spain around Valle del Alberche, with stunning views

- **Regional architecture**
  Stop in remote mountain villages, where traditional half-timbered houses lean over cobbled streets

- **Charcuterie and honey**
  Enjoy one of Spain's most noted culinary regions, Castilla y León

- **Historic Ciudad Rodrigo**
  Visit the fortified town that challenged French, Spanish and British soldiers

Peak of Peña de Francia overlooking the surrounding plains and rolling hills

The Spine of Castile

West of Madrid, the craggy heights of the spectacular Sierra de Gredos, the Sierra de la Peña de Francia and several smaller mountain ranges offer a wonderful contrast to the more familiar plains of central Spain. Between the mountains, this drive winds through traditional farming country cut by valleys and streams. En route are villages dotted with medieval houses and cobbled streets, high altitude pastures above the tree line and fine old towns full of historical sites.

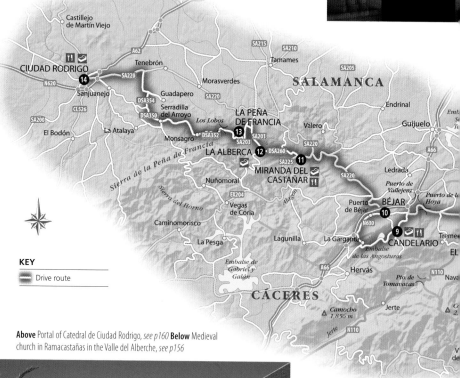

KEY

Drive route

Above Portal of Catedral de Ciudad Rodrigo, *see p160* **Below** Medieval church in Ramacastañas in the Valle del Alberche, *see p156*

0 kilometres 10

0 miles 10

ACTIVITIES

Hike on a Roman road to the pass of Puerto del Pico

Take a walk between the lakes and peaks at Hoyos del Espino

Relax in Candelario, lulled by the calming sound of rushing water in the town's canals

Walk in the footsteps of Wellington o the ramparts of Ciudad Rodrigo

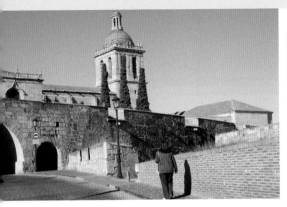

walls of Ciudad Rodrigo in Salamanca, *see p160* **Below** Ibex grazing in the Valle del Tormes, *see p158*

PLAN YOUR DRIVE

Start/finish: Toros de Guisando to Ciudad Rodrigo.

Number of days: 4, allowing a day to explore Ciudad Rodrigo.

Distance: 465 km (290 miles).

Road conditions: Mostly well surfaced; occasionally narrow and winding. Higher roads may be affected by snow closures during winter.

When to go: In summer, the mountains can be crowded, but the weather is perfect. Spring and autumn are sometimes wet, but quieter.

Opening hours: Most museums and monuments are closed on Mondays. On other days, they open from 10am to 2pm, and in some cases, reopen from 5 to 8pm.

Main market days: Arenas de San Pedro: Wed; Béjar: Thu; La Alberca: Fri; Ciudad Rodrigo: Tue, Sat.

Shopping: Dry-cured ham and honey are the regional specialities.

Major festivals: Arenas de San Pedro: Virgen del Pilar, 8 Sep; La Alberca: Fiestas de la Asunción, 15 Aug; Ciudad Rodrigo: Carnaval del Toro, Feb.

DAY TRIP OPTIONS

History buffs will enjoy a visit to the castles in the villages of Arenas de San Pedro and Mombeltrán, while **architecture enthusiasts** should head to Ciudad Rodrigo and La Peña de Francia. For details, *see p161.*

Top Stone bulls of Guisando **Above left** Hiking up to Puerto del Pico pass **Above right** Castillo de Don Álvaro de Luna, Arenas de San Pedro

VISITING TOROS DE GUISANDO

From Madrid, take the A5–E90 Carretera de Extremadura as far as Navalcarnero (exit 32). At the roundabout, take the M507 and continue on it (direction Villamanta) until Aldea del Fresno. At the next roundabout turn left towards Mendrida and then right onto the M507 towards Villa del Prado. Turn right onto the N403 (direction Ávila). After San Martin de Valdeiglesias, turn left onto the AV904 for Toros de Guisando.

WHERE TO STAY

AROUND TOROS DE GUISANDO

Hotel Toros de Guisando *moderate*
This is a good-value hotel with large rooms located 10 km (6 miles) north of the bulls in the town of El Tiemblo.
Avda. de Madrid, 05270, El Tiemblo; 918 627 192; www.torosdeguisando.com

ARENAS DE SAN PEDRO

Hosteria Los Galayos *moderate*
A decently maintained hotel, this place also has a restaurant.
Plaza Condestable Dávalos 2, 05400; 920 371 379; www.losgalayos.com

AROUND CASTILLO DE LOS DUQUES DE ALBURQUERQUE

Hotel Marji *inexpensive*
Located to the south of Mombeltrán, this hotel has great views of the castle.
C/ Calvo Sotelo 64, 05410, Mombeltrán; 920 386 031

① Toros de Guisando
Ávila; 05270
The ancient stone carvings of four life-size bulls face the hill of Guisando in the eastern foothills of the Sierra de Gredos. The bulls are examples of *verracos*, granite megalithic sculptures of animals, found in a few provinces in Spain and Portugal. Although the origins of the Bulls of Guisando are uncertain, it is believed they were carved by a pre-Celtic people called the Vettones around the 2nd century BC.
🚗 *Drive north to the N403 and turn left (direction Ávila) to follow the highway past the slip road for El Tiemblo and, on the left, the Embalse del Burgillo reservoir. Just past El Barraco, look out for the small sign for the AV905 to Béjar.*

② Valle del Alberche
Ávila; 05134
After Navarredondilla, the AV905 descends into the Alberche valley, offering a scenic route west, zigzagging over the ridges to the village of Navatalgordo. Stop at the viewpoint 7 km (4 miles) after the village. Shortly after, the route cuts sharply left onto the AVP419, crossing the Alberche river on a new bridge that stands next to an old, pretty one. Look out for the traditional, conical haystacks typical of the region. From here onward, there are several fine

viewpoints, including a superb vista from a rocky bluff on the left. At Navarrevisca, turn right onto the AV913 and drive up to the Collado de Serranillos pass (1,600 m/5,200 f) from where are more good views. At San Esteban del Valle turn left onto the AVP706 and descend into Santa Cruz del Valle, passing several shady picnic spots en route; the last of these has excellent views across the valley to the castle in Mombeltrán.
🚗 *Drive through Santa Cruz del Valle to meet the N502. Turn left and drive into Ramacastañas. At the main roundabout, exit onto the AVP708 for the Cuevas del Águila.*

③ Cuevas del Águila
Ávila; 05400
Also known as the Grutas del Águila, these interesting "eagle caves" (open daily; 920 377 107), discovered in 1963 consist of a water-formed limestone cavern. Guided tours run mornings and afternoons throughout the year, offering views of the multihued formations, coloured by mineral deposits and organic material mixing with the limestone accretions. There is a lovely picnic area, bar and restaurant outside.
🚗 *Return to Ramacastañas, take the second exit from the roundabout onto the AV925, and follow signs for Arenas de San Pedro. Park by the castle.*

Arenas de San Pedro
la; 05400

 small town of Arenas is the
nmercial hub for the southern
dos and acts as a base for visits
he Parque Regional de la Sierra
Gredos. The town is dominated
the 15th-century **Castillo de Don
aro de Luna** *(open to the public; 969
001)*. The riverside decking over-
king the Arenal and its medieval
dge is a pleasant spot to relax.

ake the AVP713 west out of Arenas
Guisando, a picturesque village well
rth a visit. From Guisando take the
?712 to **El Hornillo**, which has a
cina natural, a lovely semi-natural
mming pool, on the Cantos river.
en take the AVP711 to **El Arenal**;
easily accessible hiking route to the
dos park starts just out of the town.
*From El Arenal, follow the cobbled
eet. At the end of it, turn right onto
 unsigned Carretera Forestal de las
jadas. In Mombeltrán, turn right
to the N502, and then left.*

Castillo de los Duques de
burquerque
la; 05410

ch its lofty round towers hidden by
ne trees, the 15th-century Castillo
los Duques de Alburquerque rises
m the south side of Mombeltrán.
e tourist office on the main road can
anize short tours.
*Rejoin the N502 that runs through
mbeltrán and head north towards*

*Ávila and the Puerto del Pico pass,
via Cuevas del Valle. Be careful of the
tight hairpin bends while leaving
Cuevas del Valle.*

6 Puerto del Pico
Ávila; 05413

At 1,352 m (4,436 ft), Puerto del Pico
is the most important road pass in
the Sierra de Gredos. The Romans
constructed a robust stone road over
the mountains here, linking the basin
of the Tiétar river to the south with
that of the Tormes to the north. The
road, the Calzada Romana, has been
restored and makes for a good, if
steep, 6-km (4-mile) hike up to the
pass. Park by the church in Cuevas
del Valle and then walk up to the pass.
*From the pass, continue down the
N502 into the northern Gredos, turning left onto the AV941 for San Martín
del Pimpollar and Hoyos del Espino.*

Above At the top of the Puerto del Pico pass
in the Sierra de Gredos **Below left** Looking
down from the Puerto del Pico pass to
Mombeltrán **Below right** Towering ramparts
of the Castillo de los Duques de Alburquerque
in Mombeltrán

EAT AND DRINK

CUEVAS DEL ÁGUILA

Cuevas del Águila *inexpensive*
A restaurant that serves original,
Spanish cuisine. Highlights of the
menu are dishes such as roasts,
Chuletón (grilled meats seasoned
with sea salt).
*Ctra. Cuevas del Águila, 05418; 920 377
106; closed Mon–Fri from Dec to Feb*

ARENAS DE SAN PEDRO

Hostería Los Galayos *moderate*
This hotel in Arenas de San Pedro
also has a restaurant.
*Plaza Condestable Dávalos 2, 05400;
920 371 379; www.losgalayos.com*

Eat and Drink: inexpensive, under €20; moderate, €20–€40; expensive, over €40

Above El Barco de Ávila by the banks of the Tormes river **Below** Medieval town of Miranda de Castañar

WHERE TO STAY

VALLE DEL TORMES

El Milano Real *moderate*
Located in Hoyos del Espino, this Rusticae hotel is exceptionally stylish and welcoming.
C/ Toleo 2, 05634, Hoyos del Espino; 920 349 108; www.elmilanoreal.com

La Casa de Arriba *moderate*
This is a 17th-century stone house in Navarredonda de Gredos, which has spectacular views of the mountains.
La Cruz 19, 05635, Navarredonda de Gredos; 918 596 391; www. casadearriba.com

Parador de Gredos *expensive*
The oldest parador in the state-run group, this hotel, located near Navarredonda, is recommended for cosy stays in autumn or winter.
Ctra. AV941, Km 10, 05635 Navarredonda de Gredos; 920 348 048; www.parador.es

CANDELARIO

Centro Turismo Rural Artesa *inexpensive*
There are very comfortable rooms in this mid-18th-century house.
C/ Mayor 57, 37710; 923 413 311; www.artesa.es

MIRANDA DEL CASTAÑAR

Condado de Miranda *inexpensive*
Modest, comfortable, clean rooms, and the price includes breakfast.
Paraje de La Perdiza 13, 37660; 923 432 026; www. condadovilllademiranda.com

LA ALBERCA

Hotel Antiguas Eras *moderate*
This hotel has idiosyncratic decor and a popular bar-café in the basement.
Avda. Batuecos n°29, 37624; 923 415 113; www.antiguaseras.com

⑦ Valle del Tormes
Ávila; 05634

Enter the upper Tormes valley on the AV941 through **Navarredonda de Gredos** and stop in the next village, **Barajas**, to look at the old forge, now an occasionally open tourist office. Further down the road, **Hoyos del Espino** has several riding and activity centres, and small restaurants and modest hotels along the main road. To hike in the Gredos, turn south onto the AV931, just east of Hoyos, up to the end of the road (called La Plataforma). Either do the 3-hour round-trip walk to the Los Barrerones col and viewpoint, or the 5.5-hour round-trip hike to the spectacular Laguna Grande. Park at La Plataforma and set off before midday, equipped with good footwear and waterproofs.

🚗 *Returning from La Plataforma, turn left after 4 km (2 miles) and cross a cattle grid to follow the valley of the Garganta del Barbellido on the Camino Panoramico el Polvoroso (signed). There is a good swimming spot by an old bridge at 11 km (7 miles). To rejoin*

the AV941, cross the next cattle grid the outskirts of Navacepeda de Torn and turn left, following the road uph At El Barco, proceed into the old tow and park to the right of the castle.

⑧ El Barco
Ávila; 05600

Dominating the riverbank in the old quarter of El Barco, the massiv round-towered **Castillo de Valdecorneja** was founded in the 12th century and rebuilt in the 14 century. The castle is currently clos to the public, but it is well worth strolling around its perimeter, a sh promenade with good views acro the Tormes river to the west. The town's 14th-century parish churc the **Iglesia de Nuestra Señora de la Asunción**, which blends Gothic, Romanesque and Renaissance sty is open for visits on weekends *(Sat noon, 1pm, 5pm, 6pm & Sun 11am)*.

🚗 *Drive west out of El Barco on the AV100/SA100, following signs for Bé On the outskirts of Béjar, turn left at traffic lights for Candelario (sign-posted) and park in the Plaza Mayor*

⑨ Candelario
Ávila; 37710

A pretty mountain village full of traditional architecture – wooden-framed houses with balconies – Candelario makes for a very pleasa overnight stay. Stroll through the n row alleys that echo with the soun of running water through a netwo of small canals, called *regaderas*. These canals that traditionally cope with the blood from the winter slaug ter of thousands of pigs, now deal with rain and the spring snow mel From the Plaza Mayor, head uphill

take a right after 1 km (0.6 miles)
drive to a fine viewpoint over the
balse de las Angosturas.
*Continue on the same road. At the
age of La Garganta, take a sharp
ht, signposted Puerto de Béjar, soon
ing a country road through groves
weet chestnut. On the south side of
erto de Béjar, join the N630/A66 for
ar. Follow signs right into Béjar and
into the "Centro Urbano". Drive to
western end of town to the old
arter. Park by the square between
church and the palace.*

Béjar
amanca; 37700

It in a dramatic location on a
rrow ridge between two valleys,
e old textile town of Béjar is made
of a tight grid of streets. A few old
lls still stand in the adjacent valley
the north, a 10-minute walk from
e town centre, where a *ruta textil*
xtile route) follows the river under
e bridges. The Plaza Mayor is domi-
ted by the 12th-century **Iglesia
Santa María la Mayor** and the
naissance **Palacio Ducal**. Drive or
lk to the western end of Béjar,
here a well-presented **Museo Judío**
osed Mon and Sat) tells the history of
e town's Jewish community.
*Drive west, around the back of the
esia de Santiago, and then north, to
reach the SA220. Turn left towards
udad Rodrigo. After 25 km (16 miles),
ere is a snack bar and a petrol station
useful, as the countryside is virtually
inhabited. At the confusing junction
fore Miranda del Castañar, Ciudad
drigo is signposted right (SA220).
ay on the main road (SA225), and
ke the sudden left for Miranda.*

Miranda del Castañar
amanca; 37660

randa del Castañar's crumbling
th-century castle is emblematic of
s medieval, walled bastion's flaking
peal. The village is perched on a
l with panoramic views, and the
trance road is the only access. Its
eets are lined with ancient houses
th wide eaves. Walk up the narrow
gh street to the 13th-century Gothic
urch, calling at shops selling hams
d other local produce.
*Return to the SA225 and turn left for
peda; 2 km (1 mile) later, turn right*

onto the DSA260 (CV111) after the
bridge towards Mogarraz. About 5 km
(3 miles) later, the road leads to the
Mirador Peña de Cabra viewpoint on a
tight right-hand bend. Continue to La
Alberca; follow the main road around
the Old Town centre to park.*

⑫ La Alberca
Salamanca; 37624

The genteel capital of the Sierra de la
Peña de Francia, La Alberca is a
much-visited Spanish national monument. Its narrow streets are lined with
wood-framed houses, and its flower-
bedecked Plaza Mayor, with its arcades
and rows of granite columns, boasts
a fine cross. The terraced gardens and
old Moorish irrigation system that
underpin the town are the subject
of a popular walk – the *Senda de Los
Cortinales* – details of which are on
the board near the office of the Parque
Nacional de las Batuecas on the west
side of the town.
*Leave La Alberca on the SA201
towards Ciudad Rodrigo, turning left
after 5 km (3 miles) onto the DSA342
(CV134), and left again onto the SA203
for the Peña de Francia monastery.*

Top left Hikers going up one of the many trails
in the Sierra de Gredos **Top right** Stone archway
in the town of Miranda del Castañar **Above**
Charming mountain village of Candelario

EAT AND DRINK

CANDELARIO
Taberna El Ruedo *moderate*
A popular traditional restaurant just
off Candelario's lovely Plaza Mayor,
El Ruedo is an excellent place to find
well-prepared, hearty, cuisine served
with style. Game and mushrooms are
specialities here.
*Avda. del Humilladero 2, 37710;
923 413 422*

MIRANDA DEL CASTAÑAR
Bar Restaurante Las Petronilas
moderate
This is a much-loved local
establishment serving home-style
mountain cooking, especially beans,
patatas menéas (potatoes with bacon),
lamb, pork and various stews.
*C/ Llanitos, 3, 37660 (on the way into
town); 923 432 030*

Eat and Drink: inexpensive, under €20; moderate, €20–€40; expensive, over €40

Above Roman bridge crossing the Agueda river in Ciudad Rodrigo

VISITING CIUDAD RODRIGO

Tourist Information
Avda. de Yurramendi, 37500; 923 460 561; www.ciudadrodrigo.net

Parking
Car parks are outside the old city walls on the northeast side and by the Puerto del Conde. Alternatively, drive in and park in the Plaza Mayor.

WHERE TO STAY

CIUDAD RODRIGO

Conde Rodrigo inexpensive
Set in a fine old house, this hotel offers well-priced rooms.
Plaza San Salvador 9, 37500; 923 461 404; www.conderodrigo.com

Parador Enrique II expensive
This hotel enjoys a beautiful castle setting in the highest location in town.
Plaza del Castillo 1, 37500; 923 460 150; www.parador.es

13 La Peña de Francia
Salamanca; 37532
Visible for miles around, the peak of La Peña de Francia (1,700 m/5,650 ft) is surmounted by a huge telecom tower and a venerable Dominican monastery – although only one friar still lives here as church warden. The peak is the site of a vision of the black Madonna on 18 May 1434, o of dozens in Spain. A tiny grotto, ir which visitors can descend, marks the site of the vision.

Drive back down, but turn right after 3.5 km (2 miles) onto the DSA3 at the Los Lobos pass, signposted to the valley town of **Monsagro**. A lor sweeping descent, with dramatic views back to La Peña, becomes a narrow road that leads to the Plaza Mayor. In the first week of Septembe the town hosts the Fiestas de Monsagro, a local festival, when contestants vie to climb a greasy po and grab the ham tied to the top.

🚗 From the Plaza Mayor, take a sharp right onto the DSA352. At Serradilla take the DSA350, then the DSA354, then turn left onto the SA2 Arriving at Ciudad Rodrigo, drive in the old city via the Puerta de la Collada; turn right immediately. Park beside the walls of the castle.

14 Ciudad Rodrigo
Salamanca; 37500
A short drive from the Portuguese border, the fortified town of Ciud Rodrigo played a significant role in the early 19th-century Peninsu Wars, when it was a key bastion of defence against Napoleon's aml tions. As well as being replete with Napoleonic-era sites and referenc the town contains some magnificent Renaissance mansions.

A two-hour walking tour
Start at the car park and walk to the **Catedral de Santa Maria** ① (closed Mon) on Avenida de Yurramendi, opposite the tourist information offi The cathedral, founded in the 12th century, is a mix of styles, and the cloister features a series of grotesqu

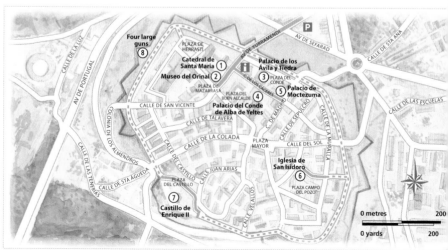

iature figures on the columns.
)-minute guided visit to the 18th-
tury Torre de las Campanas or bell
er *(Spanish only; closed Mon)* offers
at views from the belfry. Across
square the **Museo del Orinal** ②
sed Tue), housed in the Casa de los
anda, has a collection of chamber
s from all around the world. Go
vn Calle de los Cáceres, opposite
cathedral, to get to the Plaza del
ide. The first building of note, to
left, is the Renaissance **Palacio de
Ávila y Tiedra** ③ (also known as
Palacio de los Castro), a mansion
t on monumental scale. Like
**Palacio del Conde de Alba de
es** ④ (now a bank), across the
are on the right, it was built in the
century and is privately owned.
third mansion is the **Palacio de
ctezuma** ⑤ *(open daily)*, now the
n's Casa de Cultura, with a chang-
programme of events.
o back to the cathedral, turn right
limb up to the boardwalk and
t walking clockwise around the

city walls. For wheelchair access, start
from the ramp in the Plaza de Herrasti,
named for the general who was the
governor of the town when it was
besieged by Napoleon. On strolling
down the broadwalk, visitors will
come to the Romanesque **Iglesia de
San Isidoro** ⑥ down on the Plaza
Campo del Pozo. Return to the walls
and stroll around the southeast corner,
from where the panoramic view is
particularly impressive, and walk down
to street level to visit the 14th-century
Castillo de Enrique II ⑦, now the
town's parador.

Approaching the northwestern
part of the wall, where the fiercest
action took place when Wellington
recaptured the city from Napoleon's
forces, look out towards the bullring
to see **four large guns** ⑧. Plaques
mark the Great Breach where the
walls were finally stormed. Note the
pockmarks of cannon damage on
the façade of the Catedral de Santa
Maria. Descend to street level, and
relax in the Plaza del Buen Alcalde,
or head to the Plaza Mayor for a
lunch stop. Then walk back to the
car park.

Above Dominician monastery at Peña de
Francia **Below** Twelfth-century Catedral de
Santa Maria in Ciudad Rodrigo

EAT AND DRINK

CIUDAD RODRIGO

Bar Arcos *inexpensive*
Work through a variety of *raciones* in
this bar and watch the world go by
on the Plaza Mayor. This is also a good
breakfast venue, with reliable *churros*.
Plaza Mayor 18, 37500; 923 460 664

Restaurante Mayton *expensive*
This is a cool and elegant retreat
featuring exposed stonework, and
serves superb fish and meat dishes.
Try the *tostón* (suckling pig) with
baked potatoes.
*C/ Colada 7, 37500; 923 460 720;
www.ciudadrodrigo.net/mayton*

AY TRIP OPTIONS

art from either Ciudad Rodrigo or
adrid to do the following day trips.
he A5–E90 Carretera de Extremadura
asily accesses Madrid and most
her stops in this drive.

**astles in the eastern Sierra
redos**
art the drive from Toros de
uisando ❶ through the scenic

Valle del Alberche ❷ with many fine
viewpoints and little villages dotting
the way. Then stop by the small
town of Arenas de San Pedro ❹ to
see the 15th-century Castillo de Don
Álvaro de Luna. From here, head to
visit the castle in Mombeltrán ❺.

*Follow the driving instructions in the
text and bear in mind that some
sections of the route are very narrow.*

Monastery and walled city
The other alternative would be to
drive to La Peña de Francia ⓭ to
visit the Dominican monastery.
Then head to Ciudad Rodrigo ⓮
for a lazy stroll, and lunch, around
this Napoleonic-era site. The town
is rich in architecture, with beautiful
mansions scattered around it.

Return to Madrid via the A5–E90.

Eat and Drink: inexpensive, under €20; moderate, €20–€40; expensive, over €40

Roman Ruins and Unspoilt Landscapes

Trujillo to Las Hurdes

Highlights

- **Historic cities**
  Walk through the well-preserved medieval centres of Trujillo, Plasencia and Coria

- **Virgin meadows and Mediterranean forests**
  Explore the Parque Nacional de Monfragüe and see rare mammals and birds of prey

- **Rural idylls**
  Drive from village to village through rows of oak and olive trees

- **Old-world Spain**
  Visit the peaceful, pretty hamlets of Las Hurdes, a reminder of how life used to be in Spain

Panoramic view of the golden-brown city of Plasencia

Roman Ruins and Unspoilt Landscapes

Despite the baking heat and low rainfall throughout the long summer, northern Extremadura boasts regions that are wild, untamed and green, as well as rolling farmlands and mountain villages. The drive starts at Trujillo and takes visitors through the Parque Nacional de Monfragüe, which protects rare species like the European lynx and Eurasian black vulture. The tour ends at the remote villages of Las Hurdes, which lie on the steep southern flank of the Sierra de la Peña de Francia, the mountain range that separates Cáceres from Salamanca.

Above Romanesque Catedral Nueva in Plasencia, *see p168* **Top right** Salto del Gitano on the outskirts of the Parque Nacional de Monfragüe, *see p166* **Below** Ancient stone walls built by the Moors in Plasencia, *see p166*

KEY

Drive route

ACTIVITIES

Climb up to Trujillo's Moorish fortress for panoramic views of farmlands and mountains

Go hiking or biking in the Parque Nacional de Monfragüe and catch a glimpse of its rare flora and fauna

Stop for a lunch of *migas* – the regional dish of day-old bread, garlic, *pimentón*, olive oil, alfalfa and pan-fried pork ribs – in Jarandilla de la Vera

Visit the Catedral Nueva, the stunning Romanesque cathedral in Plasencia

Drive up high mountain roads to the lost world of Las Hurdes

PLAN YOUR DRIVE

Start/finish: Trujillo to Las Hurdes.

Number of days: 2–3, allowing half a day to explore Plasencia.

Distance: 310 km (190 miles).

Road conditions: Well paved and generally fairly well signposted; there are steep inclines and switch-backs around the Monasterio de Yuste and Las Hurdes.

When to go: Autumn and spring are the loveliest seasons, with notable highlights such as the cherry tree blossoms in late March in the Valle del Jerte near Plasencia; winter is often sunny and the oak-tree groves are at their greenest.

Opening hours: Shops, bars and cafés, monuments and museums are generally open from 10am to 6 or 7pm in the towns and cities; in small villages and hamlets many shops and tourist attractions close for siesta from 3 to 5pm.

Main market days: Trujillo: Thu; Plasencia: Tue; Coria: Thu.

Shopping: There are several small workshops producing ceramics, silverware, gold ornaments, wooden handicrafts and local costumes in Trujillo. Cherry liqueurs and traditional Montehermoseña caps are available in Plasencia. Homemade jams and desserts are available in Coria.

Major festivals: Jarandilla de la Vera: Las Escobazos y la Encamisá, 7 Dec; **Plasencia:** Fiesta de Árbol, first Sun after Easter Sun.

DAY TRIP OPTIONS

Nature lovers will enjoy spending a day walking around Parque Nacional de Monfragüe, observing its lush flora and abundant fauna. **Families** will be enthralled by Coria and the villages of Las Hurdes, which are steeped in history. For details, *see p169*.

Above View of the Tajo as it flows through the Parque Nacional de Monfragüe **Below** Reliefs on the corner of the Palacio Marqueses de la Conquista *(see p174)*, Trujillo

WHERE TO STAY

TRUJILLO

NH Palacio de Santa Marta *moderate*
Trujillo's most beautiful and best-run hotel, this boutique hotel has 50 spacious bedrooms, all stylishly modern, with king-size beds. The suites have some of the best views of the plaza.
C/ Ballesteros 6, 10200; 927 649 190; www.nh-hotels.com

Parador de Trujillo *moderate*
This charming 43-room hotel occupies part of what used to be a 16th-century convent, with breakfast served in the chapel. Rooms overlook patios and, while the main square is within easy walking distance, the parador is located up a quiet back street and so peace and quiet are assured.
Santa Beatriz de Silva 1, 10200; 927 321 350; www.parador.es

AROUND PARQUE NACIONAL DE MONFRAGÜE

Casa Rural Al-Mofrag *moderate*
Though built in 2006, this handsome 6-bedroom property is built from local stone near the park's information office and in a style in keeping with the traditions of rural Monfragüe.
C/ Villareal 19, 10530, Villareal de San Carlos; 686 454 393; www.casaruralalmofrag.com

① Trujillo
Cáceres; 10200

The Old Town in Trujillo *(see pp174–5)*, with its steep cobbled streets, walls and citadels, is evocative of the *reconquista*, when the Moors fought in vain against Christian attempts to recapture the town. From the Moorish fortress, at the very top of the hill on which the city is built, visitors can walk down between several medieval churches, palaces and houses dating from the 15th and 16th centuries. One of these was the home of the Pizarro family, which produced four infamous conquistadors, including Francisco Pizarro, conqueror of Peru, whose statue stands in the main plaza.

🚗 *Trujillo's traffic is controlled by a one-way system (the scheme changes at weekends) clearly marked with arrows and bollards. Follow the arrows and signs for the EX208, out of the Old Town, towards Plasencia. Follow the road for 40 km (25 miles) to reach Torrejón el Rubio.*

② Torrejón el Rubio
Cáceres; 10694

This tiny hamlet has been a way station since the 13th century. It ha[s] an impressive 16th-century church the **Iglesia de San Miguel Arcángel** *(open daily)*. As the gateway to the Parque Nacional de Monfragüe, Torrejón el Rubio gets many visitor[s] and is a good place to stop for a snack or coffee.

🚗 *Continue on the EX208 towards Villareal de San Carlos, which mark[s] the entrance to the Parque Naciona[l] de Monfragüe. Visitors can stop at th[e] Mirador del Salto del Gitano for spe[c]tacular views of the Tajo river and o[f] an impressive rocky pinnacle. From the viewpoint, continue on the EX2[0]through the national park.*

③ Parque Nacional de Monfragüe
Cáceres; 10530

Designated a national park in 2007 Monfragüe is a 200-sq-km (75-sq-mi[le]) patch of wilderness in an otherwise intensively farmed agricultural regio[n.] The Tajo and Tiétar rivers cut in fro[m] the east with their confluence insi[de] the park. The banks of the rivers crea[te] a deep green swathe through the heart of Extremadura. The area is noted for its importance as a bree[d]ing area for some rare and protecte[d] birds including the black vulture, bla[ck] stork, Imperial eagle and Bonelli's eagle. Monfragüe is also a habitat f[or] one of the world's most endangere[d] wild cats, the lynx, and it is this that l[ed] to it being upgraded from "parque natural" to "parque nacional".

Continue on the EX208 to reach Villareal de San Carlos where there [is] an information centre *(open daily)* fo[r] the Parque Nacional de Monfragüe Founded in 1784, Villareal de San Carlos is young by Extremadura sta[n]dards. It is a convivial hamlet with a[ ]small church, the **Iglesia de Nuestra Señora de la Merced** *(open only for th[e] Festividad de Mercedes on 24 Sep)* and several restaurants.

For those interested in spending a few hours exploring the park, the information centre provides walkin[g] maps, field guides and information about the weather and trail conditions. Head south on the EX208 to the **Puente del Cardenal**, constructe[d]

450 at the behest of the Bishop Plasencia to link the towns of Trujillo and Plasencia. After crossing the bridge, the trail follows the Tajo the main road bridge and then ers away from the riverbank to climb steeply up to the **Ermita y stillo de Monfragüe** *(closed Sun)*. The castle was built in 811 by the Moors, and the monastery was added after the Reconquest led by Alonso in 1180. Continue, following the line of the EX208 road, on to the Salto del Gitano. There are sweeping views of the Tajo river from here.

Immediately north of Villareal de San Carlos is a right turn onto the 389 signposted "Saltos de Torrejón", which exits the national park. This is the back road to La Bazagona, going across the Torrejón-Tiétar dam and past many panoramic view-points. More the right turn after La guijuela for Serrejón and to soon drive at La Bazagona, a main junction for both railway and road systems. Follow the EX389 to Jaraíz de la Vera 11 km (7 miles) before turning right to the EX203 towards Jaraiz de la ra and Jarandilla de la Vera.

Jarandilla de la Vera
Cáceres; 10450

is charming little village is a popular stopover for lunch for those visiting the Monasterio de Yuste or setting off on walks in the nearby countryside. It merits a stroll to see a few buildings, including the grand 15th-century **Señora de la Torre** and the house of Don Luis de Quijada, tutor of Don Juan de Austria, Charles's illegitimate son. Visitors can see remnants of the Roman presence

in a bridge and a mausoleum just outside the village. The village's one imposing building, the 15th-century **Castillo de los Condes de Oropesa**, used by Charles V for several months prior to his taking up residence in the Monasterio de Yuste, is now a parador.

🚗 *Retrace the route on the EX203 to Cuacos de Yuste and turn right onto the EX391 for the Monasterio de Yuste.*

5 Monasterio de Yuste
Cáceres; 10412

In 1556 Charles V retired from public life and took refuge in the Hieronymite **Monasterio de Yuste** *(closed Mon)*. He died here two years later. The monastery's location, in the wooded Valle de la Vera, is peaceful and idyllic. The church's Gothic and Plateresque cloisters are open to the public, as is the austere palace, but some areas, including the cloisters adjacent to the mansion, are closed, as there are still a handful of monks in residence.

🚗 *Continue on the steep EX391 following signs for Garganta la Olla.*

6 Garganta la Olla
Cáceres; 10412

This area of Extremadura is characterized by gorges and ravines. Garganta la Olla is a tiny hamlet but is better known as the name of the neighbouring wide gorge, a popular spot for families, who picnic in the woodlands at the side of the Tiétar river and bathe in its cool waters.

🚗 *The EX391 ends in a T-junction. Turn right here. Take the left fork after Garganta onto the CC17, which goes back to the EX203. Turn right and follow the road towards Plasencia.*

Above Terrace café in Jarandilla de la Vera
Below left Gardens in Monasterio de Yuste
Below right *Estatua de la Madre* in Trujillo

EAT AND DRINK

TRUJILLO

Mesón La Troya *inexpensive*
The Mesón La Troya is well liked by local residents and visitors alike. Housed in a classic and very charming 16th-century *mesón* (inn), it serves hearty meals, including good *solomillos* (steaks), *migas* (the local fry-up) with pork and a range of tapas. *Plaza Mayor 10, 10200; 927 321 364*

Nuria *inexpensive*
Opt for tapas or main meals from the à la carte menu on this restaurant's outdoor terrace.
Plaza Mayor 27, 10200; 927 320 907; www.hostal-nuria.com

JARANDILLA DE LA VERA

Puta Parió *moderate*
Set in the back streets, this little restaurant is housed in what used to be the residence of Don Luis de Quijada, and is full of history. Downstairs is a busy little tapas bar (smoking permitted) where locals watch TV while eating tasty portions of tortilla, fish and sausages. Upstairs is an intimate restaurant specializing in regional dishes, including exceptional tomato soup and bull's tail.
C/ Francisco Pizarro 8, 10450; 927 560 392; closed Mon

Above Ornate balcony of a house in Plasencia

VISITING PLASENCIA

Tourist Information
*Oficina de Turismo, C/ Santa Clara 2,
10600; 927 423 843; www.
aytoplasencia.es*

Parking
Parking is available on the corner of
Avenida del Valle and Avenida de
Calvo Sotelo.

WHERE TO STAY

PLASENCIA

Alfonso VIII *moderate*
This modern 56-room hotel is
decorated in a contemporary style.
*Avda. Alfonso VIII, 32, 10600; 927 410
250; www.hotelalfonsoviii.com*

CORIA

Hotel Palacio *moderate*
The Hotel Palacio is housed in the
17th-century Palacio Episcopal.
*Plaza de la Catedral s/n, 10800; 927
506 449; www.hotelpalaciocoria.es*

LAS HURDES

Husa Hospedería Río Hurdes Reales
moderate
This is a four-star, 30-room hotel, 10 km
(6 miles) from Vegas de Coria, with a
restaurant that serves typical hurdana
goat- and pork-based dishes.
*Ctra. Factoria s/n, 10625, Las Mestas;
927 434 139; www.husa.es*

⑦ Plasencia

Cáceres; 10600

Plasencia was founded by King Alfonso VIII as a city-fortress in 118
when the Jerte river was the southwestern frontier of Castile. The
imposing city walls date from the end of the 12th century, and there
was originally a huge Alcázar (or keep) in the northern quarter which
was demolished in the 1940s. Plasencia has been an important trading
hub since Roman times, due to its position on the Ruta de la Plata
(Silver Route) between Seville and Gijón.

A two-hour walking tour

From the car park walk up Calle
Talavera to the **Plaza Mayor** ①, the
city's main square. Many of the grand
palaces, stately ancestral homes and
churches are around this square.
Walk across the plaza and up Calle
del Rey to see the shortened tower
of **La Casa de las Argollas** ②. Go back
to the Plaza Mayor and up Calle de la
Rúa Zapatería, through the medieval
quarter, till the narrow Plaza de San
Vicente Ferrer. At one end of this
plaza is the 15th-century **Iglesia de
San Vicente Ferrer** ③, with an adjoining convent that now houses the city's
beautiful parador. The north side of
the square is dominated by the
Renaissance **Palacio de Mirabel** ④.
From the plaza, turn right into Plaza
de San Nicolás. Walk across the plaza
and turn left and then right into Calle
Blanca. Turn right into Calle Trujillo till
Plaza del Marqués de la Puebla,
which houses the **Museo Etnográfico
y Textil** ⑤ *(closed Sun)*, in a building
that served as a hospital in the 14th
century. It now has displays of local

crafts and traditional costume. Continue down Calle del Obispado to
reach the two cathedrals. The
Catedral Nueva ⑥, built in the 15th-
16th-century, has two Plateresque
façades, a Baroque organ and
beautifully carved wooden choir sta
The Romanesque **Catedral Vieja** ⑦
(closed Sun afternoon), built between
the 13th and 14th centuries, houses
museum with works by the Spanish
painter José de Ribera (1591–1652)
and a 14th-century Bible. It acquired
over the intervening centuries a
Gothic nave and rose window as well
as Renaissance elements. Walk under
the arch on the eastern side of the
cathedral square and turn left into
Avenida de Calvo Sotelo and then
almost immediately right into Calle
de Juan Gómez Pasajero. Walk across
the crossroads into Calle de San
Marcos. Continue on this road till
the right turn into Paseo Caño Soso,
which gives access to the **Parque de
la Isla** ⑧, formed naturally by the
Jerte river as it divides near the city.
This is perhaps the most popular of

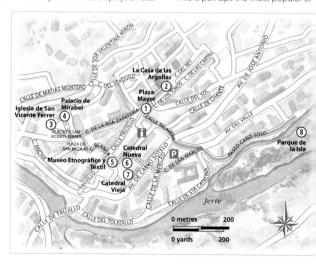

e city's green spaces and it offers
od panoramic views of the
hedrals and other monuments.
trace the route on Paseo Caño
so till the car park.

*Follow the N630 southwest from
sencia towards Cáceres. Take the
6 towards Cáceres, turn right on
t 479 and follow EX108 until Coria,
ssing through farmlands. Look
t for the walled town of Galisteo
the right and continue westwards
vards Coria.*

Coria
ceres; 10800

rrounding the old part of Coria are
pressive Roman walls. Inside these
a compact labyrinth of a city, ideal
walking. At the heart of the city is
e Gothic-Romanesque **Catedral de
nta María de la Asunción** *(open daily)*,
ilt between the 15th and 18th
nturies. Other key buildings are the
th-century Convento de Madre de
os; the Palacio Episcopal, built in
26; the Iglesia de Santiago, dating
m the 16th century; the Royal
son, site of the **Museo de la Cárcel
al** *(closed Mon, Tue)* and on the out-
rts of town, a **Jardín Botánico**
osed Sat, Sun).* Coria's Castillo de los
uques de Alba, also from the 15th
ntury, still has its keep standing.

*Continue northwest on the
108. When the road forks, turn
ht onto the EX204, which is the
uta a Las Hurdes". On the left, to
e northwest, are the hills of the
rra de Gata. Continue on the EX204
Pinofranqueado, the gateway to
s Hurdes.*

9 Las Hurdes
Cáceres; 10628

Las Hurdes' black slate mountains and
lonely hamlets have a mythic quality
for many Spaniards. The area was very
poor, depending on goat herding and
terrace farming for subsistence. In the
1950s paved roads opened up Las
Hurdes on both sides of the Sierra de
Gata and it is now easily accessible
from Salamanca and Extremadura.

Pinofranqueado is the gateway
to the region and has a campsite,
several small hotels and a public
swimming pool. Fifteen kilometres
(9 miles) along the EX204 is Vegas de
Coria, from where there is a left turn
onto the CC55 for **Nuñomoral**, a
popular base for walks up to Fragosa
and El Gasco – also accessible by car.
Eight kilometers (5 miles) to the northwest of Nuñomoral is **Casares de las
Hurdes**, where visitors can see the
slate from the mountains used on
the roofs of many local houses.

Above View of the village wall in Galisteo

EAT AND DRINK

PLASENCIA

Puerta Talavera *moderate*
Veal, lamb, roast kid, quail, a wide
range of Iberian hams and a delicious
carpaccio are served at this stylish,
modern restaurant.
*C/ Talavera 30, 10600; 927 421 545;
closed Mon*

CORIA

El Mirador de la Catedral *moderate*
This family-friendly restaurant is the
place to come to explore extremeño
classics such as *morcilla* (blood sausage),
cured ham and tasty meat dishes.
*Plaza de la Catedral s/n, 10800;
927 506 449*

LAS HURDES

La Posada del Casar *moderate*
In the south of Las Hurdes, this rural
hotel has a cosy stone dining room
where they serve traditional dishes.
*C/ Mayor 36, Casar de Palomero,
10640; 927 436 410; open daily*

DAY TRIP OPTIONS

This drive in northern Extremadura
can be broken down into two day
trips with either Trujillo (on the A5)
or Coria (near the EX–A1) as base.

Natural parkland
After breakfast and a morning stroll
around Trujillo ❶, drive to Torrejón
el Rubio ❷ to see the 16th-century
Iglesia de San Miguel Arcángel.
Continue to Villareal de San Carlos,
where there is an information centre
for Parque Nacional de Monfragüe
❸. Spend the afternoon exploring
the national park on foot; look out

for birds such as black storks, herons,
European bee eaters and Azure-
winged magpies, as well as deer
and lizards.

*From Trujillo, head northwards
towards Torrejón del Rubia on the
EX208. Continue to Villareal de San
Carlos and turn right onto the EX389
just north of the town to drive through
the Parque Nacional de Monfragüe.*

Historical villages
Start the day at the historic city of
Coria ❽, and visit the imposing
cathedral. Northwest of the city is a

road to Villanueva de la Sierra, where
visitors can take a back road to El
Bronco, Cerezo and Mohedas, before
rejoining the main road at
Caminomorisco. Head northeast
towards Vegas de Coria, Nuñomoral
and Casares de las Hurdes, villages
typical of Las Hurdes ❾.

*Leave Coria on the EX108 . When the
road forks, take the right fork onto the
EX204. At Villanueva de la Sierra, turn
right onto the EX205 to reach El Bronco,
then join the EX204 in Vegas de Coria
and the CC55 to Nuñomoral and
Casares de las Hurdes.*

Eat and Drink: inexpensive, under €20; moderate, €20–€40; expensive, over €40

Cities of the Conquistadors

Cáceres to Jerez de los Caballeros

Highlights

- **Medieval cities**
  Explore Cáceres, Trujillo and Guadalupe from where the conquistadors set out to explore the Americas

- **Palaces and mansions**
  Visit Trujillo's many stately mansions, built over centuries by Moorish and Christian nobles

- **Roman Lusitania**
  Walk through the impressive Roman ruins at Mérida, once the capital of an ancient Roman province

- **Little Andalusia**
  Stop by Zafra, the architectural and spiritual twin of Seville

Panoramic view of the castle and walls of Trujillo

Cities of the Conquistadors

Of all Spanish regions, Extremadura, which means the land beyond the Duero river, is the most remote from the modern world. It was the birthplace of many conquistadors and emigrants to the New World, and some of Spain's finest Roman architecture can be seen in this region. This winding drive takes visitors from medieval Cáceres through Trujillo to Guadalupe. After a couple of hours in real backcountry, during which visitors will drive along the valley of the Guadiana river, they will arrive in Mérida, the ancient capital of the Roman province of Lusitania. Visitors will also pass through Zafra, where they can relax in one of the plazas, surrounded by Andalusian-style buildings, and then finally arrive in Jerez de los Caballeros, with its beautiful churches.

KEY

Drive route

0 kilometres 20

0 miles 20

Above View of Trujillo on the approach from Cáceres, *see p174*

ACTIVITIES

Stroll around the stunning back streets of Cáceres

Take a tour of Trujillo and see where the Pizarro brothers, the conquistadors of Peru, lived

Enjoy drinking an ice-cold *caña* (sugarcane juice) in Guadalupe's busy plaza

Explore the medieval town of Mérida and its impressive Roman ruins

Taste the acclaimed wines of the Guadiana region

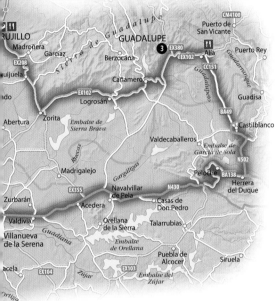

ove left Main shopping street in Zafra, *see p177* **Above right** Façade of the Monasterio Guadalupe, *see p175* **Below** Panoramic view of the Guadalupe valley, *see p175*

PLAN YOUR DRIVE

Start/finish: Cáceres to Jerez de los Caballeros.

Number of days: 3, allowing half a day each to explore Trujillo and Mérida.

Distances: 450 km (280 miles).

Road conditions: Well paved and generally well signposted; beyond Guadalupe, the road is somewhat narrower until it joins the N430.

When to go: Autumn and spring are very pleasant; winter is often sunny.

Opening hours: Shops, monuments and museums are generally open from 10am to 6 or 7pm in the towns and cities; in small villages and hamlets many shops and tourist attractions close for siesta between 3 and 5pm. Many attractions have shorter hours at weekends, and in winter.

Main market days: Cáceres: Wed; Trujillo: Thu; **Mérida:** Tue; **Zafra:** Sun.

Shopping: Buy high-quality Spanish shoes and cured ham from Cáceres; local cheese, honey and copper and *tilatón* (copper-zinc) ornaments from Guadalupe; Bellota ham and cheese from Zafra.

Major festivals: Cáceres: Extremúsika (Music Festival), Mar–Apr; Festival de San Jorge, 22–23 April; WOMAD (World of Music and Dance), May; **Mérida**: Festival de Teatro Clásico (Classical Drama Festival), Jul–Aug; **Zafra**: Feria de Ganado (Livestock Fair), first week Oct; **Jerez de los Caballeros**: La Feria del Jamón (Ham Fair), first week May.

DAY TRIP OPTIONS

History buffs will enjoy visiting Cáceres, Trujillo and Guadalupe, while **architecture lovers** will be amazed by the heritage buildings, palaces and monuments in the towns of Mérida and Zafra. For details, *see p177*.

Top View of the old city and its battlements in Cáceres **Above** Plaza in Trujillo, with Pizarro's statue in the forefront

VISITING TRUJILLO

Tourist Information
*Plaza Mayor, 10200; 927 322 677;
www.ayto-trujillo.com*

Parking
Parking is available at Paseo Ruiz de Mendoza.

WHERE TO STAY

CÁCERES

Parador de Cáceres *expensive*
The parador in Cáceres is a labyrinth of patios, gardens and corridors and has tastefully decorated rooms.
*C/ Ancha 6, 10003; 927 211 759;
www.parador.es*

TRUJILLO

NH Palacio de Santa Marta *moderate*
Trujillo's most beautiful and best-run hotel has 50 spacious bedrooms, all of which are stylishly modern.
*C/ Ballesteros 6, 10200; 927 649 190;
www.nh-hotels.com*

---

① Cáceres
Cáceres; 10001
The medieval town of Cáceres grew to prominence after 1227 when Alfonso IX of León conquered the region and established trade routes through northern and central Extremadura. Cáceres became a UNESCO World Heritage Site in 1986.

The Old Town is surrounded by walls built by the Almohad, 12th-century Muslim rulers and has perfectly preserved palaces, churches and residential buildings. The architecture here reflects a blend of Roman, Islamic, Northern Gothic and Renaissance styles. Old Cáceres is almost devoid of the taint of modern society and, as many of its streets are too narrow even for small cars, a morning stroll here is a tranquil affair. Most of today's serene Renaissance town dates back to the late 15th and 16th centuries, after which economic decline set in. There are several older parts, including

the **Casa y Torre Carvajal**, a typical Renaissance mansion with a peace garden and topped by a 13th-cent Arab tower, and the **Torre del Buja** also a beautiful Moorish construction, dating from the 12th century Other sights include the 15th-cent **Casa y Torre de las Cigüeñas** (Hous and Tower of the Storks), with its crenellated tower; the **Convento d Santa Clara**, built between the 14t and 17th centuries; the **Museo Provincial** *(closed Sun)*, housed in th atmospheric Casa de las Veletas; a the **Palacio de los Golfines de Aba** which melds Gothic, Mudéjar and the ornate Plateresque styles and features a battlemented façade. Th **Plaza de Santa María**, framed by be tiful palaces and the Iglesia de San María, is the hub of Old Town life.
🚗 *Leave town heading eastwards c the N521 and the A58 following sig to Trujillo. Parking is available at Paseo Ruiz de Mendoza.*

---

② Trujillo
Cáceres; 10200
Trujillo is an elegant, tranquil medieval city with some impressive architecture. It was the birthplace of several conquistadors, most notably Francisco Pizarro, who conquered Peru; Francisco de Orellana, the first European to sail up the Amazon river; and Gaspar de Rodas, the first governor of Antioquia, Colombia. Grandiose statues, quirky museums and fascinating bas-reliefs remind visitors of the town's connection to the Americas.

A 90-minute walking tour
From the car park walk northeast and turn left into Calle de los Herreros and then straight into Calle de las Tiendas into the **Plaza Mayor** ①, a beautiful sight in the morning, when there is likely to be no traffic and very few pedestrians, or at night, when floodlights illuminate the surrounding buildings. On all four sides, and on several of the adjoining streets, are escutcheoned palaces and mansions, some of which have been converted into restaurants and shops.

Overlooking the plaza is the **Iglesia de San Martín** ②, built in the 16th century, with its two lichen-covered bell towers. In front of the main door of the church stands an imposing

Bell tower in Iglesia de San Martin

equestrian bronze statue of Pizarro the work of the American sculptor, Charles Rumsey. Walk clockwise around the plaza from the base of the statue, taking in the Renaissance-style **Palacio de San Carlos** on the northeast corner. Th **Palacio de los Marqueses d Piedras Albas** ④, a Gothic mansion with a Renaissance gallery, is at the southeast corner of the plaza. Howeve the most impressive building is the Plateresque **Palacio de la Conquista** ⑤ located towards the southwest corner. It has the magnificent coat arms of the Pizarro family over the window. Directly opposite is the **Cas de las Cadena** ⑥, seat of the Chave Orellana family. Head for the stairs

tween the statue of Pizarro and
e church and turn left onto Calle
los Ballesteros to reach the **Torre
l Alfiler** ⑦ (Needle Tower), deco-
ed with tiles from the town of
avera de la Reina. Continue on
lle de los Ballesteros, heading past
e NH hotel, another beautiful
ace now converted into a stylish
utique hotel, to reach the **Puerta
Santiago** ⑧, a gate into the oldest
rt of the city. Straight ahead, on
lle de Santa María, is a stonewalled
urch, the **Iglesia de Santa María la
ayor** ⑨, facing the **Palacio de
zarro-Hinojoso** ⑩.

Turn left, then right into Calle de
nta María and then right into
lle de la Puerta de Coria to reach
e **Museo de la Coria** ⑪, formerly a
nvent, which is full of didactic but
ely displays on the archaeology,
story, cuisine and culture of the New
orld. Turn left into Calle Mercad to
ach the **Casa Museo de Pizarro** ⑫,
nich is full of artifacts relating to the
e of the conquistador and to every-
y life in the 15th and 16th centuries.
om here take the inclined Calle del
astillo to the **Castillo y Murallas** ⑬,
ilt in Moorish times on the remains
a Roman fort. Retrace the route to
t back to the car park in Paseo Ruiz
Mendoza.

 Take the EX208 southeast out of
ujillo. At Zorita, turn left onto the
(102 and then left again onto the
380 to Guadalupe.

❸ Guadalupe
Cáceres; 10140
The village of Guadalupe grew
around the Hieronymite **Monasterio
de Guadalupe**, founded in 1340,
which harbours an image of the Virgin
Mary, discovered here in the early 14th
century. The exterior of the main building is a mix of Gothic, Mudéjar and
Plateresque styles. In the main square
there are shops that sell traditional
monastic crafts.

🚗 *Retrace the route to the EX102 and
follow it eastwards past Alía. Turn
right onto the CC151, which becomes
the BAV7118 across the provincial border. Turn right at Castilblanco onto the
N502 and follow the road as it veers
southwards. Turn right at Herrera del
Duque, follow the brown signs indicating "Peloche" onto the BAV7114, which
becomes BAV6348 after Peloche. Fork
right and then turn left after the dam.
Follow Mérida signs on N430 and A5.*

Above left Beautiful interior of the monastery
in Guadalupe **Above right** Ruins of the
Castillo y Murallas in Trujillo

EAT AND DRINK

CÁCERES

Atrio *expensive*
This restaurant serves contemporary
takes on Extremeño and Spanish cuisine.
*Avda. de España 22, 10002; 927 242
928; www.restauranteatrio.com; closed
Sun dinner, Mon and two weeks in July*

TRUJILLO

Nuria *inexpensive*
Opt for tapas or main meals on this
restaurant's outdoor terrace.
*Plaza Mayor 27, 10200; 927 320 907;
www.hostal-nuria.com*

AROUND GUADALUPE

Mesón del Cazador *inexpensive*
About 16 km (10 miles) to the east of
Guadalupe, this place serves goat meat
chops, plain fish dishes and salads.
*Avda. Luis Chamizo 8, Alía, 10137;
927 366 265*

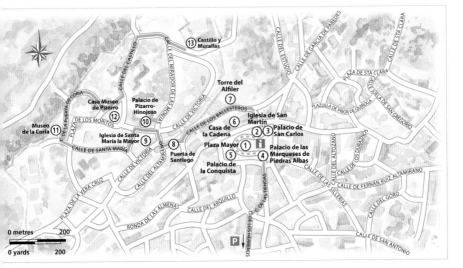

Above Teatro Romano in Mérida **Below left**
Puerta de Jerez in Zafra **Below right** Road
approaching the Old Wall in Mérida

VISITING MÉRIDA

Tourist Information
Santa Eulalia 64, 06800; 924 330 722

Parking
Parking is available in Calle de las
Atarazanas.

WHERE TO STAY

MÉRIDA

Mérida Palace *inexpensive–moderate*
Housed in a pair of elegant palaces, this
hotel maintains a regal atmosphere and
has all modern conveniences.
*Plaza España 19, 06800; 924 383 800;
www.hotelmeridapalace.com*

ZAFRA

Huerta Honda *moderate*
The Huerta Honda is stylish, yet
traditional, and has chic rooms that
are extremely comfortable.
*Avda. López Asme 30, 06300; 924 554
100; www.hotelhuertahonda.com*

Parador de Zafra *expensive*
Also known as the Hotel Duque de
Feria, this parador occupies a majestic
15th-century castle. The rooms here
are elegant and spacious.
*Plaza Corazón de María 7, 06300; 924
554 540; www.parador.es*

❹ Mérida
Badajoz; 06800

Founded by Augustus in 25 BC, Mérida, then known as Emerita
Augusta, grew into the cultural and economic capital of Lusitania,
Rome's westernmost province. The city, however, lost its eminence
under the Moors. Though a small city, Mérida has many fine Roman
monuments. Now the capital of Extremadura and a UNESCO World
Heritage Site, it has a Roman amphitheatre and theatre, aqueduct,
circus and temples. The best approach to the town is via the Puente
de Guadiana that leads to the original entrance of the Roman city.

The most concentrated set of ruins is
to the west of the city, where a tiny
gateway provides access to the huge
Teatro Romano and **Anfiteatro**. The
amphitheatre was used mainly for
displays of gladiatorial combat with
condemned prisoners, servants and
paid soldiers taking on each other as
well as wild animals but the *fossa
arenaia* (the depression at the centre
of the arena) could also be water-
proofed or flooded with
water for spectacles. The
theatre was built in 16–15
BC and is one of the best
preserved Roman theatres
in the world. Seating in this
venue was determined by
one's status in society – the
orchestra pit was reserved
for those of the highest
class, senators and officials,
while the top rows were for slaves
and the poor. The theatre is still used
for performances and is at its most
magnificent when hosting the
Festival de Teatro Clásico de Mérida,
an annual classical theatre festival, in
June and July.

Mérida's **Museo Nacional de Arte
Romano** *(closed Mon)*, just north of
the theatre, is one of the most stunning museums in Europe, boasting

**Bronze statue at
Merida's theatre**

large collections of coins, sculpture,
ceramics and mosaics. Opened in
1986 and designed by renowned
Spanish architect Rafael Moneo
(b. 1937), the museum building is a
marvel in itself – the low lights and
plain decor create a calming environ-
ment, enhancing the displays.

In the city centre are the 1st-centu-
ry BC **Templo de Diana** at Romero Leal
and the beautiful **Arco de Trajano**
at the northern end of
Calle Trajano. The **Museo
de Arte Visigodo** *(closed
Mon)* is in the Convento
de Santa Clara, which
is situated off the main
square. The **Iglesia de
Santa Eulalia**, built in
the 5th century during
the reign of Constantine
in honour of the city's
patron saint, is located on the north
side of the city. St Eulalia, martyred
during the Roman era, is believed to
have been buried here along with
several clerics.

Spain's oldest Moorish building,
the **Alcazaba de Mérida** *(open daily)*,
which has towers, a cistern and
Roman ruins, overlooks the Guadiana
river and the Roman bridge over it.
One in a series of fortresses along the

ristian border with Islamic Spain, it
ved both the Moors and the
ristians as a stronghold.
Leave town heading southwards on
A66. Turn left on the N630 at exit
 towards Los Santos de Maimona.
 before entering the town, fork
nt onto the EX101 to Zafra.

Zafra
ajoz; 06300

t west of the main highway in the
th, Zafra is a white-walled town of
tel-coloured houses, decorated
h window boxes brimming over
h flowers. At the heart of this conviv-
town, nickamed "little Seville"
cause of its Moorish character, are
arcaded squares. The large central
are, the 16th-century **Plaza**
nde, is located near the Iglesia
estra Señora de la Candelaria. On
ar corner is the **Plaza Chica**, the old
are. Once a bustling marketplace,
now a calm, intimate square with a
dful of small restaurants around it.

he largest church in town is the
thic-Renaissance Iglesia Nuestra
iora de la Candelaria. It has nine
els painted by Francisco Zurbarán
98–1664) on the retable in a
apel designed by the Spanish
hitect and sculptor, José Benito
Churriguera (1665–1725). The
57 **Alcázar de los Duques de Feria**,
ich boasts a spectacular façade,
autiful coffered ceilings and a
th-century Herreran patio, is now
overnment-run parador.
 Exit the town on the EX320
lowing signs to Salvatierra de los
rros and Barcarrota. At Barcarrota,
n left onto the N435 which leads
aight to Jerez de los Caballeros.

⑥ Jerez de los Caballeros
Badajoz; 06380

Set on a hillside, with its profile
broken by three Baroque church
towers, Jerez de los Caballeros is
one of Extremadura's most picturesque towns. This small town is
also historically important – Vasco
Núñez de Balboa, who "discovered"
the Pacific, was born here in 1475.
The old quarters of the town are
centred around the three churches –
San Bartolomé, **San Miguel** and the
Santa María de la Encarnación. Social
life in Jerez de los Caballeros, however, revolves around the plaza and
the bullring.

Above View of the Alcázar de los Duques
de Feria in Zafra **Below** Arched Plaza Chica
in Zafra

VISITING ZAFRA

Parking
Parking in the old city of Zafra is
difficult unless visitors are staying at
the parador, so park in one of the bays
around the edges of the wall.

EAT AND DRINK

MÉRIDA

Rufino *moderate*
Popular with locals, this is a friendly
tapas bar that serves ham, tortilla,
clams and a roast kid dish.
Plaza Santa Clara 2, 06800;
924 312 001; closed Sun

ZAFRA

La Rebotica *moderate*
One of Zafra's most romantic
restaurants, with each table inside an
arched alcove, La Rebotica specializes
in local dishes like *rabo de toro* (oxtail
stew) and *higos en salsa de coñac* (figs
in cognac sauce), and desserts.
C/ Boticas 12, 06300; 924 554 289;
www.lareboticadezafra.com

DAY TRIP OPTIONS

he drive can be divided into two
hort trips with either Cáceres (on
he N521) or Mérida (on the A66)
s a base.

Heritage cities
tart the day with breakfast and
a slow walk around Cáceres ❶, a
UNESCO World Heritage Site and
a beautiful city, famous for its storks.
Head east to Trujillo ❷, another
impressive historic town that is the
birthplace of Francisco Pizarro,

Francisco de Orellana and other
famous conquistadors. End the day
at Guadalupe ❸, famous for its
Monasterio de Guadalupe which
houses a 14th-century image of the
Virgin Mary. The town is also home
to some excellent restaurants.

Take the N521 from Cáceres following
signs for Trujillo. Park in Trujillo's new
town as the historic centre is a
labyrinth with narrow roads lined by
high walls. From Trujillo, take the

quiet EX208 south, then the EX102
northeast to Guadalupe.

Roman roads
Mérida ❹ was once the capital
of Lusitania and is now a UNESCO
World Heritage Site worth a morning's
exploration. In the afternoon, head
to Zafra ❺, where Extremeño and
Andaluz cultures are blended in the
architecture and local cuisine.

From Mérida, take the A66 southwards
to Zafra.

Atlantic Ocean

Bilbao
A Coruña

SPAIN Zaragoza
Barcelona

Madrid
Valencia Palma

Murcia Mediterranean
Sea
Seville

Málaga

Don Quixote's La Mancha

Puerto Lápice to Consuegra

Highlights

- **Gem-like towns**
  Visit some of Spain's most beautiful old towns, immortalized by Cervantes

- **Unusual discoveries**
  Surprise yourself in La Mancha's hills and woods

- **Wetland habitats**
  Pack a pair of binoculars to catch the rich birdlife of the Parque Natural de Lagunas de Ruidera

- **Castle-monastery**
  Explore the Castillo de Calatrava la Nueva, perched on a craggy summit

A spectacular view of the windmills of Consuegra in La Mancha

Don Quixote's La Mancha

South of Madrid, La Mancha (from *manza*, meaning "parched earth" in Arabic) seems arid and inhospitable from the motorway. Get off the *autovía* and onto the best regional roads in Spain to discover the reality of the Manchegan countryside – rolling wheat fields and stunning sunsets, white windmills and jewel-like lakes. Try wines from the biggest vineyard in the world, and look out for reminders, everywhere, of Spain's most famous literary creations, Don Quixote and Sancho Panza.

Above Fifteenth-century Santuario de Nuestra Señora de Las Virtudes, *see p184*

ACTIVITIES

Explore the windmills at Campo de Criptana before lazing over lunch

Go bird-watching at dawn and have a late breakfast followed by a swim in Laguna Concejo

Park the car and go walking to Castillo de Rochafrida and Don Quixote's Cueva de Montesinos

Have a night out at the theatre in Almagro's Corral de Comedias

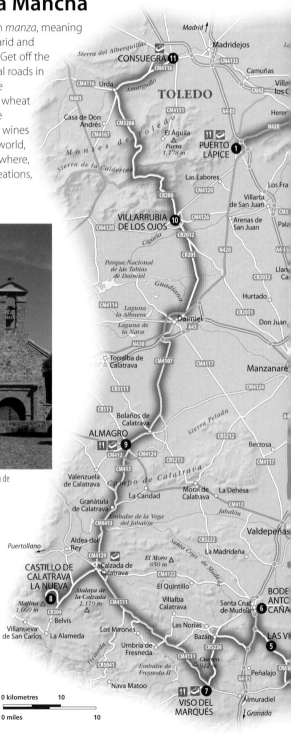

Y

Drive route

CM3105 11
Alcázar de 2 CAMPO DE
San Juan CRIPTANA N420 → *Cuenca*
CM3105 CR1222
Záncara Arenales de
San Gregorio
CM42 Los Árboles
Alameda
de Cervera CM3103
CM3102
Cinco Casas Tomelloso N310
CM3113 N310a N310
Argamasilla N310
de Alba CM3109 CR400
de N310 CM3115 CR1225
na La Pachecas El Buen Retiro
CM3109 CM3115 La Mierera
Embalse de Cañada de
Peñarroya la Manga
513 El Lobillo Ruidera
UDAD REAL CR650 *Cueva de*
La Solana CR1511 La Calera N430 3 *Montesinos*
PARQUE NATURAL *Laguna*
Alhambra DE LAS LAGUNAS 11 *Concejo*
DE RUIDERA El Ossero
Casas Blancas
Sierra de Alhambra △ Bolos
1,088 m
△ Cristo *Embalse de* Carrizosa *Cañamares*
1,010 m *Puerto de Vallebermoso* *Azuer*
CM3127 Melgarejo CR6421
CM3129
Pozo de la Serna Fuenllana
La Jarosa CM412 Alcubillas 4 VILLANUEVA DE
848 m LOS INFANTES
CM3127
Embalse de CA624 Montiel
Cabezuela
ranillo CM3129
CR6112 Cózar Casa
Los Morrones del Monte
Cabeza de Buey CR6221
Navalavaca △ 1,155 m Almedina
CR614 Torre de
as Tajoneras La Borreguilla Juan Abad
Guadalén
del Castellar CM3200
tellar de La Guadianeja
tiago

hurch of San Carlos del Valle, near Villanueva de los Infantes, *see p184*
: Vineyards rolling across the Manchegan landscape, *see p184*

PLAN YOUR DRIVE

Start/finish: Puerto Lápice
to Consuegra.

Number of days: 3–4, allowing half a
day to explore the Parque Natural de
las Lagunas de Ruidera.

Distance: 400 km (250 miles).

Road conditions: Nearly all the
roads are excellent in the region.
Some ice is possible in winter.

When to go: Summer is extremely
hot. Spring and autumn can be
delightful, with warm, sunny days
and cool nights.

Opening hours: Most monuments
are open from 9:30am to 2pm and
from 5pm to 8pm. Many of them are
closed on Mondays.

Main market days: Campo de
Criptana: Tue; Villanueva de los
Infantes: Fri; Almagro: Wed;
Consuegra: Sat.

Major festivals: Campo de Criptana:
Virgen de Criptana, Easter Mon;
Almagro: Festival Internacional de
Teatro Clasico, Jun–Jul.

DAY TRIP OPTIONS

Don Quixote enthusiasts should visit
Puerto Lápice, after which they can
head to Campo de Criptana to see the
windmills. **History buffs** could spend a
day visiting a bullring, a Renaissance
palace and a medieval castle in Las
Virtudes, Viso del Marqués and Calzada
de Calatrava. For details, *see p187*.

VISITING PUERTO LÁPICE

Start the tour through Quixotic Spain by taking the Madrid–Seville highway (Autovía del Sur), A4-E5 and leaving at Puerto Lápice (exit 134).

WHERE TO STAY

PUERTO LÁPICE

Hotel El Puerto *inexpensive*
This is a very decent, motel-style accommodation with a bar-restaurant.
Avda. Juan Carlos I, 59, 13650; 926 583 050; www.hotelpuertolapice.es

PARQUE NATURAL DE LAS LAGUNAS DE RUIDERA

Hotel Albamanjon *moderate*
Opened in the late 1970s, this delightful boutique hotel nestled on the shore of Laguna San Pedro offers a range of rooms, each with its own patio, terraced on the hillside behind the main house. It has an excellent restaurant and café.
Lagunas de San Pedro 16, 02611, Ossa de Montiel; 926 699 048; www.albamanjon.net

AROUND PARQUE NATURAL DE LAS LAGUNAS DE RUIDERA

Hotel Restaurante Entrelagos *inexpensive*
A lakefront hotel, (1 km/0.6 miles south of Ruidera along the lakeshore road) catering mostly to weekending Madrileños and bird-watchers. The rooms here are reasonably spacious and comfortable.
Crtra. de las Lagunas, Entrelagos, 13249, Ruidera; 926 528 022; www.entrelagos.com

Top left Statue of Don Quixote in Puerto Lápice **Top right** Lake Concejo in Parque Natural de las Lagunas de Ruidera **Above** Windmills scattered across the rocky hillside of Campo de Criptana **Below** Fishing in the crystal-clear lakes in Ruidera

❶ Puerto Lápice
Ciudad Real; 13650

Sleepy Puerto Lápice was immortalized by Cervantes' novel. The **Venta del Quijote**, the sprawling inn at this one-street farming town below the low hills of the Montes de Toledo, claims to have been the model for the inn mistaken by Don Quixote for a castle at the very beginning of his adventures. The cobbled courtyard where Quixote was "knighted" by the landlord is always busy with tour groups, but the inn's terraces and basement make for a cool hideaway.

🚗 *From the Venta del Quijote, drive to the town's colonnaded Plaza Mayor, then turn right, signposted Cuenca N420. Follow this road around Alcázar de San Juan to Campo de Criptana. Entering the town, follow signs for "molinos". Go straight at the Don Quixote roundabout. Turn left before the Repsol station and left again at the sign for Sierra de los Molinos. Follow the blue signs. Park by the windmills.*

❷ Campo de Criptana
Ciudad Real; 13610

The prettily whitewashed old Moorish quarter of town, the Albaicín Criptano, spreads out beneath 13 windmills on the rocky hillside, of which 10 have been restored (out of an original group of 32, the largest concentratio in the region). This is the site of Don Quixote's "terrifying and never-to-be imagined Adventure of the Windmill in which the knight jousts with a whirling sail and is flung off his hors Visit the tourist office *(open daily)*, located in Molino Poyatos, for information on visits to the restored **Molino Infante** and **Molino Culebro** *(irregular opening hours).*

🚗 *From the town centre, follow sign for Ciudad Real, then at the lights on the Don Quixote roundabout get onte the CR1222, signposted to Arenales d San Gregorio. At the railway crossing turn left before the tracks. Go over the railway bridge, through Arenales, an turn right for Tomelloso on the CM310. Join the CM3102 and bypass Tomellos for Argamasilla de Alba on the N310. On the outskirts of Argamasilla, turn left, signed CM3115 Lagunas de Ruidera. At the T-junction in Ruidera town, turn right and climb the hill an turn left, following signs for Lagunas d Ruidera. Follow the lakeshore road and turn left at the Hotel Albamanjon sign. Past the hotel there is a picnic spo under a stand of Lombardy poplars. About 1 km (0.6 miles) beyond the pop lars there is a tiny church. Park here.*

Parque Natural de las Lagunas de Ruidera

iudad Real; 13249

he Parque Natural de las Lagunas de Ruidera is one of the largest natural wetland areas in central Spain. Comprising a chain of 15 lakes, the area is naturally wooded and a significant refuge for a large number of birds, as well as other fauna and flora. Start the walk early to avoid crowds and see the lakes and wildlife at their best.

three-hour walking tour

rom the parking near **Ermita de San** dro de Verona ①, walk down to a Y-nction with wooden signs. Take the e de Enmedio trail on the left and low the green arrows, leading ross the valley and up over the hill, uthwards. The footpath winds to the est of the ridge, from where there e panoramic views, and then loops wn to the shore of **Laguna oncejo** ②. Concejo is considered the est faunal area in the lake chain. pend some time pottering along the arshy shoreline trail – here an made road – and observing the rds and other wildlife. Look out for preys fishing over the lake, harmless perine snakes at the water's edge, ure-winged magpies in colourful cks (brought to Spain from China by ilors in the 16th century) and, if lucky dawn, a wild boar or a genet. After 2 km (1 mile) of following e shore of the lake, turn east and llow the trail a further 2 km (1 mile)

through fields towards the hills. At the T-junction signposted "Ruta de Don Quijote", turn left along the trail. Then, before the small bridge, turn left and walk down the track into the poplars. Follow the footpath round to the left until the signpost indicating "Subida al Castillo", which leads up to the ruins of the medieval **Castillo de Rochafrida** ③. Retrace the path to the main trail and turn left to walk back to the car. Visitors with time can walk, 2 km (1 mile) up the road from the church, to the **Cueva de Montesinos** ④ – the limestone cave that features in Book II of *Don Quixote* – up on the plateau. Look out for Great and Little Bustards in the scrub.

🚗 *Take the CR650 back to the N430 in the direction of Manzanares, turning left after 15 km (9 miles) for Villanueva de los Infantes (CM3129). In town, follow "Centro Urbano" signs and turn left in Plaza Santísima Trinidad. Drive up, then turn left into Plaza Mayor. Park outside the square.*

Top Ruins of a medieval castle in Ruidera **Above** Renowned Venta del Quijote in Puerto Lápice

VISITING PARQUE NATURAL DE LAS LAGUNAS DE RUIDERA

Tourist Information
Centro de Recepcíon, Ctra. N-130 Badajoz, 13249; 926 528 116; closed Mon and Tue in winter

Parking
Park near the Ermita de San Pedro de Verona.

EAT AND DRINK

PUERTO LÁPICE

Venta del Quijote *inexpensive*
A popular and busy pub, tapas bar and full-blown restaurant, this place offers a good choice of *raciones* and full meals.
El Molino 4, 13650; 926 576 110; www.ventadelquijote.com

CAMPO DE CRIPTANA

Las Musas *moderate*
This top-notch restaurant on the hillside by the windmills has fine views of the old quarter of town. Try the cod or roast lamb.
C/ Barbero 3, 13610; 926 589 191; www.lasmusasrestaurante.com

LAGUNAS DE RUIDERA

Restaurante Albamanjon *moderate*
With its idyllic setting, the Albamanjon is a wonderful lunch or dinner venue. Try their game stews or slow roast lamb.
Lagunas de San Pedro 16, 02611, Ossa de Montiel; 926 699 048; www.albamanjon.net

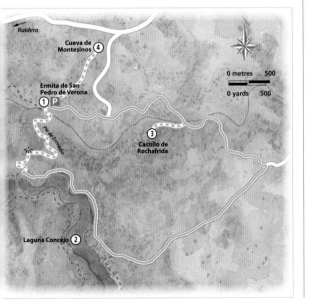

Eat and Drink: inexpensive, under €20; moderate, €20–€40; expensive, over €40

Above Patio in the Santa Cruz palace at Viso del Marqués Below Bronze statues of Don Quixote and Sancho Panza in the square in Villanueva de los Infantes

WHERE TO STAY

VISO DEL MARQUÉS

Hospederia la Almazara del Marqués *moderate*
Palatial style in keeping with its location, this hotel has an austere exterior but a very pleasant interior, with cool public areas and 18 large rooms.
C/ Almagro s/n, 13770; 926 337 154; www.hospederialaalmazara.com

AROUND CASTILLO DE CALATRAVA DE LA NUEVA

Hostal las Palomas *inexpensive*
Friendly enough, with very reasonable, clean, air-conditioned rooms above the busy bar, this place is located on one of Calzada de Calatrava's two main streets. Seafood-based *comedor* (dining room) at the back.
C/ Cervantes 10, 13370, Calzada de Calatrava; 926 876 852; www. hostallaspalomas.com

④ Villanueva de los Infantes
Ciudad Real; 13320
This small Manchegan town has a magnificent Neo-Classical arcaded Plaza Mayor, with the splendid **Iglesia de San Andrés** on its north side and wooden-balconied houses lining its south. Villanueva has a strong claim to be Cervantes' model for the home-town of Don Quixote and there are evocative modern bronzes of Don Quixote and Sancho Panza, with their animals, in the square. Just off the square, west of the church is the 16th-century **Alhóndiga**, the old corn exchange, now the Casa de Cultura. The town is full of beautiful architecture – details are available at the tourist office *(open Mon–Sat)*, on the west side of the square.

Exit Plaza Mayor on the one-way street and, at the roundabout, take the exit signposted Montiel on the CM3127. Turn right at the crossroads, signposted Cózar on the CM3129. Follow the CM3129 to Torre de Juan Abad. Turn sharp right for Castellar de Santiago on the CM3200. After 11 km (7 miles) from Castellar turn right on the rough CR6102 towards Las Virtudes. In Las Virtudes, park outside the bullring on the left.

⑤ Las Virtudes
Ciudad Real; 13730
The extraordinary 17th-century **Plaza de Toros** and the adjoining 15th-century **Santuario de Nuestra Señora de las Virtudes** *(no official opening hours)* are the only sights in tiny Las Virtudes. The square **Plaza de Toros**, (bullring) which dates from 1645, is

vibrant, with red-painted woodwo[rk] stone walls and orange sand. Bullfights are very occasionally staged here between late April and early September. The Santuario de Nuestra Señora de las Virtudes contains some of the finest Baroqu[e] frescoes in the region, many of the[m] bearing influences from those in th[e] palace in Viso del Marqués *(see p18.)*

Leave Las Virtudes on the CR610[?] until it meets the A4-E5 highway. Tu[rn] right (towards Madrid) and take exit 217 to head for Santa Cruz de Mudel[a]. Go straight on the main street until it forks. Take the left fork and turn right twice. Get onto Calle Gloria to find Bodegas Antonio Cañaveras.

⑥ Bodegas Antonio Cañaveras
Ciudad Real; 13730
The vineyards of La Mancha, centred on the region's wine capita[l] Valdepeñas, amount to more than 2,000 sq km (775 sq miles) and produce half the country's output of wine. They are locally known as "the world's biggest vineyard". Although historically viewed as a source for blending both white and red grape wines from *Denominación de Orige[n]* La Mancha and D.O. Valdepeñas ha[ve] been increasingly well reviewed sinc[e] the 1980s. Stop to taste and buy win[e] at the Bodega Antonio Cañaveras *(Santa Cruz de Mudela 42, 629 739 298).*

Return to the A4-E5 and head south. Exit at junction 223 for Bazán and fork right. At Bazán, turn left on the CR5226 to Viso del Marqués. In th[e] village, park outside the main square.

Viso del Marqués

Ciudad Real; 13770

The Renaissance palace of Viso del Marqués completely dominates this little town. Everything about the palace *(guided tours Tue–Sun, closed Mon)* is built on a huge scale. Commissioned by the Marquis of Santa Cruz in 1564 and constructed by Italian architects and artists between 1574 and 1588, it contains many vivid frescoes and a Classical patio. The palace is also home to Spain's national maritime archives. Facing the palace is the exceptionally pretty Plaza Mayor, full of greenery, a splashing fountain and noisy birdlife. For visitors without picnic supplies, the Los Leones restaurant is a good place to stop by.

Follow the CM4111 to Calzada de Calatrava and turn left after 26 km (16 miles). The road leads to the centre of Calzada de Calatrava, one block south of Plaza Mayor. Follow signs to Guardia Civil and Parque Reina Sofia (public gardens) and after passing them, leave town on a road signposted to Villanueva de San Carlos. At the huge junction, take the direction signposted CR504 for Puertollano. The castle will be on the horizon.

Castillo de Calatrava la Nueva

Ciudad Real; 13370

This brooding castle-monastery *(open Tue–Sun; winter closes earlier; be careful of steep stairs and unguarded drops)*, perched on a craggy summit, was founded in 1217 by an order of Cistercian soldier-monks in the vanguard of the Reconquest of Spain. These monks, the Knights of Calatrava, were Spain's first military-religious order. Particularly impressive is the Cistercian church; in this

remote and hostile location, its construction was a remarkable feat and, although empty inside, it is still beautiful. The ruins of **Salvatierra**, the Muslim castle captured by the Calatrava knights in the 12th century, is visible across the valley, but not accessible by road. Visitors can walk to the site, but it has no facilities. The drive from the castle towards Almagro is a good opportunity to see waterfowl, and there are usually lots of storks here, especially near the bridge over the Jabalon river.

From the castle, return towards Calzada de Calatrava, but use the bypass, towards Ciudad Real. At the roundabout, turn right into Calzada, then left at the petrol station, signposted "Almagro" on the CM4129, which becomes the CM413. In Almagro, the parador (with free parking) is signposted left. Otherwise, turn right (signed) to the car park behind the church, Iglesia Madre de Dios.

Above left Seventeenth-century square bullring of Las Virtudes **Above right** Rose window above the entrance to the church in the Castillo de Calatrava **Below** View from the remote Castillo de Calatrava, perched on a mighty crag

EAT AND DRINK

VISO DEL MARQUÉS

Restaurante Los Leones *moderate*
This informal, family-run restaurant on Plaza Mayor offers good Castillian cuisine, big on local meat and vegetables. Eat at tables in the square, or in the dining room at the back.
Plaza del Pradillo 7, 13770; 926 336 098; closed Wed

Eat and Drink: inexpensive, under €20; moderate, €20–€40; expensive, over €40

WHERE TO STAY

ALMAGRO

La Posada de Almagro *moderate*
This charmingly renovated inn around the corner from Plaza Mayor offers excellent value. The rooms, most of which face the planted courtyard, are simple but comfortable.
C/ Gran Maestre 5, 13270; 926 261 201; www.laposadadealmagro.es

Parador de Almagro *expensive*
A converted 16th-century convent in the old town, this is a good example of the Parador group. It is full of antique furniture, with 54 large rooms.
Ronda de San Francisco 31, 13270; 926 860 100; www.parador.es

CONSUEGRA

La Vida de Antes *moderate*
A perennially popular, small, family-run hotel, mixing old-style decor with modern comforts and offering an exceptionally restful ambience.
C/ Colón 2, 45700; 925 480 609; www.lavidadeantes.com

Above Shady colonnades in Plaza Mayor in Almagro **Below** Raised wooden broadwalk through the scenic wetlands of Daimiel

⑨ Almagro
Ciudad Real; 13270

This pretty town, one of the richest in Spain in the 16th century, has the largest and finest Plaza Mayor in La Mancha, featuring green window frames above the colonnades. On its south side, the fascinating 16th-century open-air theatre, the **Corral de Comedias** *(open Tue–Sun)*, is the focus of Almagro's annual theatre festival – one of the biggest in Spain. Most of the town's other notable sites are a 5-minute walk from here, including some superb Renaissance mansions. Visit the **Almacén de los Fúcares**, the 16th-century home and business house of the Fugger

Ornate knocker of a mansion in Almagro

family of Germany – bankers to Charles V (1500–58). The **Museo Etnográfico** *(closed Mon)* has displays of traditional local crafts and practices. The tourist office is at the east end of Plaza Mayor *(closed Mon)*.

🚗 *Leave the old town car park and drive around the ring road until the major roundabout on the east side of town by the Hospedería de Almagro convent. Exit on the road signposted CM4124 Daimiel. In Bolaños de Calatrava, follow the CM4107, which makes a sharp left. At the roundabout on the Daimiel bypass, turn right and drive 3 km (2 miles) before turning left again onto the CR201 for Villarrubia de los Ojos.*

The Dry Marshes of Daimiel

The town of Daimiel is the access point for the Parque Nacional de las Tablas de Daimiel *(926 693 118; http://reddeparquesnacionales.mma.es)*, whose marshlands were formed by the confluence of the Cigüela and upper Guadiana rivers. Parts of the marshlands have been dry since the late 1980s, as water has been diverted by dams for industry and agriculture. In winter, the marshes attract some migrant birds. For the best bird-watching opportunities, arrive early in the morning. The park has trails incorporating attractive wooden boardwalks linking the islands via dry reedbeds and stretches of shallow water; a good stop for drivers. Allow 90 minutes for the 2-km (1-mile) Isla del Pan trail, marked in yellow.

Spain's Golden Age of Theatre

Almagro's Corral de Comedias survives in its original form from the early 17th century, a period when public theatre first flourished in Castile, fed by the prolific output of Spain's Shakespeare, Félix Lope de Vega, and his successor, Pedro Calderón de la Barca. Both playwrights put their plots centrestage, and brought new relevance to old tales by creating characters that their enthusiastic audiences could believe in.

Villarrubia de los Ojos

Ciudad Real; 13670

A small agricultural centre, well off the tourist track, Villarrubia de los Ojos lies at the foot of the Sierra de Villarrubia, part of the Montes de Toledo. It is worth stopping to see the sculptures of vineyard workers, on two roundabouts, movingly executed in rough wood by local carpenter and artist Valentín Rodríguez Camacho (www.carpinteria-rustica. com). The inscription on the town centre sculpture translates: "To the workers of Villarrubia and all those who have left their land to bring dignity to their lives elsewhere". To the north of the town, the road twists into the hills over the pass of **Puerto de los Santos** (970 m/3,200 ft), where lynx are said to survive, and then drops through a beautiful rolling rural landscape of wheatfields, oak and thistle.

From the town centre sculpture roundabout, take the CR200/TO3268 north, direction Urda, then take the CM4116 to Consuegra. On the way to Consuegra, past the bullring, turn right to climb the hill of windmills. Park outside the tourist office.

⑪ Consuegra

Toledo; 45700

Consuegra, founded by the Romans, is famous for its photogenic ridge of 12 windmills, one of which serves as the town's tourist office *(open daily)*. It is an easy 15-minute walk to the southern end of the ridge for wonderful panoramic views. En route is the originally Moorish castle *(open daily)*, which makes a perfect short visit, with plenty of rooms and walkways to explore and views (beware of unguarded drops). The same ticket gives access to the museum located on the town's Plaza Mayor in the 17th-century **Corredores** (former town hall). Just outside town, the dead-straight 700-m (2,300-ft) stone wall across the fields is the **Presa Romana**, a Roman dam. To get to the dam, take the road to Urda past the bullring, then turn left at the blue house with the tyres and follow the track for 2 km (1 mile).

Above Moorish castle in Consuegra **Below** Façade of a superb Renaissance mansion in Almagro

SHOPPING

ALMAGRO

Manzano Gracia
Stop here for lacework made on the premises or locally, including decorative embroidered items, bedspreads and curtains.
C/ Gran Maestre 3 (ring the bell), 13270; 926 882 487

EAT AND DRINK

ALMAGRO

Bar Donde Sea *inexpensive*
A variety of generous free tapas, served with beers and wines, makes Donde Sea a reliable standby. Try the *queso manchego* (Spanish sheep cheese).
Plaza Mayor (south side, near the Corral de Comedias), 13270

Méson El Corregidor *expensive*
This restaurant is located in a smart 19th-century family house with a variety of dining areas, and serves dishes which innovate on local traditions. Try the spinach and garlic cod, or one of the aubergine dishes.
C/ Jerónimo Ceballos 2, 13270; 926 860 648; closed Mon

DAY TRIP OPTIONS

With a base in Puerto Lápice and using the N420 and the A4-E5, one day could be spent visiting the windmills and another day at the palace at Viso del Marqués and the bullring in Las Virtudes.

Quixotic Spain and windmills
Start the day in the sleepy town of Puerto Lápice ①, visiting the cobbled courtyard where Quixote was "knighted" by the landlord. Then

head to the whitewashed old Moorish quarter of Campo de Criptana ②, before taking a stroll among the windmills.

Follow directions in the itinerary starting from Puerto Lápice and return on the same route.

Bullrings, palaces and castles
Visit the 15th-century Sanctuary of Las Virtudes ⑤ in Santa Cruz de Mudela, which contains some of the finest

frescoes in the region, and the 17th-century bullring. Then head to the palace of Viso del Marqués ⑦. If visitors have time, they can go a little further to the Castillo de Calatrava la Nueva ⑧.

Drive 80 km (50 miles) south of Puerto Lápice at junction 220 of the A4-E5, and from there visit Las Virtudes. Follow instructions in the itinerary to Viso del Marqués and to Calatrava la Nueva before driving back to the A4-E5.

Eat and Drink: inexpensive, under €20; moderate, €20–€40; expensive, over €40

White Pueblos

Arcos de la Frontera to Jimena de la Frontera

Highlights

- **Classic Andalusia**
  Drive through the land of rolling fields, with Moorish whitewashed villages perched on dramatic cliff tops

- **Green Grazalema**
  Enjoy picnics and trekking in the Parque Natural de la Sierra de Grazalema

- **Wonderful architecture**
  Take in the dramatic setting and the Moorish and Renaissance architecture of Ronda, beside a spectacular gorge

- **Fiestas, ferias and romerías**
  Watch flamenco and bullfights, and enjoy the cuisine at celebrations throughout the region

Puente Nuevo across the El Tajo gorge in Ronda

White Pueblos

One of the classic images of Andalusia is that of its *pueblos blancos* – fortified hillside towns which are whitewashed in traditional Moorish style. The "frontera" in the names of some settlements refers to the fact that this was once the border between Christian and Muslim kingdoms. This drive starts from the handsome town of Arcos de la Frontera, through less-visited and smaller settlements, to Grazalema, which lies at the centre of one of Spain's most popular hiking areas. The tour also weaves through dramatically located white villages such as Gaucín and Jimena de la Frontera and ends in one of the region's most atmospheric towns, Ronda.

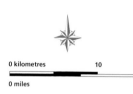

0 kilometres   10

0 miles

Above Picturesque Gaucín in the Sierra del Hacho, see *p197* **Above right** Parador de Ronda, beside the El Tajo gorge, see *p196* **Below** Gate in Ronda's city walls, see *p196*

ACTIVITIES

See wonderful architecture – Gothic, Mudéjar and Renaissance – in Arcos de la Frontera

Hike around the foothills of the Sierra del Pinar in Grazalema

Watch a bullfight in Ronda

Eat classic Andalusian tapas with chilled sherry all over this region

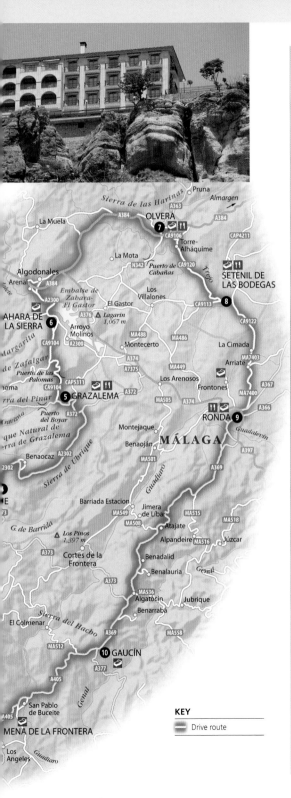

PLAN YOUR DRIVE

Start/finish: Arcos de la Frontera to Jimena de la Frontera.

Number of days: 3–4, allowing half a day each to explore Arcos de la Frontera and Ronda.

Distances: 225 km (140 miles).

Road conditions: Roads are well signposted and smoothly paved. Many parts of the route are winding hill roads; there are no barriers in some sections of the road.

When to go: The region is great to visit all year round, but July and August can be very hot, and many places are crowded.

Opening hours: Shops and monuments are generally open from 10am to 7pm, with many attractions having shorter hours on weekends.

Main market days: Arcos de la Frontera: Fri; Grazalema: Tue; Ronda: Sun; Jimena de la Frontera: Fri.

Shopping: There are many shops selling leather goods in the lively shopping district in Ronda.

Major festivals: Arcos de la Frontera: Toro del Aleluya, Easter Sun; Ronda: Corrida Goyesca (traditional bullfight), first Sat Sep; Jimena de la Frontera: Festival Internacional de Música, Jun/Jul.

DAY TRIP OPTIONS

History buffs and **nature lovers** will enjoy visits to Ronda, Guacín and Jimena de la Frontera, while **adventure lovers** will enjoy walking the hill trails around Zahara de la Sierra, Grazalema and Ubrique. For details, *see p197.*

Above View of Arcos de la Frontera and its hilltop castle **Below** Courtyard of the Hotel Casa Grande in Arcos de la Frontera

VISITING ARCOS DE LA FRONTERA

Tourist Information
Plaza del Cabildo, 11630; 956 702 264; www.ayuntamientoarcos.org

Parking
There is limited parking around the Plaza del Cabildo and only a couple of hotels have their own parking areas – it may be wise to park in the New Town and walk into the Old Town of Arcos.

WHERE TO STAY

ARCOS DE LA FRONTERA

El Convento *moderate*
This 17th-century convent has only 11 rooms, most with amazing views. There is a rooftop terrace for basking in the evening sun.
C/ Maldonado 2, 11630; 956 702 333; www.hotelelconvento.es

Casa Grande *moderate*
Elegant and intimate, Casa Grande offers the best accommodation in Arcos. There are just four doubles and two suites in this 18th-century mansion, all decorated with a fusion of Moroccan and local design.
C/ Maldonado 10, 11630; 956 703 930; www.lacasagrande.net

Parador de Arcos de la Frontera *expensive*
Housed in the Casa del Corregidor, the parador has views of the Guadalete river and the plains surrounding it. The parador's restaurant offers traditional dishes such as corvina a la roteña (sea bass in red pepper sauce).
Plaza del Cabildo s/n, 11630; 956 700 500; www.parador.es

① Arcos de la Frontera
Cádiz; 11630

A whitewashed town typical of the region, Arcos de la Frontera is one of the most spectacular of the *pueblos blancos*, positioned along a sheer cliff that overlooks the valley of the Guadalete river. Although legend has it that a son of Noah founded Arcos, it is more probable that it was the Iberians. Known as Arcobriga during Roman times, the town grew considerably under the Moors who built a labyrinthine quarter that twists up to the town's castle.

The **Plaza del Cabildo**, the pretty main square, is at the heart of Arcos de la Frontera and easily found by following the signs for the parador that occupies the east side of it. The opposite side is occupied by a lovely 11th-century Moorish castle, rebuilt by the Christians after the *reconquista*. The third side is dominated by the impressive late Gothic-Mudéjar **Iglesia de Santa María de la Asunción** *(closed Sat and Sun afternoon)*, noted for its choir stalls and altarpiece. The church has different styles as various generations have added to, improved or repaired the building, which was originally built in the 13th century.

Iglesia de Santa María de la Asunción

The final side of the square is most remarkable for not being there at all – the sheer walls of the *peña nueva* (New Rock) plunge down from here. Stand on the edge to take in sweeping views of the river valley below and of the rolling hills.

A string of narrow streets, Calle Escribanos, Calle Boticos and Calle Nuñez de Prado, lead to the 17th-century **Convento de las Mercedarias Descalzas**, home to a closed order of nuns who sell cakes and biscuits. Ring the bell, give the order through a grille and the baked goodies will be delivered on a revolving lantern, all without any face to face contact. Find the entrance on the right-hand side of the narrow passageway leading from the parador to the Hotel El Convento.

For some down-to-earth delights, stroll to the **Galería de Arte Arx-Arcis** *(closed Sun)* on Calle Marqués de Torresoto near Plaza Boticos. A crafts museum and shop, housed in a labyrinthine building, it displays locally fashioned carpets, blankets, artwork

and ceramics. Near Plaza Boticos is the unfinished church that was started in the 18th century by the Jesuits, who were forced to abandon it on their expulsion from Spain. Further along the road is the precariously perched Gothic **Iglesia de San Pedro**, built between the 16th and 18th centuries. Its thick-set tower provides stunning views over the sheer drop down to the Guadalete river.

For more breathtaking views of the Guadalete river, go to the **Mirador de Abades** on Calle Abades. On Calle Almirante are two palaces, the **Casa Palacio de Cuenca** on the left and the **Antigua Casa Palacio del Marqués de Torresoto**, now a hotel, a 17th-century Renaissance palace which has a richly decorated exterior and beautiful interior patios.

🚗 *Leave Arcos heading northwards on the A393. Then join the A384 and follow it northeast towards Bornos.*

956 716 063; open daily). El Bosque is also a popular site for hunting and fishing and houses a trout farm.

🚗 **Drive back to the A373 and continue southwards on it. At the fork after Travizna, bear right, still on the A373, to Ubrique.**

④ Ubrique
Cádiz; 11600

A picturesque *pueblo blanco* in the Serrania de Ronda mountains, Ubrique has a long, interesting history which stretches over many empires and centuries. Its origins can be traced back to Palaeolithic times or earlier. Much of the area's finest architecture was burned down during Napoleon's invasion but **Ocuri**, a Roman city 1 km (0.6 miles) from Ubrique, is still remarkably preserved and excavations have unearthed a 1st-century BC crematorium and irrigation aquifers. The town is well-known for its flourishing leather industry. Leather handbags and shoe shops along the streets in the centre hark back to the 18th century, when immigrants from southern Italy brought the leather trade with them.

This beautiful and tranquil town is also known for its flamboyant bull-fighter, Jesulín de Ubrique, now retired, who has an estate nearby.

🚗 **Drive back to where the road forks and turn right onto the A2302 towards Grazalema. When the road forks again, just before the town, bear left onto the A372 to Grazalema.**

Left Iglesia de San Pedro in Arcos de la Frontera **Below** Ubrique at the foot of the Sierra de Ubrique

Bornos
…diz; 11640

…rawled across a wide open valley, …rnos is primarily an agricultural …wn. The centre of this small town …illed with stately houses and small, …anicured gardens. The dam on the …adalete river makes it look like a …e here and the well-watered fields …rounding the town produce a …ge of fruits and vegetables. …rnos is famous for its cabbage …ws as well as its basket-making.

Continue on the A384 following …ns for Villamartín, 12 km (7 miles) …the northeast. At Villamartín turn …ht onto the A373 and then, after …ssing the road to Prado del Rey, …n left onto the A372 to El Bosque.

El Bosque
…diz; 11670

…is picturesque village has a few …teworthy 18th-century buildings …cluding the Ermita del Calvario, the …esia de Nuestra Senora de …adalupe and the Molino del Duque …l. However, El Bosque is better …own to travellers as one of the main …teways to the **Parque Natural de la …erra de Grazalema**, a nature reserve …vering 535 sq km (205 sq miles). …alking permits are required for some …eas of the park because some spe-…es of flora found here, such as the …llenarian *Abies pinsapo* (Spanish fir) …e, are rare. Information and permits …r the walks are available at the park's …itor centre (*Avenida de la Diputación;*

EAT AND DRINK

ARCOS DE LA FRONTERA
Peña Flamenca de Arcos *moderate*
Put on your dancing shoes and head on down to Arcos' flamenco club. There are shows occasionally.
Plaza de la Caridad s/n, 11630; 956 701 251

EL BOSQUE
Enrique Calvillo *moderate*
Fresh trout with ham, dark bull's tail and classic Spanish ham are some of the standards at this lively, friendly restaurant housed in a *hotel rural.*
Avda. Diputación 5, 11630; 956 716 105; www.hotelenriquecalvillo.com

Eat and Drink: inexpensive, under €20; moderate, €20–€40; expensive, over €40

Above Panoramic view from the Puerto de las Palomas pass **Below** Quiet village of Zahara de la Sierra dominated by its ruined castle

WHERE TO STAY

GRAZALEMA

Hotel Puerta de la Villa *expensive*
A smart hotel for the price, this place boasts a pool, jacuzzi, gym and sauna.
Plaza Pequeña 8, 11610; 956 132 376; www.grazalemahotel.com

ZAHARA DE LA SIERRA

Hotel Arco de la Villa *inexpensive*
On the edge of the Parque Natural de la Sierra de Grazalema, this charming, cosy hotel has just 17 rooms, all with views of the nearby lake. Breakfast of bread, oil and jams is included.
Paseo Nazarí, 11688; 956 123 230

OLVERA

Sierra y Cal *inexpensive*
This quietly stylish 33-room hotel has a large terrace with a swimming pool and a tea lounge. Its restaurant is acclaimed for its local cuisine.
Avda. Nuestra Señora de los Remedios 2, 11690; 956 130 542

SETENIL DE LAS BODEGAS

El Almendral *inexpensive*
A friendy, typically Andalusian hotel, this place has an outdoor pool, a tennis court and a manicured lawn.
C/ Setenil-Ronda, 11692; 956 134 029

⑤ Grazalema
Cádiz; 11610

The village of Grazalema is set in the centre of the **Parque Natural de la Sierra de Grazalema**. It was very prosperous between the 17th and 19th centuries, when it became famous for its textile manufacturing industry, that it was called *Cádiz el Chico* (Little Cádiz). A number of grand houses and churches are testimony to this wealthy era. The village's Artesania Textil de Grazalema guild is busy reviving the traditional methods of cloth-making and blanket-weaving.

The Parque Natural de la Sierra de Grazalema has some of the highest rainfall in Spain and a walk around Grazalema offers impressive views over the green hills that surround the village on all sides. There are a number of walking and horse riding trails from here, as well as an array of mountain sports, including bungee jumping, potholing and abseiling. The influx of visitors to the village from Cádiz and Seville means that restaurants and other facilities are sometimes over-stretched at weekends and in the peak summer season.

🚗 *Continue westwards on the A372 from Grazalema, then turn right onto the CA9104 (still signed as the CA531 in some stretches) towards Zahara de la Sierra. Rising through a series of switchbacks to the pass at Puerto de las Palomas (1,360 m/4,450 ft), the road offers outstanding panoramic vistas. Visitors can park up at the pass and marvel at the impressive bit of road construction. At the junction after the pass bear right, still on the CA9104, to Zahara de la Sierra.*

The White Towns

Western Andalusia is instantly recognizable by its classic white villages and towns. The houses are painted in traditional Moorish style. Many of these fortified hillside villages were founded by Berber tribes who settled in the area during the eight centuries of Moorish presence. These flat-roofed houses, often built of baked clay, are usuall[y] whitewashed in spring mainly for a practical reason: to deflect the sun's harsh rays. They also have few windows to help keep the interiors cool. The Andalusian Moorish legacy is also evident in the exquisite ubiquitous glazed tiles, patios and wrought iron work.

⑥ Zahara de la Sierra
Cádiz; 11688

The houses of Zahara de la Sierra a[re] scattered on a hillside beneath the ruins of a castle that sit high above on the mountain peak. The Moor[ish] castle *(open daily)* gives spectacular views over this village and the artificial lake that spans the foot of the hill. Declared a historic monument [in] 1983, the town has many attractive sights such as the Torre del Homen[aje,] a 16th-century watchtower, the Iglesia de Santa María de la Mesa with its Baroque altarpiece and the **Arco de la Villa**. There is a restored olive mill, **Molino El Vinculo** *(open Fri–Sun)*, just outside Zahara de la Sierra, where visitors are shown ho[w] olive oil is traditionally produced. T[he] reservoir just outside the town give[s] visitors the option of water sports and swimming.

🚗 *Leave Zahara on the A2300 and follow signs for Algodonales. Turn right onto the eastbound A384 and*

en the road forks, bear left, still on
e A384, for Olvera. At the cross-
ıds near the town, turn left onto
e A363 to reach Olvera.

Olvera

diz; 11690

the early 20th century this town's
onomy received a boost as Olvera
came a key station on a new rail
k between Almargen and prosper-
ıs Jerez de la Frontera. Today this
andoned track bed still nourishes
e town's economy, providing visi-
ʳs with an interesting hiking and
king route to Puerto Serrano. Other
ːeresting sights in Olvera include
recently renovated castle and
e **Iglesia de la Encarnación** with
small but fascinating museum
ɔen daily). Also worth a visit is the
mita de Nuestra Senora de los
medios (open daily), just 2 km
mile) from Olvera. It has a room
ʋplaying interesting offerings such
photographs, trophies and wed-
ɪg dresses, all dedicated to the
ɪgen de los Remedios to thank
r for her "miracles".
  Drive back on the A363 and turn
t onto the A384. Turn right south-
ırds, onto the CA9106, a quiet
untry road, which becomes the
ʌ9120 after the small white village
Torre-Alháquime. On the outskirts
Setenil de las Bodegas, turn left
to the CA9113 which will take
ʋitors into the town.

Setenil de las Bodegas

diz; 11692

ɪenil de las Bodegas is a *pueblo*
ʌnco with a difference, with many
its streets carved into the side of

an overhanging gorge of volcanic
tufa rock formed by the Trejo river.
Depending on the time of year, this
town's tourist office *(open daily)*,
housed in a medieval building, can
arrange visits to some local cave
homes. The town's ruined Moorish
castle has a vestigial tower that is
worth a careful climb. The "bodegas"
in the town's name hark back to the
town's wine trade, which flourished
from the 15th century onwards but
was wiped out in the 1860s by
phylloxera (insects that destroy
vines). Olives and almonds are still
important local industries. Setenil
also produces quality meat products
and is known for its fine pastries.
  🚗 *Leave town on the CA9113*
eastwards and almost immediately
turn right onto the CA9122, which
becomes the MA7403 when entering
the Málaga province. Continue on the
MA7403 to Arriate, a tiny, quiet town
overlooking the Ronda mountain
range. Just south of Arriate the road
becomes the MA7400, which joins the
A367 to Ronda.

Above Picturesque walking trail in the Sierra
de Grazalema **Below left** Sign at the entrance
to Setenil de las Bodegas **Below right** Church
in the white village of Olvera

EAT AND DRINK

GRAZALEMA

Mirador El Tajo *moderate*
Great rabbit, quail and lamb dishes and
dramatic views of the surrounding hills
are the attraction here.
Avda. Juan de la Rosa s/n, 11610; 666
502 957; www.eltajo.com

OLVERA

El Puerto de los Arbolitos *moderate*
Charcoal-grilled meats, traditional
cuisine, stews and homemade
desserts in a country-style atmosphere
in the heart of the beautiful white
town of Olvera.
C/Cordel 2, 11690; 956 120 532

SETENIL DE LAS BODEGAS

El Mirador *moderate*
Set slightly away from the main
restaurant cluster on Plaza de
Andalucía, this restaurant serves
great *paella* and other rice dishes.
C/Callejon, 11692; 956 134 527

SETENIL
DE LAS
BODEGAS

Above El Tajo gorge within Ronda

VISITING RONDA

Tourist information
Paseo de Blas Infante, 29400; 952 187 119; www.turismoderonda.es

Parking
Parking is available on the Plaza del Socorro.

WHERE TO STAY

RONDA

Parador de Ronda *expensive*
Book in advance to get a room here. The views are amazing, the decor innovative and the experience palatial.
Plaza de Espana s/n, 29400; 952 877 500; www.parador.es

AROUND RONDA

Hotel La Fuente de la Higuera *expensive*
This luxurious hotel 10 km (6 miles) north of Ronda, is cool and chic and the Mediterranean cuisine using organic produce is top-class too.
Partido de los Frontones s/n, 29400; 952 114 355; www.hotellafuente.com

GAUCÍN

El Nobo *moderate*
With superb views of the surrounding countryside, this place has gorgeous rooms and villas.
Camino de Gibraltar, 29480; 952 151 303; www.elnobo.co.uk

JIMENA DE LA FRONTERA

Posada La Casa Grande *inexpensive*
This small hotel is run by a Norwegian expat. Rooms are spacious and bright.
C/ Fuentenueva 42, 11330; 956 640 297; www.posadalacasagrande.es

⑨ Ronda
Málaga; 29400

Rainer Maria Rilke (1875–1926), the great German poet, called Ronda the "dream city". Ronda's cliff-top buildings sit astride a high limestone cleft, parted by the Guadalevín river and surrounded by mountains. The town's adopted symbol is the 18th-century Puente Nuevo (New Bridge) that spans the gorge and links the old Moorish citadel in the south (La Ciudad) to the newer town (the Mercadillo quarter), home to one of Spain's oldest bullrings. It is here that the walking tour begins.

A three-hour walking tour

From the car park walk down Calle de Espinel to Calle Virgen de la Paz. Turn left into it to reach the **Puente Nuevo** ①, which spans the jaw-dropping El Tajo gorge created by the Guadalevín river. It links the old Moorish citadel in the south to the newer town in the north and was completed in 1793 after four decades of impressive work by stonemasons and labourers. Civil War prisoners were forced to jump to their deaths from the bridge and the pre-jump jail, above one of the arches, has now been converted into a museum.

Turn left into Calle de Santo Domingo to reach the inaccurately named **Casa del Rey Moro** ② (House of the Moorish King), actually built in 1709. Beneath the house is a rock-cut stairway, which does date back to Moorish times, leading to beautiful French landscaped gardens. Continue down Calle de Santo Domingo and then turn right into Calle Marqués de Salvatierra to see the 18th-century

Palacio del Marqués de Salvatierra ③. The palace is closed to the public but look for the figurines on the façade which were inspired by Latin American native art. Beside the palace is a stone cross marking the spot where Don Vasco Martín de Salvatierra camped after the Reconquest of Ronda in June 1485. Take in views of the Puente de San Miguel, Ronda's oldest bridge, and the 13th-century Baños Árabes (Arab Baths) from here.

Continue along Calle Marqués de Salvatierra and turn left down Calle de Armiñán to arrive at the picturesque orange-tree-lined **Plaza de la Duquesa de Parcent** ④. Stroll in the shade towards the northern end of the square to visit the **Iglesia de Santa María la Mayor** ⑤, once a Roman temple, then a mosque and now the town's main church. The local archaeology museum is housed in the **Palacio de Mondragón** ⑥, a fine building to the west of the church on Calle de Manuel Monter. From here, walk across the Plaza de

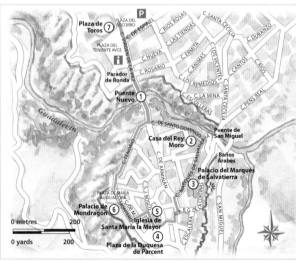

áría Auxiliadora to the narrow,
nding Calle Tenorio and follow it
ck to Calle de Armiñán and the
ente Nuevo.
Walk back down Calle Virgen de la
z to the **Plaza de Toros** ⑦, one of
e oldest and most beautiful bull-
gs in Spain, inaugurated in 1785. It
here that the classic Ronda style of
ullfighting was developed by Pedro
mero, one of the fathers of bull-
hting. Walk back down Calle de
pinel, to the right of the bullring,
reach the car park.
█ *Leave Ronda on the A369 which
ads to Gaucín, 37 km (23 miles) to
e southwest.*

⑩ **Gaucín**
álaga; 29480
cated more than 600 m (2,000 ft)
gh in the Serrania, Gaucín offers
ews over the Mediterranean, the
lantic, the Rock of Gibraltar and
e Rif mountains of North Africa
n clear days. Gaucín takes its name
om the Arab word *guazan* (strong
ck), a reference to the Sierra del
acho on which it is perched. The

Romans made use of its unique strategic position and built the **Castillo del
Aguila** (Eagle's Castle) which also has
later Moorish additions.
The heart of the village is a tangle
of narrow, twisting streets and was
once a haven for brandy and
tobacco smugglers who travelled
through the surrounding hills.
Gaucín was popular with British
officers in the 19th century, who used
to stop here on the way to Gibraltar.
Today, many wealthy expats reside
here, served by an ample choice of
bars, restaurants and art shops.
🚗 *Leave Gaucín on the A405. In San
Pablo de Buceite take the road to the
right, still the A405, and head westwards on it to Jimena de la Frontera,
re-entering the province of Cádiz.*

⑪ **Jimena de la Frontera**
Cádiz; 11330
Jimena de la Frontera is set beneath
an extensive ruined Moorish castle,
amid hills where wild bulls graze in
the shade of olive and cork trees. The
Moors used the village as a strategic
military point. Jimena de la Frontera
is also popular with expats, and approximately one in nine of its residents is
foreign. However, it still retains its
local whitewashed charm and steep
cobbled streets.
Beneath the village is the
Hozgarganta river valley, which is a
spectacular place for hiking and
swimming if the weather is favour-
able. The surrounding countryside
also has several game reserves and
rich forest land.

EAT AND DRINK

RONDA

Almócabar *moderate*
This is one of the best places in Ronda
for tapas, served in the front bar, or a
full meal in the restaurant. The latter
has interesting Arab-Andalusian
dishes. Drink the excellent local red
wine, Cortijo de las Monjas.
*Plaza Ruedo Alameda 5, 29400;
952 875 977; closed Tue*

La Gota de Vino 13 *moderate*
Serving a large range of great wine,
this restaurant also has an excellent
menu with dishes made with
ingredients from the local market.
C/ Sevilla 13, 29400; 952 875 716

El Escudero *expensive*
Near the bullring, this stylish restaurant
has refined modern Andalusian cuisine
and spectacular views typical of Ronda.
*Paseo Blas Infante 1, 29400; 952 871
367; closed Sun evening*

Above Field of flowers on the outskirts of
Jimena de la Frontera

DAY TRIP OPTIONS
This drive can be divided into two
shorter day trips for those who do
not have the time to attempt the
full drive. Visitors can use either
Ronda (near the A397) or Zahara de
la Sierra (near the AP4) as a base
for these trips.

Beautiful white villages
Start at Ronda ⑨, the city of bridges
and the most popular of the *pueblos
blancos*. The town is a great place to
walk around in. Head south to
Gaucín ⑩ for views of the Costa del
Sol and, on a clear day, Morocco.
Continue to Jimena de la Frontera ⑪,

a pretty hilltop hamlet with an
impressive Moorish castle.

*Leave Ronda on the A369, which heads
southwest to Gaucín. Continue on the
A369 till the road forks. Take the A405,
the road to the right, and head westwards on it to Jimena de la Frontera.*

High roads and hiking
Start off at Zahara de la Sierra ⑥, a
striking white village on a steep hillside topped by a Moorish castle,
from which there are spectacular
views over the town and the lake on
the outskirts of the town. Head south
to Grazalema ⑤, a lively town known

for its carpet-weaving and textile
industry and the hub of arguably the
best hillwalking region in the whole
of Andalusia. Head south towards
Ubrique ④, which provides access
to other hill trails in the Parque
Natural de la Sierra de Grazalema.

*Take the CA9104 southwards from
Zahara de la Sierra towards Grazalema
and then turn left onto the A372 to
reach Grazalema. From Grazalema
continue on the A372 to the southwest
and then turn right onto the A2302
towards Ubrique. Turn left when the
road forks onto the A373 to reach the
hillside town of Ubrique.*

Eat and Drink: inexpensive, under €20; moderate, €20–€40; expensive, over €40

Coast of Light

Jerez de la Frontera to Tarifa

Highlights

- **Sherry stops**
  Explore old bodegas all over this region and sample *fino* and *manzanilla* sherry

- **Europe's oldest city**
  Discover the secret alleyways and laid-back ambience of old Cádiz

- **Secret beaches**
  Enjoy the long ocean beaches between Rota and Zahara de los Atunes

- **Windsurfer's paradise**
  Take a boat trip to see whales or go windsurfing and kitesurfing in Tarifa

Catedral Nueva by the waterfront in Cádiz

Coast of Light

The Costa de la Luz is the western stretch of the Andalusian coastline facing the Atlantic Ocean. The beaches here are wide and long and the sand is finer and more golden than on the neighbouring Costa del Sol – the special light makes it extraordinarily beautiful. Strong Atlantic winds and waves attract windsurfers and surfboarders from all over Europe to this region. This drive goes through some lovely seaside towns and, just inland, sleepy white *pueblos*, starting with the sherry-making city of Jerez. The tour ends at Tarifa, the windsurfing capital of Europe.

Above Enjoying the beach at Rota, *see p204* **Below** Domes of the Catedral Nueva in Cádiz, *see p205*

KEY

Drive route

ACTIVITIES

Watch and hear flamenco in Jerez de la Frontera during the Festivales de Flamenco

Go sherry tasting and bodega-hopping in Sanlúcar de Barrameda

Explore Cádiz and its Old Town

Wander through the pretty white villages of Medina-Sidonia and Vejer de la Frontera

Swim, surf, windsurf or kitesurf on the beach at Tarifa

Above Ornate façade of Catedral de San Salvador in Jerez de la Frontera, *see p202*

Map labels:
Junta de los Ríos
La Barca de la Florida
Torrecera
Gigonza
Paterna de Rivera
MEDINA-SIDONIA
Los Badalejos
Benalup-Casas Viejas
Cantarranas
VEJER DE LA FRONTERA
Barbate
AHARA DE OS ATUNES
Atlanterra
Pta. Camarinal
Ensenada de Bolonia
Ensenada de Valdevaqueros
TARIFA
Punta Marroquí o de Tarifa
Strait of Gibraltar

Embalse del Guadalcacín
San José del Valle
Pto. de Galis 417 m
La Sauceda
Alcalá de los Gazules
CÁDIZ
Embalse del Barbate
El Jautor
P. del Castraño
Embalse del Guadarranque
Castellar de la Frontera
Embalse del Celemín
Sierra Blanquilla
Parque Natural de los Alcornocales
Almoraima
Embalse de Charco Redondo
Sierra del Niño
Taraguilla
Tahivilla
La Zarzuela
Facinas
Los Barrios
Algeciras
Bahía de Algeciras
El Lentiscal
La Peña
El Cuartón
El Bujeo
Punta Carnero
Ensenada del Tolmo

ATLANTIC OCEAN

0 kilometres 10
0 miles 10

PLAN YOUR DRIVE

Start/finish: Jerez de la Frontera to Tarifa.

Number of days: 3–4, allowing half a day each to explore Jerez de le Frontera and Cádiz.

Distances: 220 km (140 miles).

Road conditions: Well paved and signposted throughout; some busy roads around Jerez and Cádiz.

When to go: The ideal time to visit the Costa de la Luz is March to June and mid-September to October when it is not too hot and there are not too many visitors. July to mid-September is the peak season and can be very hot, especially inland.

Opening hours: Shops, monuments and museums are generally open from 10am to 6 or 7pm. Many attractions have shorter hours at weekends, and in winter.

Main market days: Jerez de la Frontera: Mon; Sanlúcar de Barrameda: Wed; Cádiz: Mon; Tarifa: Tue.

Shopping: Antiques and antiquarian books, jewellery and handicrafts can be purchased in Cádiz.

Major festivals: Jerez de la Frontera: Festival de Flamenco, Feb/Mar; Festival de Jerez, first Sat Sep; Sanlúcar de Barrameda: Exaltación del Río Guadalquivir (horse racing on the beach), mid-Jul to mid-Aug; Cádiz: Carnaval de Cádiz, Feb/Mar; Tarifa: Romería de la Virgen de la Luz (traditional pilgrimage on horseback), first Sun Sep.

DAY TRIP OPTIONS

Wine lovers will enjoy driving the sherry circuit from Jerez de la Frontera to El Puerto de Santa María through Sanlúcar de Barrameda, Chipiona and Rota. **Families** and **adventure enthusiasts** will enjoy a drive to the beaches at Zahara de los Atunes and Tarifa. For details, *see p207*.

Above Tio Pepe vineyard on the road from Jerez de la Frontera to Arcos

❶ Jerez de la Frontera

Cádiz; 11407

Jerez first rose to prominence under the Moors who ruled it until 1264. Their greatest architectural achievement in the city is the 11th-century Alcázar which encompasses a well-preserved mosque now a church. The capital of sherry production, Jerez is surrounded by a countryside blanketed with rows of vines. The city has several world-famous sherry bodegas. It is also famous for its flamenco and there are flamenco venues to suit all budgets. The city is the region centre for equestrian skills and horse-lovers from all see the performances at the Real Escuela Andaluza the Royal Riding School.

VISITING JEREZ DE LA FRONTERA

Tourist Information
Alameda Cristina s/n, 11403; 956 338 874; www.turismojerez.com

Parking
Parking is available in Los Cisnes on Calle Larga.

SHERRY BODEGAS

Bodegas Gonzáles-Byass
C/ Manuel Maria González 12, 11403; 902 440 077; www.gonzalezbyass.com; open daily

Bodegas Fundador-Pedro Domecq
C/ San Ildefonso 3, 11403; 956 151 500; www.bodegasfundadorpedrodomecq. com; closed Sun; reservations recommended

EQUESTRIAN DISPLAYS

Real Escuela Andaluza de Arte Ecuestre
Avda. Duque de Abrantes, 11407; 956 319 635; www.realescuela.com; open Mon–Sat

WHERE TO STAY

JEREZ DE LA FRONTERA

La Fonda Barranco *moderate*
An old house in the heart of Jerez has been carefully restored to house this elegant and comfortable small hotel.
C/ Barranco 12, 11403; 956 332 141; www.lafondabarranco.es

Casa Viña de Alcántara *expensive*
Housed in a stately mansion 21 km (13 miles) from Jerez, Casa Viña has extensive grounds and sherry vineyards.
Ctra. Jerez-Arcos; 956 393 010; www.vinadealcantara.com

SANLÚCAR DE BARRAMEDA

Hotel Posada de Palacio *moderate*
Luxury and a traditional Andaluz ambience are combined in this mansion in Sanlúcar's Old Town.
C/ Caballeros 9, 11540; 956 364 840; www.posadadepalacio.com

A two-hour walking tour

From the car park walk northwards on Calle Larga, the main shopping artery. Turn right into Alameda Cristina to reach the **Palacio Domecq ①** which is typical of the 18th-century late Baroque sherry barons' homes. Next to the palace, on Calle Rosario, is the **Convento de Santo Domingo ②** *(open for Mass only)*. The Baroque altar here is worth seeing. Go back to Calle Larga and continue southwards on it to a distinctive circular building, the popular **Gallo Azul Café ③**. From Plaza Esteve, the square in front of the café, head southwest down Calle Lanceria to the **Plaza del Arenal ④** where horse races are sometimes held. Head up Calle Consistorio, to the north of the plaza, to reach the **Plaza de la Asunción ⑤**, home to Jerez's *ayuntamiento viejo* (old town hall). From the plaza turn left to walk down Calle de José Luis Díez, which

becomes Calle Cruces, to visit the **Catedral de San Salvador ⑥** *(open daily; Sat, Sun Mass only)*, that is built on the site of an old mosque and is a mix of Gothic, Renaissance and Baroque styles. The towers of the cathedral offer views of the surrounding area. Southwest of the cathedral, down Plaza del Arroyo, is the **Puerta del Arroyo ⑦**, a 16th-century city gate. Two of the town's largest sherry bodegas, González-Byass and Fundador-Pedro Domecq, are on either side of the gate and both offer tours. Go back towards the cathedral and turn right on Calle Encarnación to the 12th-century **Alcázar de Jerez ⑧** *(open daily)*. The fortress has a camera obscura, a small round darkened room with a rotating angled mirror at the apex of the roof, projecting images of the landscape onto a flat surface inside. From the alcázar, walk eastwards down Calle de Manuel María

doorway. A short walk away, on Calle Caballeros, is the **Castillo de Santiago**, the 15th-century Moorish castle, flanked on two sides by *manzanilla* sherry bodegas, including the town's largest sherry maker, **Barbadillo**, founded in 1821. *Manzanilla*, a light, dry sherry, is said to owe its salty tang to the local sea breeze.

Sanlúcar is also home to some of the oldest horse races in Europe. The 1,500 m (1,650 yd) and 1,800 m (2,000 yd) races take place just before sunset, along the beach at the mouth of the Guadalquivir river, every August, with thousands of spectators in attendance.

Across the Guadalquiver river to the west of Sanlúcar is the vast Parque Nacional de Doñana. Boat trips run at regular intervals from the Sanlúcar waterfront to the park.

🚗 *Return to the A480 and follow signs to Chiopiona, 9 km (6 miles) to the west.*

The Rules of Sherry

Real sherry can only be produced in the triangle formed by Sanlúcar de Barrameda, El Puerto de Santa María and Jerez de la Frontera, and gets its name from Jerez. It is made from two main varieties of grapes, Palomino and Pedro Ximénez, and also gets its special qualities from the region's white *albariza* soils. Andalusians drink the light, pale *fino* and *manzanilla* styles of sherry, which are 15.5 percent alcohol (only a little stronger than many table wines), with tapas. The longer-aged, richer, yet still dry styles of *amontillado* and *oloroso* sherry, with a higher percentage of alcohol, are traditionally made mainly for export.

ɔnzález to the Plaza de Arenal. Walk ɔross the plaza and to the car park.

🚗 *From central Jerez follow signs r the NIVa Cádiz road and in the ɔtskirts of the city turn right onto ɔ A480, which becomes the A471 ɔar Sanlúcar de Barrameda.*

ɔ Sanlúcar de Barrameda
ɔdiz; 11540

ɔe city of Sanlúcar is famous as the ɔeparture port for Columbus's third ɔyage in 1498 and for Magellan's ɔ19 expedition – during which his ɔutenant, Juan Sebastián de Elcano, ɔmpleted the first circumnavigation ɔf the globe.

The town is divided into two main ɔstricts: the Barrio Alto, the old part of ɔe town up on the hill, and the Barrio ɔjo beneath it. The centre proper is ɔ the Barrio Bajo, and has elegant ɔedestrian thoroughfares and a series ɔf pretty plazas. There is a long prome-ɔde, Bajo de Guía, beside the ɔadalquiver river, lined with outdoor ɔafood restaurants that are great ɔaces for an atmospheric feast.

Sanlúcar has a number of impressive ɔurches, including the 16th-century ɔlesia de Santo Domingo and 17th-ɔntury **Iglesia de San Francisco**, both ɔ the Barrio Alto. The Old Town also ɔs two palaces – the **Palacio de los ɔuques de Medina-Sidonia**, still inhab-ɔed by the current bearer of the title, ɔd the **Palacio de Orleans y Borbon** ɔe town hall). Next door to the ɔtter is the town's oldest church, the ɔth-century **Iglesia de Nuestra ɔenora de la O** *(open daily)*, which ɔatures a richly decorated Mudéjar

VISITING SANLÚCAR DE BARRAMEDA

Tourist Information
C/ Calzada del Ejército, 11540; 956 366 110

Parking
There is convenient underground parking at La Calzada, just opposite the Hotel Guadalquivir.
Avda. la Calzada del Ejército, 11540; 956 385 408

SHERRY BODEGAS
Bodegas Barbadillo
C/ Luis de Eguilaz, 11, 11540; 956 385 500; www.barbadillo.com

EAT AND DRINK

JEREZ DE LA FRONTERA
Cafetería La Vega *inexpensive*
This is the place to come to soak up some real local atmosphere, and the tapas and traditional fish dishes can all be recommended.
Plaza Estévez, 11540; 956 337 748

Bar Juanito *moderate*
An atmospheric tapas bar and restaurant, this place has a reputation for its exceptionally large portions.
C/ Pescardería Vieja 8; 956 341 218; www.bar-juanito.com; closed Sun dinner

SANLÚCAR DE BARRAMEDA
Casa Bigote *expensive*
This is a former sailor's tavern that is the most famous of the terrace restaurants on the Bajo de Guía, with a fine view of the mouth of the Guadalquivir.
C/ Bajo de Guía 10; 956 362 696; www.restaurantecasabigote.com

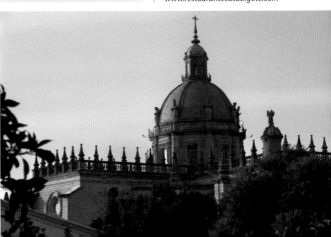

Above Wooded park near Playa de la Castilla in Rota **Below** Statue at the Catedral Neuva in Cádiz

VISITING BODEGAS IN EL PUERTO DE SANTA MARÍA

Bodegas Osborne
C/ de los Moros, 11500; 956 869 100; www.osborne.es; open Mon–Sat; advance booking required

Bodegas Terry
C/ Toneleros s/n, 11500; 956 151 500; www.bodegasterry.com; closed Sun

WHERE TO STAY

CHIPIONA

Hotel Brasilia moderate
With its pleasant garden, swimming pool and solarium, this is one of Chipiona's most enjoyable hotels.
Avda. del Faro 12, 11550; 956 371 054; www.brasiliahotel.net

ROTA

Hotel Caribe moderate
This hotel is a peaceful refuge after a day of swimming and sunbathing.
Avda. de la Marina 60, 11550; 956 810 700; www.hotel-caribe.com

CÁDIZ

Hotel Argantonio moderate
Mosaic floors and warm stone interiors make this elegant boutique hotel one of the most romantic refuges in Cádiz.
C/ Argantonio 3, 11002; 956 211 640; www.hotelargantonio.com

Pension Centro-Sol moderate
A tiny pension housed in a refurbished Neo-Classical buiding, this hotel is situated in one of Cádiz's lovely alleyways.
Manzanares 7, 11004; 956 283 103; www.hostalcentrosolcadiz.com

❸ Chipiona
Cádiz; 11550

Situated on one of the quieter stretches of the Costa de la Luz, Chipiona offers 12 km (7 miles) of golden beaches. Playa de Regla is one of the best beaches, but for a quieter experience Playa Cruz del Mar or Las Canteras are worth a try. Popular with Spanish tourists, Chipiona is known for its bracing waters along its beaches and good seafood restaurants: white crabs and lobster are two popular local products. This seaside town is home to the **Faro de Chipiona** (guided visits; 956 377 263), Spain's tallest lighthouse and the third-highest in the world. It dates from 1867, but a lighthouse was first built on this spot by the Romans in 140 BC to guide ships to the entrance of the Guadalquivir. The town has attractive buildings such as the 16th-century **Parroquia de Nuestra Senora de la O** and the 14th-century former **Monasterio de Nuestra Senora de la Regla**.

🚗 Take the A491 southwards out of Chipiona. After 12 km (7 miles) follow signs onto the A2075 to Rota.

❹ Rota
Cádiz; 11520

Founded by the Phoenicians, Rota derived its name from the Moorish Rabita Rutta (watchtower of Rota). This attractive seaside resort has some lovely beaches including the Playa de la Costilla, an EU blue-flagged beach and a conservation area for

dune landscapes and pine forests. The town also has a 13th-century Moorish castle, the **Castillo de la Luna** (guided visits by reservations only on Tue and Thu 7pm, Sat and Sun at 10am and 8pm; 956 846 345). The 16th-century **Iglesia de Nuestra Senora de la O** illustrates a mix of architectural styles – Gothic/Renaissance, the ornate Plateresque and Baroque. The local wine, tintilla, made from dark, ripe grapes in local bodegas, such as El Gato.

🚗 Return to the A491 via the A2075 and turn right. When the road forks, turn right onto the CA603, which leads to El Puerto de Santa María.

❺ El Puerto de Santa María
Cádiz; 11500

Situated on the bay of Cádiz, at the mouth of the Guadalete, El Puerto de Santa María is surrounded by picturesque beaches such as Vistahermosa, La Puntilla and Valdelagrana. The town is well known for the excellent seafood and tapas served at the restaurants along the **Avenida de la Bajamar**, the main promenade. El Puerto de Santa María exports large quantities of sherry and was once the most important sherry exporting town in Spain. It is home to many bodegas such as Terry and Osborne, which produce fino, a dry, pale sherry, as well as moscatel, oloroso and amontillado and are open to the public.

The town is famous for its bullring, **Plaza de Toros**, built in 1880 and one of the largest in Spain. Bullfights are organized during the Feria season in August and the Feria de la Primavera (Spring Fair) in May, which is dedicated to sherry. The town also has a 18th-century fountain, **La Fuente de las Galeras**, which used to supply water to ships bound for the Americas. A few archaeological remains from the Palaeolithic era can be found in the **Museo Arqueólogico Municipal** (closed Sun). A short distance from the museum is the 13th-century **Castillo de San Marcos** (guided visits only, Mon–Sat; 956 851 751), built on the site of a mosque and watchtower.

🚗 Take the CA32 out of the town and drive towards the Parque Natural Bahía de Cádiz. Follow signs for the N443 and on crossing the Puente de José León de Carranza, turn right onto the CA33 to Cádiz.

Where to Stay: inexpensive, under €70; moderate, €70–€120; expensive, over €120

Above Imposing bullring at El Puerto de Santa María **Below** Baroque Catedral Nueva in Cádiz

Cádiz

iz; 11002

nost entirely surrounded by water,
ting into the Bay of Cádiz, Cádiz lays
ims to being Europe's oldest city.
iile legend names Hercules as
founder, history credits the
ɔenicians with establishing the
ɔn of *Gadir* (walled city) in 1100 BC.
haeologists have found remnants
almost every major maritime cul-
e since then in the Old Town.
Modern Cádiz is made up of two
rts – the compact Old Town and
sprawling New Town. Most of the
d Town's architecture dates back to
e 18th and early 19th centuries,
ren Cádiz rose to prominence as a
go port. From the sea wall there are
ews of the surrounding regions –
e **Torre de Telefonica** stands high
ove everything else – and also of
e sweeping bulge of the peninsula.
diz briefly became Spain's capital
1812 when the nation's first consti-
ion was drafted here.
Wandering along the waterfront is
good preamble to viewing Cádiz's
es. The **Catedral Nueva** was con-
ived as a Baroque masterpiece by
e Spanish architect Vicente Acero;
e building project was curtailed sev-
al times as funds ran out. A smaller
thedral, the **Catedral Vieja**, was orig-
ally built in the 13th-century but was
idly damaged during the English
sault on Cádiz in 1596. On Calle del
arqués del Real Tesoro is the **Torre
ıvira** *(open daily)*, the city's watch-
wer; there are splendid views over
idiz through its camera obscura. A
9th-century church, **Oratorio de San
elipe Neri**, and the **Museo de Cádiz**

(open Tue–Sun), which maps the city's
history, are other sites worth visiting
in the city. The museum is in Plaza de
Mina and houses exhibits dating back
to Phoenician, ancient Greek and
Roman times, and also has one of the
largest art collections in Andalusia.

Head up Calle Compañia to the
Plaza Topete, which is locally known
as the Plaza de las Flores, for all the
florists that have stalls here. There is a
handsome Correos (post office) here
too. The Carnaval *(Feb–Mar)* in the city
is one of the largest and the most
colourful in Europe, with much sing-
ing, dancing and all-night partying.

🚗 *Exit on the wide Avenida de
Andalusia, which becomes the well-
signposted CA33. This will lead past
the junction for the Puente de José
León de Carranza and on to San
Fernando. Take the A48 from the
junction after San Fernando and then
turn right onto the A390 for Chiclana
de la Frontera. Pass through this town
and turn left at the next junction, still
on the A390, for Medina-Sidonia.*

VISITING CÁDIZ

Tourist Information
*Avda. Ramón de Carranza, 11006; 956
203 191; www.andalucia.org; www.
cadizturismo.com*

Parking
Parking is available in San Jose in
Avenida Ana de Viya.

EAT AND DRINK

CHIPIONA

Restaurante La Belle Cuisine
moderate
With an artful, innovative approach to
classic tapas, this place is very popular.
*Avda. de la Laguna 43, 11550; 956 374
781; www.labellecuisine.es*

ROTA

Restaurante El Fresquito *moderate*
The blood sausage, the seafood and
fish tapas, *piriñacas* pepper, tomato and
onion salads here are delicious.
*Plaza de las Canteras 13, 11520; 956
840 832*

CÁDIZ

Freiduría Cervecería Las Flores
inexpensive
This friendly neighbourhood bar-
restaurant serves up the Andalusian
dish of *pescaito frito* (fried fish).
Plaza Topete 4, 11001; 956 226 112

Ventorillo del Chato *expensive*
A picturesque inn in an 18th-century
staging post by the sea, this restaurant
specializes in authentic Andalusian
cuisine. Recipes use fresh fish from the
bay often in combination with local
meat and vegetables.
Via Augusta Julia, 11011; 956 250 025

Above left Castilo de Guzmán el Bueno, Tarifa
Above right Vejer de la Frontera atop its
mountain crag **Below left** Decorated porch in
Medina-Sidonia **Below right** Iglesia de Santa
María la Coronada in Medina-Sidonia

WHERE TO STAY

VEJER DE LA FRONTERA

Casa Cinco *moderate*
This is a smart hotel in a typical
Andalusian-Arabic style house.
No children under the age of 17
are allowed.
*C/ Sancho IV El Bravo 5, 11150; 956
455 029; www.hotelcasacinco.com*

ZAHARA DE LOS ATUNES

El Varadero *moderate*
The 10 rooms at this original, hip hotel
are right on the beach, with an innovative restaurant and balconies for
watching the superb sunsets.
*Urbanización Atlanterra, 11393;
956 439 038; www.el-varadero.com*

TARIFA

Posada La Sacristia *moderate*
This 17th-century inn has individually
styled rooms, many with a distinct
Moorish and Oriental touch in the
decor. It also has an in-house restaurant.
*San Donato 8, 11380; 956 681 759;
www.lasacristia.net;*

Hotel Misiana *expensive*
The rooms of this chic boutique
property feature modern art and
Moroccan furnishings. The hotel also
has a bar and a café.
*C/ Sancho IV El Bravo 16, 11380; 956
627 083; www.misiana.com*

AROUND TARIFA

Mesón de Sancho
inexpensive–moderate
This is a classic, family-friendly roadside
inn-cum-restaurant, 8 km (5 miles)
from Tarifa, serving hearty Andalusian
meat and fish dishes.
*Ctra. Cádiz-Málaga, Km 94, 11380; 956
684 900; www.mesondesancho.com*

⑦ Medina-Sidonia
Cádiz; 11170

This peaceful, small town is situated
off the main *pueblos blancos* trail, on
a hill overlooking rolling fields. The
Guzman family, who took the town
from the Moors, were granted the
dukedom of Medina-Sidonia in the
15th century. The town then became
one of the most important ducal
seats in Spain. The town is surrounded
by medieval walls within which there
are narrow, cobbled streets of whitewashed houses with traditional iron
rejas or grills on their windows.

Medina-Sidonia contains some
interesting buildings, including a
ruined **Castillo** *(open daily)* and Roman
sewers. The Gothic **Iglesia de Santa
Maria la Coronada** is the town's most
notable and important building. Inside
it is a collection of religious works of
art dating from the Renaissance,
including paintings and a spectacular retable with beautifully
carved panels.

🚗 *Take the CA2032, then the CA203,
out of the town and head southwards
onto the A396. Turn left onto the N340
and when the road forks, right onto
the A393/A314 for Vejer de la Frontera.*

⑧ Vejer de la Frontera
Cádiz; 11150

High up on a hill above the steep
gorge of the Barbate river, this brig
white village was first built up in
Phoenician and Roman times to pr
tect the fishing grounds below from
barbarian tribes from further north.
later became an important agricultu
centre under Moorish influence – th
original Moorish gates are still stanc
ing. Surrounded by pastures and
orange groves, Vejer has a
commanding position overlooking
the coast from Tarifa to Cádiz.

Vejer was largely undiscovered by
the outside world until the 1980s.
Interesting buildings to visit include
the 14th-century **Iglesia de Divino
Salvador**, built on the site of an old
mosque; the **Santuario de Nuestra
Senora de la Oliva**, a local chapel tha
houses a 16th-century sculpted imag
of the Virgin Mary; and the restored
16th-century Renaissance **Convento
de las Monjas Concepcionistas**. The
plaza on the edge of the old Mooris
village offers a number of good
restaurants and bars.

🚗 *Continue on the A314 to Barbate.
Then take the A2231 into Zahara.*

Zahara de los Atunes

Cádiz; 11150

Once a thriving tuna-fishing port, Zahara de los Atunes ("of the tunas") is now a low-key resort with a magnificent, long beach, mainly used by Spaniards. It is also home to two noteworthy buildings: the spectacular 15th-century **Iglesia de Nuestra Señora Carmen**, and the ruins of 15th-century **Castillo de las Almadrabas**, which was built to protect the town from pirates and was also the residence of the Dukes of Medina-Sidonia. This town's other claim to fame is the local belief that Miguel de Cervantes (1547–1616), the Spanish author and poet, was imprisoned here for espionage. He mentions the town in *La Pegona Ilustre* (The Illustrious Mop).

Leave Zahara de los Atunes eastwards on the A2227 passing La Zarzuela en route. After 11 km (7 miles) turn right onto the N340 to Tarifa.

Tarifa

Cádiz; 11380

Windsurfing and kitesurfing capital of Europe, Tarifa is the liveliest town on the Costa de la Luz. The town was named after its Moorish conqueror, Tarif ibn Malik, who conquered the town in AD 710 making it the first Moorish possession in Spain. It is home to an assortment of brightly-painted bars and sunny plazas that give it an atmosphere reminiscent of the Caribbean. The constant wind feeds the hundreds of power-generating windmills erected in the area. The smoky-blue outline of Africa's Rif Mountains can be seen from the ramparts of the town's 10th-century **Castillo de Guzmán el Bueno** *(open daily during summer)*. The 15th-century **Iglesia de San Mateo** houses a late Gothic interior, hidden behind its 18th-century Baroque exterior. Two-thirds of the city walls, built after the Castilians took Tarifa from the Moors in 1292, and the main gate, the **Puerta de Jerez**, are still standing.

Winds and Whales

Tarifa's strong winds are ideal for wind- and kitesurfing and the sandy beaches make the experience especially enjoyable. A multitude of other day-trip activities are also available, including scuba diving, fishing, hang-gliding and, away from the water, free climbing, trekking and horse riding. Tarifa's location is ideal for whale- and dolphin-watching and daily boat trips are available for viewing these cetaceans. Long-finned pilot whales, bottlenose dolphins, common dolphins, and striped dolphins are commonly sighted in this region.

WHALE-WATCHING IN TARIFA

Foundation for Information and Research on Marine Mammals
The FIRMM conducts daily whale- and dolphin-watching boat trips.
Pedro Cortés 4, 11380; 956 627 008; www.firmm.org; book at least two or three days in advance

EAT AND DRINK

VEJER DE LA FRONTERA

Venta Pinto *expensive*
This former staging post is now a chic but rustic restaurant serving elaborate country dishes and tapas.
La Barca de Vejer s/n, 11150; 956 450 877; www.ventapinto.com

TARIFA

La Vaca Loca *moderate*
Hugely popular – so visitors often have to wait for a table – this very Tarifa-style restaurant specializes in generous grills of excellent meats.
C/ Cervantes 6, 11380; 605 281 791; closed for lunch

Below Windsurfer off the beach at Tarifa

DAY TRIP OPTIONS

There are plenty of spots along the Costa de la Luz worth a day trip. This drive can be divided into two day trips with either Jerez de la Frontera (near the A4) or Vejer de la Frontera (near the A48) as base.

Sherry circuit
Start at Jerez de la Frontera ①, famous for its sherry, and head northwest to Sanlúcar de Barrameda ② where all *manzanilla* sherry is made. Sanlúcar also has a great equestrian tradition. Follow the coast from here, passing the small resorts of Chipiona ③ and

Rota ④ before reaching El Puerto de Santa María ⑤, once the most important sherry-exporting port and a great spot for sampling sherries and seafood dishes.

From Jerez, take the A480 to Sanlúcar and Chipiona. Then follow the A491 and the A2075 to Rota. From Rota take the A491 and then the CA603 to El Puerto de Santa María.

Sea and sand
After spending the morning in Vejer de la Frontera ⑧ and visiting its church, the Iglesia de Divino

Salvador, drive down to the coast at Barbate. From here, drive to the Cabo de Trafalgar before heading down the coast to Zahara de los Atunes ⑨, one of the prettiest spots on the Costa de la Luz. End the day at Tarifa ⑩, which offers some excellent windsurfing and kitesurfing opportunities.

From Vejer de la Frontera, take the A314 southwards to Barbate and the Cabo de Trafalgar. Then follow the A2231 to Zahara de los Atunes. From Zahara de los Atunes, take the A2227, then the N340 to Tarifa.

Eat and Drink: inexpensive, under €20; moderate, €20–€40; expensive, over €40

The Mudéjar Route

Almuñécar to Salobreña

Highlights

- **Ancient Almuñécar**
  Wander around the ancient
  Phoenician port, and then relax
  by the beach

- **Picturesque villages**
  Follow the Mudéjar route, which
  winds through a string of villages
  in the Axarquía

- **Arab baths**
  Visit the baths hidden beneath a
  spa hotel in Alhama de Granada

- **Castle town**
  Walk through the picturesque streets
  of Salobreña to the Moorish castle

Village of Frigiliana, nestled amid rugged hills

The Mudéjar Route

The coast of the province of Granada is known as the Costa Tropical because of its microclimate, which permits the cultivation of exotic fruits. Only a short hop from the Costa del Sol, it has a rugged shoreline punctuated by often unfrequented beaches. This route follows the most scenic part of the coast and then heads inland to the picturesque villages of the Axarquía, a region said to have the best climate in Europe. After a visit to the spa of Alhama de Granada, the route returns to the coast via a dramatic mountain descent to end the journey with a walk around the old town of Salobreña.

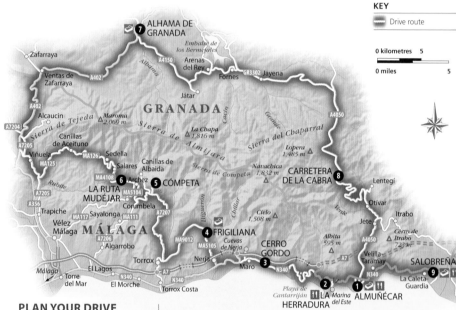

KEY

— Drive route

0 kilometres 5

0 miles 5

PLAN YOUR DRIVE

Start/finish: Almuñécar to Salobreña.

Number of days: 2.

Distance: 220 km (135 miles).

Road conditions: Generally good, although some parts of the road to Torrox are badly surfaced.

When to go: June and September are ideal. July and August are holiday months and can be crowded.

Opening hours: Most museums are open from 9:30am to 1:30pm, and from 4:30 to 6 or 8pm.

Main market days: Almuñécar: Fri; Alhama de Granada: Fri.

Major festivals: Almuñécar: Le Noche de San Juan, Jun; **Frigiliana:** Festival de las Tres Culturas, Aug.

Above Sandy beach surrounded by rocky cliffs in Nerja, *see p211*

Almuñécar

ranada; 18690

settlement was founded on the
e of Almuñécar, now a cosmopoli-
n resort, by the Phoenicians in the
h century BC. It was later taken over
y the Romans who constructed an
queduct and a fish-salting plant –
e ruins of the latter can be seen in
arque del Majuelo, a pretty garden
subtropical plants. Situated above
e garden is the **Castillo de San
iguel** *(closed Mon and Sun afternoon)*,
uilt by the Romans and developed
to an impressive fortress by the
oors in the Middle Ages.

 *Head west along the coast and turn
ght towards Málaga on the Avenida
el Mediterráneo. At the crossroads,
rn left on the N340 for La Herradura,
assing the turn off for Marina del Este.*

La Herradura

ranada; 18697

here are views of the beautiful bay
La Herradura as the road descends
wards the sea. A detour to the left
to Calle de la Carretera de la Playa,
ter crossing the tunnel before La
erradura, leads to the pretty yacht
arbour of **Marina del Este**, a base for
nderwater excursions. The same
ad leads to a lighthouse, above the
arbour, from which there are pano-
mic views of the countryside and
e coast. La Herradura itself has a
lendid beach and some restau-
nts that serve great seafood.

 *Retrace the route to the N340 and
rn left. Go straight over the round-
bout, where most of the traffic leaves
e N340 to join the motorway. A tun-
el pierces through the headland of
erro Gordo, marking the beginning
perhaps the most beautiful stretch
road on Spain's southern coast.*

③ Cerro Gordo

Granada, Málaga; 18697, 29787

The N340 winds along the coast
offering a scenic drive crossing the
magnificent headland of Cerro Gordo,
which has a succession of beaches.
Several 16th- and 17th-century watch-
towers still stand guard along the
coast. Turn right at the roundabout
after Maro to visit the **Cuevas de Nerja**,
a series of vast caverns discovered in
1959. Back on the N340, cross the
viaduct over the Chillar river. You will
see the 19th-century **Acueducto del
Aguilar**, to which the viaduct runs
parallel, on the right.

 *Drive over a series of roundabouts,
past Nerja, to turn right onto the
MA5105 for Frigiliana. Go through the
first, more modern part of town and
descend to the parking area in Plaza
de la Cañada del Ingenio. Park here to
take a walk in the Old Town.*

④ Frigiliana

Málaga; 29788

Frigiliana is by far the prettiest of the
many whitewashed towns in the
Axarquía. The old quarter of the town
is a delightful complex of small
streets, alleyways, steps and tunnels,
often leading nowhere, decorated
with potted plants.

 *Leave on the MA9012 for Torrox.
Pass beneath the Caracoles hotel,
descend into a valley, cross a small
bridge and climb again to reach Torrox.
A green metal fence on the left con-
firms the route. Turn right for Cómpeta
on the A7207. Just before reaching
Cómpeta, there is a **mirador** (viewpoint) over the town. At the next
junction, turn right on the Avenida
Sayalonga (MA112). In the town, the
tourist office is on the right. Go up the
slope to Plaza Axarquía and park.*

Above left Colourful doors around a
courtyard, Frigiliana **Above right** Long
curving beach at La Herradura

WHERE TO STAY

ALMUÑÉCAR

Los Laureles *inexpensive*
A small four-bedroom guesthouse in
the backstreets of the town, this place
also has a swimming pool.
*La Ribera Baja 14, 18690; 958 069 132;
www.loslaureles.net*

AROUND FRIGILIANA

Los Caracoles *moderate–expensive*
With igloo-like bungalows arranged on
a hillside, Los Caracoles, 5 km (3 miles)
from Frigiliana, has spectacular views.
*Ctra. Frigiliana-Torrox, 29788; 952 030
609; www. hotelloscaracoles.com*

EAT AND DRINK

ALMUÑÉCAR

Horno de Candida *moderate*
This restaurant-school is located in
the old part of the town near Plaza
de las Constitución. The chefs may
be trainees under supervision, but
the standards are high.
*C/ Orovia, 3, 18690; 958 883 284;
www.hornodecandida.es*

LA HERRADURA

El Pilon *inexpensive–moderate*
Tucked away in a side street with a
shady terrace with superb views, this
town-centre restaurant has a menu
that includes options for vegetarians.
C/ Laberinto, 18697; 952 553 512

El Chambao de Joaquin *moderate*
Although it looks like a humble beach
bar, this is a fairly sophisticated restaurant. On Saturdays and Sundays, a
giant **paella** is cooked over a wood fire.
*Paseo de Andrés Segovia 2, 18697;
958 640 044*

Eat and Drink: inexpensive, under €20; moderate, €20–€40; expensive, over €40

Top Typical Andalusian farm outside sleepy Cómpeta **Above** Placid waters of the spa in Alhama de Granada **Below** Andalusian spa town of Alhama de Granada

WHERE TO STAY

ALHAMA DE GRANADA

La Seguiriya *inexpensive*
A small hotel-restaurant in the Old Town, La Seguiriya is run by a flamenco singer and his family. There are six individually decorated rooms. It also has a restaurant with a terrace.
C/ Las Peñas 12, 18120; 958 360 801; www.laseguiriya.com

SALOBREÑA

Jayma *inexpensive*
This is a family-run hotel on one of the main streets of the Old Town. One room is equipped for the disabled. There are no meals served here but there are bars and restaurants nearby.
C/ Cristo 24, 18680; 958 610 231; www.hostaljayma.com

AROUND SALOBREÑA

La Casa de los Bates *expensive*
The Casa de los Bates, a 19th-century country mansion, sits on a hill over-looking the Costa Tropical, 10 km (6 miles) to the east of Salobreña. It has personalized rooms, a lovely garden and a large swimming pool.
Ctra. N340, Km 329, 5, 18600, Motril; 958 349 495; www.casadelosbates.com

5 Cómpeta
Málaga; 29754
The pleasant mountain of town Cómpeta acts as a service centre for the villages and houses spread across the surrounding hillsides. Its main economic activity, apart from tourism, is the production of sweet dessert wines. The sloping rectangular enclosures, used for drying the grapes, are a common feature of the home-steads of the Axarquía region.

🚗 *Retrace your route back out of Cómpeta, but continue straight at the junction towards Torre del Mar and Algarrobo on the MA112 and MA111. After 5 km (3 miles), take the right turn onto the MA5104 for Archez. Continue on this road across the bridge and then on the MA4108 to Salares.*

6 La Ruta Mudéjar
Málaga; 29753 & 29714
The Mudéjars were Muslims who stayed back in Christian territory after the *reconquista* (Reconquest of Spain), continuing to apply their artistic and architectural skills in accordance with their own traditions. Visitors can still see examples of Mudéjar craftsman-ship in Archez and Salares. Stroll around these towns to see exquisite ornate brick church towers, which are minarets in all but name.

🚗 *Continue on the road past Sedella and Canillas de Aceituno and follow signs for Vélez Málaga. At the bottom of the hill, turn right for Granada onto the A7205. Cross the bridge to meet the A402. Turn right and keep on the same road through Ventas de Zafarraya. In Alhama de Granada, follow signs for "Centro Urbano" to the tourist information office.*

7 Alhama de Granada
Granada; 18120
The ancient spa town of Alhama is built on the lip of a gorge; there are great views of the canyon from behind the Iglesia del Carmen. The town is built around the main parish church, the **Iglesia de Santa Maria de la Encarnación** *(closed Sun)*. In the ce[llars] of the the spa hotel of Balneario Alhama de Granada below the tow[n] are perfectly preserved 13th-centu[ry] Arab baths *(visits possible only while sp[a] patients are at lunch from 2 to 4pm).*

🚗 *Retrace your route on the A402 towards Ventas. After leaving town, turn left onto the A4150 for Játar, cros[s]ing the Alhama river and passing a reservoir. Before Játar, take the bad[ly] signed left turn onto the GR3302. Sk[ip] Arenas del Rey and continue to Forne[s] taking the left turn signposted to Granada and then onto Jayena. Tur[n] right at the next junction onto the A4050 – the Carretera de la Cabra.*

8 Carretera de la Cabra
Granada; 18127, 18698 and 18699
The route goes through a rolling landscape high above the coast, wi[th] a sudden dramatic descent, passing under greyish-white cliffs. There are endless curves and great views all th[e] way down the so-called "Road of th[e] Goat", which goes through **Otívar** an[d] **Jete** and passes a few Roman remain[s].

🚗 *On reaching Almuñécar, do not g[o] under the N340, but turn left and follo[w] it parallel to a junction to pick up the N340 east towards Salobreña. Take th[e] second marked entrance into Salobreña to reach the roundabout, next to which is the tourist infor-mation office, and park nearby.*

Salobreña

ranada; 18680

he old white town of Salobreña is spread over a large rock located little way back from the sea. This walk goes through a warren of :eep, narrow streets and steps, to the Moorish castle at the top. The >wn is best explored in the morning and early evening to avoid the eat of an Andalusian summer's day.

Above Charming old town of Salobreña overlooking the beach

VISITING SALOBREÑA

Tourist Information
Plaza de Goya, 18680; 958 610 314

Parking
Parking is available on the streets near the tourist information office.

EAT AND DRINK

SALOBREÑA

El Peñon *inexpensive–moderate*
The menu has a wide selection of seafood, some of which is barbecued over an open fire on the beach.
Playa del Peñón, 18680; 958 610 538; www.elpenon.es

Pesetas *inexpensive–moderate*
This restaurant offers good seafood and stunning views of the coast.
C/ Bóveda 13, 18680; 958 610 182; closed Mon

two-hour walking tour

om the car park, walk to the **Tourist ıformation Office** ① and follow the avement past the roundabout, on ʰhich stands an old sugar-milling ʰachine. Go down Avenida de ederico García Lorca. Pass y the church and ʰarket; turn right etween the hardware ʰop and the Santander ank, up the short Calle e los Hermanos Álvarez ʷuintero. Go straight on ʰis road and up Calle ʷuestra Señora del Rosario >wards the fountain. Take ʰe two flights of steps to ʰe Plaza del Antiguo Mercado. ear right to a hairpin bend from ʷhere a flight of steps begin. Go up ʰe steps and into a modern arcade ʷutside the **Museo Historico** ② *(open ʲaily, closed Mon in winter)*, a museum f Salobreña's history, on Plaza del ʸyuntamiento.

Turn left around the square and gain immediately left through Calle e la Bóveda, a 16th-century barrel-aulted tunnel. Continue a few steps ʲo the Pesetas restaurant for a lunch top, which has superb views from its ʲooftop terrace. Otherwise, take the ʲight of brick steps to the right, eaving the Bóveda, and turn right at ʰe top towards the Arab-influenced ʲudéjar church, **Iglesia de Nuestra Señora del Rosario** ③. Turn left up ʰe steps at the corner of the church. ʲt the top of the steps, stop either at ʰe refreshments stall located on the ʲight, halfway up the cobbled and ʲtepped Calle Andrés Segovia, or ʲurn left to visit Salobreña's restored **Castillo Arabe** ④ *(open daily, closed ʲon in winter)*, which has panoramic ʲiews from its magnificent ramparts.

From the castle, go down Calle ʸndrés Segovia and turn left at the ʲottom into Calle Girona, then imme-ʲiately left again. This goes to the ʲorseshoe-arched Puerta del Postigo

Colourful tile from Salobreña

gate; fork left through it for a park, the **Paseo de las Flores** ⑤.

Take the narrow steps across the street from the Puerta del Postigo, slightly to the left and downhill. There is no option but to turn left at the bottom of the first flight of steps. Take the next set of steps to the right, which leads out to a balcony. Bear right along this through an unkempt park overhung by eucalyptus trees. At the bottom of the next flight of steps, bear left down ano-ther very short zigzag flight of steps. Get on to Calle Carmen, which is just around the corner. Turn right and continue straight down Calle Bodegon to reach Calle del Cristo. At the cross-roads at the bottom of this street, turn right to reach a pedestrianized triangle on which stand the outdoor tables of the bar-restaurant Porteria. Turn left at the corner just after the bar to approach the tourist informa-tion office, where the car is parked.

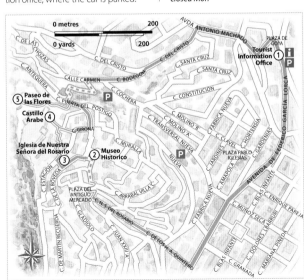

Eat and Drink: inexpensive, under €20; moderate, €20–€40; expensive, over €40

Atlantic Ocean
Bilbao
A Coruña
Zaragoza
SPAIN
Barcelona
Madrid
Valencia
Palma
Murcia
Mediterranean Sea
Seville
Málaga

Historic Mountain Villages

Granada to Puente de Tablate

Highlights

- **Moorish Spain**
  Wander through the streets of the Alabaicín, the old Moorish quarter of Granada, up to the Alhambra

- **Cave houses**
  Visit the famous troglodyte quarter of Guadix

- **Renaissance fortress**
  Climb up to Castillo de La Calahorra, which stands guard over the plains

- **Villages of the Alpujarras**
  Explore the tiny villages on the slopes of the Sierra Nevada

The Alhambra and the Sierra Nevada, seen from the Mirador de San Nicolás, Granada

Historic Mountain Villages

The city of Granada, famous for the unmistakable castle-palace of the Alhambra, sits at the foot of the northern slopes of the Sierra Nevada. This route crosses the mountains at the first available pass to the east, after visiting the cave quarter of Guadix and the Renaissance castle at La Calahorra. The gentle, green southern slopes of Las Alpujarras are a rural region of beautiful walks and peaceful villages. This route makes an excellent relaxed and unhurried drive.

Above Intricate Portico del Partal inside the Alhambra, Granada, *see p218*

Below View over the rooftops of the old Moorish quarter, the Albaicín, in Granada, *see p218*

0 kilometres 5

0 miles 5

PLAN YOUR DRIVE

Start/finish: Granada to Puente de Tablate.

Number of days: 2, allowing a day for the walk around the Albaicín and the Alhambra.

Distance: 235 km (145 miles).

Road conditions: Some of the roads on this route are narrow and winding.

When to go: The best time to visit this region is from spring to autumn. The road over Puerto de la Ragua may be inaccessible in winter.

Opening hours: Most museums and monuments are generally open from 10am to 2pm, and from 5 to 8pm, and are closed on Mondays.

Main market days: Granada: Sat, Sun; Guadix: Sat; Lanjarón: Sat.

Shopping: The region is famous for *jarapas* (rag rugs). Look for ceramics in Purullena and cured hams in Trevélez.

Major festivals: Granada: Día de la Cruz, 3 May; Corpus Christi, May/Jun; Guadix: Feria, end Aug; Lanjarón: Fiesta de San Juan, 24 Jun.

DAY TRIP OPTIONS

The route splits into two halves: north of the Sierra Nevada and south of it. **History buffs** will enjoy a visit to the Alhambra and the cave houses in Guadix. **Mountain lovers** should head south to visit the tiny villages for a breath of fresh air. For details, *see p223*.

ACTIVITIES

Visit the Alhambra – one of the most extraordinary sights in Spain

Shop for traditional ceramic items in the road side shops of Purullena

Taste the hams of Trevélez, dry-cured in the mountain air, and wash them down with local wine

Stroll along the dense wooded paths of the Alpujarras

Right Arid La Peza countryside en route to Purullena, *see p220*

Above Patio de los Leones inside the Alhambra

❶ Granada

Granada; 18009

First occupied by the Moors in the 8th century, Granada's golden period came during the rule of the Nasrid dynasty from 1238 to 1492, when artisans, merchants and scholars all contributed to the city's reputation as a centre of culture. The city is overlooked by one of the most impressive sights of Spain – the fortress-palace of the Alhambra. This walk goes through the streets of Granada's Moorish quarter, the Albaicín, and then up to the Alhambra and its gardens. Avoid doing this walk in the afternoon as it can get very hot.

A two-hour walking tour

Start from the car park and walk to **Plaza Nueva** ①, below the Alhambra. Start walking down Calle de Elvira (at the end of the square, signed for Plaza de San Gil) but fork right almost immediately up Calderería Vieja. Turn right at the top to emerge onto the Plaza de San Gregorio. Keep going in the same direction, always uphill, on Calle de San Gregorio and double back at the first corner on the left. At the end of this short street turn left again; this will lead to Placeta de San José, beneath a graceful 10th-century minaret, now a church tower of the **Iglesia de San José** ②. Continue uphill from the Placeta de San José beside the minaret on Calle San José, past the door of Carmen San Luis – *carmen* being the name of a typical well-to-do house in the Albaicín – its garden secluded behind high walls. Turn right and immediately left across

Calle de Bocanegra and straight up hill into **Placeta de San Miguel Bajo** ③. Here the route turns right on Calle de Santa Isabel la Real beside the wall of the whitewashed church. Go past the 16th-17th-century monaster of the same name. From here, the tower of Iglesia de San Nicolás on top of the hill can be seen. Turn left just before the road starts to go downhil to get to the square (up the steps) in front of the church, where there is the viewpoint, the **Mirador de San Nicolás** ④. There is a panoramic vie of the Alhambra across the Darro valley from here.

Turning left at the bottom of the Mirador de San Nicolás, go past the modern mosque on the left, down the steps through Cuesta de las Tomasas and down to the **Placeta del Aljibe de Trillo** ⑤, which has a 14th-century cistern. At the bottom of the square, turn left on Azacayuel

VISITING GRANADA

Parking

Parking is restricted in the centre of Granada (especially in the Albaicín) and it is best to park a little way outside the centre. There is a car park next to the ticket office of the Alhambra on the hill above Plaza Nueva. From here visitors can either walk down the hill to Plaza Nueva or take a minibus. There is a car park on Acera de Darro from which it is a 10-minute walk to Plaza Nueva.

VISITING THE ALHAMBRA

A visit to the Alhambra is best planned well ahead because visitor numbers are limited. Tickets can be booked in advance through various outlets, details of which are on the website. Tickets can also be acquired online (*www.alhambra-tickets.es*) or by phone. *902 888 001; www.alhambra-patronato.es; open daily 8:30am to 8pm, closes 6pm in winter, night visits 10 to 11:30pm Tue–Sat in summer (from Mar to Oct), 8 to 9:30pm Fri–Sat in winter*

WHERE TO STAY

GRANADA

Santa Isabel la Real *moderate*
Located in a restored 16th-century house, this hotel consists of 11 individually styled rooms around a patio. *C/ Santa Isabel la Real Nº19, 18009; 958 294 658; www.hotelsantaisabellareal.com*

Parador de Granada *expensive*
Part of the state-run parador chain, this hotel enjoys a fabulous setting next to the gardens of the Alhambra. *Real de la Alhambra s/n, 18009; 958 221 440; www.parador.es*

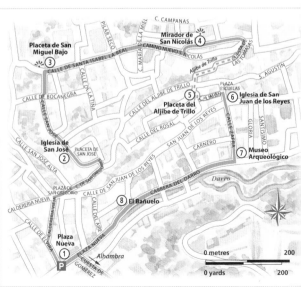

e San Pedro. Go down the steps and
und the corner. Turn left on the
nsigned Calle Limón to reach Plaza
cuelas, where the **Iglesia de San
an de los Reyes** ⑥ acts as a land-
ark. Cross the street into Calle Zafra
d go straight down it to the banks
 the Darro river. At the end of the
reet, on the left, is the **Museo
rqueológico** ⑦ *(closed Mon)*, which
 housed in the Casa de Castril, a
enaissance mansion with a lovely
ateresque portal. Turn right along
e Darro and further along on the
ght, there is the **El Bañuelo** ⑧ *(open
e–Sat)*, 11th-century Arab baths
hose vaults are lit by star-shaped
les in the roof. Continue in the same
rection to return to Plaza Nueva.
 From here, head towards the
hambra. Those with the day to
are can get to the Alhambra on
ot from Plaza Nueva but it is a long
eep walk up the Cuesta de Gomérez
d not suggested. A minibus goes
 the same route here. By car, the
hambra is approached along an
cess road from the southeast, which
oids the city centre. There is a car
rk at the entrance of the Alhambra.
 Built under Ismail I, Yusuf and
uhammad V – kings of the Nasrid
nasty – the Alhambra is the most
nsual piece of architecture in Spain.
 though it has an austere defensive
terior when seen from the Albaicín,
e Alhambra has an exquisitely deco-
ted suite of royal chambers and
urtyards at its heart. On the hill
de above it is the summer palace,
eneralife, which stands in water

gardens. The Generalife now provides
a magical setting for some events of
Granada's annual music and dance
festival. After the visit, go back to
Plaza Nueva and then to the car park.
🚗 *Get onto the bypass (indicated by
blue signs) south towards Motril. After
taking exit 132 for Sierra Nevada keep
to the left and follow signs. Keep to
the right lane through the tunnel and
look out for a right turn for Pinos Genil
and Quentar. An access road leads to
a T-junction outside Cenes de la Vega.
Turn right here on the A4026. Before
Pinos Genil turn left for Dudar, Quentar
and La Peza on the GR3201 for the
Embalse de Quéntar. A right turn will
lead to the car park, which is off a
bend going left.*

❷ Embalse de Quéntar
Granada; 18192, 18519

This attractive turquoise-blue
reservoir comes up suddenly after
the town of Quéntar. From the car
park, walk around and across the
dam. There are some good views of
the lake. The route then continues
over the scenic pass of **Puerto de los
Blancares** (1,300 m/4,250 ft).
🚗 *Continue on the same road (the
GR3201, which is sometimes also
numbered GR-SE-39) beside the lake
for Purullena. Take a right turn in La
Peza towards Purullena. Continue
through the town to the crossroads
which has a large statue of a bull. Turn
left downhill on Calle Rio and continue
down and then out of town on the
GR4104. Keep on this road past Los
Baños and Graena onto Purullena.*

Above Rugged terrain of the Sierra Nevada
Below left Belfry of the Iglesia de San José in
Granada **Below right** View of the Alhambra

EAT AND DRINK

GRANADA

Mesón El Yunque
inexpensive–moderate
An agreeably informal place for tapas
or a meal, in a square in the Albaicín.
*Plaza San Miguel Bajo 3, Albaicín,
18009; 958 800 090; www.
vivagranada.com/yunque*

Mirador de Morayma *moderate*
This charming patio-restaurant
specializes in typical dishes of Granada,
such as *remojón* (a salad of oranges
and codfish).
*C/ Pianista Garcia Carnillo 2, 18010;
958 228 290; closed Sun evenings*

Eat and Drink: inexpensive, under €20; moderate, €20–€40; expensive, over €40

Above Renaissance Castillo de La Calahorra, with its domed turrets against the Sierra Nevada **Below left** Distinctive chimney of a cave house in Guadix **Below right** Streets of La Calahorra with the castle in the background

SHOPPING IN PURULLENA

La Esperanza and Cueva La Inmaculada
Ctra. de Granada; 958 690 181

ACTIVITIES IN THE SIERRA NEVADA

Hiking
Lanteira is a popular departure point for hikes. The tourist office for the area is in Guadix.
Ctra. de Murcia, 18510; 958 665 070

WHERE TO STAY

AROUND GUADIX

Cuevas La Granja *moderate*
Several caves around Guadix have been transformed into womb-like hotels. This hotel in Benalúa, (8 km/5 miles) from Guadix, has 11 self-contained cave houses, a restaurant and a pool.
Camino de la Granja, 18510, Benalúa; 958 676 000; www.cuevas.org

Casa Las Chimeneas
inexpensive– moderate
The owners of this bed-and-breakfast in a restored village house organize walking tours. Each of the large bedrooms has a private balcony or terrace.
C/ Amargura 6, Mairena, 18493; 958 760 089; www.alpujarra-tours.com

③ Purullena
Granada; 18519
Until the motorway was built, Purullena was on the main road between Murcia/Almeria and Granada. This explains the existence of the large open-fronted shops specializing in local ceramics on the way out of town. The brightly coloured crockery comes in all shapes and sizes. Famous for its cave houses, Purullena still has a large number of people who live in these cave homes today. The cave quarter is located above the town.

🚗 *Leave on the A4100 towards Guadix. In Guadix, go straight over the roundabout and down the broad modern avenue. The tourist inform-ation office, a squat brown building, is on the left.*

④ Guadix
Granada; 18500
Founded in Roman times, Guadix thrived under the Moors and after the Reconquest but declined in the 18th century. Although it has a hand-some monumental town centre, most visitors make straight for the famous *barrio de cuevas*, the troglo-dyte quarter with 2,000 inhabited caves. These caves have been used as dwellings since prehistoric times, when people first hid in them for safety. The **Museo de Alfarería** and **Museo Etnológico** (*open weekends*

*only) museums show how people here live underground. For an overview, follow the "barrio de cuevas" signs beyond the church to the **Mirador Cerro de las Balas**. Steps from a small car park lead up to a constructed balcony overlooking the town and its mud hills pockmarked with cave dwellings. Two sights worth visiting are the 16th-century Baroque **Cathedral** and the **Iglesia de Santiago**, which has a fine coffered ceiling and Mudéjar tower.

🚗 *From the cave quarter, return to the town centre and leave on the N324 towards Almeria. Just after leaving the town, turn right onto the GR5104 (also marked GR-SE-19) for Jerez del Marquesado and Lanteira. Keep on the same road past Jerez to Lanteira.*

⑤ Lanteira
Granada; 18518
A pleasant town of winding streets lined with white houses, Lanteira serves as a departure point for hikes into the Sierra Nevada. Its name is derived from the Ibero-Roman Argentaria, City of Silver, a reminder that there was once a prosperous mining industry here, which sup-ported two castles. Both are ruins now.

🚗 *Continue on the same road, the GR5104, into La Calahorra. Either walk from the town up to the castle or take the car further up the hill, but there are no signs on the route to help.*

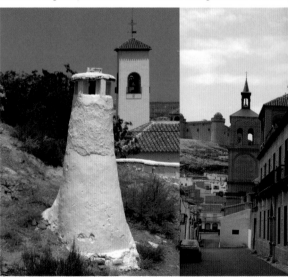

EAT AND DRINK

GUADIX

Comercio *inexpensive–moderate*
A comfortable restaurant which
specializes in traditional Spanish and
international cuisine.
*C/ Mira de Amezcua 3, 18500; 958 660
500; www.hotelcomercio.com*

AROUND CASTILLO DE LA CALAHORRA

Hospederia del Zenete *moderate*
This hotel-restaurant in the town
below the castle claims to preserve the
culinary traditions of Moorish Andalusia.
Olives, figs, rabbit and lamb all figure
prominently on the menu.
*Ctra. La Ragua 1, 18512; 958 677 192;
www.hospederiadelzenete.com*

PUERTO DE LA RAGUA

Posada de los Arrieros
inexpensive–moderate
An isolated inn tucked into a sheltered
fold of the Sierra Nevada, it offers spectacular views and great food.
*Ctra. de Bayarcal, 04479; 950 524 001;
www.posadadelosarrieros.com*

Castillo de La Calahorra
Granada; 18512

Standing on the summit of an
isolated hill from which to control
the plains below, at the foot of the
Sierra Nevada, the magnificent Castillo
de La Calahorra *(open Wed only)* was
the first Renaissance building in Spain.
The construction of the castle was
ordered by Rodrigo de Mendoza, son
of Cardinal Mendoza, for his bride, and
was completed between 1509 and
1512. The defiantly military exterior of
La Calahorra, with its four cylindrical
corner towers, is in complete contrast
with the Carrara marble pillars and
the palatial courtyard inside.

*Take the road towards Granada
and Almeria but at the end of the town
turn off right onto the A337 for Ferreira
and Puerto de la Ragua.*

Puerto de la Ragua
Granada; 18512, 18494, 18460

The ascent to the tree-shrouded
2000-m (6,550-ft) pass across the
slopes of the Sierra Nevada has some
beautiful views looking back over
the plains and fertile valleys. Far from
the crowds of Alpine ski resorts,
visitors can indulge in the many
sports activities such as cross-country
skiing and mountain biking. In the
summer, the pass is a great place to
pick up the hiking trails that set off
from the visitors' centre here. The
pass is usually snowbound in the
winter months when the slopes are
used for cross-country skiing.

*Coming down from Puerto de la
Ragua, turn right for Válor on the
A4130, passing over the top of Laroles.
Stay on this road through Válor to
Yegen, Mecina Bombarón as it passes*

*Bérchules and on to Juviles. After
Juviles turn right on the A4132 to the
town of Trevélez.*

Troglodyte Residences

In and around Guadix, a cave house
is considered just as good a place
to live in as a house or flat, if not
better. The soft clay is easy to
excavate so an extra room can be
added if needed. Underground, the
temperature remains at an agreeably constant 18° C (64° F) meaning
that the cave feels relatively warm
in winter and cool in summer. The
only drawback is the lack of natural
light, but despite this, caves here are
much in demand and are bought
and sold (at surprisingly high prices)
just like any other piece of good
real estate.

Above left Flower pots decorate the walls of
a house in La Calahorra **Above right** Colourful
ceramic pottery in a shop in Purullena **Below**
Cave houses against a rock face, Guadix

Above Flat roofs of Pampaneira huddled together on the mountainside **Below left** Ruins of Lanjarón's castle on a lone hill **Below right** Spray of flowers adding colour to a house in Trevélez

the road enters the Poqueira Valley. Turn right by the petrol station to get onto the A4129 to visit Bubión and Capileira above. To get to Pampaneira retrace the route on the A4132 and turn right.

⑨ Poqueira Valley
Granada; 18411, 18412, 18413
The attractive little villages tucked into the folds of the southern slopes of the Sierra Nevada are a must-visit. Bubión, Capileira and Pampaneira are the prettiest villages in Las Alpujarras surrounded by dazzling views. All share similar architectural characteristics – white houses piled on top of each other seemingly at random, all with flat gravelled roofs and sprouting eccentric chimneys. The streets are quiet and some disappear down short tunnels beneath the houses – one in Pampaneira has a stream gurgling down the middle. From Capileira, the furthest point that can be driven to independently, take a national park minibus *(bookings recommended; 671 564 407)* into the heights of the Sierra Nevada. 🚗 *Leave Pampaneira on the A4132. At the bottom of the hill outside Orgiva turn right for Lanjarón on the A348.*

⑧ Trevélez
Granada; 18417
The highest town in Spain, Trevélez stands at an altitude of 1,450 m (4,750 ft) beneath the highest mountain on the Spanish mainland, Mulhacén (3,500 m/11,500 ft). Trevélez is divided into three parts: a nondescript area of shops at the bottom selling the town's trademark cured hams, and two more *barrios* (quarters) up the hill. Calle Cuesta, starting beside the church, is the most direct way to walk up into the prettier streets. 🚗 *Continue on the A4132 to Pórtugos – where there is an unusual iron-rich spring – and Pitres. Rounding a corner,*

⑩ Lanjarón
Granada; 18420
On the threshold of Las Alpujarras, Lanjarón has a long history as a spa. It is known throughout Spain as the source of one of the country's most

WHERE TO STAY

TREVÉLEZ

Hotel La Fragua *inexpensive*
This simple whitewashed *mesón* (inn) is located in one of the highest villages in Spain, which has spectacular views from the rooftop. It has a lovely open fire in winter.
C/ San Antonio 4, 18417; 958 858 626; www.hotellafragua.com

POQUEIRA VALLEY

El Cascapeñas *inexpensive*
Located in one of the prettiest villages of the Alpujarras, Capileira, this is a charmingly decorated small hotel and restaurant. It also has a well-stocked wine cellar.
Ctra. de la Sierra 5, 18413, Capileira; 958 763 011; www.elcascapenas.com

popular brands of mineral water. From June to October, visitors flock to the town for various water treatments for many ailments. There are several springs and fountains where visitors can fill up a bottle – one of the most convenient is beside the road shortly after leaving town. A major festival, the Fiesta de San Juan, begins on the night of 24 June and includes a water battle. Lanjarón's only monument is a ruined castle on a bluff, south of the town. The roads to and from Lanjarón wind slowly and dizzily around the slopes.

Follow the A348 straight down from Lanjarón past the wind farm. Turn left at the bottom of the hill for Puente de Tablate.

Puente de Tablate

Granada; 18660

Curiously, this name applies to three bridges of three different generations, bestriding over the same gorge,

which is 45 m (150 ft) deep, at the same point. The oldest, **Puente Nazari**, was built between the 16th and 17th centuries and is used only by pedestrians. Next to it is the 19th-century bridge (with a white shrine beside it), which replaced it. Above both of these older bridges is a functional modern viaduct over which traffic passes noisily.

Above Craft shop displaying its wares in Pampaneira in the high Alpujarras **Below** View of Capileira in Las Alpujarras

EAT AND DRINK

TREVÉLEZ

La Fragua *inexpensive*
This restaurant concentrates on the traditional food of the Alpujarras, which includes dry-cured ham.
C/ San Antonio 4, 18417; 958 858 573; www.hotellafragua.com

POQUEIRA VALLEY

Hostal Pampaneira Casa Alfonso *inexpensive*
A small *hostal* in Pampaneira which specializes in braised meats and serves local Alpujarra wines.
Avda. de la Alpujarra 1, 18411; 958 763 002; www.hostalpampaneira.com

LANJARÓN

Alcadima *inexpensive–moderate*
The highlights of the menu are local recipes such as baby kid in garlic sauce, broad bean soup and fennel stew.
C/ Francisco Tarrega 3, 18420; 958 770 809; www.alcadima.com

DAY TRIP OPTIONS

Using Granada as a base, the itinerary can be split into two independent day trips. A third option is to head south from Granada to the Alpujarras. The A44 and A92 motorways are easy access roads to most of the sights in this drive.

Magnificent Alhambra
The Alhambra, in Granada ①, can take the best part of a day to see properly, with a lazy lunch in the middle. Dip into the city centre monuments and stroll around the fabulous gardens of Generalife. Then

take a walk around the atmospheric streets of the Albaicín.

With a little planning, and using a bus or two, go around the Alhambra.

Castles and cave houses
Either wander along the back road to Guadix ④ and return along the motorway or, if time is really short, use the motorway to go straight to Guadix to see the extraordinary cave houses. The trip can be extended to see Castillo de La Calahorra ⑥.

Take the motorway, A92, from Granada to Guadix and return the same way.

Mountain lovers
The best of Las Alpujarras can be seen if the last part of the route is done backwards. Take a walk around the mountain town of Lanjarón ⑩ and then Pampaneira, Bubión and Capileira – picturesque villages of the Poqueira Valley ⑨.

Take the A44 south from Granada towards Lanjarón. Continue towards Orgiva but before getting there, turn off left onto the A348 for Lanjarón. Continue on the A348 and at Orgiva, get onto the A4132 to visit Pampaneira, Bubión and Capileira.

Andalusian Renaissance and Wooded Mountains

Baeza to Sabiote

Highlights

- **Colleges and palaces**
  Explore Baeza with its old university and ornate Palacio del Jabalquinto

- **Renaissance towns**
  Stroll around the superb Andalusian town of Baeza and visit the Palacio del Deán Ortega in Úbeda

- **Woods and mountains**
  Drive down the valley of the Guadalquivir river in the Parque Natural Sierras de Cazorla, Segura y Las Villas or take a hike on one of the park's many trails

Courtyard of the Palacio del Deán Ortega in Úbeda

Andalusian Renaissance and Wooded Mountains

Two preserved Renaissance towns, Baeza and Úbeda, sit on adjacent hills among the endless olive groves of Jaén province. This route crosses the plains, taking visitors up into one of Spain's best-known nature reserves, the Parque Natural Sierras de Cazorla, Segura y Las Villas. Much of the itinerary goes through dramatic landscapes and there are plenty of opportunities to stop and enjoy the views or set off on foot with a pair of binoculars in search of wildlife. Game and freshwater fish figure on menus everywhere in this region, as do some of the world's best olive oils.

Above Ornate Isabelline-style façade of the Palacio del Jabalquinto, Baeza, *see p228*

Below Panoramic view of the Collado del Almendral, *see p230*

ACTIVITIES

Take an organized nature trek or photo safari in a 4WD vehicle into restricted areas of the Parque Natural Sierras de Cazorla, Segura y Las Villas

Follow one of the many marked footpaths, which vary from easy to demanding, of the Parque Natural Sierras de Cazorla, Segura y Las Villas

Try climbing or hang-gliding in the Parque Natural Sierras de Cazorla, Segura y Las Villas

Taste the olive oils of the region, which to connoisseurs, have just as much individual character as fine wines

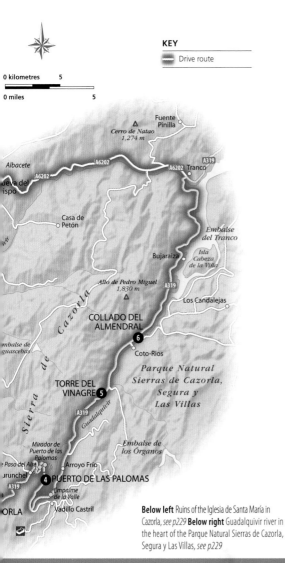

KEY

Drive route

0 kilometres 5

0 miles 5

Fuente
Pinilla

△ Cerro de Natao
1,274 m

Albacete

A6202

A6202

A6202 Tranco

A319

ueva del
ispo

A6202

Casa de
Petón

Embalse
del Tranco

Bujaraiza

Isla
Cabeza
de la Viña

Alto de Pedro Miguel
1,830 m
△

A319

Los Candalejas

**COLLADO DEL
ALMENDRAL**

6

Coto-Ríos

mbalse de
guascebas

*Parque Natural
Sierras de Cazorla,
Segura y
Las Villas*

**TORRE DEL
VINAGRE** 5

A319

Guadalquivir

Mirador de
Puerto de las
Palomas

Embalse de
los Órganos

Paso del Aire

Arroyo Frío

urunchel

4 **PUERTO DE LAS PALOMAS**

A319

Empalme
de la Valle

ORLA

Vadillo Castril

Below left Ruins of the Iglesia de Santa María in
Cazorla, *see p229* **Below right** Guadalquivir river in
the heart of the Parque Natural Sierras de Cazorla,
Segura y Las Villas, *see p229*

PLAN YOUR DRIVE

Start/finish: Baeza to Sabiote.

Number of days: 2, allowing half
a day to explore Úbeda.

Distance: 190 km (120 miles).

Road conditions: Generally good,
although some roads are very windy.

When to go: June and September
are ideal; the weather is warm but
there are few people around. July and
August are holiday months and on
the weekends the roads can be busy
with traffic.

Opening hours: In the winter, most
museums are open from 9:30 or
10am to 6 or 8pm. In the tourist
season, most museums remain
open all day long.

Main market days: Baeza: Thu;
Úbeda: Thu; Cazorla: Wed.

Shopping: Olive oil is a speciality in
this region.

Major festivals: Baeza: Feria, second
week Aug; Romería de la Yedra, early
Sep; Úbeda: San Miguel, 28 Sep;
Sabiote: Fiesta de Virgen de la
Estrella, May.

DAY TRIP OPTIONS

For those interested in **architecture**
and **culture**, Baeza and Úbeda
together can make up a day's sightseeing. The nature reserve in Cazorla
can make a self-contained day out for
nature lovers. For details, *see p231*.

Above Sunlight filtering into the courtyard of the Palacio del Deán Ortega in Úbeda

① Baeza
Jaén; 23440

Baeza has a compact monumental centre, which makes it easy to explore on foot. Begin in the **Plaza del Pópulo** (Plaza de Los Leones), a square overlooked by two arches and two other handsome buildings, one of which is the tourist information office. From here the cathedral is uphill through the arch to the left and, opposite it,

the former university with the name of students daubed on it in bull's blood. The town's most visited building, the **Palacio del Jabalquinto** (open Mon–Fri) is a splendid Gothic palace.

🚗 *Leave town on the J3040, then turn left onto the A316 which leads to Úbeda. Follow the purple signs for "Centro Monumental" or the yellow signs for the "tourist office". Park in or near the tiny Plaza de Santa Lucía.*

② Úbeda
Jaén; 23400

Úbeda is a remarkable assembly of Renaissance architecture with an Andalusian flavour. Much of it is due to the combination of a gifted 16th-century architect, Andrés de Vandelvira, and his two patrons – Francisco de los Cobos, secretary to Emperor Charles V, and Cobos' nephew and successor in the post, Juan Vázquez de Molina.

VISITING ÚBEDA

Tourist Information
C/ Baja del Marqués 4, 23400; 953 779 204

Parking
Parking is available in and around the Plaza de Santa Lucía.

WHERE TO STAY

BAEZA

Puerta de la Luna *expensive*
This 17th-century mansion was formerly the residence of the cathedral's canons. It has a large courtyard with a library, a swimming pool, a spa and a small gym.
C/ Canonigo Melgares Raya, 23440; 953 747 019; www. hotelpuertadelaluna.com

ÚBEDA

Parador de Úbeda *expensive*
The former residence of the Dean of Málaga, this is a comfortable place centred around an elegant patio.
Plaza de Vázquez Molina, 23400; 953 750 345; www.parador.es

AROUND CAZORLA

Parador de Cazorla
moderate–expensive
This modern hotel, in a privileged and secluded forest setting south of the village, is a good base for walks.
23470, Sierra Cazorla; 953 727 075; www.parador.es

A one-hour walking tour

From the car park, walk up Calle Baja del Salvador to the **Plaza Vázquez de Molina** ① and take time to look at the four main buildings that delineate it. At the eastern end stands the **Sacra Capilla del Salvador** ②, a funerary chapel by Vandelvira (1509–75), with an ornate façade and interior. Framing the northern side of the square are the town hall, **Palacio del Deán Ortega** ③ *(open daily)*, former residence of the Dean of Málaga, now a parador hotel and the **Palacio de las Cadenas** ④. Across the square is the somewhat discordant church complex of **Santa Maria de los Reales Alcazares** ⑤, constructed in a mixture of styles. The doorway, for example, is Romanesque, and the cloister, Gothic

Leave the square on Calle Juan Montilla, to the left of the town hall

Where to Stay: inexpensive, under €70; moderate, €70–€120; expensive, over €120

s you face it. Turn left at the corner of the Plaza del Ayuntamiento into Calle Corazón de Jesús. Turn right up Baja el Marqués. The tourist information office is housed in the 18th-century **alacio de Marqués del Contadero** ⑥ on the left of this street. Turn right into the next street to return to the Plaza el Ayuntamiento beneath the **alacio Vela de los Cobos** ⑦, a handsome urban mansion, distinguished by a gallery on the top floor and a corner balcony right below it. Turn left up Calle Juan Montilla and then left up Calle Real, the main street through the Old Town, and turn right up Calle Las Parras. At the top, turn right down Calle de las Ventanas but first take a few steps left to see **Torre Octagonal** ⑧, a remnant of Úbeda's medieval Arab wall.

Turn right off Calle de las Ventanas, through Plazuela Josefa Manuel then right into Calle de Hernán Crespo and quickly left down Calle de Cervantes. Just off this street on the right is the **asa Mudéjar** ⑨. This rebuilt 14th-century house is entered through a porch framed by horseshoe arches. The rooms, built around the patio inside, are now occupied by the own's archaeology museum.

Continue down Calle Cervantes ast the 13th-century **Iglesia de San ablo** ⑩. In the square beside the church (Plaza del Primero de Mayo) a monument of the same name to **an Juan de la Cruz** ⑪, who died in beda in 1591. He is best remembered for his mystical poetry.

Continue downhill past the *ayuntamiento viejo* (old town hall) back to the Plaza Vázquez de Molina. From here, retrace the route down Calle Baja del Salvador to the car park at Plaza de Santa Lucía.

🚗 *Exit Úbeda on Calle de Valencia and turn right onto the N322a. Turn right onto the N322 eastwards towards Torreperogil and Albacete. Turn right at Torreperogil onto the A315. From the roundabout before Peal de Becerro, turn left onto the A319 to Cazorla. Park in or near one of the two squares before entering the streets of the old town.*

③ Cazorla
Jaén; 23470

The town clings to a steep slope beneath a rocky ridge and looks out over endless olive groves. The *casco historico* (old town) is a warren of narrow streets leading to the **Plaza de Santa María** and the gutted but impressive ruins of the **Iglesia de Santa María**. The Moorish **Castillo de la Yedra** *(open Tue–Sat)* stands slightly out of the urban area. This mountain town serves as an access point to the nature reserve, the **Parque Natural Sierras de Cazorla, Segura y Las Villas**. On the road leading to the park are the remains of **La Iruela** castle, dramatically sited on a rock outcrop.

🚗 *Leave Cazorla on the A319, which runs beside the thin triangular park next to the tourist office, towards the nature reserve (following the brown signs). Follow the road through Burunchel to the Puerto de las Palomas.*

Above Medieval archways framing the streets of Baeza **Below left** Façade of a *posada* (inn) in Plaza de Santa María, Cazorla **Below right** Fountain in Plaza de Vázquez de Molina, Úbeda

EAT AND DRINK

BAEZA

Juanito *moderate*
This renowned restaurant has served bullfighters, politicians and other VIPs.
Paseo del Arca del Agua, 23440; 953 740 040; www.juanitobaeza.com

ÚBEDA

Meson Navarro *inexpensive*
A centrally located restaurant, this place serves a well-priced *menu del día*.
Plaza del Ayuntamiento 2, 23400; 953 790 638; www.casaventura.es

CAZORLA

Las Vegas *inexpensive*
This is one of the most popular bars in town, serving tapas prepared with game, fish, mushrooms and olive oil.
Plaza de la Corredera 17, 23470; 953 720 277

Eat and Drink: inexpensive, under €20; moderate, €20–€40; expensive, over €40

Above left Botanical garden at Torre del Vinagre
Above right Street decorated with potted plants, Iznatoraf **Below left** Nature reserve visitor centre at Torre del Vinagre **Below right** House with a carved stone portal, Sabiote

VISITING PARQUE NATURAL SIERRAS DE CAZORLA, SEGURA Y LAS VILLAS

Safaris
Turis Nat Paseo del Santo Cristo 17, 23470, Cazorla; 953 721 351; www.turisnat.org

Hang-gliding centre
Estación de Vuelo Libre El Yelmo, Segura de Sierra; 953 480 280; www.fiaelyelmo.com

WHERE TO STAY

SABIOTE

Palacio las Manillas *moderate*
Housed in a 16th-century Renaissance mansion, this hotel has 15 rooms.
C/ Castillo 1, 23410; 953 774 346; www.palaciolasmanillas.com

④ Puerto de las Palomas
Jaén; 23470

There are two miradors (constructed viewpoints) at the top of the wooded Puerto de las Palomas (1,140 m/ 3,750 ft). The first, on the right, is the **Mirador de Paso del Aire**, with a view northwest over olive groves near Cazorla and La Iruela. A little further on is the **Mirador de Puerto de las Palomas**, which has impressive views over the thickly wooded Guadalquivir valley – the heart of the nature reserve.

🚗 *The A319, still passing through the Sierras de Cazorla park, descends to a crossroads, the Empalme de la Valle. Turn left here to continue on the A319, through the Guadalquivir river valley, towards Torre del Vinagre. After crossing the Guadalquivir river, the road goes through the tourist complex of Arroyo Frío. Follow the road across the Guadalquivir a second time to the Torre del Vinagre.*

⑤ Torre del Vinagre
Jaén; 23470

The Torre del Vinagre is the Parque Natural Sierras de Cazorla, Segura y Las Villas' visitor centre. It has exhibitions on the various ecosystems of the surrounding mountains and valleys. Across the road (and to the left) is a pleasant botanical garden in which threatened, locally endemic species, such as the Cazorla violet, are protected and propagated. The garden is at its most colourful in spring. A short road from the Torre del Vinagre leads across the river to another visitor centre, next to a fish farm, where displays deal with fish and other aquatic life.

🚗 *Stay on the same road through the valley but look out for the next stop a* *Collado del Almendral, on the right. A handwritten sign indicates "Parque Cinegético" and "Kiosco". Park here or, to skip the 800-m (875-yd) on foot, continue on the road and park near the gate on the right.*

⑥ Collado del Almendral
Jaén; 23470

This fenced-in area of woodland is the closest visitors will get to Cazorla's wild life without going on a guided excursion. A footpath leads through the trees, past pens in which deer are kept. The animals will probably be dozing in the shade but at the very least there will be views of the **Embalse del Tranco** reservoir in the distance. The reservoir expands and contracts depending on how wet the year has been. Trek up to the viewpoint at the top of the hill in the

middle of the Collado del Almendral or more spectacular views.

🔁 *After the Collado del Almendral, the A319 winds around the reservoir and crosses the Embalse del Tranco, exiting the Sierras de Cazorla park. Turn left onto the A6202 at Tranco for Villanueva del Arzobispo. Turn left onto the N322 towards Úbeda then right onto the A8103 for Iznatoraf.*

7 Iznatoraf
Jaén; 23338

There are panoromic views of the countryside from this small hilltop town – Cazorla and La Iruela are visible to the south and Sabiote to the southwest. The shady streets, decorated with potted plants, converge on the 16th-century church. Several houses have their coat of arms set into their façades. All or part of the five arched gateways, which formed part of the city's 11th-century Arab walls, still survive.

🔁 *Retrace the route to the N322 and turn right for Úbeda. After skirting around Villacarrillo, continue for another 21 km (13 miles) and then turn right onto the JV6106 to Sabiote. Park in the square beside the castle.*

8 Sabiote
Jaén; 23410

Sabiote is a gem of an old town with beautiful streets winding uphill from its Renaissance castle and the **Iglesia de San Pedro** to the *ayuntamiento* (town hall). Many of the houses in Sabiote have ornately carved stone portals and grilled windows. Two-thirds of the town's medieval walls remain intact along with six gateways. The views from the walls and the lookouts are spectacular.

Above Breathtaking view from the Mirador de Puerto de las Palomas **Below** Façade of a house in Sabiote

EAT AND DRINK

SABIOTE

La Antigua Fabrica
inexpensive–moderate
A restaurant based on traditional cooking using ingredients such as salt cod, peppers and garlic to the fullest. Specialities include stuffed artichokes and bean stew.
C/ San Ginés 99, 23410; 953 773 703

DAY TRIP OPTIONS

An alternative to one long drive is to break the route into one or two separate day trips. One of these could be dedicated to the two splendid Renaissance towns with either Baeza or Úbeda (on the A316) as a base, the other to the nature reserve with Cazorla (on the A319) as the base.

Architecture and culture

The superb Renaissance towns of Baeza ❶ and Úbeda ❷ are close enough for them to easily be visited in the same day, allowing more time for the latter. There will almost certainly be time to make the short drive to visit Sabiote ❽ as well.

Leave Baeza on the A316 straight to Úbeda. From Úbeda, follow the A6103 into Sabiote.

Nature and adventure

Visit the ruins of the church and the Moorish castle in the hillside Renaissance town of Cazorla ❸. With Cazorla as base, visit the Parque Natural Sierras de Cazorla, Segura y Las Villas, a nature reserve, which makes a self-contained tour. Visitors can go climbing and hang-gliding or take a safari through the park to discover its flora and fauna.

Enter the Parque Natural Sierras de Cazorla, Segura y Las Villas from Cazorla and follow the A319 to Torre del Vinagre and return along the same road.

Eat and Drink: inexpensive, under €20; moderate, €20–€40; expensive, over €40

Atlantic Ocean

A Coruña

Bilbao

SPAIN

Zaragoza

Barcelona

Madrid

Valencia

Palma

Murcia

Mediterranean Sea

Seville

Málaga

Secret Beaches

Carboneras to Vela Blanca

Highlights

- **Rocky peninsula**
  Visit the remains of Spain's last gold mines in Rodalquilar

- **Quiet beaches**
  Find a deserted beach on this fascinating coastline

- **Breathtaking views**
  Take in the beauty of the coast from one of several viewing points

- **Eighteenth-century tower**
  Explore Torre de Vela Blanca, set amid jagged cliffs

Dark volcanic rocks at Cabo de Gata, east of Almeria

Secret Beaches

Spain's Mediterranean coastline still has spectacular, remote places to get away to. This route goes through the Parque Natural de Cabo de Gata in the dry southeast province of Almeria. The nature park has seen only light development, leaving many sandy beaches and secret coasts virtually untouched by tourism. The drive visits few monuments but passes through dramatic desert landscapes with breathtaking views.

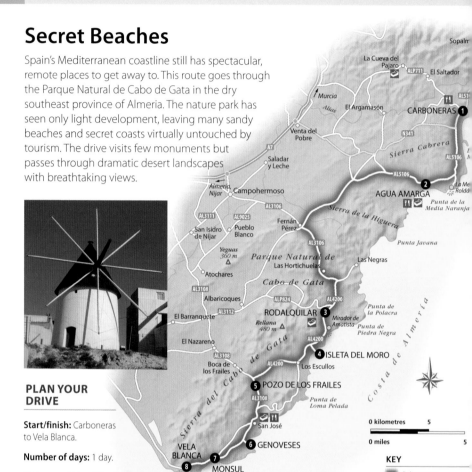

PLAN YOUR DRIVE

Start/finish: Carboneras to Vela Blanca.

Number of days: 1 day.

Distances: 60 km (40 miles).

Road conditions: All the roads in this region, except for the final stretch, are surfaced.

When to go: June and early September are ideal to visit. Ask about sea conditions at the nearest resort before swimming.

Opening hours: Museums in this region do not have fixed times, so it is best to check before visiting.

Main market days: Carboneras: Thu.

Shopping: Pick up pottery from around the region.

Major festivals: Carboneras: San Antonio, Jun; **Agua Amarga:** Santiago, Jul; **Rodalquilar:** Fiesta del Turista, Jul; **Isleta del Moro:** Virgen del Carmen, Jul.

Above Windmill at the holiday resort of Carboneras, *see p235* **Below** Whitewashed houses stretching out around the beach in Agua Amarga, *see p235*

Carboneras
meria; 04140

amed after its previous industry
f charcoal-burning and towered
ver by a power station chimney, this
rmer fishing village is now a boom-
g holiday resort. It is also a point of
ccess to the **Parque Natural de Cabo
e Gata**. The Plaza de Castillo is the
eart of this town. However, the main
ttractions of Carboneras are its
everal long, sandy beaches, which
retch for almost 17 km (11 miles)
ong its coast, and a rocky islet, the
la de San Andrés.

Leave Carboneras along the
eafront on the AL5106 towards
gua Amarga. Go past the Almeria
urn-off and continue straight.
hortly after leaving the urban area,
here is a car park for **Los Muertos**
each on the left. Next to this is a
ttle road signposted for **La Mesa
oldán**. Turn up this road and go up
o the lighthouse and watchtower
or some spectacular views.

🚗 *Return to the AL5106 and resume
n the road to Agua Amarga. In Agua
marga, park on the main road.*

➋ Agua Amarga
lmeria; 04149

small resort of white houses, barely
nore than a hamlet on the edge of
he Parque Natural de Cabo de Gata,
gua Amarga has adapted to tourism
vithout losing its charm. It is a great
blace for water sports and scuba
living, and for visitors who feel like a
valk, the nature reserve is a stone's
hrow away. Behind the beautiful
andy beach, there are streets worth
exploring for their picturesque
orners. The houses, both old and
nodern, are in the typical white-
vashed, cubic style of Almeria. In the
hills around Agua Amarga are several
old farmsteads with attractive
domed wells.

🚗 *Leave Agua Amarga for Almeria,
Murcia and Venta del Pobre on the
AL5106. Look out for an inconspicuous
urning to the left, which only has a
signpost for Fernán Pérez. At the end of
the road, there is a T-junction in Fernán
Pérez. Turn left for San José and
AL3106 and then right on the AL4200
after Las Hortichuelas for Rodalquilar.
Turn right to enter the town, fork right
and head towards the church to park.*

➌ Rodalquilar
Almeria; 04115

Once a run-down town, Rodalquilar
is now the headquarters of the Parque
Natural de Cabo de Gata. There is an
information office next to the church
and the **Jardín Botánico El Albardinal**
nearby. Continue on the road, passing
the nature reserve's buildings, to a
geology museum. Beyond the museum is the site of the somewhat eerie,
dilapidated remains of the peninsula's
last gold mines, the **Minas de Oro de
Rodalquilar**. Visitors are free to wander around the wash pans and crumbling buildings but extreme care is
needed as there are no safety pre-
cautions here.

Just outside Rodalquilar, on the
AL4200, is the **Mirador de Amatista**,
a viewing balcony high above the
sea, from which there are spectacular
views of the sea.

🚗 *Leave Rodalquilar on the AL4200
and turn right for San José. Continue
on this road for 4 km (2 miles) and
turn left down to Isleta del Moro.*

➍ Isleta del Moro
Almeria; 04118

This picturesque fishing village of
low-lying white houses on an isthmus leading to an outcrop of rock
and an island (the *isleta* of the name)
has changed little under the impact
of tourism. Most people come here
to combine a day on the beach with
a meal of fried or grilled fish in one of
Isleta's few restaurants. Another small
resort worth a stopover, just down
the road, is **Los Escullos**.

🚗 *Return to the AL4200 and turn left.
After Los Escullos, the road leads to a
T-junction. Turn left on the AL3108 for
Pozo de los Frailes.*

Above left Church in the town of Rodalquilar
Above right Turquoise blue waters seen from
the Mirador de Amatista

WHERE TO STAY

AROUND CARBONERAS

Casa Concha de Fazahali
inexpensive–moderate
Located 9 km (6 miles) in the hills
behind Carboneras, this hotel is built
in the shape of a giant shell.
*Cueva del Pájaro, 04140, Carboneras;
950 130 812; www.fazahali.com*

AGUA AMARGA

El Tio Kiko *moderate*
All the rooms in this small Rusticae hotel
have large windows and terraces with
great views.
*C/ Embarque, 04149; 950 138 080;
www.eltiokiko.com*

RODALQUILAR

Los Patios *moderate*
A minimalist hotel close to the sea,
with partly-glass roofs in some of the
rooms so visitors can watch the stars.
*Camino del Playazo, 04115; 950 525
137; www.lospatioshotel.es*

EAT AND DRINK

CARBONERAS

El Dorado *moderate*
This charming restaurant and hotel is
a good place for breakfast by the sea.
*C/ Camino Vieja de Garrucha 24,
04140; 950 454 050; www.eldorado-
carboneras.com*

AGUA AMARGA

La Chumbera *moderate*
A restaurant in a traditional farmhouse
just outside Agua Amarga. The cuisine
is Mediterranean with an Italian accent.
*Paraje los Ventorrillos, 04149; 950
168 321; www.lachumbera-
aguamarga.com*

Eat and Drink: inexpensive, under €20; moderate, €20–€40; expensive, over €40

Top Faro de Gata on the headland of Cabo de Gata **Above** Waterwheel in Pozo de los Frailes

⑤ Pozo de los Frailes
Almeria; 04117

At the centre of this tiny village is a restored waterwheel surrounded by a circular wall. Step inside to appreciate the ingenuity with which water was managed in the arid regions of Almeria. Visit the **Los Galeria de los Frailes** (www.lagaleriadelosfrailes.es), a gallery displaying contemporary works of art by artists living in the Cabo de Gata area. Continue on the AL3108 into San José. Back on the coast south of El Pozo, **San José** is the main town in this area, where all the hotels and restaurants in the southern Cabo de Gata are located.

🚗 *From San José, follow signs for Genoveses and Monsul. The road goes around the back of San José to the start of a dirt road to the beaches of Genoveses and Monsul. Take this dirt road over a saddle until the fork. Take the left turn down to the car park of the Genoveses beach.*

⑥ Genoveses
Almeria; 04118

An arc of sand between two prominent headlands, this beach is named after the Genoese fleet that took part in the Christian attack on Moorish Almeria in 1147. In commo with all the beaches west of San Jos no development has been permitte and there are no bars or restaurants here. Despite its lack of facilities, Genoveses is hugely popular in the summer. There are two more small beaches further down the road.

🚗 *Go back to the fork and turn left on to the upper road to Monsul, 2 km (1 mile) further on. There is a car park on the road and another one near the beach, turning left from this road.*

⑦ Monsul
Almeria; 04118

If Monsul, with its large rock placed in the middle of the sand, looks familiar, it may be because it was used as the location for a scene in *Indiana Jones and the Last Crusade* starring Harrison Ford, Sean Connery and a flock of imported pigeons. The sandy beach stretches for a long distance with calm tranquil water, perfect for diving and snorkelling. The coastline is studded with dramatic volcanic rocks.

🚗 *The track continues a little way beyond Monsul. After Monsul, the track leads to a gate. Park here to do the walk.*

⑧ Vela Blanca
Almeria; 04118

Due to the fragility of its ecosystem, the stretch of coast between Cala Carbón (near Monsul) and the headland of Vela Blanca is closed to traffic. A broad track runs along the steep slopes from one gate to another (approximately 2 km/1 mile apart), offering easy walking and spectacular views all the way. Avoid doing the walk in the hottest part of the day as there is no shade along the route. The views are different in the morning, afternoon and evening as the sun shifts round the whole day long. For views of the cape ahead, visitors need to do the walk before midday. Later in the day the sun shines on the beaches of Monsul and Genoveses.

A three-hour walking tour

From the car park go to the **eastern gateway** ① and take the broad track ahead. This track follows the contours of the coast without turning off it, so there is no possibility of getting lost.

At first glance it looks as if little life survives here, but this is a surprisingly rich habitat. The most conspicuous plant is the dwarf fan palm (*Chamaerops humilis*), Europe's only native palm tree. There is always some species or other in flower among the xerophytic flora along the side of the track and on the steep slopes. Some plants, such as the pink snapdragon (*Antirrhinum charidemi*), grow here and nowhere else in the world.

Around the first corner of the track there is a spectacular viewpoint looking back eastwards over the beaches and headlands between here and San José. Below, the steep slopes fall into the Mediterranean as

VISITING VELA BLANCA

Tourist Information
There are tourist information offices en route and in San José. They provide information regarding Vela Blanca and also about visiting the Parque Natural Cabo de Gata.
Avda. de San José 27, 04118; 950 380 299; www.cabodegata-nijar.com

WHERE TO STAY

AROUND POZO DE LOS FRAILES
Cortijo el Sotillo
moderate–expensive
This is both a hotel and restaurant built around an early 18th-century farmhouse 2 km (1 mile) from Pozo de los Frailes, when entering San José. On the menu are fresh fish, kid and lamb.
Ctra. Entrada a San José, 04118, San José; 950 611 100; www. cortijoelsotillo.com

inaccessible cliffs. Hidden beneath the waves is a marine nature reserve rich in coral reefs and beds of seagrass in contrast to the arid and deserted hillsides around.

From here the track swings away from the sea and continues to climb leading to a ravine, the **Barranco del Negro** ②. Once across this ravine, continue to walk up to the **western gateway** ③. This is located on a saddle below the Torre de Vela Blanca, offering stunning views in both directions. Westward is the cape itself on which stands a lighthouse. Beneath it are some jagged rocks, the Arrecife de las Sirenas (Mermaids' Reef), the name referring to monk seals which used to inhabit these waters. Walk up the road to the **Torre de Vela**

Blanca ④, although it is closed to visitors there are spectacular views. The tower was built in the 18th century under Charles III as part of the coast's defences against pirate attacks. If a belligerent vessel was sighted, a fire would be lit and a smoke signal transmitted to the next towers in the chain. It is said that such a message could be sent from Málaga to Mojácar in 30 minutes.

For a longer walk (6 km/4 miles there and back), take the same road down from the saddle, descending in hairpins and passing over the top of two beaches to reach a junction near the Faro de Gata lighthouse. The only way back is by the same route; downhill from the saddle to the lower gate and to the car park.

Above left Rocky Monsul coastline in Almeria
Above right Secluded beach of Genoveses

ACTIVITIES IN CABO DE GATA

SCUBA DIVING

ISUB
Although this centre is mainly for experienced divers, there is also a beginner's "Discover Scuba Diving" course for those who want to progress. There are more than 20 diving sites along the coast of the Parque Natural Cabo de Gata – Carboneras, Agua Amarga, Las Negras, La Isleta del Moro and San José being a few of them.
C/ Babor 3, 04118, San José; 950 380 004; www.isubsanjose.com

---

EAT AND DRINK

AROUND POZO DE LOS FRAILES

Casa Miguel *moderate*
A rice and fish restaurant on the main street at the centre of San José, 3 km (2 miles) from Pozo de los Frailes. The menu is strong on local fish and seafood. *Paella* is another good choice.
C/ Correo, 04118, San José; 950 380 329; www.restaurantecasamiguel.es

El Tempranillo *moderate*
This is a restaurant on San José's marina, 3 km (2 miles) from Pozo de los Frailes, specializing in fish and seafood, and in locally reared meat.
Puerto Deportiveo de San José, 04118; 950 380 206; www.tempranillo.com.es

La Taberna del Puerto *moderate*
Located by the waterside marina in San José, 3 km (2 miles) from Pozo de los Frailes, this restaurant offers a choice of sun and shade.
Puerto Deportivo de San José, 04118; 950 380 042

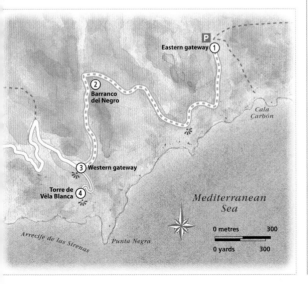

Eastern gateway ①

② Barranco del Negro

Cala Carbón

③ Western gateway

Torre de Vela Blanca ④

Mediterranean Sea

Arrecife de las Sirenas   *Punta Negra*

0 metres   300
0 yards   300

Eat and Drink: inexpensive, under €20; moderate, €20–€40; expensive, over €40

Mallorca's Cliffs and Coves

Palma to Alcúdia

Highlights

- **Historic city**
  Explore the capital of Mallorca, Palma, an ancient seaport with a beautiful Gothic cathedral

- **Fishing village**
  Stop by Sant Elm, a small coastal resort, by the crystal-clear waters of the Mediterranean

- **Mountain scenery**
  Take in the spectacular mountain scenery of the Serra de Tramuntana along Mallorca's northwest coast

- **Hidden beaches**
  Relax in a hidden cove by a dazzling turquoise sea

The cathedral, La Seu, overlooking the town and the harbour of Palma

Mallorca's Cliffs and Coves

The largest island of the Balearic archipelago, Mallorca offers visitors wonderful beaches, rural retreats, quiet coves and historic architecture. Beginning in the capital city of Palma, this drive weaves its way through the green foothills of the Serra de Tramuntana before emerging on the north coast. The road threads through steep valleys and past rearing peaks, where there are exquisite views out across the Mediterranean, to explore the beguiling old town of Pollença, the walled town of Alcúdia and the craggy mountains of the Península de Formentor.

Above Exterior of the Palau de l'Almudaina in Palm p242 **Left** Open-air market stalls in Alcúdia, see p.

ACTIVITIES

Take a walk around the historic town of Palma and visit its spectacular cathedral

Go for a swim at Sant Elm, one of the island's most charming resorts

Enjoy the spectacular views around the Gorg Blau and its reservoirs

Explore the holiest place in Mallorca, the Santuari de Monastir de Lluc

See the island's wildest scenery on the Península de Formentor

Right Looking down on the cove at Banyalbufar, *see p243*

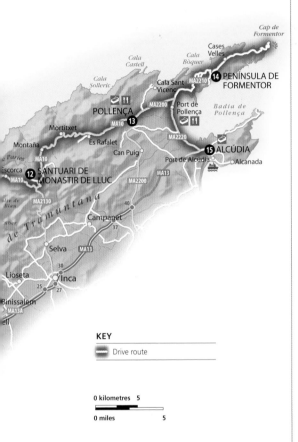

KEY

— Drive route

0 kilometres 5

0 miles 5

low Town and monastery of Valldemossa, *see p244*

PLAN YOUR DRIVE

Start/finish: Palma to Alcúdia.

Number of days: 2, including half a day on Illa de Sa Dragonera.

Distance: 230 km (145 miles).

Road conditions: Roads and lanes are generally very narrow but are well paved and signed. There are many steep sections, especially the ascent/descent into Sóller on the northeast and southwest side. There are a lot of hair-raising bends down to Sa Calobra, the Península de Formentor, and between Andratx and Banyalbufar.

When to go: Spring (from Apr to May) and autumn (from late Sep to Oct) are the best times to enjoy the drive. Temperatures can be too hot for comfort and the roads very crowded during summer (from Jul to Aug).

Opening hours: Museums and historic monuments are usually open from Mon to Fri, from 10am to 1pm and again from 4 to 6pm. Most churches, however, have no fixed opening hours.

Market days: Palma: Sat; Valldemossa: Sun; Sóller: Sat; Pollença: Wed, Sun; Alcúdia: Tue.

Shopping: Shoppers should head to Palma which has a range of shops. Local specialities include glassware, lanterns, chandeliers, leather goods, Mallorcan textiles and ceramic tiles.

Major festivals: Palma: Sant Sebastià, 20 Jan; Carnival, Feb; **Valldemossa:** Santa Catalina Thomàs, 28 Jul; **Sóller:** Festes de Moros i Cristians, second Sun May; **Pollença:** Sant Antoni, 17 Jan, Corpus Christi, mid-Jun; **Alcúdia:** Romeria de la Victòria, 2 Jul.

DAY TRIP OPTIONS

Visitors can explore the area covered in the drive in a series of day trips. **Wildlife enthusiasts** can head off to Sant Elm and then to the Illa de Sa Dragonera nature reserve; **architecture buffs** can enjoy the echoing cloisters of Valldemossa monastery; and **families** will delight in the safe, gently shelving beach at Port de Pollença. For details, *see p247*.

Above Rows of sun beds lining the beach at Sant Elm Below left Shops along a shady street in Palma Below right Majestic façade of the Gothic cathedral in Palma

VISITING PALMA

Tourist Information
The main tourist office is called the Oficina d'Informaticio Turistica. *Avda. Argentina 1, 07013; 902 102 365; www.illesbaleros.es*

Parking
For on-street parking, visitors have to buy a ticket from the ORA ticket machines, which are ubiquitous. Alternatively, there are about ten underground car parks in and around the city centre; just follow any of the signs. One of the handiest car parks is right next to the cathedral on Avenida Antoni Maura.

WHERE TO STAY

PALMA

Hotel Born *moderate*
Located in the centre of Palma, this is an appealing hotel in a lovely refurbished old mansion. *C/ Sant Jaume 3, 07012; 971 712 942; www.hotelborn.com*

Hostal Brondo *moderate*
This stylish hotel occupies an old house complete with stone arches and traditional whitewashed plaster work. *C/ Ca'n Brondo 1, 07001; 971 719 043; www.hostalbrondo.net*

Palacio Ca Sa Galesa *expensive*
Set in a privileged location just a stone's throw from Mallorca's cathedral, this is a 16th-century palace. *Miramar 8, 07012; 971 715 400; www.palaciocasagalesa.com*

GALILEA

Scott's Galilea *expensive*
All the rooms in this lovely hotel have fabulous views. *Sa Costa Den Mandons, 3, 07195; 971 870 100; www.scottsgalilea.com*

❶ Palma
Mallorca; 07012

Palma's pride and joy is its cathedral, **La Seu** *(closed Sun)*, which dominates the waterfront from the crest of a hill. The interior, renovated by Antoni Gaudí (1852–1926), is the epitome of the Catalan Gothic style, its yawning nave flanked by tall and slender columns. It is regarded as one of Spain's outstanding Gothic structures. Next door is the **Palau de l'Almudaina** *(closed Sun)*, a royal residence from Moorish times. The current Gothic palace was rebuilt in the 13th century after the Moorish fortress was destroyed, and it is still sometimes used as a royal residence. Spreading northeast behind the cathedral are the narrow lanes and ageing mansions of the old town. Tucked away among the side streets are two detours – the Baroque **Basílica de Sant Francesc** *(open daily)*, notable for its exquisite Gothic cloister, and the 10th-century Moorish bathhouses, the **Banys Àrabs** *(open daily)*. About 3 km (2 miles) west of the city centre, stands the Gothic **Castell de Bellver** *(open daily)* with great views of the city and bay.

🚗 *Head west around Palma's outer ring road, the Via Cintura, and take the MA1040 north to get to Esporles.*

❷ Esporles
Mallorca; 07190

A world away from the teeming resorts of the coast, Esporles is a lea little town whose elongated main street, the Passeig del Rei, follows th line of an ancient stone watercourse This street is lined with a handful of cafés and restaurants. The town's principal sight is the 16th-century stone church.

From Esporles, drive 1 km (0.6 mile north along the MA1100 and turn le onto the MA1101 to reach **La Granj** *(open daily)*, a handsome *finca* (countr house) nestled in a tranquil woode and terraced valley. It belonged to a order of Cistercian monks from the 13th to the 15th centuries and then to the Fortuny family. Highlights of the interior include an antique kitche the dining room with its paintings and the first-floor loggia. Look out also for the finely crafted, green-tinte Mallorcan chandeliers and the beau tiful majolica tile-panels that embel lish the walls. There are folk dancing displays here *(Wed and Fri)* throughout the summer.

🚗 *Leave La Granja and turn south onto the MA1101, a winding country road, towards Puigpunyent. Go throug Puigpunyent on the MA1032 to Galile Park on the street.*

❸ Galilea
Mallorca; 07195

Offering a spectacular view of the southwestern Mallorcan coast, the tir village of Galilea is a favourite haunt for artists from all over Europe. It has few whitewashed farmsteads dottin the valley and clambering up the su rounding hills. The main sight in the village is the sturdy 19th-century church, as many of its older building

d not survive the attentions of arauding pirates.

Leave Galilea on the MA1032 to Es pdellà. At Capdellà, turn right onto e MA1031 to reach Andratx. From ndratx, take the MA1030 straight to nt Elm. Park on the street at the trance to the village.

Sant Elm
allorca; 07159

nt Elm's main street strings along e seashore with a sandy beach at he end and a tiny harbour at the her. This small resort town has a ood selection of cafés and restau-nts and beautiful scenery.

From the harbour, passenger boats ke 15 minutes to shuttle across to e austere offshore islet of **Sa ragonera**, a craggy hunk of rock, km (2 miles) long and 700 m 65 yd) wide, that lies at an angle to e coast. A nature reserve since 1988, a Dragonera is home to a variety of rd life and wild flowers. An imposing dge of cliffs dominates its north-estern shore. Behind the ridge, a ough track travels the length of the and, linking a pair of craggy capes nd their lighthouses. Boats dock at a ove-harbour halfway up the east ore, which puts both ends of the and within comfortable walking stance, though the excursion north Cap de Tramuntana is prettier.

From Sant Elm, retrace the route n the MA1030 to Andratx. At the undabout in Andratx, take a left nto the main coastal road, the MA10. ollow this road for 18 km (11 miles) ortheast to Estellencs. Park on the reet in Estellencs.

⑤ Estellencs
Mallorca; 07192

With its steep coastal cliffs and handsome terraced fields, Estellencs is the prettiest of the coastal villages. It has narrow winding alleys adorned by old stone houses and an 18th-century parish church *(no fixed opening hours)*. The church has an exquisite pinewood and candle-lit interior, where villagers gathered for hundreds of years, seeking shelter from pirates and invaders.

A steep, but driveable, 2-km (1-mile) lane leads down from the village to **Cala Estellencs**. Quiet and undeveloped, Cala Estellencs is a rocky, surf-buffeted cove that has a beach and a summertime bar.

🚗 **Return to the MA10 and continue (7 km/4 miles) to Banyalbufar.**

⑥ Banyalbufar
Mallorca; 07191

The terraced fields of Banyalbufar cling to the coastal cliffs beside the MA10. The land here has been culti-vated since Moorish times, with a spring above the village providing a water supply that is still channelled down the hillside along slender watercourses into open storage cisterns. The village's main street, flanked by whitewashed houses and narrow cobbled lanes, culminates in the main square, which is overlooked by the 15th-century parish church.

🚗 **From Banyalbufar, continue on the MA10. At the junction with the MA1100, stay on the same road. At Valldemossa, park in one of the two municipality car parks. They are paid car parks, but are safe.**

Above Quiet cove of Cala Estellencs, lapped by the blue-green waters of the sea
Below Rooftop view of Galilea

VISITING SA DRAGONERA

Ferry Services
There is a passenger boat service to Sa Dragonera from Sant Elm three times a day from Feb to Apr and from Oct to Nov, as well as a more frequent service (four times a day) from May to Sep.
Plaça de la Reina 2, 070120; 639 617 545, 627 966 264; 971 100 866

EAT AND DRINK

PALMA

Ca'n Joan de S'Aigo *inexpensive*
This long-established coffee house serves freshly baked *ensaimadas* (pastry buns) and excellent fruit-flavoured mousses.
C/ Can Sanç 10, 07012; 971 710 759; closed Tue

La Taberna del Caracol
inexpensive–moderate
Housed in a charming old premise with wooden beams and ancient arches, this is an excellent tapas bar.
C/ Sant Alonso 2, 07012; 971 714 908; www.taberna.name; closed lunch and Sun; reservations advised at peak times

Ca'n Carlos *moderate*
A delightful family-run restaurant, the highlights of the menu are its first-class Mallorcan cuisine that takes in delights such as cuttlefish and snails.
C/ Aigua 5, 07012; 971 713 869; closed Sun

SANT ELM

Vista Mar *moderate*
Located on the harbour, this restaurant does an excellent fish soup as well as seafood main courses.
Sant Elm, 07159; 971 237 547

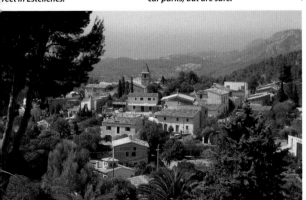

Eat and Drink: inexpensive, under €20; moderate, €20–€40; expensive, over €40

Above People relaxing on the beach at Cala Deià, Deià **Below** Monastery complex of Reial Cartoixa de Valldemossa overlooking the town

WHERE TO STAY

VALLDEMOSSA

Es Petit Hotel Valldemossa *expensive*
This restored hotel has a welcoming atmosphere and it combines old and modern decorative elements.
Uetam 1, 07170; 971 612 479; www.espetithotel-valldemossa.com

DEIÀ

Pensión Miramar *moderate*
Perched high above and signposted from the road, this is a family-run *pensión* in a traditional stone *finca*.
C/ Ca'n Oliver s/n, 07179; 971 639 084; www.pensionmiramar.com

La Residència *expensive*
Nestled in the foothills of the Tramuntana, this is a beautiful luxury hotel which has several ivy-covered stone buildings and villas.
Son Canals s/n, 07179; 971 639 011; www.hotel-laresidencia.com

AROUND DEIÀ

Hotel Costa d'Or *expensive*
Overlooking an undeveloped slice of coast just 2 km (1 mile) east of Deià, this is a splendid four-star hotel.
Lluc-Alcari s/n, 07179; 971 639 025; www.hoposa.es; closed Nov–Mar

SÓLLER

Hotel El Guía *moderate*
Set behind a pretty little courtyard near the train station, this is a long-established, family-run hotel.
C/ Castanyer 2, 07100; 971 630 227; www.sollernet.com/elguia; closed Dec–Feb

AROUND SÓLLER

Hotel Ca's Xorc *expensive*
Located in the hills, just off the MA10, this is an intimate boutique hotel with a beautiful swimming pool.
Ctra. Sóller–Deià MA-10; 971 638 280; www.casxorc.com

⑦ Valldemossa
Mallorca; 07170

The ancient hill town of Valldemossa is a jumble of houses and monastic buildings. Valldemossa's status was transformed in the early 14th century, when the asthmatic King Sanç built a royal palace here in the hills where the air was easier to breathe. In 1399, the palace was gifted to Carthusian monks from Tarragona, who converted and extended the original buildings into a sprawling monastery, the **Reial Cartoixa de Valldemossa** *(open daily)*. The monastery also houses the **Museu Municipal Art Contemporani** which has a small collection of works by Spanish artists such as Miró, Picasso and Tàpies.

🚗 *Leave Valldemossa on the MA1130 and then take a right onto the MA10. Drive along the coast to Son Marroig. It comes up on the left of the road. Park in the car park.*

Sand and Chopin
The Reial Cartoixa de Valldemossa monastery owes its present fame almost entirely to the French writer George Sand (1804–76), who, with her companion, the composer Frédéric Chopin, lived here for four months in 1838–9. Visitors can look around Sand and Chopin's old quarters as well as the church and the echoing cloisters, where the first port of call is the antique pharmacy. There are free concerts of Chopin's piano music.

⑧ Son Marroig
Mallorca; 07179

An imposing L-shaped mansion perched high above the seashore, Son Marroig *(closed Sun)* was the favourite residence of the Habsburg Archduke Ludwig Salvatore (1847–1915), who lived here long enough to immerse himself in all things Mallorquín. The house is now a museum dedicated to his life and work. The Son Marroig estate comprises the house, its gardens and the wild and wonderful Sa Foradada headland, a 40-minute walk away.

🚗 *Continue on the MA10 from Son Marroig along the coast to Deià. Park on the street in Deià.*

⑨ Deià
Mallorca; 07179

Dramatically surrounded by mountains, Deià is a beautiful village located at the spot where the mighty Puig d'es Teix mountain (1,050 m/ 3,450 ft) meets the sea. Alleys of old peasant houses curl up to a country church, in the precincts of which the village's most famous resident, British poet and novelist Robert Graves (1895–1985), is buried. His old home **Ca n'Alluny** *(closed Mon)*, beside the main road, northeast of the village, was opened to the public in 2006. Known also for its artistic community and up-market cafés, Deià attracts a big international crowd.

Drive out of Deià on the MA10 and take the signed turn to reach **Cala Deià** on the left. A lovely cove flanked by jagged cliffs, Cala Deià is a great place for a swim. There is a ramshackle beach bar to keep the swimmers happy.

🚗 *Return to the MA10, which wriggles its way over the mountains before emerging at Sóller. Park on the Avinguda Gran Vía while driving into town.*

⑩ Sóller

Mallorca; 07100, 07101

Sóller is one of the most elegant towns on Mallorca and it is also an ideal base for exploring the surrounding mountains. The town's sloping lanes are lined with 18th- and 19th-century fruit merchants' stone houses, many of which are adorned with ornate grilles and doors – examples of Catalan Modernism. This walk starts at Sóller and steps out of town through the countryside to visit the hamlet of Biniaraix.

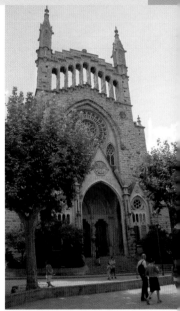

A two-hour walking tour

From the spot where the car was parked, head down Carrer Bauza towards **Plaça Constitució** ①, a lively square and the centre of Sóller, which is flanked by a gaggle of cafés and bisected by the tramlines that carry on down to Port de Sóller. Overlooking the square is the Gothic-Baroque **Església de Sant Bartomeu** ②, which dates back to 1236. Its most appealing features are its attractive rose window, high in the main Art Nouveau façade, and the sweeping balustrade up above. The façade was designed by the celebrated Catalan Modernist architect Joan Rubió i Bellver (1870–1952), a disciple of Antoni Gaudí. From the square, head north along Avinguda Cristòfol Colom to reach the **market** ③ with its racks of local produce and glistening fish. The market is something of a social hub for locals, who gather here to drink coffee and cognac while nibbling on the island's *ensaimadas* (pastries). Take Carrer Palou from near the market and turn right onto Carrer 11 de Maig to reach **Can Prohom** ④, one of the grandest mansions in town at Carrer de Sa Lluna. The gentry used to stay here when they came to town, donning their top hats and canes before strolling out into town. From here retrace the route to the car park.

Hop into the car and drive along Carrer Bauza and then Carrer de Sa Lluna up the valley to the tiny and extremely pretty hamlet of Biniaraix. On the way, pass orchards and farmland flanked by dry-stone walls. At Biniaraix, look out for the tiny main square, where there are lovely cafés under the shade of the palm trees. The village is popular as the starting point for long and strenuous hikes up into the surrounding mountains. After relaxing for a while, retrace the route to return to Sóller.

🚌 *Leave Sóller on the MA11. At the roundabout, turn right onto the MA10. The road climbs up into the mountains before tunnelling through to the Gorg Blau, a distance of 13 km (8 miles).*

Above Façade of the Església de Sant Bartomeu in Plaça Constitució

VISITING SÓLLER

Tourist Information
The tourist office is right in the centre of town, a few metres down from the train station in an old train carriage. *Plaça d'Espanya, 07100; 971 638 008; www.sollernet.com*

Parking
Park on the street on Avinguda Gran Vía just on entering the town.

EAT AND DRINK

VALLDEMOSSA

Restaurant Ca'n Mario *inexpensive*
Located just a few minutes from the Valldemossa monastery, this restaurant serves delicious traditional Mallorcan food at affordable prices. *C/ Uetam 8, 07170; 971 612 122; closed end-Dec–end-Jan*

DEIÀ

Restaurant Buganvilla *expensive*
The highlight of this smart restaurant is a creative menu using the very best of local ingredients, from island fish to home-grown vegetables. *Ctra. Deià-Valldemossa s/n, 07179; 971 639 000; closed Sun and Nov–Mar*

SÓLLER

Restaurant Don Cipriani *inexpensive*
Probably the best restaurant in Sóller, this amenable Italian place specializes in homemade pastas and pizzas. *Gran Via 43, 07100; 971 633 049*

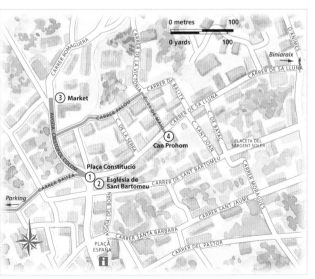

0 metres 100
0 yards 100

Biniaraix

③ Market
④ Can Prohom
PLACETA DEL SÀRGENT SOLER
Plaça Constitució
① ② Església de Sant Bartomeu
Parking
PLAÇA ESPANYA

CARRER ROMAGUERA
CARRER DE LA VICTORIA
AVINGUDA CRISTÒFOL COLOM
CARRER PALOU
C. DE LA SERRA
CARRER BAUZA
AVGDA. DEL BORN
CARRER SANTA BÀRBARA
CARRER DE SA LLUNA
CARRER D'ORMINO
C. DE BALITX
C. SANT JOAN
C. DE BATLX
CARRER DE SANT BARTOMEU
CARRER DEL PASTOR
CARRER SANT JAUME
CARRER MORAGUES
D'ANIMES

Eat and Drink: inexpensive, under €20; moderate, €20–€40; expensive, over €40

WHERE TO STAY

POLLENÇA

Posada de Lluc *expensive*
This is a chic hotel in an immaculately restored old stone town house.
C/ Roser Vell 11, 07460; 971 535 220; www.posadalluc.com

Son Brull *expensive*
A very comfortable hotel that combines ancient architecture with avant-garde design.
Ctra. Palma–Pollença PM220, Km 50, 07460; 971 535 353; www.sonbrull. com; closed Dec–Jan

AROUND POLLENÇA

Hostal Bahía *moderate*
Located right on the seafront, this is an attractive *hostal* that offers 30 rooms in one of the port's older villas.
Passeig Voramar 31, 07470, Port de Pollença; 971 866 562; www.hoposa. es; closed Nov–Mar

ALCÚDIA

Ca'n Simó *moderate*
This is an appealing hotel occupying a 19th-century Mallorcan manor house.
C/ Sant Jaume 1, 07400; 971 549 260; www.cansimo.com

AROUND ALCÚDIA

Hostatgeria Ermita de la Victòria *inexpensive*
The old monastic quarters behind the Ermita de la Victòria, just 5 km (3 miles) from Alcúdia, have been converted into a charming *hostal*.
07400, Ermita de la Victòria; 971 549 912; www.lavictoriahotel.com

Above left Portal of the Monestir de Nostra Senyora de Lluc **Above right** Breathtaking view from the Mirador des Colomer **Below** Looking down the Via Calvari from the shrine at Pollença

⑪ Gorg Blau
Mallorca; 07315

A well-known beauty spot, the Gorg Blau (Blue Gorge) offers a harsh and craggy landscape in the heart of the mountains. Two reservoirs dot the bottom of the gorge. The largest reservoir is the Embalse de Cúber, which is located southwest of Gorg Blau. There is rich bird life here and this is a good spot to see different kinds of birds of prey. To visit the gorge, visitors need to look out for the sign to Embalse de Gorg Blau.

🚗 *Continue on the MA10. After Escorca, turn left to stay on the MA10. Turn left onto the MA2140 to reach the Santuari de Monastir de Lluc.*

⑫ Santuari de Monastir de Lluc
Mallorca; 07315

Located in a valley in the middle of the mountains is the Santuari de Monastir de Lluc *(open daily)*, Mallorca's most important place of pilgrimage for over 800 years. Tourists now mingle with the pilgrims who arrive here every year to pay homage. The object of devotion, inside the basilica, is a much-revered statue of the Virgin, *La Morenta de Lluc*. The monastery's boys' choir, nicknamed *Els Blauets* (The Little Blue Boys), for the colour of their cassocks, performs in the basilica. There is a museum which houses local handicrafts and works of art.

🚗 *Leave the monastery on the MA2140 to reach the MA10. Keep on this road to arrive at Pollença. Park on the street on the south side of town.*

⑬ Pollença
Mallorca; 07460; 07470

Inordinately pretty, the narrow cobbled lanes and honey-coloured stone mansions of Pollença are a delight. Pollença has retained much of its old-world charm with narrow, twisting streets and beautiful houses. At the centre of town is the **Plaça Major**, a genial main square, which houses a cluster of laid-back cafés and is the site of a lively fruit and vegetable market on Sundays. Overlooking the square is the 13th-century **Església de Nostra Senyora dels Angels**, with a fine rose window. Pollença's most dramatic attraction is its **Via Calvari** (Way of the Cross), a long and steep stone stairway that climbs up to a tiny hilltop shrine.

Drive out of Pollença on the MA2200 to Pollença's port 5 km (3 miles) northeast of the town. **Port de Pollença** was actually built just inland to guard against surprise attacks from pirates and this town curves through the flatlands behind its bay, the **Badia de Pollença**. The beach is the centre of attention here, a narrow sliver of sand enhanced by its sheltered waters, which are ideal for swimming. The prettiest part of the resort is to the north of the marina, where a portion of the old beachside road has been pedestrianized and planted with pine trees, known as the "Pine Walk".

🚗 *Leave Port de Pollença and drive northeast on the MA2210, Carretera de Formentor, to reach the next stop, Península de Formentor.*

⑭ Península de Formentor
Mallorca; 07470

The Carretera de Formentor goes through an extravagantly scenic route to Península de Formentor. Located at the northern end of the Serra de Tramuntana, this peninsula is a 20-km (12-mile) long headland of steep mountains. Three lookout points, such as the **Mirador des Colomer**, oversee plunging, north-facing sea cliffs. The peninsula also boasts one of the island's finest beaches, the **Platja de Formentor**. The rocky, wind-battered tip of the peninsula, the **Cap de Formentor**, is guarded by a lighthouse, rising to 260 m (850 ft), from where there are magnificent views. On a clear day visitors can see Menorca and its former capital, Ciutadella.

🚗 *Leave Cap de Formentor on the MA2210 back along the bay back to Port de Pollença. Continue on the MA2220 through Port de Pollença to Alcúdia. Park in the big car park not far from the main entrance to town.*

⑮ Alcúdia
Mallorca; 07400

The town of Alcúdia, with its old stone mansions surrounded by the sturdy remains of the old city wall, cuts a handsome profile. Situated on a neck of land separating two large and sheltered bays, Alcúdia's strategic location was first recognized by the Phoenicians and then by the Romans, who built their island capital here. The beautifully restored town is entered through the vast **Porta de Moll** gate. The town's best-looking building is the *ajuntament* (town hall), a finely proportioned 17th-century structure with an elegant stone balcony. Located on the edge of town, a 10-minute walk away, is Alcúdia's **Museu Monogràfic** *(closed Mon)*, which is packed with an assortment of archaeological bits and pieces, including Phoenician jewellery and a multitude of Roman artifacts. Right next to the museum are the Roman ruins, Alcúdia's most famous sight.

EAT AND DRINK

POLLENÇA

Restaurant Clivia *moderate*
Located in the heart of Pollença, this is a friendly restaurant offering an excellent range of Spanish dishes.
Avda. Pollentia 5, 07460; 971 533 635

AROUND POLLENÇA

Café La Balada del Agua del Mar *inexpensive*
This is an appealing, little beachside café-restaurant, 5 km (3 miles) from Pollença, occupying an old villa. The highlights of the menu are the salads and seafood.
Passeig Voramar 5, 07470 ; 971 864 276

Restaurant Stay *expensive*
Set beautifully on the pier, this restaurant combines contemporary design with a good international menu, which includes Mallorcan dishes, seafood and lots of big salads.
Moll Nou, 07460; 971 864 013; www.stayrestaurant.com

Below left Roman ruins at Alcúdia **Below right** Nostra Senyora dels Angels overlooking the main square, Pollença

DAY TRIP OPTIONS
Mallorca is a small island with a dense road network, so getting from one place to another rarely takes time. The MA10 accesses most of the stops in this drive. Visitors can base themselves either in Palma or Alcúdia.

Beaches and island
Spend a lazy morning on the beach in Sant Elm ④ and then take a boat to the uninhabited nature reserve island of Sa Dragonera.

Take the MA1 from Palma, southwest towards Andratx. At Andratx, get onto the MA1031 and then the MA1030 to Sant Elm. Return to Palma the same way.

Ancient monastery and resort
Take a stroll around the Santuari de Monastir de Valldemossa ⑦ and then head to Deià ⑨ to spend the rest of the day in this resort town.

Leave Palma on the MA1040 towards Esporles. After Esporles take the MA1100

left and then get onto the MA10, right, to Valldemosa. Continue on the MA10 to Deià. Return to Palma the same way.

Port town and spectacular views
Spend the day on the golden sands of Port de Pollença and then head up the Península de Formentor ⑭ for some spectacular views.

Take the MA2220 from Alcúdia to Port de Pollença and then the MA2210 to the Península de Formentor.

The White Island

Santa Eulària des Riu to Eivissa Town

Highlights

- **Charming port town**
  Explore Santa Eulària des Riu, a colourful old town in a delightful seaside setting

- **Sparkling beaches**
  Catch the sun on Cala Mastella, one of Ibiza's best beaches

- **Spectacular views**
  Take in the views at Port de Sant Miquel, a former smugglers' hideaway

- **Stunning town**
  Stroll around Dalt Vila, the exquisite heart of the island's capital

Tourists on the beach at Port de Sant Miquel

The White Island

For many, the most beautiful of the Balearic islands, Ibiza, or Eivissa in the island's Catalan language, has a 200-km (125-mile) long coastline punctuated with small coves and pristine beaches. The island is celebrated for its nightlife, but while most tourists are bound for its bars and clubs, discerning visitors know that Ibiza has much more to offer. The island has a backbone of beautiful hills and, away from the big resorts, tiny, beguiling villages dot the landscape. This drive, which can easily be done in a day, takes in the most scenic parts of rural Eivissa.

PLAN YOUR DRIVE

Start/finish: Santa Eulària des Riu to Eivissa Town.

Number of days: 1–2, allowing for a walk around Eivissa Town.

Distances: 65 km (40 miles).

Road conditions: Generally well paved and signed with some steep sections in the hills approaching Sant Miquel.

When to go: Spring (Apr–May) and autumn (late Sep–Oct) are the best times to enjoy the drive. Temperatures can be too hot for comfort and the roads very crowded during July and August.

Opening hours: Most monuments are generally open daily from 10am to 2pm, and from 4 to 6pm. None of the churches mentioned in the drive have set opening times. Most clubs open late at night and stay open until morning.

Market days: Santa Eulària des Riu: daily.

Major festivals: Santa Eulària des Riu: Anar a Maig, first Sun May; Sant Joan de Labritja: Nit de Sant Joan, 23 Jun.

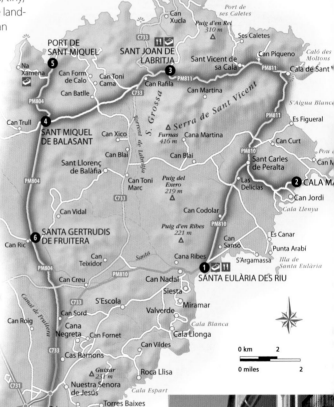

Above Old city walls of Dalt Vila in Eivissa Town, see 253 **Right** Tourists at one of La Marina's many outdoor restaurants, Eivissa Town, see 253

KEY

 Drive route

① Santa Eulària des Riu

Ibiza; 07840

The island's third largest town, Santa Eulària des Riu is an attractive place, whose neat centre spreads along the seashore. Santa Eulària is crowned by the **Puig de Missa** church and cemetery. The main street, Passeig de s'Alamera, is lined with market stalls selling everything from T-shirts to jewellery. There are two town beaches, whose sands slope down into the sea, making them ideal for children. The town is at its busiest on Wednesdays as tourists make their way to the large hippy market at Punta Arabí, just 3 km (2 miles) northeast of Santa Eulària.

🚗 *From the town, take the PM810 northeast to Sant Carles de Peralta, and turn right on the country lane signed for Cala Llenya. Follow this road for some distance, and look out for signs pointing to Cala Mastella.*

② Cala Mastella

Ibiza; 07840

Located in a beautiful cove, Cala Mastella is one of northern Ibiza's prettiest beaches. Its yellow-white sands back onto a lovely terraced valley of orchards and olives. Pine trees provide shade and the waters are crystal clear. The snorkelling is among the best in the Mediterranean. Sun beds are available for hire and there is a beach bar selling soft drinks. Swimmers should beware of jellyfish and sea urchins.

🚗 *From Cala Mastella, head back towards Sant Carles de Peralta to rejoin the PM810. Proceed north on the PM810, which then becomes the PM811. Continue on this road until the T-junction and turn left, following the PM811 into Sant Joan de Labritja.*

③ Sant Joan de Labritja

Ibiza; 07810

Once a hippy hangout, Sant Joan de Labritja is a lovely little village of just 950 people, nestled in the foothills of northern Ibiza. The most distinctive sight of the village is its large 18th-century church, the **Església de Sant Joan**, whose thick walls dominate proceedings. The village is still a favourite haunt of expatriate writers and artists. Many of them live in tastefully modernized, bright white old peasants' cottages with nifty wrought-iron balconies and handsome wooden doors. The farms surrounding Sant Joan are proud of their organic credentials.

🚗 *From Sant Joan, drive west on the PM811 till the C733. Turn onto it and after a short distance turn right onto the country lane, Carretera de Sant Miquel de Sant Joan, which cuts west. Turn right onto the PM804 signed for Sant Miquel to reach the next stop.*

Above left Tranquil beach of Cala Mastella **Above right** Whitewashed houses lining a street in Sant Joan de Labritja **Below** Colourful flea market at Punta Arabí, Santa Eulària des Riu

WHERE TO STAY

AROUND SANTA EULÀRIA DES RIU

Agroturismo Xarc *expensive*
This is a finely appointed country hotel just 5 km (3 miles) north of Santa Eulària, which amalgamates the best of modern style – a gorgeous pool – with traditional features, including stone walls and wooden beams.
Es Nuvells, 07840, Santa Eulària des Riu; 971 339 178; www.agroxarc.es; a minimum stay of five nights in summer

AROUND SANT JOAN DE LABRITJA

Can Martí *expensive*
An environmentally conscious country hotel just 2 km (1 mile) south of Sant Joan de Labritja. The four apartment-sized rooms are individually decorated and seductively charming.
Venda de Cas Ripolls 29, 07810; 971 333 500; www.canmarti.com

EAT AND DRINK

SANTA EULÀRIA DES RIU

Agroturismo Atzaró *expensive*
This luxury hotel in an old Ibizan-style house, set in an orange grove a few minutes outside town, serves great Mediterranean dishes with creative touches. A selection of tapas is available and they have an excellent collection of red and white South African wines.
Ctra. Sant Joan, Km 15, 07840; 971 338 838; www.atzaro.com

SANT JOAN DE LABRITJA

El Corsario Negro *inexpensive*
Right down on the marina, this informal café-restaurant has a wide-ranging menu, offering everything from pizza to tapas.
Port Esportiu s/n, 07810; 971 319 358

Eat and Drink: inexpensive, under €20; moderate, €20–€40; expensive, over €40

Above Spectacular view over the harbour of Eivissa Town from Dalt Vila **Below left** Courtyard leading to the Església de Sant Miquel in Sant Miquel de Balasant **Below right** Way up to the 14th-century cathedral in Dalt Vila, Eivissa Town

SHOPPING IN EIVISSA TOWN

Eivissa Town has the best shopping on the island, with many boutiques and shops lining up along the main streets of the city centre. In particular, look out for the handsome ceramics of Ceramica Es Test (*C/Mar 15, 07800; 971 191 600*); the designer clothes of Babaz – Antik Batik (*Plaça Constitució 8, 07800*) and the artwork and jewellery of Natura (*C/Major 20, 07800; 971 390 674*).

WHERE TO STAY

AROUND PORT DE SANT MIQUEL

Hacienda Na Xamena *expensive*
Set in the heart of a nature reserve, this is a luxury spa-hotel 3 km (2 miles) to the west of Sant Miquel. It also has a poolside gourmet restaurant.
Buzón 11, 07815, Na Xamena; 971 334 500; www.hotelhacienda-ibiza.com

EIVISSA TOWN

Hostal La Marina *inexpensive*
Right on the waterfront, this long-established *hostal* occupies three port-side buildings dating back to the 1920s.
C/ Barcelona 7, 07800; 971 310 172; www.hostal-lamarina.com

La Torre del Canonigo *expensive*
Spectacular views and a smooth ambience can be found here in this small, plush hotel, which occupies an old stone tower that was once part of the city wall.
C/ Major 8, Dalt Vila, 07800; 971 303 884; www.latorredelcanonigo.com

④ Sant Miquel de Balasant
Ibiza; 07815

Located high up in the hills, the small village of Sant Miquel de Balasant was founded in the 13th century. A must-see is the large and imposing **Església de Sant Miquel**, a 16th-century church that once provided shelter during the frequent raids by pirates. The interior of the church is unusual in that it has two chapels, one of which is adorned with bright, modern frescoes. Every Thursday at 6pm there is a music and dance show performed by a local folklore group in front of the church. From the church there are lovely views of the olive groves and pine forests in the surrounding country-side and of the huddle of artisans' cottages that make up the village.
🚗 *Heading north from Sant Miquel, it is just 4 km (2 miles) along the PM804 to Port de Sant Miquel.*

⑤ Port de Sant Miquel
Ibiza; 07815

The main road from Sant Miquel to Port de Sant Miquel cuts a scenic route through a verdant valley before weaving its way down to the coast at this tiny port that was once a smugglers' hideaway. The port has a spectacular setting with jutting promontories sheltering a tiny inlet, and there is a first-class sandy beach with all the accoutrements – a beach bar, pedalos and a brace of large hotels. Nearby, on one of the hills, stands the exclusive hotel Hacienda Na Xamena hotel, which offers magnificent views.
🚗 *Doubling back from Port de Sant Miquel on the PM804, it is 12 km (7 miles) south to Santa Gertrudis.*

⑥ Santa Gertrudis de Fruitera
Ibiza; 07814

This ancient agricultural village is surrounded by apricot, peach and orange orchards, and hence its name "de Fruitera", which means "of the fruits". Now a centre of expat life, it has an excellent selection of bars and restaurants, plus the very popular Casi Todo auctioneers (*www.casitodo.com*) where visitors can pick up anything from clocks to paintings and doors to old cars. Visit the **Església de Santa Gertrudis**, a stern structure dating back to medieval times and long the centre of village life, though it is much less so today.
🚗 *Leave Santa Gertrudis de Fruitera going south on the PM804. After 5 km (3 miles), it joins the C733, which goes straight to Eivissa Town (Ibiza).*

⑦ Eivissa Town

Ibiza; 07800

Glued to a rocky outcrop overlooking the Mediterranean, the oldest and most interesting part of Eivissa (or Ibiza) Town, Dalt Vila, dates back to the 17th century. This part of town boasts a Gothic cathedral, honey-coloured stone walls, attractive squares and chic bars and restaurants. There are fine views over the city from its walls.

A two-hour walking tour

Park the car and start exploring Eivissa by the waterfront with its cafés, fishing boats, ferries and yachts. Halfway along the waterfront is a distinctive stone **obelisk** ①, which was erected in honour of those local corsairs who long protected the island from marauding pirates. Head south from near the obelisk along Carrer de Sant Elm. Turn left at the end and take the first right up Carrer de Joan Mayans to reach **Mercat Vell** ②, the Old Market.

From the Old Market, walk south up the hill to the monumental stonework of the **Portal de Ses Taules** ③, the main gateway into the old town, the Dalt Vila. Beyond the gateway, turn right for **Plaça de la Vila** ④, a broad, pedestrianized piazza, flanked by old mansions and alive with art galleries, boutiques, bars and restaurants. Down the slope from the plaza is the

A statue in the Portal de ses Taules

Baluard de Sant Joan, a stone bulwark that juts out over the town.

Go up the hill from Plaça de la Vila and take the second left along Carrer de Sant Carles, which leads into Carrer de Ignasi Riquer. This leads to the square abutting both the medieval church, the **Església Sant Pere** ⑤, and the **ajuntament** ⑥, the town hall. A narrow walkway to the left of the town hall leads up to Carrer de Santa María. Follow it up and round to a second gateway, the **Sa Portella** ⑦. Beyond the gateway, turn left and ascend to the 14th-century **Catedral de Santa María** ⑧, rebuilt in Baroque style in the 18th century. From here, go southwest along the ramparts to the **Baluard de Sant Bernat** ⑨, one of Dalt Vila's several surviving bastions. From here the neighbouring island of Formentera in the distance is visible. After the walk, go back to where the car is parked.

Above View across the port towards the upper town of Eivissa

VISITING EIVISSA

Tourist Information
Passeig Vara de Rey 1, 07800; 971 301 900; www.ibiza.travel

Parking
Park on the streets close to the pier, on the area that lies between Avinguda de Bartomeu de Rosselló and Passeig de Vara de Rey.

EAT AND DRINK

EIVISSA TOWN

El Faro *moderate*
Located on the harbourfront, this is one of the best places to eat fish and take in the quayside atmosphere.
Plaça Sa Riba 1, 07800; 971 313 233

La Oliva *moderate*
A smashing Dalt Vila restaurant serving a creative menu that mixes Spanish and French cuisines. Located in the heart of the Eivissa scene, it is a very popular spot, so book ahead.
C/ Santa Creu 2, 07800; 971 305 752; www.laoliviaibiza.com

La Brasa *moderate*
This first-rate restaurant, in between the port and the city walls, has a lovely garden terrace for summer dining and a well-designed interior. Meat and seafood dishes are highly recommended and the daily specials stick firmly to seasonal ingredients.
C/ Pere Sala 3, 07800; 971 301 202; www.labrasaibiza.com

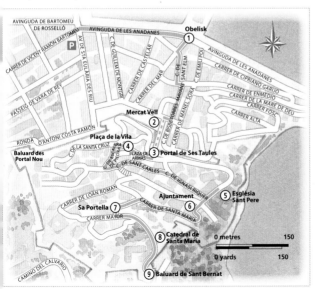

Eat and Drink: inexpensive, under €20; moderate, €20–€40; expensive, over €40

General Index

Page numbers in **bold** refer to main entries.

The information in this
DK Eyewitness Travel Guide is checked annually.
Even though every effort has been made to ensure that this book is as up-to-date as possible at the time of going to press. Some details, however, such as telephone numbers, opening hours, prices, gallery hanging arrangements and travel information are liable to change. The publishers cannot accept responsibility for any consequences arising from the use of this book, nor for any material on third-party websites, and cannot guarantee that any website address in this book will be a suitable source of travel information.
We value the views and suggestions of our readers very highly. Please write to: Publisher, DK Eyewitness Travel Guides, Dorling Kindersley, 80 Strand, London WC2R 0RL.

Acknowledgements

Dorling Kindersley would like to thank the many people whose help and assistance contributed to the preparation of this book.

Contributors
Mary-Ann Gallagher has written more than 20 travel guides. She has written for and edited numerous guidebooks for DK, *National Geographic* and *Footprint Handbooks*, among others.
Nick Inman is a full-time author, editor and photographer. He has written for or contributed to over 50 travel guides, mainly on Spain and France.
Phil Lee has been a travel writer for over 20 years and his work has been published in many magazines and newspapers. He also writes regularly for *Rough Guides*.
Chris Moss is the travel editor at *Time Out* magazine, London. He contributed to DK *Eyewitness Travel Guide to Argentina* and is the author of *Patagonia: A Cultural History*.
Nick Rider has a Ph.D. in history and has written books on France, Spain and Mexico. He has also contributed to DK *Eyewitness Travel Guides to France, Spain, Mexico, Great Britain and Poland*.
Richard Trillo is a travel writer and editor. He is the author of *Rough Guides to Kenya, West Africa, The Gambia* and *World Music* and was formerly Rough Guides' Director of Communications.
Suzanne Wales is a freelance writer who writes for publications such as *Wallpaper*, Vogue* and *The Australian Newspaper*, and contributes to documentaries and television reports on various Spanish issues.
Greg Ward has written several different guides to Hawaii, as well as books on the USA, the Southwest USA, the Grand Canyon, the Blues, American History and many other topics.

Fact Checker
Paula Canal
Proofreader
Devabrata Kar
Indexer
Cyber Media Services Ltd.

Design and Editorial
Publisher Douglas Amrine
List Manager Vivien Antwi
Managing Art Editor Jane Ewart
Project Editor Michelle Crane, Georgina Palffy
Project Designers Shahid Mahmood, Kate Leonard
Senior Cartographic Editor Casper Morris
Cartographer Stuart James
Managing Art Editor (Jackets) Karen Constanti
Senior Jacket Designer Tessa Bindloss
Jacket Designer Meredith Smith
Senior DTP Designer Jason Little
DTP Designers Jamie McNeill, Natasha Lu
Picture Research Ellen Root
Production Controller Linda Dare

Special Assistance
Bernard Byrne, Paula Canal, Juan Marcos Carillo, Serge Defaix, Lara Dunston, Elizabeth Furbear, Cristina Garcia, Maribel Izcue, Arma Kleinepier, Cécile Landau, Kate Leonard, Xavier Ribas, Marie Aude Serra, Matt Wright

Photography
Alex Havret, Nick Inman, Chris Moss, Alex Robinson, Tara Stevens
Additional Photography
Max Alexander, Stephen Bere, Joe Cornish, Lydia Evans, Joan Farre, Emma Firth, Heidi Grassley, Neil Lukas, Malcolm McGregor, John Miller, Kim Sayer, Colin Sinclair, Tony Souter, Linda Whitwam, Peter Wilson, Bartlomies Zaranek. Rough Guides: Ian Aitken, Demetrio Carrasco, Neville Walker.

Photography Permissions
Dorling Kindersley would like to thank the following for their assistance and kind permission to photograph at their establishments:
Casa Leonardo, Casa-Museo Rosalía de Castro, Caudalíe Vinothérapie Spa at Hotel Marqués de Riscal, Elciego, Hotel el Convento Parador de Cambados, Parador de Sto. Estevo, Posada el Bosque.

Picture Credits
Placement Key- t=top; tc=top centre; tr=top right; cla=centre left above; ca=centre above; cra=centre right above; cl=centre left; c=centre; cr=centre right; clb=centre left below; cb=centre below; crb=centre right below; bl=bottom left; bc=bottom centre; br=bottom right; ftl=far top left; ftr=far top right; fcla=far centre left above; fcra=far centre right above; fcl=far centre left; fcr=far centre right; fclb=far centre left below; fcrb=far centre right below; fbl=far bottom left; fbr=far bottom right.
Every effort has been made to trace the copyright holders, and we apologize in advance for any unintentional omissions. We would be pleased to insert the appropriate acknowledgments in any subsequent edition of this publication.
The publisher would like to thank the following individuals, companies, and picture libraries for their kind permission to reproduce their photographs:
4Corners Images: SIME/Schmid Reinhard 9br; **Alamy Images:** Graham Lawrence 79tl; [Holandaluz] Vincent de Vries 20tr; **The Bridgeman Art Library:** Map of Spain, from 'Blaeus Grooten Atlas, Oft Werelt-Beschryving...' by Joan Blaeu (1596-1673) 1648-65 (coloured engraving), Spanish School, (17th century) / © Royal Geographical Society, London, UK 28-29; **Photolibrary:** Jeronimo Alba 224-225; Paco Ayala 17tr; Alan Copson 2-3; Kevin George 162-163; Jose Antonio Jimenez 6cl; Sabine Lubenow 248-249; Juan Carlos Munoz 38-39; Fabian von Poser 1c; Jose Fuste Raga 8; Antonio Real 30-31

Cover Picture Credits
Front: 4Corners Images: SIME/Olimpio Fantuz.
Back: DK Images: Nick Inman c; Chris Moss l; Tara Stevens r.
Spine: 4Corners Images: SIME/Olimpio Fantuz t
All other images © Dorling Kindersley
For further information see: www.dkimages.com

Phrase Book

IN AN EMERGENCY

Help!	¡Socorro	soh-koh-roh
Stop!	¡Pare!	pah-reh
Call a doctor!	¡Llame a un médico!	yah-meh ah oon meh-dee-koh
Call an ambulance!	¡Llame a una ambulancia!	yah-meh ah oo-nah ahm-boo-lahn-thee-ah
Call the police!	¡Llame a la policía!	yah-meh ah lah poh-lee-thee-ah
Call the fire brigade!	¡Llame a los bomberos!	yah-meh ah lohs bohm-beh-rohs
Where is the nearest telephone?	¿Dónde está el teléfono más próximo?	dohn-deh ehs-tah ehl teh-leh-foh-noh mahs prohx-ee-moh
Where is the nearest hospital?	¿Dónde está el hospital más próximo?	dohn-deh ehs-tah ehl ohs-pee-tahl mahs prohx-ee-moh

COMMUNICATION ESSENTIALS

Yes	Sí	see
No	No	noh
Please	Por favor	pohr fah-vohr
Thank you	Gracias	grah-thee-ahs
Excuse me	Perdone	pehr-doh-neh
Hello	Hola	oh-lah
Goodbye	Adiós	ah-dee-ohs
Goodnight	Buenas noches	bweh-nahs noh-chehs
Morning	La mañana	lah mah-nyah-nah
Afternoon	La tarde	lah tahr-deh
Evening	La tarde	lah tahr-deh
Yesterday	Ayer	ah-yehr
Today	Hoy	oy
Tomorrow	Mañana	mah-nya-nah
Here	Aquí	ah-kee
There	Allí	ah-yee
What?	¿Qué?	keh
When?	¿Cuándo?	kwahn-doh
Why?	¿Por qué?	pohr-keh
Where?	¿Dónde?	dohn-deh

USEFUL PHRASES

How are you?	¿Cómo está usted?	koh-moh ehs-tah oos-tehd
Very well, thank you.	Muy bien, gracias.	mwee bee-ehn grah-thee-ahs
Pleased to meet you.	Encantado de conocerle.	ehn-kahn-tah-doh de koh-noh-thehr-leh
See you soon.	Hasta pronto.	ahs-tah prohn-toh
That's fine.	Está bien.	ehs-tah bee-ehn
Where is/are …?	¿Dónde está/están …?	dohn-deh ehs-tah/ehs-tahn
How far is it to …?	¿Cuántos metros/ kilómetros hay de aquí a …?	kwahn-tohs meh-trohs/ kee-loh-meh-trohs eye deh ah-kee ah
Which way to …?	¿Por dónde se va a …?	pohr dohn-deh seh bah ah
Do you speak English?	¿Habla inglés?	ah-blah een-glehs
I don't understand	No comprendo	noh kohm-prehn-doh
Could you speak more slowly please?	¿Puede hablar más despacio por favor?	pweh-deh ah-blahr mahs dehs-pah-thee-oh pohr fah-vohr
I'm sorry.	Lo siento.	loh see-ehn-toh

USEFUL WORDS

big	grande	grahn-deh
small	pequeño	peh-keh-nyoh
hot	caliente	kah-lee-ehn-the
cold	frío	free-oh
good	bueno	bweh-noh
bad	malo	mah-loh
enough	bastante	bahs-tahn-the
well	bien	bee-ehn
open	abierto	ah-bee-ehr-toh
closed	cerrado	thehr-rah-doh
left	izquierda	eeth-key-ehr-dah
right	derecha	deh-reh-chah
straight on	todo recto	toh-doh rehk-toh
near	cerca	thehr-kah
far	lejos	leh-hohs
up	arriba	ah-ree-bah
down	abajo	ah-bah-hoh
early	temprano	tehm-prah-noh
late	tarde	tahr-deh

entrance	entrada	ehn-trah-dah
exit	salida	sah-lee-dah
toilet	lavabos, servicios	lah-vah-bohs, sehr-bee-thee-ohs
more	más	mahs
less	menos	meh-nohs

SHOPPING

How much does this cost?	¿Cuánto cuesta esto?	kwahn-toh kwehs-tah ehs-toh
I would like …	Me gustaría …	meh goos-ta-ree-ah
Do you have?	¿Tienen?	tee-yeh-nehn
I'm just looking, thank you.	Sólo estoy mirando, gracias.	soh-loh ehs-toy mee-rahn-doh grah-thee-ahs
Do you take credit cards?	¿Aceptan tarjetas de crédito?	ah-thehp-tahn tahr-heh-tahs deh kreh-dee-toh
What time do you open?	¿A qué hora abren?	ah keh oh-rah ah-brehn
What time do you close?	¿A qué hora cierran?	ah keh oh-rah thee-ehr-rahn
This one	Éste	ehs-the
That one	Ése	eh-she
expensive	caro	kahr-oh
cheap	barato	bah-rah-toh
size, clothes	talla	tah-yah
size, shoes	número	noø-mehr-oh
white	blanco	blahn-koh
black	negro	neh-groh
red	rojo	roh-hoh
yellow	amarillo	ah-mah-ree-yoh
green	verde	behr-deh
blue	azul	ah-thool
antiques shop	la tienda de antigüedades	lah tee-ehn-dah deh ahn-tee-gweh-dah-dehs
bakery	la panadería	lah pah-nah-deh ree-ah
bank	el banco	ehl bahn-koh
book shop	la librería	lah lee-breh-ree-ah
butcher's	la carnicería	lah kahr-nee-theh-ree-ah
cake shop	la pastelería	lah pahs-teh-leh-ree-ah
chemist's	la farmacia	lah fahr-mah-thee-ah
fishmonger's	la pescadería	lah pehs-kah-deh-ree-ah
greengrocer's	la frutería	lah froo-teh-ree-ah
grocer's	la tienda de comestibles	lah tee-yehn-dah deh koh-mehs-tee-blehs
hairdresser's	la peluquería	lah peh-loo-keh-ree-ah
market	el mercado	ehl mehr-kah-doh
newsagent's	el kiosko de prensa	ehl kee-ohs-koh deh prehn-sah
post office	la oficina de correos	lah oh-fee-thee-nah deh kohr-reh-ohs
shoe shop	la zapatería	lah thah-pah-teh-ree-ah
supermarket	el supermercado	ehl soo-pehr-mehr kah-do
tobacconist	el estanco	ehl ehs-tahn-koh
travel agency	la agencia de viajes	lah ah-hehn-thee-ah deh bee-ah-hehs

SIGHTSEEING

art gallery	el museo de arte	ehl moo-seh-oh deh ahr-the
cathedral	la catedral	lah kah-teh-drahl
church	la iglesia la basílica	lah ee-gleh-see-ah lah bah-see-lee-kah
garden	el jardín	ehl hahr-deen
library	la biblioteca	lah beh-blee-oh-teh-kah
museum	el museo	ehl moo-seh-oh
tourist information office	la oficina de turismo	lah oh-fee-thee-nah deh too-rees-moh
town hall	el ayuntamiento	ehl ah-yoon-tah-mee-ehn-toh
closed for holiday	cerrado por vacaciones	thehr-rah-doh pohr bah-kah-cee-oh-nehs
bus station	la estación de autobuses	lah ehs-tah-thee-ohn deh owtoh-boo-sehs
railway station	la estación de trenes	lah ehs-tah-thee-ohn deh treh-nehs

STAYING IN A HOTEL

Do you have a vacant room?	¿Tienen una habitación libre?	tee-eh-nehn oo-nah ah-bee-tah-thee-ohn lee-breh

double room	habitación doble	ah-bee-tah-thee-ohn doh-bleh
with double bed	con cama de matrimonio	kohn kah-mah deh mah-tree-moh-nee-oh
twin room	habitación con dos camas	ah-bee-tah-thee-ohn kohn dohs kah-mahs
single room	habitación individual	ah-bee-tah-thee-ohn een-dee-vee-doo-ahl
room with a bath	habitación con baño	ah-bee-tah-thee-ohn kohn bah-nyoh
shower	ducha	doo-chah
porter	el botones	ehl boh-toh-nehs
key	la llave	lah yah-veh
I have a reservation.	Tengo una habitación reservada.	tehn-goh oo-na ah-bee-tah-thee-ohn reh-sehr-bah-dah

EATING OUT

Have you got a table for …?	¿Tienen mesa para …?	tee-eh-nehn meh-sah pah-rah
I want to reserve a table.	Quiero reservar una mesa.	kee-eh-roh reh-sehr-bahr oo-nah meh-sah
The bill please.	La cuenta por favor.	lah kwehn-tah pohr fah-vohr
I am a vegetarian	Soy vegetariano/a	soy beh-heh-tah-ree-ah-no/na
waitress	camarera	kah-mah-reh-rah
waiter	camarero	kah-mah-reh-roh
menu	la carta	lah kahr-tah
fixed-price menu	menú del día	meh-noo dehl dee-ah
wine list	la carta de vinos	lah kahr-tah deh bee-nohs
glass	un vaso	oon bah-soh
bottle	una botella	oo-nah boh-teh-yah
knife	un cuchillo	oon koo-chee-yoh
fork	un tenedor	oon teh-neh-dohr
spoon	una cuchara	oo-nah koo-chah-rah
breakfast	el desayuno	ehl deh-sah-yoo-noh
lunch	la comida/ el almuerzo	lah koh-mee-dah/ ehl ahl-mwehr-thoh
dinner	la cena	lah theh-nah
main course	el primer plato	ehl pree-mehr plah-toh
starters	los entremeses	lohs ehn-treh meh-sehs
dish of the day	el plato del día	ehl plah-toh dehl dee-ah
coffee	el café	ehl kah-feh
rare	poco hecho	poh-koh eh-choh
medium	medio hecho	meh-dee-oh eh-choh
well done	muy hecho	mwee eh-choh

MENU DECODER

al horno	ahl ohr-noh	baked
asado	ah-sah-doh	roast
el aceite	ehl ah-thee-eh-teh	oil
las aceitunas	lahs ah-theh-toon-ahs	olives
el agua mineral	ehl ah-gwa mee-neh-rahl	mineral water
sin gas/con gas	seen gas/kohn gas	still/sparkling
el ajo	ehl ah-hoh	garlic
el arroz	ehl ahr-rohth	rice
el azúcar	ehl ah-thoo-kahr	sugar
la carne	lah kahr-neh	meat
la cebolla	lah theh-boh-yah	onion
la cerveza	lah thehr-beh-thah	beer
el cerdo	ehl therh-doh	pork
el chocolate	ehl choh-koh-lah-teh	chocolate
el chorizo	ehl choh-ree-thoh	red sausage
el cordero	ehl kohr-deh-roh	lamb
el fiambre	ehl fee-ahm-breh	cold meat
frito	free-toh	fried
la fruta	lah froo-tah	fruit
los frutos secos	lohs froo-tohs seh-kohs	nuts
las gambas	lahs gahm-bahs	prawns
el helado	ehl eh-lah-doh	ice cream
el huevo	ehl oo-eh-voh	egg
el jamón serrano	ehl hah-mohn sehr-rah-noh	cured ham
el jerez	ehl heh-rehz	sherry
la langosta	lah lahn-gohs-tah	lobster
la leche	lah leh-cheh	milk
el limón	ehl lee-mohn	lemon

la limonada	lah lee-moh-nah-dah	lemonade
la mantequilla	lah mahn-teh-kee-yah	butter
la manzana	lah mahn-thah-nah	apple
los mariscos	lohs mah-rees-kohs	seafood
la menestra	lah meh-nehs-trah	vegetable stew
la naranja	lah nah-rahn-hah	orange
el pan	ehl pahn	bread
el pastel	ehl pahs-tehl	cake
las patatas	lahs pah-tah-tahs	potatoes
el pescado	ehl pehs-kah-doh	fish
la pimienta	lah pee-mee-yehn-tah	pepper
el plátano	ehl plah-tah-noh	banana
el pollo	ehl poh-yoh	chicken
el postre	ehl pohs-treh	dessert
el queso	ehl keh-soh	cheese
la sal	lah sahl	salt
las salchichas	lahs sahl-chee-chahs	sausages
la salsa	lah sahl-sah	sauce
seco	seh-koh	dry
el solomillo	ehl soh-loh-mee-yoh	sirloin
la sopa	lah soh-pah	soup
la tarta	lah tahr-tah	pie/cake
el té	ehl teh	tea
la ternera	lah tehr-neh-rah	beef
las tostadas	lahs tohs-tah-dahs	toast
el vinagre	ehl bee-nah-greh	vinegar
el vino blanco	ehl bee-noh blahn-koh	white wine
el vino rosado	ehl bee-noh roh-sah-doh	rosé wine
el vino tinto	ehl bee-noh teen-toh	red wine

NUMBERS

0	cero	theh-roh
1	uno	oo-noh
2	dos	dohs
3	tres	trehs
4	cuatro	kwa-troh
5	cinco	theen-koh
6	seis	says
7	siete	see-eh-the
8	ocho	oh-choh
9	nueve	nweh-veh
10	diez	dee-ehth
11	once	ohn-theh
12	doce	doh-theh
13	trece	treh-theh
14	catorce	kah-tohr-theh
15	quince	keen-theh
16	dieciséis	dee-eh-thee-seh-ees
17	diecisiete	dee-eh-thee-see eh-the
18	dieciocho	dee-eh-thee-oh-choh
19	diecinueve	dee-eh-thee-nweh-veh
20	veinte	beh-een-the
21	veintiuno	beh-een-tee-oo-noh
22	veintidós	beh-een-tee-dohs
30	treinta	treh-een-tah
31	treinta y uno	treh-een-tah ee oo-noh
40	cuarenta	kwah-rehn-tah
50	cincuenta	theen-kwehn-tah
60	sesenta	seh-sehn-tah
70	setenta	seh-tehn-tah
80	ochenta	oh-chehn-tah
90	noventa	noh-vehn-tah
100	cien	thee-ehn
101	ciento uno	thee-ehn-toh oo-noh
102	ciento dos	thee-ehn-toh dohs
200	doscientos	dohs-thee-ehn-tohs
500	quinientos	khee-nee-ehn-tohs
700	setecientos	seh-teh-thee-ehn-tohs
900	novecientos	noh-veh-thee-ehn-tohs
1,000	mil	meel
1,001	mil uno	meel oo-noh

TIME

one minute	un minuto	oon mee-noo-toh
one hour	una hora	oo-na oh-rah
half an hour	media hora	meh-dee-a oh-rah
Monday	lunes	loo-nehs
Tuesday	martes	mahr-tehs
Wednesday	miércoles	mee-ehr-koh-lehs
Thursday	jueves	hoo-weh-vehs
Friday	viernes	bee-ehr-nehs
Saturday	sábado	sah-bah-doh
Sunday	domingo	doh-meen-goh

Driver's Phrase Book

SOME COMMON ROAD SIGNS

aduana	customs
apagar luces de cruce	headlights off
aparcamiento	car park
atención al tren	beware of trains
autopista	motorway
autovía	dual carriageway
callejón sin salida	no thoroughfare
calle peatonal	pedestrians only
calzada deteriorada	bad surface
calzada irregular	uneven surface
cambio de sentido	crossroads
carretera cortada	road closed
ceda el paso	give way
centro ciudad	city centre
centro urbano	town centre
circule despacio	slow
circunvalación	circular road
cruce	crossroads
desvío	diversion
desvío provisional	temporary diversion
encender luces de cruce	headlights on
escalón lateral	no hard shoulder
escuela	school
final de autopista	end of motorway
firme en mal estado	bad surface
hielo	black ice
información turística	tourist information
obras	road construction
ojo al tren	beware of trains
paso a nivel	level crossing
paso subterráneo	subway
peaje	toll
peatón, circule a la izquierda	pedestrians, keep to the left
peatones	pedestrians
peligro	danger
peligro deslizamientos	slippery road surface
precaución	caution
prohibido aparcar	no parking
prohibido el paso	no trespassing
puesto de socorro	first-aid post
salida de camiones	construction exit
vado permanente	in constant use (no parking)
vehículos pesados	heavy vehicles
velocidad controlada por radar	automatic speed monitor
zona azul	restricted parking zone
zona de estacionamiento limitado	restricted parking area

DIRECTIONS YOU MAY BE GIVEN

a la derecha/izquierda	on the right/left
después de pasar el/la ...	go past the ...
la primera a la derecha	first on the right
la segunda a la izquierda	second on the left
todo recto	straight on
tuerza a la derecha	turn right
tuerza a la izquierda	turn left

THINGS YOU'LL SEE

aceite	oil
agua	water
aire	air

apague el motor	turn off engine
aparcamiento subterráneo	underground car park
área de servicios	service area, motorway services
cola	queue
completo	car park full
entrada	way in
estación de servicio	service station
garaje	garage
gas-oil	diesel
gasolina	fuel
gasolinera	petrol station
introduzca el dinero exacto	exact change
nivel del aceite	oil level
presión	air pressure
presión de los neumáticos	tyre pressure
prohibido fumar	no smoking
recoja su ticket	take a ticket
reparación	repairs
salida	exit
sin plomo	unleaded
solo para residentes del hotel	hotel guests only
taller (de reparaciones)	garage (for repairs)

THINGS YOU'LL HEAR

¿Lo quiere automático o manual?
Would you like an automatic or a manual?

Su permiso/carnet de conducir, por favor
May I see your driving licence?

Su pasaporte, por favor
Your passport, please

USEFUL PHRASES

I would like some petrol/oil/water.
Quería gasolina/aceite/agua.
keh-ree-a gassoh-leena/athay-teh/ahg-wa

Fill it up, please!
¡Lleno, por favor!
yeh-noh por fa-vor

35 litres of 4-star petrol, please
Póngame treinta y cinco litros de extra
ponga-meh traynti theenkoh leetross deh extra

Would you check the tyres, please?
¿Podría revisar los neumáticos, por favor?
podree-a revee-sarmeh loss neh-oo-mateekoss por fa-vor

Do you do repairs?
¿Hacen reparaciones?
ah-then reparrath-yoh-ness

Can you repair the clutch?
¿Pueden arreglarme el embrague?
pweh-den arreh-glarmeh el embrah-geh

There is something wrong with the engine.
Hay algo que no va bien en el motor.
i algoh keh noh va byen en el moh-tor

The engine is overheating.
El motor se calienta demasiado.
el moh-tor seh kal-yenta deh-massyah-doh

I need a new tyre.
Necesito un neumático nuevo.
neh-thessee-toh oon neh-oo-matikoh nweh-voh

Can you replace this?
¿Pueden cambiarme esto?
pweh-den kam-byar-meh es-toh

The indicator is not working.
El intermitente no funciona.
el een-tair-mee-ten-teh noh foon-thyoh-na

How long will it take?
¿Cuánto tiempo tardarán?
kwan-toh tyem-poh tar-da-ran

I'd like to hire a car.
Quería alquilar un coche.
keh-ree-a alkee-lar oon kot-cheh

How much is it for one day?
¿Cuánto cuesta para un día?
kwan-toh kwesta parra oon dee-a

Is there a mileage charge?
¿Tiene suplemento por kilómetro?
tyeh-neh soo-ple-men-toh por kee-lo-met-roh

When do I have to return it?
¿Cuándo tengo que devolverlo?
kwan-doh teng-goh keh devo-lvair-loh

Where is the nearest garage?
¿Dónde está el taller más cercano?
don-deh esta el tayair mass thair-kah-noh

Where is the nearest petrol station?
¿Dónde está la gasolinera más cercana?
don-deh esta la gas-soh-lee-neh-ra mass thair-kah-na

Where can I park?
¿Dónde puedo aparcar?
don-deh pweh-doh appar-kar

How do I get to Seville?
¿Cómo se va a Sevilla?
koh-moh seh va a sevee-ya

Is this the road to Malaga?
¿Es ésta la carretera de Málaga?
ess esta la karreh-teh-ra deh malaga

Which is the quickest way to Madrid?
¿Cuál es el camino más rápido para Madrid?
kwal ess el kam-ee-noh mass rapee-doh parra madreed

USEFUL WORDS

automatic	**automático**	*owtoh-mateekoh*
bonnet	**el capó**	*ehl kapo*
boot	**el maletero**	*ehl malleh-teh-roh*
brake	**el freno**	*ehl freh-noh*
breakdown	**una avería**	*oo-nah avveh-ree-a*
car	**el coche**	*ehl kotcheh*
car park	**el aparcamiento**	*ehl apar-ka-myen-toh*
caravan	**la caravana**	*lah karra-vah-na*
clutch	**el embrague**	*ehl embrah-geh*
crossroads	**el cruce**	*ehl kroo-theh*
driving licence	**el permiso/**	*ehl pair-meesso/*
	el carnet	*ehl kar-neh*
dual carriageway	**la autovía**	*lah owtoh-vee-a*
engine	**el motor**	*ehl moh-tor*
exhaust	**el tubo**	*ehl too-boh*
fanbelt	**la correa del**	*lah korreh-a del*
	ventilador	*ven-teela-dor*
garage (for repairs)	**un taller**	*oon tay-air*
gear	**la marcha**	*lah mar-tcha*
gears	**las marchas**	*lahs mar-tchass*
headlights	**las luces**	*lahs loo-thess*
	de cruce	*deh kroo-theh*
indicator	**intermitente**	*een-tair-mee-ten-teh*
junction	**el cruce**	*ehl kroo-theh*
mirror	**el (espejo)**	*ehl esspeh-hoh*
	retrovisor	*retroh-vessor*
motorway	**la autopista**	*owtoh-peesta*
number plate	**la matrícula**	*matree-koola*
petrol	**la gasolina**	*gassoh-leena*
petrol station	**una gasolinera**	*gassoh-leeneh-ra*
rear lights	**las luces traseras**	*loothess-trasseh-rass*
road	**la carretera**	*karreh-teh-ra*
spare parts	**los repuestos**	*reh-pwestoss*
spark plug	**la bujía**	*boo-hee-a*
speed	**la velocidad**	*velothee-da*
speedometer	**el cuenta-**	*kwenta-*
	kilómetros	*keelomeh-tross*
steering wheel	**el volante**	*voh-lanteh*
tow	**remolcar**	*reh-molkar*
traffic lights	**el semáforo**	*seh-mafforoh*
tyre	**el neumático**	*neh-oo-mateekoh*
van	**la furgoneta**	*foorgoneh-ta*
wheel	**la rueda**	*rweh-da*
windscreen	**el parabrisas**	*para-bree-sass*
windscreen	**el limpia-**	*leempya-*
wiper	**parabrisas**	*parabreessass*

Road Signs

SPEED LIMITS AND GENERAL DRIVING INDICATIONS

Give way

Compulsory stop

Your route has priority

Your route no longer has priority

Give way to oncoming traffic

Your lane has priority over oncoming traffic

Speed limit

No overtaking

No stopping

Crossroads ahead

Roundabout

Minimum distance separation required

No entry

Traffic light

60 KPH maximum speed

WARNING SIGNS

Caution, left-hand bends

Slippery road surface

Risk of snow and ice or slippery road

Road works

Risk of rockfalls

Wild animals

Children crossing

Pedestrian crossing

Speed bumps

Unspecified danger

Level crossing without barriers

High winds

Steep downhill decline

Road narrows

Road narrows on right